Medieval Robots

THE MIDDLE AGES SERIES

Ruth Mazo Karras, Series Editor
Edward Peters, Founding Editor

A complete list of books in the series
is available from the publisher.

Medieval Robots

Mechanism, Magic, Nature, and Art

E. R. Truitt

PENN

UNIVERSITY OF PENNSYLVANIA PRESS

PHILADELPHIA

ART HISTORY
PUBLICATION INITIATIVE

This book is made possible by a collaborative grant
from the Andrew W. Mellon Foundation.

Published by
University of Pennsylvania Press
Philadelphia, Pennsylvania 19104-4112
www.upenn.edu/pennpress

Printed in the United States of America on acid-free paper
5 7 9 10 8 6 4

Library of Congress Cataloging-in-Publication Data
ISBN 978-0-8122-4697-1

To Katharine Park, doctor mirabilis

CONTENTS

Color plates follow page 140

ABBREVIATIONS

ACMRS	Arizona Center for Medieval and Renaissance Studies
AHR	*American Historical Review*
AN	Archives Nationales de France
BGPM	Beiträge zur Geschichte der Philosophie des Mittelalters
BL	British Library
BnF	Bibliothèque Nationale de France
CCM	*Cahiers de Civilisation Médiévale*
CNRS	Éditions du Centre National de la Recherche Scientifique
Dehaisnes, Lille	*Inventaires-Sommaires des Archives départmentales antérieures à 1790, Nord: Archives civiles, Série B,* ed. Chrétien Dehaisnes, Lille, 1881
EETS	Early English Text Society
GRA	*Gesta regum Anglorum*
HDT	*Historia destructionis Troiae*
MGH, SS. F. et Q.	*Monumenta Germaniae Historica, Scriptores in Folio et Quarto*
MGH, SS. Ldl.	*Monumenta Germaniae Historica, Scriptores Libelli de lite imperatorum et pontificum*
MGH, SS. rer. Ger.	*Monumenta Germaniae Historica, Scriptores rerum Germanicarum*
MGH, SS. rer. Mer.	*Monumenta Germaniae Historica, Scriptores rerum Merovingicarum*
MRTS	Medieval and Renaissance Texts and Studies
MT	*Mandeville's Travels,* ed. M. C. Seymour. Oxford: Clarendon, 1967
OED	*Oxford English Dictionary*
PIMS	Pontifical Institute of Medieval Studies

PL	*Patrologiae cursus completus, Series Latina*, ed. Jean-Paul Migne, Paris, 1844–64
PMLA	*Proceedings of the Modern Language Association*
Richard, Arras	*Inventaire-Sommaire des Archives départmentales antérieures à 1790, Pas-des-Calais, Archives civiles, Series A*, ed. Jules-Marie Richard, Arras, 1878
RS	Rerum Britanicarum Medii Aevi, Rolls Series
SAC	*Studies in the Age of Chaucer*
SATF	Société des Anciens Textes Français
TAPS	*Transactions of the American Philosophical Society*
TBJM	The Book of John Mandeville

Medieval Robots

The Persistence of Robots:
An Archaeology of Automata

Golden birds and beasts, musical fountains, and robotic servants astound and terrify guests. Brass horsemen, gilded buglers, and papier-mâché drummers mark the passage of time. Statues of departed lovers sigh, kiss, and pledge their love. Golden archers and copper knights warn against danger and safeguard borders. Mechanical monkeys, camouflaged in badger pelts, ape human behavior in the midst of a lush estate. Corpses, perfectly preserved by human art, challenge the limits of life. Brazen heads reveal the future, and a revolving palace mimics the revolution of the spheres. Medieval robots, both actual and fictional, take many forms.

And they were far more than delightful curiosities. Automata stood at the intersection of natural knowledge (including magic) and technology, and they embodied many themes central to medieval learned culture. Indeed, automata were troubling links between art and nature. They illuminated and interrogated paired ideas about life and death, nature and manufacture, foreign and familiar. They performed a multitude of social and cultural functions: entertainment, instruction, prophecy, proxy, discipline, and surveillance. Automata enlivened courtly pageantry and liturgical ritual throughout the Middle Ages. They appear in *historia* and *romanz*, in travelogues and encyclopedias, in chronicles and *chansons*. By excavating the complex history of medieval automata, we can begin to understand the interdependence of science, technology, and the imagination in medieval culture and between medieval culture and modernity.

Medieval Robots identifies and explores the multiple kinds and functions of automata in the Latin Middle Ages, and demonstrates that these objects have long been used to embody complex ideas about the natural world. Automata were the products of both intellectual and artisanal labor, and could draw their power from demons, the movement of the cosmos, the secret powers of natural substances, or mechanical technology. They epitomized the transformative and threatening potential of foreign knowledge and culture, and were only gradually decoupled from such problematic origins and inscribed into a Latin Christian cultural patrimony. As people living in the Latin Christian West developed the ability to build complex machines similar to those they encountered in foreign places, they began to interpret these objects within a framework of mechanical technology, although magical and demonic causality remained equally plausible. The different methods by which automata—actual or imagined—were or were imagined to be created in this period raise important questions concerning the boundaries between licit and illicit knowledge, and between experiential and textual knowledge. The long history of medieval automata demonstrates also that the turn toward mechanism—to using mechanical models to explain and understand the body, the universe, and the laws that govern both—which is usually taken as one of the hallmarks of modernity of seventeenth-century natural philosophy, stretches back to antiquity.[1] Thinking with automata persisted throughout the Byzantine regions and the Islamicate world through late antiquity and the medieval period. Yet in the Latin Christian West, mechanistic thinking largely disappeared as a way of knowing until the turn of the fourteenth century. Before that, mechanical objects from outside the Latin West were understood within it according to a different intellectual framework, one in which magic predominated. The chronological scope of this book encompasses this intellectual transformation: I begin at the start of the ninth century, with the arrival of the first mechanical automaton in the Latin West, from Baghdad, and conclude in the middle of the fifteenth century, when mechanical knowledge in Europe allowed for the design and construction of automata within a framework of local, familiar knowledge.

All the objects in this book have two things in common: they were apparently self-moving or self-sustaining manufactured objects, and they mimicked natural forms. Medieval writers, artisans, and artists did not have a fixed term, or even a set of terms to refer to these objects. "Automaton" is an early modern coinage. It came into popular use in sixteenth-century France after Rabelais used *"automate"* to denote a machine with a self-contained principle of motion in *Gargantua* (1532), and it ramified in the twentieth century to encompass a variety of more specialized terms, including "robot," "android," and "cyborg."[2] The objects I refer to as medieval robots or automata thus comprise a group that is broader and more heterogeneous than current usage suggests. While our own definition of automata focuses on mechanical (and, increasingly, electronic) objects, because the medieval category was not limited to mechanical causality, it allowed for more variation in terms of structure and operation. Despite the multiple forms and causes of medieval automata, and despite the fact that medieval writers did not have a fixed set of terms to refer to them, these seemingly disparate objects display a powerful cultural coherence and are often grouped together in medieval texts. In legend, drama, and historiography, medieval sorcerers use magic to create prophetic metal heads or statues, and these appear alongside copper archers or golden musicians. The makers of these strange wonders also embalmed the corpses of dead heroes, encasing them in gold; no longer alive, but not consigned to death. Artisans built elaborate fountains and mechanical angels based on reports of similar objects as well as fantastical objects from legend and romance.

The medieval period is central to understanding the cultural associations of modern robots. Automata are the focus of recent literary and art historical scholarship and that of the history of science.[3] Most of this excellent scholarship focuses on automata either in antiquity or from the early modern period until now. By excavating the missing millennium, *Medieval Robots* extends the historical context for thinking about the cultural and imaginative work that machines undertake. This book also engages with several key recent works in medieval studies on marvels and geography in which automata figure, enriching those conversations by delving further into the cultural, chronological, and philosophical contexts.[4] However different from the robots and cyborgs of modernity, medieval robots also sponsor inquiry into the definitions of life, the natural, and the artificial. In any age, automata are potent symbols of human understandings of nature. Automata permeate multiple discourses as embodiments of foreign craft, scientific superiority, and guile. They externalize the awesome and morally dubious powers of medieval philosophers; they serve as manufactured representations of political prestige. They are mimetic objects that dramatize the structure of the cosmos and humankind's role in it.

The Legacy of Ancient Automata

The first automata in the Western intellectual tradition appear in ancient Greece. According to Homer, Hephaestus, the smith-god of the Greeks, made twenty tripedal servants to serve the gods on Mount Olympus, mounting them on golden wheels "so they could scurry of their own accord to the gods' gatherings."[5] In addition to these wheeled servants, he forged two golden female assistants, endowed with sense, speech, and strength, to help him in his workshop.[6] By the third century before the Common Era engineers and architects based in Alexandria began designing automata to illustrate mechanical principles, and documenting their creations in texts that detailed their construction.[7] Ktesibios (fl. ca. 300–ca. 270 B.C.E.), the earliest engineer of the Alexandrian school, wrote a technical manual that described the construction of a force pump, a catapult powered by compressed air, a water-powered organ, and pneumatic birds to sound the hours on a water clock.[8] Philo of Byzantium, who flourished during the latter half of the second century B.C.E., may have been familiar with Ktesibios's oeuvre; certainly his own books, which detail the building of an air pump and a compressed air-powered catapult, cover similar ground. Philo's work brought pneumatic principles to life with automata, including a singing bird and a mechanical wine-servant.[9]

Hero of Alexandria, the latest of the Alexandrian school of automaton-makers, flourished in the second half of the first century of the Common Era and wrote treatises on pneumatics, mirrors, catapults, and mechanical principles. In his extensive work, *On Automaton-Making*, he cites a now-lost treatise of Philo's on automata as the "best 'and most suitable to didactic purposes.' "[10] *On Automaton-Making*, a detailed treatise, describes how to build two kinds of automata: the first is a mobile shrine to Dionysus, with small figures of the god and attendant maenads. The second is a small fixed theater that stages a complete tragedy, complete with proscenium, changing scenery, and sound effects.[11] The motive power of Hero's automata (and, one assumes, of Philo's) is a counterweight enclosed in a tube or shaft. The flow of small grains through a hole, as in a sand-glass, regulates the descending counterweight, and the energy of the falling weight makes the automata move. Like some of his other mechanical constructions, Hero's automata were designed to illustrate physical principles such as leverage and the transformation from one kind of motion to another, as well as to elicit amazement and wonder.[12]

The lone surviving automaton from antiquity is the Antikythera Mechanism (ca. 80 B.C.E.), a precisely geared analog computer, about the size of a briefcase. It dates from roughly the same period as Hero's designs, and was discovered in a shipwreck in the Aegean Sea at the start of the twentieth century. It seems to have been powered by a hand crank, and it was likely intended to model complicated celestial movements and predict astronomical events, such as eclipses.[13] The existence of the Antikythera Mechanism and the detailed designs in the texts from the Alexandrian School (and the changes the authors made to previous designs) are sufficient proof that these objects were actually built in the ancient period. The Alexandrian texts were not fully translated into Latin until the late fifteenth century. Before then, automata built in the Latin Christian West were not directly influenced by the textual tradition of the Alexandrian School.[14] However, the Alexandrian treatises were, at least in part, the basis for the theory and practice of automaton making in the Byzantine Empire and the Islamicate world, and automata from these places were the inspiration for objects eventually built in medieval Europe. Caliphs and emirs had mechanical animals and lush fountains installed in their palaces, and Byzantine court ceremony included automata. The rapid expansion of Islam in the seventh and eighth centuries brought many areas where Greek culture had remained vibrant under Muslim political control. Scholars in the Dar al-Islam amended, challenged, and enriched many ideas set forth in Greek texts and incorporated them into an intellectual framework that also drew from Persian, Sanskrit, and Hebrew textual traditions.

Although automata were not built in far western Eurasia until the late thirteenth century, they appear there as a result of military, diplomatic, or commercial encounters with foreign powers as early as the start of the ninth century. These automata captivated and tantalized Latin Christians with the potential of scientific knowledge from long ago or far away. They incarnated technological savvy, extensive knowledge of and power over natural forces, and material wealth and luxury. Yet automata originated in places that Latin Christians viewed with a mixture of envy and suspicion. At least until the fourteenth century, most automata and the knowledge needed to create them were associated with places viewed as repositories of scientific knowledge and natural wonders, but also of un- or anti-Christian beliefs. This tension dramatically shaped the ways automata were portrayed in medieval European texts.

Automata in Medieval Texts

After Harun al-Rashid, the caliph of Baghdad, sent Charlemagne, the Holy Roman Emperor, an elaborate water clock with moving figures in the early ninth century, descriptions of automata began to appear in Latin annals and travel narratives. By the twelfth century fictional automata, located at distant courts or based on historical accounts of foreign devices, appeared in romances and *chansons de geste*. Legendary or fantastic automata were also mentioned in twelfth-century encyclopedias, chronicles, and philosophical treatises, which described their creation and puzzled over their moral and intellectual legitimacy. Some of these texts formed the basis of magnificently illuminated manuscript books, which include spectacular paintings of automata of all sorts. By the second half of the thirteenth century, European artisans began to devise and build their own automata. Very few mechanical automata from the medieval period are extant; however, archival documents detailing their construction do survive.

I use all these sources to document the prevalence and persistence of automata in medieval culture, and to explore the essential issues that they embody. Drawing on such a wide array of sources inevitably raises questions concerning the relationship between literary genres and between "factual" and "fictional" materials, and the ways that medieval writers configured these concepts, however alien they may seem to modern readers. Imaginary or legendary automata that appear in twelfth- and thirteenth-century texts reveal as much about medieval attitudes to natural knowledge as the actual objects that were created to enliven courtly pageantry or to adorn monumental clocks in the fourteenth and fifteenth centuries. Many of the accounts of automata in natural history treatises, travelogues, encyclopedias, and chronicles contain elements that are very similar to, and often just as fantastic as, descriptions of such objects found in medieval romance. This is evidence of a capacious understanding of causality. To a medieval audience natural, preternatural, and supernatural events had different causes (manifest and hidden powers of natural objects, demons, or divine intervention), and occurred with varying frequency. They did not, however, differ in their plausibility. Miracles, such as the parting of the Red Sea, were just as possible as sorcerers' use of astrology or demonic magic to create prophetic statues.[15]

There were real generic differences between fiction and nonfiction: Isidore of Seville (ca. 560–636) included all literary endeavors, including history, as part of grammar, and divided all prose into *fabula* (things that had not happened, but had been invented) and *historia* (a narrative of past deeds).[16] Some *fabulae* have no purpose other than to delight an audience, but other *fabulae* offer an interpretation of natural things or the customs of humankind. Tales intended merely to captivate are commonly called "fiction."[17] According to Isidore, history refers to events that did happen; drama to events that did not happen, but could have; and *fabula* to events that could not have happened, because they recount things that are contrary to nature.[18] Some romances, such as the *romans antiques* (stories of the ancient world that were fashioned into origin-myths for French and Anglo-Norman nobility in the second half of the twelfth century) were set in the distant past and took ostensibly historical events as their subjects. They were based on prior literary texts, such as the *Aeneid*, and on historical sources. By the same token, travel narratives, like histories, often relied on a mixture of personal testimony—either of the author or of people to whom the author had spoken—and prior written sources, neither of which may have been factual. The boundary between fiction and nonfiction genres was marked and often policed by medieval writers; however, fiction and nonfiction alike report and accept as true many types of events that many modern readers do not recognize as credible, such as tales of demons, witchcraft, miraculous healing, divine intervention, and astral portents.

The resemblances among these genres highlight strong links between them. Historiography, often in the form of historical chronicle, is one of the genres that contributed to the development of romance. Latin chronicles and annals provided not only a set of conventions, but also *matière*—characters, events, narrative devices, and colorful details and digressions—for vernacular authors. The sources for historiography and romance could be the same; previous historical accounts, epics, and legend could be recounted as deeds from the past or joined with a specific plot to entertain or instruct. Writers of historical narrative (as opposed to annals) do indeed display self-consciousness about their methodology and disparage fictional accounts of historical events.[19] Because accounts of automata in historical chronicles, travel narratives, and encyclopedias emerge from the same wellspring as accounts of automata in romances, epic poems, and drama, all can be read as historical texts that offer insight into medieval beliefs and practices.

Many of the examples of medieval automata in this book are from French texts, were found at French-speaking courts, or were written about by French-speaking authors. The linguistic Frenchness of literary texts in which automata play a role is striking and meaningful. Automata do appear in the literature of other European vernaculars, but generally later than in French.[20] What accounts for the strongly French character of literary texts and automata in the early and high medieval period? I still find this question puzzling and provocative—and address it in more detail in my second chapter—but I believe the answer lies at least in part in the sheer size and diversity of the medieval Francophone world, which encompassed much of northern and western continental Europe, England, parts of Italy, and the Mediterranean. This large geographic area, unified to some degree by a shared language and textual heritage, enabled the exchange of books, ideas, and artifacts that in turn promoted the appearance of automata in narrative texts, and later at courts. The cultural prestige and reach of the French language also meant that some English and Italian writers, in England and Italy, wrote in French.

Organization of This Book

The narrative of *Medieval Robots* proceeds both chronologically and thematically: it traces the story from the appearance of automata in the medieval Latin West, as gifts from foreign courts, to the literary manifestations of these objects, to the eventual creation of elaborate mechanical automata in medieval Europe. In the early medieval period, elaborate hydraulic clocks with moving figures came as gifts to Christian rulers from foreign courts. Pilgrims, soldiers, and diplomats wrote of the apparently self-propelled artificial humans and animals they saw at foreign palaces. Writers and scholars grappled with the alien origins of these objects and worked to place them in a Latin Christian context and to understand them according to a scientific framework that did not privilege mechanical knowledge. Automata from historical texts were translated to literary texts, and then reinscribed into historical legend and biography. Automata populate twelfth- and thirteenth-century literature, where they are most often represented as the products of astonishing erudition in the liberal arts and natural philosophy. The men who made them were philosophers as well as sorcerers, while medieval philosophers with particular interests in the *quadrivium* in later periods were characterized as sorcerers for having created automata. By the middle of the fourteenth century, artisans and engineers began to create richly ornamented self-moving machines that incorporated human and animal figures as centerpieces for courtly pageantry or for the glory of the Church. During this period, the elaboration of mechanical devices such as gears, levers, and counterweights permitted the fabrication of increasingly complex mimetic machines.

This chronology reveals three themes. The first is the relationship between the Latin Christian West and places beyond it: the Islamicate world, and the Byzantine and Mongol empires. Because automata appeared in those places much earlier than in the Latin West (though not the Hellenic world of antiquity), and because they first entered the Latin West as gifts or in the pages of travelogues, automata were explicitly foreign. Latins regarded them in much the same way as they viewed foreign places, people, and customs—with amazement, suspicion, desire, and fear. Furthermore, throughout much of the medieval period, automata in Europe remained linked to their distant origins. It was not until the mid-fifteenth century, almost a hundred and fifty years after the construction of the first mechanical automata, that they were fully disconnected from their associations with foreign knowledge. Second, automata are important liminal objects. They identify and patrol boundaries of many different kinds: between courtly and churlish behavior, between good and evil, living and dead. In many cases automata also comment on categories, often calling them into question by their very existence. In all cases, they reveal their own in-betweenness: surpassingly lifelike copies of natural objects, or eternal bodies that hover between life and death. Third, medieval automata complicate the natural/artificial binary, as when mechanical monkeys are disguised to appear alive. These themes enrich and complicate the chronological narrative about the evolving understanding of natural knowledge in medieval Europe, including its potential, its limitations, and its risks.

Each chapter is devoted to one kind of automaton and the topics it raises. These include the nature of marvels, the constitution of natural knowledge, the text-based transformation of Latin intellectual culture, definitions of life and death, the spectacle of court, and the mechanics of the universe. Throughout, medieval robots enact interest in and concerns about the importation of knowledge from outside Christendom into a Latin Christian framework. At the same time, they reveal concerns about mimesis and manufacture, and the morality of these undertakings. Automata interrogate the boundaries between life and death and pose important questions about the nature of human identity and individuality.

The first chapter examines medieval automata as objects that symbolize the movement of knowledge across cultures, because automata first entered the Latin West as gifts from foreign rulers. Prevailing scientific theories that rationalized the connection between geographic location and powerful natural substances allowed scholars and writers in the Latin West to explain these mechanical objects in ways that reflected contemporary ideas about natural laws, and exposed anxieties about alien technology. These theories also accounted for the different kinds of knowledge available outside the Latin West and for the persistent view of automata as inherently foreign and marvelous objects.

The second and third chapters explore natural philosophical theories for how automata work and what work they could do in the twelfth and thirteenth centuries. The mechanical arts ranked lowest in the hierarchy of knowledge; instead, natural philosophy, the goal of which was the total understanding of natural laws and processes, privileged text-based, learned knowledge, generally available only to a very select group of people. The hidden powers of natural substances, like the ability of certain gems to detect or safeguard against poison, which could be used to make moving figures, were available only to those who had spent time studying the liberal arts and the mysteries of Nature. In twelfth- and thirteenth-century literary texts, especially learned men created automata using esoteric knowledge, although the philosophical trope of *Natura artifex* (Nature as artisan) described Nature's labor in artisanal terms. The second chapter demonstrates that this metaphor obscures the rarefied intellectual ability that underpinned ideas about the invention of automata; and it extends the semantic field that denotes automaton-making, exploring the importance of esoteric knowledge to construct these objects. Sorcerers, philosophers, and poets, acting as Nature, were responsible for creating automata that displayed judgment and perception in surveilling and correcting human behavior and in delimiting certain spaces. Automata were a staple of *romans antiques*, and were consciously presented in these texts as part of the legitimate Trojan and Roman legacy bequeathed to the French and Anglo-Norman ruling elites. In this way, writers and their patrons began to claim these foreign objects as familiar, if temporarily lost.

From accounts of fictional sorcerers and philosophers who can create automata I move, in the third chapter, to the legends attached to historical learned men from the twelfth to the fourteenth centuries. This chapter explores another facet of the tension between foreign and familiar knowledge undergirding medieval automata. The tales of philosophers and the oracular metal statues they forged reflect concerns about the rapid importation and assimilation of newly imported astral science into the Latin intellectual tradition. Medieval scholars such as Gerbert of Aurillac, Robert Grosseteste, and Albertus Magnus were widely known for their erudition in astral science, mathematics, and natural philosophy, whether from Arabic sources or ancient sources transmitted to the Latin West via Arabic translations. All were also posthumously reputed to have made, either through demonic or astral magic, oracular heads or statues that would reveal to them both future events and further occult knowledge. Unlike the automata that were part of courtly pageantry in twelfth- and thirteenth-century literature, these legends attest to anxieties about the uses of new knowledge for purposes that were at best hubristic, and at worst diabolical.

The fourth chapter illustrates the imaginative movement from understanding automata within a framework of natural philosophy to one that included mechanics from the twelfth to the mid-fifteenth century, through an examination of automata, drawn from textual examples, that guard or memorialize the dead. Automata in these settings demonstrate the ways the boundaries between nature and art, between verisimilitude and fraud, and between life and death were contested and negotiated. This chapter opens with twelfth-century literary examples and then moves into a case study of Hector's tomb in three fictional accounts of the story of Troy, documenting the way that increasingly mechanical explanations of Hector's preserved corpse replace magical explanations, and coincide with a heightened emphasis on technical skill. The final example, from John Lydgate's *Troy Book* (ca. 1420), anticipates Hobbes's characterizations of the artificial life of mechanical things and the mechanical nature of the body, as in it Hector's body is kept artificially alive by a complicated system of tubes and wires that replace his nerves and blood vessels.

The growing emphasis on technical skill and fine technology found in Lydgate's version of Hector's preserved corpse reflects the development of complex machinery in the fourteenth century, and the more widespread appearance of mechanical marvels at princely courts in Europe in the fourteenth and fifteenth centuries. Beginning with the notional automata in the notebook of Villard de Honnecourt in the mid-thirteenth century, mechanical automata became more common, albeit still the province of the very wealthy. The fifth chapter probes the consequences of the diffusion of mechanical knowledge in the form of mechanical marvels. I argue that the human and animal automata created for the public display of majesty at the courts of Artois and Burgundy, Richard II of England, and the Valois are central to understanding the reappearance of mechanistic thinking, as well as for the technological developments that allowed for the creation of increasingly complex machines.

Finally, I explore the development of complex mechanical clockwork technology and the link between clockwork and automata. Horological innovations in the fourteenth century enabled the construction of astronomical clocks that were accurate reproductions of the cosmos. These macrocosmic models were conjoined with microcosmic models—mechanical animals and people—to demonstrate the glory of divine creation in its entirety. The most famous example, the clock in the cathedral of Notre-Dame de Strasbourg, used automata to dramatize the interpenetration of sacred and secular time and a cosmology centered on divine majesty and the hope of eternal salvation. Yet this clock and others like it are part of a genealogy that stretches back to an 'Abbasid water-clock and an imaginary palace, to which we now turn.

CHAPTER I

Rare Devices: Geography and Technology

In the mid-twelfth-century *chanson de geste*, *Le Voyage de Charlemagne*, Charlemagne and his barons travel to Constantinople, where they encounter King Hugo and the fantastic marvels at his court. These include a rotating palace and two musical automata, made of copper.[1] The interior of the palace is blue and is decorated with paintings of birds, beasts, serpents, and "every kind of creature."[2] In the center of the palace a massive silver pillar forms the axis around which the entire structure revolves, "like a chariot wheel."[3] Philosophers and wise men fluent in the science of the stars had erected the palace; they used their knowledge and skill to make the palace mimic the circular motion of the celestial spheres. Two copper children grace the apex of the palace roof; each one holds an ivory horn to its mouth.[4] These automata are so expressive "that you would have believed they were actually alive."[5] The west wind makes the palace turn like the shaft of a mill, and the statues "blew their horns and smiled at one another. You would have sworn they were alive. One blew loud, the other clear. [The music] is so lovely to hear that the listener would imagine himself in paradise, where the angels sing sweetly and gently."[6]

The edifice is a monumental automaton that resembles the earth and the heavens, while the musical statues represent the microcosm. Hugo the Strong, the Byzantine emperor, and the learned men of his court have made these marvels using "*cumpas* and lofty secrets."[7] *Cumpas* is the branch of astral science that enables accurate predictions of the lunar cycle and eclipses, as well as the establishment of the liturgical calendar.[8] The wind causes the palace to revolve and also brings a violent storm that rages outside the palace walls, "frightening and overpowering."[9] Charles and his barons are wholly unfamiliar with this kind of technology; they are taken by surprise and lose their footing once the palace begins to turn. "[Charles] sits down on the marble floor, unable to stand. The Franks are thrown to the ground."[10] Their total unfamiliarity with anything like the emperor's palace reflects their ignorance of technological marvels and the *cumpas* responsible for their creation. The spinning palace reimagines space in a way that confuses and disorients Charlemagne and his barons. In this example, learned knowledge and specific geography combine to produce moving, mimetic objects that are disconcertingly foreign to the Latin Christians.

After a lavish banquet at Hugo's expense, the Franks retire to their quarters where, drunk and boisterous, they exchange a series of outrageous boasts about their abilities.[11] One after another, the knights make a series of absurd, outlandish, and hyperbolic vows: to blow down Hugo's palace, steal his wealth, violate his daughter over a hundred times in one night, and make a nearby river flood its banks.[12] A spy from Hugo's court overhears these vows and reports them to Hugo, who confronts Charlemagne and swears that if Charlemagne and his knights cannot fulfill their vows then Hugo will have them beheaded. Charlemagne, desperate, prays to the relics he received earlier from the Patriarch of Jerusalem and has carried with him to Constantinople. Through the relics, God miraculously saves the Franks: he fulfills Bernard's boast to cause a nearby river to flood. "It came into the city and flooded the cellars and soaked King Hugo's people, and forced the king to run on foot to the tallest tower [of his castle, for refuge]."[13] Hugo, trapped in his tower, agrees to become Charles's vassal, and God reverses the flood.[14] Both emperors use spatial and geographic dislocation to gain the upper hand. Hugo makes the ground move by using particular, abstruse knowledge, while Charlemagne, thanks to God, changes the landscape.

The author of *Le Voyage de Charlemagne* based his Byzantine marvels on earlier descriptions from travel accounts of extraordinary technology at the Byzantine court; however, this unfamiliar technology, though impressive, is overmatched in the *chanson* by Latin Christian piety. In a number of *chansons de geste* from the twelfth and early thirteenth centuries, Latin Christians triumph—through faith and divine favor—over their enemies' superiority in natural philosophy and advanced technology. *Chansons de geste* are vernacular, literary accounts of past deeds or heroes. In terms of setting and story, *chansons de geste* look backward in time and beyond the borders of Latin Christendom, and are similar in subject matter to the epics that predate them. But the past also looked like the present in *chansons*, as authors changed aspects of history to reflect or comment on contemporary (late eleventh- to thirteenth-century) mores and anxieties.

The strange and wonderful self-moving objects from Baghdad, Constantinople, and Karakorum described and appropriated by writers from the Latin West embody contemporary concerns about foreign knowledge and its uses. Arabic and Greek courts were known for their automata, which employed a combination of hydraulic, pneumatic, and mechanical technology. Writers in the Latin Christian West, trying to explain or understand these exotic and unfamiliar objects, often did so by invoking extremely complex theories of natural philosophy (the branch of inquiry directed toward all God's physical creations, including the cosmos) or extremely simple examples of agricultural technology. Until the fifteenth century, automata in the Western imagination most often come from foreign lands or the strange geography of the past. Natural philosophy in this period explained how geographic location could confer special qualities on natural substances. Furthermore, different kinds of knowledge were available outside of Latin Christendom. What could be known and what could be observed were highly dependent on place.

In this chapter I explore the connection between geography, both real and imagined, and automata. Descriptions in Latin and vernacular texts of historical automata (automata that likely existed, but are not extant) from the eighth to the thirteenth century reveal the extent to which automata were known in the Latin West. Authors of autoptic accounts highlight the mechanical nature of automata in the Byzantine Empire and the Islamicate world, while also expressing wonder about how the automata function. This knowledge and these objects were located outside of Latin Christendom, in foreign places that were rich in knowledge and natural substances unavailable to Latins. Drawing on a textual tradition that encompassed ancient natural philosophy, early Christian philosophy and theology, *itineraria*, and encyclopedic knowledge, twelfth- and thirteenth-century natural philosophy held that greater natural variation occurred at the distant edges of the earth. This was in part because Nature expressed her many abilities more freely at the margins, and in part because the orientation of the planets toward faraway lands conferred potencies on natural objects, like gemstones, found in those places.[15]

The appearance of the Mongols in the Balkans in the mid-thirteenth century disrupted the established narrative of where automata came from and how they worked. Given the Mongols' status as real and present conquerors and threats, missionary and mercenary reports of moving statues, musical fountains, and mechanical birds came to emphasize both the manufactured element of these creations and an aspect of deceit and cunning. The author of

Mandeville's Travels, in the mid-fourteenth century, based parts of his arm-chair *itineraria* on reports from Franciscan missionaries like Odoric of Porde-none and William of Rubruck.

Whatever their cause, wherever they were located, and in whatever kind of texts they appear, the examples to come have in common their status as marvels. Authors of chronicles and *chansons*, as well as soldiers, diplomats, pil-grims, and merchants use words like *merveille, mirabilia*, and *mirifice* to de-scribe these objects. These words, and other related ones, connote objects that elicit wonder, an emotional response to objects or phenomena that ranges from awe to pleasure to terror.[16] Wonder is highly contingent on perspective, and is often evoked by the uncommon and the unfamiliar. The most robust consid-erations of wonder from medieval writers occur outside literature, in natural philosophy and theology.[17] Aristotle claimed wonder as the spark that lights the fire of philosophy. "It is owing to their wonder that men both now begin and at first began to philosophize."[18] Gervase of Tilbury, the early thirteenth-century Anglo-Norman writer, asserts in his didactic compendium of wonders, *Otia imperialia* (ca. 1211), that marvels are natural objects that defy explanation or categorization. "We embrace those things we perceive to be strange; first be-cause of the variation in the course of nature, at which we marvel; then because of our ignorance of the cause [of that wonder], the reason for which is impen-etrable to us."[19] Because marvels are natural objects that invite curiosity regard-ing their causes, natural philosophy is the proper discipline for their investigation. Marvels, including automata, appear routinely in narrative sources—*chansons de geste*, romance, chronicle, and travelogue—and the wonder they occasion often motivates inquiry into their causes.[20] Those causes were not always or completely understood as mechanical; as the examples to come demonstrate, automata were strongly correlated to foreign (or ancient) knowledge and pow-erful natural objects, such as gemstones, that drew their power from a spe-cific geography. The marvelous status of automata in the Latin West in this period was due in part to their comparative rarity, as well as to the uncom-mon knowledge and substances used to create them.

Marvelous Geography

Medieval geographic tradition held that more extreme natural variation (in people, animals, plants, and environments) was found at the edges of the world.

To the ancient Greeks, who came into contact with Asia and Africa through political conflict, India, Persia, and parts of Africa were places rich with the strange, the wonderful, the unknown, and the dangerous. Furthermore, Greeks believed that people, plants, and animals varied more widely in extreme climates than in the temperate zone (e.g., Greece).[21] This belief was repeated in the medieval period, and was combined with a flourishing body of literature that recounted the many natural wonders of India, Ethiopia, and central Asia. Therefore, that the rulers of foreign lands had access to the kind of esoteric knowledge required to build automata was seen by Latin Christians in part as a function of geographic location, as those lands had long been seen as rich in material wealth and natural diversity.

The two main medieval cartographic traditions were the T-O map (also called the *mappamundi*) and the climate zone map (also called the Macrobian map). T-O maps, so-called because the O of the world is inscribed with the T of the known Eurasian bodies of water, are oriented with east at the top (rather than north) and Jerusalem at the center. They depict the physical world and sacred history "from alpha to omega."[22] The three known continents, Asia, Africa, and Europe, echo the perfect number of the Trinity, and some maps vividly illustrate the idea "that the entire ecumene is, in a spiritual sense, contained within the body of Christ," by placing the head, feet, and hands of Jesus around the perimeter of the O.[23] The *mappaemundi* depict a world that is simultaneously centrifugal and centripetal. The three land masses are the inheritances of the three sons of Noah after the Flood, and the descendants of each populate the continents.[24] The postdiluvian diaspora radiates out from Jerusalem, the center. Yet, in a spiritual context, the inhabitants of this tripartite world will eventually to return to the center, Jerusalem, which is the site of the Crucifixion and will be the setting of the Last Judgment.

In contrast, the Macrobian tradition, based on the fifth-century scientific treatise *The Commentary on the Dream of Scipio*, prioritizes natural philosophy over theology. According to Macrobian maps, the world comprises five climatic zones: frigid and uninhabitable at the polar extremes, then two temperate zones in the northern and southern hemispheres, divided by a central torrid zone that is in turn bisected by the ocean. William of Conches, the Anglo-Norman natural philosopher of the first half of the twelfth century, gave a Macrobian account of terrestrial geography in his natural philosophical treatise, *De philosophia mundi*.[25] The text covers physics, astral science, geography, meteorology, and medicine. In an early copy from France in the second half of the twelfth century, a Macrobian map accompanies the section on geography, yet it is oriented eastward, like a *mappamundi*[26] (Plate 1).

The idea that natural wonders occur more at the margins of the world than at the middle remained central to medieval geography, regardless of cartographic system. As Gerald of Wales (ca. 1146–1223) wrote, "Just as the countries of the East are remarkable and distinguished for certain prodigies peculiar and native to themselves, so the boundaries of the West are also made remarkable by their own wonders of Nature. For sometimes tired, as it were, of the true and the serious, [Nature] draws aside and goes away, and in these remote parts indulges herself in these shy and hidden excesses."[27] Ranulf Higden (ca. 1280–1364), a Benedictine monk and author of a widely copied universal history chronicle, wrote a century later, "At the farthest reaches of the world often occur new marvels, as though Nature plays with greater license in secret afar than she does openly and nearer."[28]

Both Ranulf and Gerald were writing about Ireland, at the northwestern margin of the known world. However, the lands at the eastern margins—India and Babylon—and the southern margins—Ethiopia—were the richest repositories of natural wonder and excess. This belief was due in part to Latins' unfamiliarity with the topography, flora, and fauna of those places; as Gervase of Tilbury explained, the unfamiliar was more often marvelous than the mundane. But this belief was also due to the idea, as Gerald of Wales and Ranulf Higden noted, that Nature played at the margins, and created rare natural wonders there.[29] An account of Alexander the Great's travels and conquests, which circulated in a letter attributed to him and addressed to his tutor Aristotle, both encouraged and reflected interest in the natural wonders of India and Ethiopia from late antiquity throughout the medieval period. The letter began to circulate sometime between the late second and early fourth centuries, and was translated from Greek into Armenian, Syriac, Hebrew, Latin, Old English, Middle Irish, Icelandic, Old French, and Middle English—many vernacular languages of the "margins."[30] Alexander describes the many wonders he has seen on his campaign in India, including abundant and large gemstones and amazing fauna: hippopotami, giant tigers and panthers, three-headed snakes, and griffins. India, like Africa, was home to fabulous peoples, like the Fauni, who ate only raw fish and drank only water, and the Cynocephali, dog-headed giants.[31] Other early medieval texts echoed Alexander's letter, seeing India, parts of Asia, and Africa as places of vast wealth and magnificent natural wonders, as well as home to dangerous beasts, treacherous terrain, and monstrous races.[32]

Interest in India grew in the twelfth and thirteenth centuries, as versions of the Alexander legend, such as the *Liber Floridus*, an encyclopedic work of Alexandreana compiled by Lambert of St. Omer, and the *Roman d'Alexandre*, a late twelfth-century Old French history of Alexander, proliferated.[33] William of Auvergne (ca. 1180–1249), bishop of Paris and also part of the first generation of Latin Christian natural philosophers to incorporate previously unknown ideas and texts from the Greek and Arabic traditions into Latin Christian theology and philosophy, referred to the many natural marvels in India, and how they could be put to use by skilled artisans. "In parts of India and other adjoining regions, there is a great quantity of things of this sort [i.e., natural marvels], and on account of this, natural magic can particularly flourish there. And it thrives on account of the many experimenters there above [in India], and people who make marvelous things through skill of this sort."[34] The elaborate fountains and mechanical contrivances that flourished in courtly settings in India appear in Sanskrit literature in the tenth century and in Sanskrit technical handbooks in the eleventh, and include artificial animals, female attendants (fembots!), and musical automata.[35]

At the extreme eastern margin of the world, beyond the delights, treasures, and terrors of India, lay Eden, the earthly paradise. Like Jerusalem, the bifurcated concept of paradise encompassed both past and future. Eden was the place of origin for humankind, while the celestial Paradise (not found on the map) was the eventual destination of all who were to be saved. According to Augustine and others, the earthly paradise was a real physical place, but inaccessible to fallen humanity. It was often placed at the top of the map, although it could appear elsewhere.[36] On *mappaemundi*, the east, found at the top of the map, "marks the temporal and spatial point of origin, the birthplace of mankind and the fountainhead of the rivers of Eden, which water the earth both literally and spiritually."[37] The natural delights of paradise were unknown to humankind; however, not too far away, in India, natural variation demonstrated the glories of divine creativity.

Jerusalem, the site of Jesus' sacrifice for humankind, was at the center of the map; it contained things that were holy, and thus, rare. Accounts of Latin Christians' journeys to Jerusalem can focus on relating strangeness rather than holiness, but what was strange was often holy, and vice versa.[38] Jerusalem and its domains had long been controlled by Muslims, whose reach extended into India, while Byzantium was the heir to the ancient wisdom of the Greeks. The rulers of the Dar al-Islam and the Byzantine Empire, and, slightly later, the Mongols, had far greater access to occult forces of nature, and used them to erect magnificent buildings, create lush gardens in the middle of the desert, and build astonishing artificial people and animals.[39]

Greek and Arabic Automata

Automata, a particular kind of marvel, participate in the geographic imaginary outlined above. Throughout much of the medieval period, Latin Christians associated automata with the Arab, Greek, and Mongol courts and saw them, as I have said, as the products of foreign knowledge and exotic materials not easily available to themselves. The successive waves of large-scale Latin Christian contact with the distant lands of Byzantium and the Islamicate world forced Latin Christians to recognize and grapple with their own economic and technological inferiority. At the same time, sustained contact between Latin Christians and the lands and people beyond Latin Christendom also allowed them to see these lands as worthy of desire and fantasy.[40] No automata from antiquity survived into the medieval period, and of the texts on automaton making by the engineers of the Alexandrian school only Philo's *Pneumatica* was partially available in Latin.[41] However, these texts were copied, translated, expanded, and amended in the Islamicate world, as Hellenic culture and knowledge had spread to Mesopotamia, Egypt, and the eastern Mediterranean—all areas that became part of the Dar al-Islam during the Arabic conquests in the seventh and eighth centuries.

Automaton making flourished in the Islamicate world, along lines initiated by the Alexandrian writers. By the eighth century, Arab Muslims had gained political control over the formerly Greek-speaking Syria, Egypt, and Palestine, as well as most of the Persian Sasanid Empire, which was also strongly influenced by the Hellenic intellectual tradition. This Arabic expansion "made the translation of Greek into Arabic inevitable both in government circles and in everyday life throughout the Umayyad period."[42] Slightly later in the eighth century, in Baghdad, 'Abbasid elites were strongly influenced by Sasanian culture, which prioritized the establishment of a royal archive. Bureaucrats and courtiers under caliph Harun al-Rashid (r. 786–809/170–194 AH) carried out translations of Persian texts into Arabic as part of a "caliphal policy to project Sasanian imperial ideology."[43] Harun al-Rashid's son and successor al-Ma'mun (r. 813–833/198–218 AH) began to support the translation of texts that fell outside the project to translate and appropriate Sasanian culture. This additional focus was in part driven by administrative concerns, as courtly secretaries needed to master practical subjects such as mathematics, surveying, astro-meteorology, timekeeping, and engineering. During al-Ma'mun's reign, this central archive employed the astronomer and mathematician al-Khwarizmi and the three engineers and automaton-makers known as the Banu Musa.[44] These three sons of Musa ibn Sakir (a former bandit, astronomer, and boon companion to al-Ma'mun) grew up at the 'Abbasid court, where they received a thorough education in astral science, mathematics, and engineering. Their automaton-making treatise, *Kitab al-Hiyal* (*Book of Ingenious Devices*), was written around 850. It contains designs for almost a hundred trick vessels and automata, the effects of which "were produced by a sophisticated, if empirical, use of the principles of hydrostatics, aerostatics, and mechanics. The components used included tanks, pipes, floats, siphons, lever arms balanced on axles, taps with multiple borings, cone-valves, rack-and-pinion gears, and screw-and-pinion gears."[45] Hero's work was studied in ninth-century 'Abbasid Baghdad, and the chief translation of the *Mechanics* was made at the behest of 'Abbasid caliph al-Motassim (r. 862–866/248–252 AH).[46]

Given its interest in automaton making, the 'Abbasid court featured automata that were larger and more elaborate than those detailed in the Alexandrian treatises: artificial birds, musical fountains, and water clocks with elaborate moving parts. As early as 827, caliph al-Ma'mun, patron to the Banu Musa, had at his palace an artificial tree decorated with mechanical birds, similar in its outlines to Hero's design.[47] A century later, caliph al-Muqtadir (r. 908–932/296–320 AH) made a similar automaton the centerpiece of his palace in Samarra. The central courtyard had scented fountains, an artificial tree, and mechanical birds. Visiting Greek dignitary and future Byzantine emperor Romanos Lekapenos described this automaton during a visit in 917: A tree with gold and silver branches and enameled leaves stood in the middle of an artificial pool, and artificial birds sang on the branches.[48] In gardens such as these, fantasy was privileged over naturalism. The goal was "to evoke the imaginary and the mythic, and to test the limits of credulity." [49] The bird automata at Muslim courts testified to the caliph's wealth and ability to control natural forces.

'Abbasid caliphs not only featured automata at their courts, they exported them as diplomatic gifts to foreign rulers. Diplomatic contact between the 'Abbasids and Frankish rulers goes back at least to 768, when, according the continuations of the *Chronicle of Fredegar*, Pepin the Short, Charlemagne's father, received emissaries and gifts from al-Mansur, the caliph and founder of Baghdad.[50] The earliest detailed description of an automaton in the Latin West is from 807, of a clepsydra, or water clock, sent to Charlemagne by Harun al-Rashid. A Carolingian chronicler at the Frankish court described the gift in detail. It was made of brass, and

> marvelously contrived by mechanical art, on which the course of the twelve hours was marked by a clepsydra, with the right number of little bronze balls, which would fall into a basin when the hour was complete and make it sound. [This clock] also had the same number of horsemen, and they would, through twelve windows, come forth at the end of the hours. With the force of their exit they would close the proper number of windows, which had before been open.[51]

Harun al-Rashid's clepsydra, or water clock, embodied many of the intellectual differences between the 'Abbasid and Carolingian empires. Arabic engineers had refined the technology of the clepsydra in the eighth and ninth centuries and often ornamented them with moving people and animals.[52] In contrast, horological technology in Charlemagne's empire was limited at that time to sundials, hourglasses, and candle-clocks.[53] This water clock, intended as a mark of diplomatic civility from one ruler to another, demonstrated the artistic and technological superiority of the caliph's court. The gift was beautiful, useful, and costly. The annalist mentioned the "mechanical art" needed to make such an object. At the time this Frankish chronicler recorded his description of the clock, understanding of the mechanical arts came primarily from Isidore of Seville's *Etymologiae*, an encyclopedic work based on pagan and late antique Christian sources. According to Isidore and later commentators, the mechanical arts were necessary knowledge; however, they were not considered as important as knowing Scripture or the liberal arts.[54] It is possible that to the Franks, the clepsydra showed facility in a branch of knowledge they considered trivial. But even if it is an example of frivolous knowledge, the clock—and by extension, the principles and skill responsible for it—is also wonderful [*mirifice*]. The clock and automata were extraordinary and unusual to the Frankish audience, and demonstrated that Harun al-Rashid ruled an empire that had access to and significant understanding of natural principles, as his scholars and craftsmen were able to measure and represent the passage of time more accurately and beautifully than could their Frankish counterparts.

The Byzantine Empire (Greece, the southern Balkans, Asia Minor, and the islands of the eastern Mediterranean), the continuation of the eastern half of the Roman Empire, was another source for knowledge about automata for the Latin West. The Greek texts that had been so enthusiastically translated in the Dar al-Islam remained relevant in the Byzantine Empire. As was the case with the Islamic courts, mechanical marvels, including automata, played an important role in Byzantine imperial pageantry. Disagreements in the eighth through tenth centuries over the control of northern Italy, as well as the right to the title of Roman Emperor, meant that diplomatic contact between the Franks and the Byzantines was common. Emperor Constantine V sent envoys, along with an organ, previously unknown in Francia, to the court of Pepin the Short in 757.[55] Although we do not have extensive details about the instrument, it was likely a steam organ, and used some of the same technology as the marvelous artificial singing birds in the palaces of al-Mam'un and al-Muqtadir over a century later.

The most famous example of Byzantine automata is the Throne of Solomon, attested as early as the tenth century. Although nothing of the throne remains, it is "centrally important to the modern myth of the Byzantine court."[56] What Byzantinist James Trilling has called "conspicuous virtuosity" was a vital element of Byzantine court culture and the portrayal of majesty.[57] Contemporary Greek and Latin sources describe this arresting marvel. Liudprand of Cremona, the courtier and diplomat, traveled to Constantinople in 949 for Berengar II of Italy. He later fell out with Berengar, and wrote a travelogue/ tell-all memoir, *Antapodosis* ("Revenge"), of his diplomatic mission and his experiences at the court of Constantine VII Porphyrogennetos to embarrass his former patron. In Liudprand's description of his presentation to the emperor, he recalls the Throne of Solomon in the Magnaura, a room in the great palace in Constantinople, that resembles the striking automata at the Palace of the Tree in Baghdad described thirty years earlier by Lekapenos in 917.[58]

> Before the emperor's seat stood a tree, made of bronze gilded over, whose branches were filled with birds, also made of gilded bronze, which uttered different cries, each according to its varying species. The throne itself was artfully wrought, so that at one moment it seemed a low structure, and at another it rose high into the air. It was of immense size and was guarded by lions, made either of bronze or wood covered over with gold, who beat the ground with their tails and gave a dreadful roar with open mouth and quivering tongue. . . . At my approach [to the emperor] the lions began to roar and the birds to cry out, each according to its kind; but I was neither terrified nor surprised, for I had previously made enquiry about all these things from

people who were well-acquainted with them. So after I had three times made obeisance to the emperor with my face upon the ground, I lifted my head, and behold! The man whom just before I had seen sitting on a moderately elevated seat had now changed his raiment and was sitting on the level of the ceiling. How it was done I could not imagine, unless perhaps some such sort of device lifted him up as we use for raising the timbers of a wine press.[59]

Although Liudprand "was neither terrified nor surprised" by the roaring lions, the cheeping birds, and the moving throne, it was only because he, a wily courtier, had made sure to find out beforehand, "from people who were well-acquainted," what to expect from his audience with the emperor. However, even though he had been warned about what to expect, Liudprand still took the marvel seriously and reported it in a straightforward manner. Furthermore, his description of his own unfazed reaction implies that such marvels would occasion surprise or terror in one who was not prepared for them. Unfamiliar with the ascending throne, he could only venture a guess that it might operate in the same manner as a wine press. Although it is possible that his suggestion is a rhetorical device intended to demystify the throne and place it on the same level as a humble technology, it is more likely that he attempted to describe the motion of the throne to his audience using familiar terms.[60] However, he can offer no speculation as to the workings of the birds and lions.

In contrast to Liudprand's speculation on how the throne and its automata worked, Byzantine writers never expressed wonder or curiosity about the movement of ceremonial automata. The Throne of Solomon was also mentioned in the contemporaneous Byzantine courtly text *De ceremoniis* (ca. 956–959), written by Emperor Constantine VII Porphyrogennetos. The text covers all aspects of imperial court ritual, and the emperor's aim was to convey a sense of permanence and authority, after a time of political instability and dynastic infighting.[61] The emperor formally received foreign ambassadors while seated on a throne in the great hall of the Magnaura, within the imperial palace complex in Constantinople. According to a precisely scripted performance of diplomatic contact, the foreign ambassador approaches the enthroned emperor, accompanied by organ music and Byzantine court functionaries. The music ceases as the visitor makes his obeisance.

When the *logothete* puts the customary questions [to the envoy], the lions begin to roar, and the birds on the throne and likewise those in

the trees begin to sing harmoniously, and the animals on the throne
stand upright on their bases. While this is taking place in this way,
the foreigner's gift is brought in by the protonotary of the post and
again, after a little while, the organs stop and the lions subside and
the birds stop singing and the beasts sit down in their places. After
the presentation of the gift the foreigner, directed by the logothete,
makes obeisance and goes out, and while he is moving away to go
out, the organs sound and the lions and birds each make their own
sound and all the beasts stand upright on their bases. When the foreigner goes out through the curtain, the organs stop and the birds
and the beasts sit down in their places.[62]

This Greek version omits any mention of the rising throne or any explanation
of how it worked.[63] The lack of emphasis on automata in Greek texts about
the Byzantine court, as well a lack of emphasis on wonder in the infrequent
descriptions of Byzantine automata in other Greek texts, suggests that these
devices were much more common in the Byzantine Empire—especially in
Constantinople—than anywhere in the Latin Christian West. Liudprand's description foregrounds the throne itself; Constantine's description embeds
the throne in the larger ceremony, and reveals that the automata around the
throne are central to the production and conveyance of imperial power. During the formal presentation of foreign envoys the *logothete* speaks, the ambassador speaks, and the emperor remains silent and somewhat at a remove
from the proceedings. But the lions roar and "the birds on the trees sing harmoniously" at specific intervals, punctuating the ambassador's presentation
of credentials and gifts. The automata are part of a ritualized conversation
between the emperor, his court, and the foreign visitor, and like the emper-
or's other servants, the automata speak in his stead.[64] Constantine VII employed the automata and the Throne of Solomon in imperial ceremony to
convey to foreign visitors and to members of his Senate, which witnessed
these formal audiences, his power over nature and his technological advance-
ment. The Throne of Solomon, the pneumatic organ sent to Pepin, and the
hydraulic clepsydra sent to Charlemagne were to their Latin contemporaries
potent and mystifying examples of the scientific and technological superiority of Arab and Greek culture in the early medieval period.

Although contact between European courts and markets and those in the
eastern Mediterranean and Asia Minor occurred from the eighth to the eleventh century, the establishment of the Latin Kingdom of Jerusalem after the

first crusade (1096–1099), as well as other permanent settlements of Latin Christians in the Middle East and Asia, brought soldiers, merchants, pilgrims, and diplomats more familiarity with the customs, cultures, and courts of Orthodox Christians and Muslims. Kings Baldwin III (r. 1143–1163) and Amalric I (r. 1163–1174) of Jerusalem both were born there and had diplomatic relations with the courts of Baghdad and Cairo. They were also both allied by marriage with the rulers of the Byzantine Empire.[65] Norman Sicily was another area of cultural exchange in the medieval world. King Roger II (r. 1130–1154), stepson of Baldwin I of Jerusalem, spoke French, Arabic, and Greek at his court at Palermo, and surrounded himself with philosophers, physicians, and historians from all over Europe, North Africa, and the Middle East.[66]

One of the geopolitical effects of the first crusade and the establishment of the Latin Kingdom of Jerusalem was heightened and increasingly hostile contact between Latin and Greek Christians. This hostility is reflected and, some argue, satirized in the contest between emperors Charlemagne and Hugo in *Le Voyage de Charlemagne*.[67] Latin Christians had, since the strained relations during the first crusade, increasingly viewed Byzantine Christians as duplicitous and malign. During the third crusade (1189–1192), which regained much of the territory lost to Salah ad-Din, founder of Ayyubid dynasty, in 1187 but failed to reconquer Jerusalem, Latin Christian leaders, such as Frederick Barbarossa (1122–1190), openly allied against the Byzantine Empire with its enemies, including the Seljuk Turks.[68] By the fourth crusade, launched to retake Jerusalem from the Ayyubids in 1202, Latin mistrust of Greek Christians was entrenched. The Byzantine Empire was, at this point, in the midst of an extended contest over the throne. One of the claimants, Alexios Angelos, son of the recently deposed emperor, urged one of the Frankish leaders, Boniface of Montferrat, to divert the crusading army to Constantinople in order to help push out the pretender, Alexios III, and restore the throne to the rightful ruler. The crusading army, nominally led by Boniface, was in massive debt to Venice, which had built a large naval fleet to carry the army to Egypt; thus, Boniface was largely subordinate to the Venetian doge, Enrico Dandolo. Dandolo saw the opportunity that Constantinople presented: a city of enormous wealth and position that offered treasure enough to replenish Venice's coffers and a base for commerce throughout the eastern Mediterranean. The doge extracted a promise from Alexios Angelos, made to the pope, Innocent III: submit the Byzantine Empire to the authority of the Roman Church once Alexios had been installed as emperor.[69] This gave the leaders of the crusading army a measure of moral and theological cover for diverting the army to a Christian

empire and purported ally. In 1203 the Frankish armies traveled to Constantinople instead of the Holy Land. They besieged the city for months, before
burning and looting the city and murdering many of its Christian inhabitants
over three days in 1204.

One of the crusaders, an obscure soldier from Picardy, Robert of Clari,
wrote an account of his experience in the fourth crusade. This text is one of
the two major sources for that event available to historians, and one of the
few texts in this period written by a common soldier.[70] Robert's account is
vivid, personal, and often unfavorably contrasted to the detached, high style
of his contemporary chronicler Geoffrey of Villehardouin, a knight and Frankish envoy.[71] Robert, unlike Geoffrey, took time to describe the marvels of Constantinople, including the many automata at the Hippodrome:

> there were figures of men and women, and of horses and oxen and
> camels and bears and lions and of many manner of beasts, all made
> of copper, and which were so well made and so naturally formed that
> there is not a master in heathendom or Christendom who has enough
> skill as to make figures as good as these figures were made. And in
> the past they used to perform by enchantment [*par encantement*],
> but they do not play any longer. And the Franks looked at the Games
> of the Emperor [the Hippodrome] in wonder [*a mervelle*] when
> they saw it.[72]

Robert of Clari may have meant that these frozen statues were corroded
mechanical automata; however, these statues may have been thought to move
by ancient enchantment. They closely resemble the ancient statues, which were
believed to have been enchanted by Apollonius of Tyane in the first century
C.E., on the spina of the Hippodrome.[73] Robert emphasized how like their
natural counterparts the statues appeared, and this emphasis, along with the
fact that they required magic [*encantement*] to "play," suggests that, when fully
functional, the statues could have fooled observers into mistaking them for
real animals.

Technology to Text

To Latin Christian natural philosophers and chroniclers like William of Auvergne and Ranulf Higden, the lands in the East, approaching paradise, were

the loci of magical substances, mechanical skill, natural knowledge, aesthetic delight, and un-Christian morality. Harun al-Rashid's early ninth-century clepsydra and the mid-tenth-century Byzantine Throne of Solomon both demonstrated to Latin Christians that these places were also the sites where automata could be found. Medieval literary texts, beginning in the twelfth century, often contain automata in a foreign setting, at the courts of Byzantine or Muslim despots, or in the distant pagan classical past. In some instances, the writers gestured toward hydraulic power as the engines of these marvels (echoing, though perhaps inadvertently, the mechanism of Harun al-Rashid's clock); however, pneumatic power, astral science, magic, and hidden human agency were also used to make automata. Examples, though fictional, from two *chansons de geste* illustrate that automata flourished in the Byzantine Empire and the Dar al-Islam, though they remained strange in the Latin West. Automata in these *chansons* recall the glorious past of the Carolingian Empire as well as the time of their composition; automata were known in the Carolingian period mainly through contact with the Arabic and Byzantine realms, and were imagined but not built in the Latin Christian West of the twelfth and thirteenth centuries.[74]

Chansons de geste were narrative poems intended to illustrate the valor of Frankish nobility and provide heroic origin myths for noble families. *Chansons* are verse tales of heroism and battle, offering idealized accounts of the deeds of past rulers or legendary warriors, but with political and cultural themes resonant to the period of their composition. In subject they share many qualities with earlier oral epics. *Chansons de geste* were both written down and performed to an audience.[75] The martyred Roland in the *Chanson de Roland* expressed the pervasive moral sentiment of *chansons de geste*: "Pagans are in the wrong and Christians are in the right."[76] The enemy, variously known as the Saracen, Slav, Greek, Turk, Arab, or Persian, was defined in terms of his un- or anti-Christianity, and also his superior technology, which was usually ascribed to specialized or esoteric knowledge that was unavailable to his Frankish counterparts.[77] Given this representation of the alien opponent, *chansons* often present a binary struggle between foreign cleverness and Christian miracles. Two such *chansons*, *Le Voyage de Charlemagne à Jérusalem et à Constantinople* (mid-twelfth century) and *Aymeri de Narbonne* (early thirteenth century), are set in the time of Charlemagne and focus on military clashes and cultural interaction with the Byzantine Empire and Muslim Spain respectively.

Le Voyage de Charlemagne satirizes many elements of the *chanson de geste*; however, it also expresses a desire for a renewal of the Carolingian Empire and

the elevation of secular rule over papal authority.[78] Charlemagne's queen wounds
his pride by telling him that she has heard that Hugo the Strong of Greece is
the finest knight in the entire world. Stung and eager to prove his superiority,
Charles sets out with his barons to Constantinople, with a pilgrimage to Jerusalem along the way. While in Jerusalem, Charles is so impressive that a
Jew, catching a glimpse of Charles and mistaking him for God, rushes to the
Patriarch to be baptized. This incident, parodic or not, places Charlemagne
on the same footing as Jesus, as the conversion of the Jews is considered a necessary precedent to the Second Coming.[79] Due to his status as a Christian emperor and his support of the Church, Charles and his party are accorded the
highest honors, and receive many relics from the Patriarch of Jerusalem, including a nail from the True Cross and the Crown of Thorns. The relics given
to Charles are important in the structure of the narrative, and the author takes
time to establish their efficacy. Upon bestowing them, the Patriarch assures
Charles that the relics will perform great miracles; later, they heal a man unable to walk for the last seven years.[80]

The vast differences between Hugo's realm and Charlemagne's are immediately apparent to the Franks, both in the text and to the audience. Constantinople, a wealthy city [*une citez vaillant*] has stunning architecture and
beautiful orchards and gardens.[81] The court is large and extremely fine: twenty
thousand knights, dressed in furs and silks, diverted themselves with games,
falconry, and hawking, and three thousand beautiful women, dressed in silk,
"clung to their lovers in ecstasy."[82] Charles encounters Hugo riding on a golden
litter behind a giant golden plow. "In his hand the king held a scepter of pure
gold and he drove his plough so skillfully that his furrow is in a perfectly straight
line. Here comes Charles approaching him on an ambling mule!"[83] The golden
artifacts signify Hugo's wealth and his mastery of the mechanical arts. Furthermore, his work at the plough is symbolic of his position as the protector
of the vitality and fertility of his realm.

Hugo welcomes Charles and his entourage warmly, and offers them lavish gifts. Unconcerned about theft or vandalism, he leaves his plough unpro-
tected in the fields as Charlemagne's barons gape like rubes at Hugo's wealth.
"If I had that [plough] in France and [another baron] were there, it would be
dismantled with pikes and hammers," William of Orange observes.[84] The
Franks, already impressed by Hugo's wealth and refinement, are stunned when
they encounter the spinning palace described earlier. Large, luxurious, and
beautifully decorated, the palace is unlike anything they have seen before. Once

they step inside, the palace begins spinning on its axis and the musical automata begin to perform, muffling the howling winds outside.

Inside the palace, Hugo becomes the Cosmocrator in the center of the cosmos, claiming authority over the entire universe. The Byzantine emperor, according to Byzantine political theology, was God's anointed viceroy on earth. As such he had dominion over the entire universe, regardless of any interlopers who contested or denied his lordship.[85] The narrator stresses the lifelike appearance of the automata twice in similar language, drawing attention to Hugo's ability to mimic nature to an astonishing and unusual degree.[86] The lifelike automata underscore Hugo's role as a thaumaturgical ruler, able to perform miracles. The emperor has mastered nature in ways that are unknown or unavailable to Charles, who is both amazed and floored by the wonders of Hugo's court.

Hugo learns of the boasts, or *gabs*, of the Franks, confronts his guests with their rude behavior, and threatens to behead all of them. Taking counsel with his barons, Charles prays before the relics and petitions God to intervene on their behalf. "Then, lo, there came an angel sent by God, and he came to Charlemagne and raised him up. 'Charlemagne, do not fear, Jesus sends you this [message]: To jest as you did last night was an act of great foolishness. Never mock anyone again; this Christ commands you. Go, let it begin, none of them will fail.' "[87] Acting through relics they were given in Jerusalem, God causes a flood; Hugo, trapped in a tower by the rising water, agrees to become Charles's vassal.[88] Charles is ignorant of the natural knowledge that Hugo has mastered, and, furthermore, does not rule over a territory that is rich in natural diversity or naturally inclined toward extraordinarily potent natural substances. However, Charles has relics, bodily remains of or personal objects closely associated with holy people. Relics can travel, as their power does not derive from their geographic origin. It comes instead directly from God, the ultimate authority over nature, who acts through saintly intermediaries to perform miracles.[89] God, having created nature, is thus able to overturn or break natural laws to perform miracles.

The description of Hugo's palace and automata emphasizes the different kinds of power available to the two Roman emperors, Eastern and Western. The author compares the wondrous technology behind the automata to more mundane technology (as did Liudprand) when he compares the rotation of the palace to the movement of a chariot wheel and a mill wheel.[90] This comparison effectively reduces the palace and its automata from the level of the marvelous to the level of the banal. However, just a few lines later, the author calls the horn music of the copper youths angelic, conflating the artificial with the celestial.[91] Charles reacts to Hugo, his palace, and the automata with curiosity, concern, envy, and wonder. Yet one of the purposes of the poem is to demonstrate the supremacy of Charlemagne over Hugo. Despite his wealth, majesty, technological superiority, knowledge of *cumpas*, and position as Cosmocrator, Hugo, in submitting to vassalage, suffers a political defeat brought on by Charlemagne's relics. The might of God and his favor for the Latin Church allow the technologically backward and poorer empire to prevail over the more scientifically advanced, schismatic one; the *cumpas* of Hugo's court is outdone by supernatural power. Hugo can create a working copy of terrestrial geography because he understands natural laws, and because he uses astral science and esoteric natural knowledge. But God, acting through the holy relics, changes the original geography.

Charlemagne's warriors also triumph over the combined advantages of natural knowledge, demonic power, and advanced technology in the early thirteenth-century French *chanson de geste*, *Aymeri de Narbonne* (ca. 1205–1225). It is one of twenty-four poems in the William of Orange cycle (also known as the cycle of the Aymerides and the Garin de Monglane), which details the exploits of an illustrious family, in which each successive scion is driven from home by his father to seek land and glory. By the early thirteenth century, *chansons* were longer and resembled romances in terms of plot.[92] Probably written by Bertrand de Bar-sur-Aube, *Aymeri de Narbonne* survives in five manuscript copies, and its plot is linked to the narrative of the *Chanson de Roland*.[93] The poem contains avian automata made by necromancy and powered by the wind at the court of the caliph of Babylon (Cairo).

Aymeri de Narbonne opens after the treachery of Ganelon and the deaths of Roland and Olivier in Roncesvalles, detailed in the *Chanson de Roland*. As Charlemagne and the remnants of his army march on their way back home, they catch sight of Narbonne, a Muslim-controlled jewel in the Languedoc region of southern France. Narbonne is fortified with twenty tall towers, the tallest of which is crowned with a golden dome, embedded with a carbuncle that shines as bright as the sun.[94] Charles glimpses the town and immediately yearns to claim it; however, his barons, tired and longing for home, refuse to invade it.[95] At last, his vassal Aymeri vows to conquer Narbonne. He succeeds, imprisons the four Muslim rulers of Narbonne, and then travels to Pavia to make an advantageous marriage. While he is in Pavia, a spy releases two of the Muslim kings, who then escape to Babylon, seeking reinforcements from the caliph so they can retake Narbonne in Aymeri's absence.

The Muslims in this story are associated with marvels, including automata. In medieval lore, the carbuncle, in this text found on one of the towers of Narbonne, is a red gemstone that grows on or inside the head of a serpent or dragon and gives off a glowing light. Known sometimes as the "oriental ruby," it was in the Latin West considered extremely precious and magically powerful.[96] The caliph's court in Babylon also brims with marvels, "so wondrous [*merveillex*] that I will have a hard time recounting them to you."[97] The centerpiece of the caliph's palace is a tree, made by magicians [*enchanteres*], built of a copper and gold alloy and cast [*tresgiter*] in a mold. The fabricators of this marvel took gemstones from a river, named Paradise, and used them to ornament the numerous artificial birds that perched on the branches. "The wind is made to enter the flue [of the tree] by necromancy [*par nigromance*]; when the wind blows the birds begin to sing . . . clearly and gaily."[98] The birdsong is so lovely that the sound of it can banish angry thoughts from the listener's mind.[99] To help reconquer Narbonne, the caliph calls on the devil to send favorable winds to speed his fleet back to the shores of Narbonne, in order to reach the city before Aymeri can return with reinforcements.[100] Yet, as in *Le Voyage de Charlemagne*, the Christian army defeats the realm of the ruler with the power to control, mimic, and perfect nature. Despite the caliph's giant army and diabolical assistance, Aymeri has God on his side, and both he and Narbonne are rescued at the last minute by the army of his uncle Girart of Vienne.

The caliph of Babylon is refined and wealthy, and has the treasures of Paradise. He controls nature and uses necromancy, a term that in the early thirteenth century could refer to acting with demons, trying to change the outcome of future events (using an array of different techniques), or a more general definition of magic.[101] His councilors are able to harness and enchant nature in order to replicate and even surpass it. The artificial birds are distinguishable from real birds only in that they sing more beautifully than real birds. Art surpasses nature, buttressed by the special powers of the geographically specific gemstones. The narrator does not directly attribute the creation of the tree with the avian automata to demonic intervention; in fact, the description of the mechanism that channels moving air is fairly straightforward. The metal tree with bird automata resembles the tree at the court of the Byzantine emperor reported by Liudprand of Cremona, and also the similar object from the tenth-century Palace of the Tree in Samarra reported by Romanos Lekape-nos.[102] Yet the insistence that the tree has been made by magicians [*enchan-teres*] and that the central mechanism of the tree which made the birds sing has been made by necromancy [*par nigromance*], coupled with the interven-tion of the devil on behalf of the caliph, suggests strongly that although how automata *work* can be explained in familiar mechanical terms, how automata are *made* requires invoking mysterious, occult knowledge of questionable moral legitimacy.

Technology and Trickery at the Mongol Court

Automata appear at foreign courts from Baghdad to Byzantium in historical chronicles and *chansons de geste*. However, by the mid-thirteenth century, a new group, equally threatening to the Byzantines, the Muslims, and the Latin Christians, appeared—the Mongols. Contact between Christian Europe and the Dar al-Islam had been constant, if not always peaceful, since the first half of the eighth century. The Mongols (also called Tartars) were entirely unknown to Christian Europe until the thirteenth century, when they swept across the steppes of central Asia and quickly took control of southern Russia and the Balkans. At that time, little was known about them except their reputation for barbarity and cruelty.[103]

The Mongols disrupted Latin Christian viewpoints about foreignness. They were a new kind of non-Christian, and they were equally threatening to Mus-lim rulers in central Asia and to the Byzantine emperor. Additionally, the Mon-gols were nomads, with a fluid relationship to geography. The Jews were another group of non-Christians with no fixed place on the map. However, the Jews were monotheists, were not politically cohesive or militarily threatening, and were also familiar to Latin Christians, even if only as a conceptual category.[104] Unlike the Jews, the Mongols were new and had no place in Christian his-tory. They controlled a massive territory, but had few established cities, living instead in vast impermanent encampments across the Asian steppe. Yet the khan and his court had artificial marvels similar to those found in Baghdad and Byzantium.

Missionaries and merchants traveled to Mongol courts in the late thir-teenth and fourteenth centuries, and described the automata they saw there in terms of the mechanical arts, demons, or human trickery. While *chan-sons de geste* often portrayed the un-Christian, foreign enemy as fairly one-dimensional, medieval travel accounts were written in prose and thus closer to the norms of the chronicle. The "pagans are wrong and Christians are right" mentality in *chansons de geste* was muted or entirely absent from travel narratives. Travelers to Eastern lands between the mid-thirteenth and late fourteenth centuries were less interested in conquest than in forging diplomatic and military alliances, and in seeking adventure and profit. Their *itineraria* are ethnographic and descriptive, intended to convey important information about the topography and inhabitants of the lands to the east, and remark on the differences between familiar audience and foreign subjects.

Due to internal political struggles, the Mongol invasion of Europe halted after the death of the Mongol emperor Ögedei Khan in 1241, the second Great Khan of the Mongol Empire. Once the Mongols were no longer considered an active threat to the borders of the Latin Christian West, missionaries began to travel to Mongol territories in the hopes of offering succor to Christians who lived within them, and to missionize the pagan Mongols. Friar William of Rubruck, a Flemish Franciscan, left on a mission to the Mongols in 1253. He wrote an account of his journey after he returned in 1255, for his patron, Louis IX of France, whom he had accompanied on crusade to Egypt in 1248. His account of the Mongols and their lands, although less hyperbolic and hysterical than that of Matthew Paris just a few years earlier, emphasizes the binary distinction between the monotheism of the Abrahamic faiths and the animism of the Mongols, and, more broadly, the familiar world of Latin Christendom and the unfamiliar world of Asia.[105] He described the land of Tebet, where gold littered the ground and the people practiced necrophagy; the people of Cathay, "the most excellent artisans in all manner of crafts;" Bulgai, the chancellor of emperor Mangu Khan, who practiced the art of scapulomancy (divination by reading the burnt shoulder-blades of animals); and the priests at the khan's court, who had mastered the science of the stars and the ability to predict solar and lunar eclipses.[106]

When William reached Karakorum, the capital, in present-day central Mongolia, in 1254 he compared it unfavorably to St. Denis, just outside Paris and home to one of the most spectacular artificial marvels in medieval Europe, the Basilica of St. Denis.[107] Yet Karakorum contained a few marvels at the khan's palace. The center of the palace was taken up with an elaborate fountain, built (according to William) by a Frank, "master William the Parisian," a smith who had studied with the Mongols.[108] The fountain for the khan was wrought of silver and shaped like a tree, containing automata that worked by hidden human agency in conjunction with pneumatic and hydraulic technology. Four silver lions at the base of the tree spouted mare's milk from their mouths, while four gilded serpents, twining around the tree, belched forth wine, clarified mare's milk, honey, and rice mead.

> Between these four conduits in the top, [William] made an angel hold-ing a trumpet, and underneath the tree he made a vault in which a man can be hid. And pipes go up through the heart of the tree to the angel. In the first place he made bellows, but they did not give enough wind. Outside the palace is a cellar in which the liquors are stored, and there are servants all ready to pour them out when they hear the angel trumpeting. . . . When then drink is wanted, the head butler cries to the angel to blow his trumpet. Then he who is concealed in the vault, hearing this blows with all his might in the pipe leading to the angel, and the angel places the trumpet to his mouth, and blows the trumpet loudly. Then the servants, who are in the cellar, hearing this, pour the different liquors into the proper conduits.[109]

Friar William clearly took the time to learn exactly how the mechanism of the fountain worked. The level of detail William provides to his patron, Louis IX, reveals his perception of this marvel as something appropriate to a ruler. His reaction to the fountain clearly reflects the contemporary ideas held by natural philosophers and clerics about wonder. Both Adelard of Bath, writing a century earlier in the *Quaestiones naturales*, and Franciscan friar Roger Bacon, in his commentaries on Aristotle's *Metaphysics* written in Paris in the 1240s, attributed the emotional response of wonder to ignorance of the proper cause of the object that evoked it.[110] Wonder was ultimately per-spectival: either due to geographic perspective and the natural variation that granted special qualities to landscapes, or explained by the abundance of cer-tain substances (such as the abundance of gold in Tebet), or due to the famil-iarity of the beholder with the cause(s) of the marvel at hand. Wonder might disappear if one understood the cause of whatever had occasioned it in the first place. Yet wonder was also productive. Not only did it motivate intel-lectual inquiry, as in the passage from Aristotle quoted above, but it also led one to contemplate deeper mysteries and more difficult concepts. According to Thomas Aquinas, writing in the mid-thirteenth century, "investigation does not rest until the first cause is reached . . . . The first cause of everything is God. Thus, the ultimate goal of humanity is to know God."[111]

William also emphasized that the Mongols were known for their artisanal and divinatory skill, and it seems likely that the artificer, William the Parisian, learned how to make the fountain while living among the Mongols. Since automata and fountains in northern Europe at this time were at best notional, it is unlikely that he learned this in Paris. For example, Villard de Honnecourt's book of drawings is almost exactly contemporaneous with William of Rubruck's account, and the automata in that notebook are much less elaborate (see Plates 24–25). However, the applied science behind the fountain is combined with hidden human agency. The hidden "blower" makes the angel appear to move on its own: this is a kind of trickery.

Several decades later, the Venetian merchant Marco Polo mentions the large table fountain at the court of Kublai Khan in Shangdu. Polo had made two extensive voyages to Asia in the second half of the thirteenth century, but did not recount his experiences until he told them to a fellow prisoner in Genoa in 1298. His interlocutor, Rustichello of Pisa, was an author of romances, and he took the stories, polished some of them, and rendered them in French prose.[112] The resulting volume, entitled *Devisament du monde* (*Description of the World*), was hugely popular, and was soon translated into Latin and given a title that emphasized the geographic reach and marvelous aspects of Polo's journey: *Liber Milionis de magnis mirabilibus mundi* (*Il Milione's Book of the Great Wonders of the World*). Polo describes the large table fountain, similar to the one described earlier by William of Rubruck, as fully three paces long on each side, gilded, and adorned with animal figures. "The middle is hollow, and in it stands a great vessel of pure gold, holding as much as an ordinary butt; and at each corner of the great vessel is one of smaller size of a capacity of a firkin, and from the former the wine or beverage flavored with fine and costly spices is drawn off into the latter."[113] The khan and his court drank the wine out of giant vessels "big enough to hold drink for eight or ten persons."[114] In the late fourteenth-century manuscript painting that depicts this marvel (Plate 2), the khan's fountain is the focal point of the feast, and of the image itself.

Just a few decades after William of Rubruck's mission, another Franciscan, Odoric of Pordenone, traveled for over a decade through eastern and southern Asia. He spent several years in China and traveled to the khan's court in Cambalu—modern-day Beijing—(it had moved farther east from Karakorum in 1260), where he saw the artificial birds he later described in his *Itinerarium de mirabilibus orientalium Tartarorum* (1330). He viewed these marvels as the result of either demonic knowledge or expertise in engineering.

In the hall of the palace also are many peacocks of gold. And when
any of the Tartars [Mongols] wish to amuse their lord then they go
to one after the other and clap their hands; upon which the peacocks
flap their wings, and these appear to leap about. Now this must be
done either by demonic art [*arte diabolica*], or by some engine [*in-genio*] underground.[115]

Odoric mentions the birds in a list of observations he makes concerning
the khan's court. According to Odoric, in addition to the avian automata, the
khan also had several mechanical drinking fountains, similar to those described
by William and Marco Polo. Odoric asserts that human ingenuity could be
responsible for the birds' movements (perhaps with a mechanism similar to
the angel and fountain mentioned at Karakorum by William of Rubruck),
but also admits that demons might be the cause. Thus he acknowledges the
difficulty of distinguishing, from identical effect, the proper cause. Odoric
here expresses a tenet of late medieval philosophy, which attributed marvels
not to divine causation (as opposed to miracles, directly caused by supernatural intervention), but rather to causes in the fallen world, artificial or
demonic.[116] The artificial birds could not be miraculous, because the Mongols were pagan. Therefore, as marvels, they must have had as their cause
either human manufacture or demonic involvement. However, it was difficult for an observer to determine which cause produced the marvelous artificial birds.

Relocation and Recapitulation:
 The Travels of Sir John Mandeville

The author of *The Travels of Sir John Mandeville* relied heavily on the *itiner-aria* of earlier travelers, such as Odoric and Marco Polo, for his spectacularly
popular account. Written in Anglo-Norman French around 1357, the book pur-
ports to be an account of the travels of "Sir John Mandeville," pilgrim, soldier
of fortune, and traveler. Yet the text is a deft recombination of earlier material,
some of which was based on eyewitness testimony and some of which existed
only in the literary tradition.[117] The chief group of sources for the book com-
prises a number of autoptic *itineraria* (including Odoric of Pordenone's *Rela-tio*) that had been translated into French by Jean de Long, a monk at St. Omer,
in 1351.[118] The author included many different kinds of marvels, including

strange beasts, plants, and races, as well as divine marvels—miracles—and manufactured marvels that prompted delight and fear.

Suspicion or fear was often commingled with an appreciation of Eastern cleverness and technological skill in *The Travels of Sir John Mandeville*. The narrator recounts the amazing fountain at the court of the Great Khan, as well as the mechanical birds, but with some important changes. In "Mandeville's" *Travels*, the narrator reports that the khan's great hall has at the center an ascending throne or dais ["mountour"] made of gold, decorated with pearls and gems, with a golden serpent at each corner. Hidden conduits under the dais carry drink to the golden vessels just underneath.[119] The Mandeville-narrator also echoes and alters Marco Polo and Odoric in his account of the peacocks and "many other maner of dyuerse foules alle of gold and richely wrought and enameled" at the khan's palace.[120] These birds appear to be controlled by human agency: "Mandeville" says that "men maken hem" dance and sing, although he does not say how. He marvels at the ability to create such lifelike and richly decorated mechanical marvels and, like Odoric, links automata to human ingenuity and demonic knowledge: "And whether it be by craft or be nygromancye I wot nere . . . and it is gret meruayle how it may be."[121] The learned reader of *The Travels of Sir John Mandeville* would have recognized the citation of Odoric, and may have read it as parodic.[122] But when "Mandeville" considers the reputation of the Mongols, known for their cunning, ingenuity, and specialized knowledge, alongside the more ignorant but less devious Christians, he finds their marvels less surprising.

> But I haue the lasse meruaylle because that thei ben the most sotyle men in all sciences and in all craftes that ben in the world, for of so-tyltee and of malice and of fercastynge they passen alle men vnder Heuene. And therefore thei seyn hemself that thei seen with ii eyen, and the Cristene men see but with on, because that thei ben more sotylle than thei. For all other nacouns thei seyn ben but blynde in conynge and worchinge in comparisoun to them.[123]

The Mongols possess the qualities attributed by Latin Christians to the inhabitants of all foreign lands to the east: fabulously wealthy, artistically gifted, full of malice, and with expertise in applied arts, theoretical knowledge, and the predictive sciences. The narrator attributes the automata to several different causes: superior abilities in engineering ("crafte"); more extensive knowledge of the natural world ("science"); or demonic means ("nygromancye" and "fercastynge").[124] This echoes the causes indicated by the *chansons* mentioned earlier. Hugo's rotating palace was made by *cumpas*; the caliph in *Aymeri* had access to both demonic power and greater technological ability.

The Mandeville-author also relocates anecdotes and information from his source material to completely different places in his text. According to Marco Polo, Aloadin, also known as the Old Man in the Mountain, was the leader of the feared Ismaili Assassins, who were based in the Alborz Mountains between the Caspian Sea and Tehran.[125] Aloadin constructed an elaborate pleasure garden to convince a group of young men, highly trained killers, that his garden was Paradise, and that he was a compeer of Muhammad. According to Polo, in the most temperate part of the valley he cultivated a garden with every kind of fruit and fragrant plant he could find. He erected palaces of different sizes, furnished with gold, silk, and silver, throughout the grounds of the garden. Beautiful young women, who could "play on all manner of instruments, and sung most sweetly, and danced in a manner that it was charming to behold," lived in the palaces.[126] An elaborate network of fountains, which spouted milk, honey, wine, and water, ran throughout the garden (Plate 3). Eager to return to the sensuous delights of Aloadin's garden, his assassins fearlessly risked their own lives to kill his enemies.

The same story is retold in *The Travels of Sir John Mandeville*. In this version, "Mandeville," in India, ruled by the Christian king Prester John, encounters the territory of Gatholonabes.[127] A previous account of Prester John's sexual continence contrasts with Gatholonabes's garden, dedicated to sensual and sexual pleasure.[128] The false paradise contains halls and rooms painted in gold and blue, and decorated with automata in the forms of animals and birds "that songen fulle delectabely and meveden by craft, that it semede that they weren quyke."[129] In addition to the automata, Gatholonabes has dug three wells, richly decorated with gold and precious gems. "And he had made a conduyt vnder erthe so that the iii welles at his list, on scholde renne mylk, another wyn, and another hony. And that place he clept 'paradys.'"[130] As in *Le Voyage de Charlemagne*, the narrator emphasizes the lifelike attributes of the automata, but in this example also mentions the "craft" (which can mean both artisanship and trickery) that makes the automata move. Furthermore, the narrator earlier refers to Gatholonabes's cunning [*cauteles*] and deceit [*sotylle disceytes*]. The mention of guile, the reference to the false nature of the garden, and the "craft" which cause the automata to move affirm the fraudulent and wicked purpose of the false "Paradys."

Similar to Hugo's palace and central hall in *Le Voyage de Charlemagne*, Gatholonabes's garden is a microcosm of the earth, with pavilion ceilings painted as blue as the sky, and with automata so mimetically accurate that they seem "quyke." Additional musical marvels sound at his command that were "ioye for to here, and no man scholde see the craft therof," and which he "seyed weren aungeles of God." The garden, filled with beautiful women and replete with fountains of milk, honey, and wine, resembles the Muslim paradise. But the garden is a false paradise; the animals move and the music sounds by "craft," and the wine flows only at the bidding of Gatholonabes, who, in an imitation of Scripture, says, "Dabo vobis terram fluentem lacte et melle."[131] In this case, Gatholonabes perverts the Scripture of his Christian ruler, just as he perverts the Christian (and Muslim) idea of paradise.

The prose travel narratives and the epic *chansons* I have discussed in this chapter foreground foreign knowledge, and contrast that knowledge with familiar Latin Christian knowledge. The descriptions of the automata, whether in an eyewitness or fictional account, illustrate Latin Christian attitudes towards these places and the knowledge and marvels they engendered. Automata abounded in lands understood to be rich in flamboyant excesses of nature, unimaginable wealth, both material and intellectual, and access to ancient knowledge and magical objects; these lands are populated with clever, talented, devious people. These elements were all necessary to accounts of foreign automata; these automata are animated variously by or in combination with mechanical know-how, control of the forces of nature, hidden knowledge about the natural world, and demonic influence.[132]

CHAPTER 2

Between Art and Nature: *Natura artifex*, Neoplatonism, and Literary Automata

A richly dressed woman stands before a forge and, using a hammer and anvil, fashions people out of existing parts: this is *Natura artifex*, or Nature the artisan (Plate 4). The metaphor of *Natura artifex* was commonly used in the early and high medieval periods to convey Nature's role in a three-tiered system of creation that included the works of God, Nature, and human beings. Broadly speaking, the metaphor turns on the idea that Nature acts as an intermediary between the world of ideal forms and the world of matter. This metaphor is grounded in late antique secular Neoplatonism from the fourth and fifth centuries, but became in the twelfth century one way for Latin Christian natural philosophers to understand and explain the work of Nature in human terms. The metaphor of *Natura artifex* depicts Nature's role—to create material objects out of preexisting forms—and renders it visually (the preexisting forms are in this image the body parts) and in the vocabulary of manufacture (Nature uses a hammer, anvil, and forge to do her work).

The combination of natural and human work reveals much about how automata were understood and described in twelfth- and thirteenth-century literary culture. Appearing in the Latin Christian West mainly as textual objects in this period, automata were self-propelled metal copies of natural forms—humans, animals, even the universe itself. Yet the automata found in medieval *romans* and *chansons* do not sit easily alongside other examples of human craft. Indeed, the comparison of the Throne of Solomon to a wine press in Liudprand's *Antapodosis* and the comparison of King Hugo's revolving palace to a mill- and chariot-wheel only highlight the differences between these kinds of objects. The revolving palace, Throne of Solomon, and attendant musical avian automata are much more complex in terms of operation, and much more beautiful to look at, than a capstan, such as would be used in a wine press. Because of these differences in complexity and register, automata are usually presented as the product of intellectual rather than artisanal endeavor. Although sometimes described in artisanal terms, they are more often characterized (e.g., in *Aymeri de Narbonne*) as the result of complicated intellectual work involving natural knowledge that is mysterious, difficult, and arcane. Likewise, their creators are scholars and magicians, rather than artisans. Despite the fact that automata were often created for a specific end, such as the assertion of power or to provoke wonder, they also embody the possibility that humans can usurp Nature's prerogative. And, as discussed previously, in poetic texts this knowledge came from outside Latin Christendom, and was considered morally and intellectually ambiguous.

By emphasizing the extent to which philosophical ideas of the time explained the work of Nature and the work of the artist, I demonstrate in this chapter how automata were understood in the twelfth and early thirteenth centuries. Beginning in the fourth century, philosophers, distinguishing among the powers and products of God, Nature, and humankind, used the metaphor of *Natura artifex* as a way to describe Nature's labor. This metaphor became increasingly central in the twelfth century, due to the influence of natural philosophers associated with the cathedral school of Chartres, near Paris. There were numerous and overlapping ties between the students and scholars at Chartres and the Anglo-Norman court who were the patrons of the *romans antiques* that used the metaphor of *Natura artifex* in conjunction with automata.[1] In French *romans* in this period descriptions of automata, their creators, and the methods used to make them expose apparently overlapping categories of mimesis and natural creation, which cohere around intellectual rather than artisanal skill. The creators of automata in these literary examples are philosophers, priests, and magi: men who can manipulate celestial forces, use the hidden properties of natural objects, and call on demons to create and control artificial copies of natural forms.

Automata appear in twelfth- and thirteenth-century texts (*romans* as well as *historiae*) as marvelous objects, and they evoke a complicated network of emotions. Some of the wonder they elicit is due to the knowledge they embody. Yet equally, the copper and gold knights, archers, acrobats, and courtiers are marvelous because their abilities so perfectly mimic, and in some cases surpass, human ability. Not only can they play music or fight, they can also monitor and correct people's behavior. While some automata were wondrous because of their exotic or foreign origins, others, in histories and legends of European antiquity, were stunning incarnations of the cultural inheritance that ruling dynasties in northern Europe sought to claim through the poets who enjoyed their patronage.

The Hierarchy of Creation

The medieval image *Natura artifex* is based on a syncretic tradition of medieval neoplatonism. Three late antique authors in particular, Chalcidius (fl. 325), Macrobius (ca. 354–430), and Boethius (ca. 480–524), were most influential in the development of medieval neoplatonism in the eleventh and twelfth centuries.[2] A central principle of platonism is what C. S. Lewis called Plato's "Principle of the Triad," which found expression in Chalcidius's commentary on Plato's *Timaeus* and in Macrobius's *Commentary on the Dream of Scipio*.[3] According to the *Timaeus*, Nature, which had been created by the divine craftsman (the Demiurge), translated the ideal world of forms into the sensible world, for "it is impossible that two things should be joined together without a third. There must be some bond in between both to bring them together."[4] Nature is the bridge between perfect, immaterial archetypes and the physical manifestations of those ideas. Chalcidius's translation into Latin of part of the *Timaeus* and his extensive commentary on the entire work were the only major Platonic texts available in the Latin West through much of the medieval period. His explanation of the Principle of the Triad was enormously influential in the development of medieval Latin Neoplatonism. Chalcidius explained that Nature is the intermediary between form and matter, and linked the triad of form, nature, and matter to the Aristotelian classification of the three kinds of creative endeavor: "For all things which exist are either the work of God, or of Nature, or of a human artificer imitating Nature."[5] Macrobius, writing slightly later, echoed this idea when he attributed the creation of physical bodies to what he called the "world-soul."[6] Natura takes forms or archetypes and translates them into materiality, as in the *artifex* part of the metaphor.

This tripartite framework, as expressed by Macrobius and Chalcidius, formed the basis for the medieval Neoplatonist movement, which was located mainly at the Chartrian and Victorine schools in and around Paris in the twelfth century. The earliest and most important of the works associated with this movement was Hugh of St. Victor's (1096–1141) *Didascalicon*.[7] Hugh wrote the didactic treatise in the late 1120s at the newly founded monastery school at the abbey of St. Victor. The *Didascalicon*, a guide to students, teaching them what they should read, how they should read, and to what purpose, both in the arts and in Scripture, is Hugh's attempt to select the areas of knowledge important to humanity, and to show how mastery of these subjects is crucial to attaining spiritual perfection. The work is extant in over one hundred manuscripts, held in over forty-five libraries throughout Europe, in testament to its philosophical and spiritual importance.[8] In addition to being a practical manual for students, and thus indicative of the rise of cathedral and monastery schools in the Île-de-France, the *Didascalicon* heralded the resurgence of the philosophy of aesthetics, which had languished since John Scot Eriugena (ca. 800–877), the most influential philosopher of the Carolingian period and the key figure in Neoplatonist philosophy and aesthetics between Macrobius and Hugh of St. Victor. Medieval aesthetics reached a peak in the twelfth and thirteenth centuries, due in part to an analysis of the arts (such as found in the *Didascalicon*) and also to a foundation in Neoplatonism.[9]

In the *Didascalicon*, Hugh presented a view of knowledge and creation that followed the tripartite division first put forth by Plato. He divided knowledge into four types: theoretical (philosophy), practical (liberal arts), and mechanical (manual work), with logic providing the framework to assess the truth and clarity of conclusions in the other three types of knowledge. Hugh granted the mechanical arts more epistemological legitimacy than had earlier writers, such as Cassiodorus, Isidore of Seville, and Bede, who viewed the mechanical arts as indicative of the uses of mathematics.[10] Because they were less important than the theoretical arts, the mechanical arts had never before been classified separately. The seven mechanical arts in Hugh's taxonomy are fabric-making (*lanificium*), arms (*armatura*), commerce (*navigatio*), agriculture (*agricultura*), hunting (*venatio*), medicine (*medicina*), and theatrics (*theatrica*).[11]

In addition to this trinitarian hierarchy of knowledge, Hugh also proposed a pyramid of kinds of things: eternal, perpetual, and temporal.[12] The first category—eternal—contains one thing: God. The eternal "has no distinct cause and effect; it draws its existence not from something apart from it, but from itself alone. Such alone is the progenitor and creator [*artifex*] of Nature."[13] The second category—perpetual—also contains one thing: Nature. "Perpetual," according to Hugh, refers to that thing in which its essence and its principle of existence are separate. Nature was created on a divine principle, yet has no end, which is why it is called perpetual.[14] The third category—temporal things—"comprises those things which have both beginning and end and which come into being not through themselves but as works of Nature."[15] Thus, God is eternal and created Nature; Nature, in turn, is responsible for creating all temporal things.

Each of these three kinds of things (eternal, perpetual, and temporal) has a different kind of creative power: "the work of God, the work of Nature, and the work of the artificer, in imitation of Nature."[16] God, eternal, creates ex nihilo; Nature makes temporal things from templates (forms, in platonic parlance) created by God. Nature exists as an extrinsic, perpetual principle that gives temporary existence to things in the sublunar realm through the movement of a "creative fire" that flows down to earth.[17] Humanity, Nature's creation, is temporal, and human creative endeavor is the third kind of work in Hugh's hierarchy: "the work of the craftsman is to unite things kept separate or to disjoin those put together . . . for the earth cannot create the heaven, nor can man, who is unable to add even an inch to his height, produce the herb."[18] God creates both divine archetypes and Nature; Nature then uses these archetypes to create natural objects in the sublunary world. The human artificer, one of Nature's creations, manufactures material objects in imitation of natural forms. The artificer can create *only* composites of preexisting forms, for anything he could possibly imagine is based on something that already exists from Nature.

Hugh suggested that human work, however impressive, was always degraded. He called this creative work "not nature but imitative of nature; it is called mechanical, that is to say, counterfeit, just as it is said that a key, secretly introduced, is called 'mechanical.' "[19] Hugh's conflation of "counterfeit" and "mechanical" may reflect a translation error from Greek to Latin in the late ninth century. Martin of Laon, who had studied under John Scot Eriugena, directed the copying at Laon of a Latin-Greek thesaurus and has also been credited as the author of another lexical text from Laon in this period, the *Scholica graecarum glossarum*, a compilation of several hundred words, with accompanying definitions and etymologies.[20] According to Martin,

> "Moechus" means adulterer, a man who secretly pollutes the marriage bed of another. From "moechus" we call "mechanical art" any object which is clever and most delicate and which, in its making or operation, is beyond detection, so that beholders find their power of vision stolen from them when they cannot penetrate the ingenuity of the thing.[21]

All mechanical art is intrinsically fraudulent, and it can blind one with its ingenuity.

Automata, such as the birds on the Throne of Solomon in Constantinople or in the Palace of the Tree in Samarra, are copies of natural objects and would thus seem to be easily categorized in this period as the product of human craft. However, the distinction between Nature's work and humanity's work was sometimes difficult to make, as the metaphor *Natura artifex* both elevates human labor and diminishes Nature's creative work. Several related metaphors linking Nature's work with craft, especially metalworking, were repeatedly employed in Neoplatonist texts from late antiquity through the thirteenth century. Macrobius, in his *Commentary on the Dream of Scipio*, first personified Nature as *Natura artifex* and compared the process of human reproduction to that of a coiner minting money. "Once the seed has been deposited in the mint where man is coined [the uterus], *Natura artifex* first begins to work her skill upon it so that on the seventh day she causes a sack to form around the embryo."[22] Hugh, familiar with Macrobius, also used the coining metaphor, but to describe the maturation of the human mind rather than the generation of the human body. He equated the human mind with metal that then becomes a coin. Both the unformed mind of the infant and the lump of metal become changed into something very different: the mature human intellect and the tangible power of the sovereign respectively.[23] Both are created in a similar manner: an undifferentiated lump of plastic material comes into (violent) contact with a preexisting form, which gives its shape or contours to the material. Once minted, the coin is no longer a piece of metal like any other. It has a specific value, it can be exchanged for goods or services, and, most importantly, it represented in this period the power of the sovereign. Similarly, according to Hugh, the mind, by receiving the imprints of natural archetypes over the course of maturation to adulthood, is transformed from an unshaped, plastic material into the human intellect. However, both the coin and the human mind owe their existence to previously created external forms. The fully formed and trained human intellect of an adult is different from the pliable, merely receptive mind of an infant, but it is still only capable of viewing the world through previously seen archetypes.

Hugh influenced later Neoplatonist philosophers and theologians, especially Bernard Silvestris and Alain de Lille, both of whom used the metaphor *Natura artifex*. Bernard and Alain were associated with the cathedral school at Chartres, which represented the assimilation of several centuries of Neoplatonism from the early medieval period.[24] Bernard Silvestris (fl. 1115–1150), the earlier of the two wrote *Cosmographia* (also known as *De mundi universitate*), a natural philosophical *prosimetrum*—alternating passages of prose and classical meter—about the creation of the world. In it, Bernard personifies Nature as the "artisan who compounds bodies" for the souls provided by Endelechia, the world-soul.[25] Although the Chartrian and Victorine schools were seen by some contemporaries as rivals, their geographic proximity and similarity of purpose ensured that texts and ideas circulated fairly easily between them. The *Didascalicon* was probably a source for Bernard, as Bernard's definition of Nature is very similar to Hugh's.[26] A few decades later, Alain de Lille (ca. 1128–1203) established Nature an important character in his philosophical poems *De planctu naturae* and *Anticlaudianus*, both written between 1165 and 1185.[27] As with his Neoplatonist predecessors, Alain employs the metaphor of Nature stamping or coining natural objects; in *Anticlaudianus* Nature coins people into species from matter.[28] In *De planctu*, modeled on Boethius's *Consolatio Philosophiae*, the hammer and anvil are everywhere as Alain extends the coining metaphor to speech and verbal expression: a man who knows how to use grammar well is as much an artificer as one who works with his hands.[29] Alain also uses coining imagery to explain the creation of people, as when he compares human generation to artisanal craftsmanship. As Nature describes her role:

> Me, therefore, He appointed as His deputy; a coiner for stamping the types of things, so that I, minting the copies of things on the appropriate anvils, would not allow the shape to deviate from the shape of the anvil, but that, through my skilled labor, the face of the copy would in no aspect, defrauded by the endowments of any other elements, deviate from the face of the exemplar.[30]

The painting of *Natura artifex*, taken from a fifteenth-century manuscript of Jean de Meun's continuation of Guillaume de Lorris' poem *Le Roman de la Rose*, illustrates this extended metaphor of human generation.[31] The image depicts Nature creating new people at her forge out of existing limbs and appendages. Jean de Meun drew heavily on ideas in Chartrian Neoplatonist texts, especially *De planctu*. Nature (the creative impulse) works with Genius (sexual desire), to renew humankind in the face of mortality: "But when sweet and compassionate Natura sees that envious Death and Corruption come to destroy whatever they find within her forge, [she] continues always to hammer and forge and to renew the pieces with a new generation . . . . From these,

Art makes her examples, but does not make the forms as true."[32] Nature's divine forms are true, but human art can only make imperfect copies.

The metaphor of *Natura artifex* runs in both directions, explaining natural and human creative work. Nature's work is much more mysterious than the work of the artificer, but it can only be explained and understood in the language of human art. The metaphor is an attempt to explain her work to an audience in recognizable terms, just as the author of *Le Voyage de Charlemagne* compared Hugo's palace to a rotating mill-shaft.[33] *Natura artifex* describes Nature's singular power to give material form to divine archetypes, yet the coining imagery, as well as the trope of Nature's forge and anvil, evoke human art and metalworking. However, Nature can make humans; the artificer can make only a similitude. The image of Nature hammering together separated limbs recalls Hugh's assertion that the work of the artisan is "to bring together things disjoined or to disjoin those put together."[34] Interestingly, the work of *Natura artifex* is visually and verbally described as "forging," a term that meant both joining disparate things together and creating a counterfeit object intended to deceive.[35] The terms of human art, deployed in metaphor to explain Nature's special and important creative role, carry with them the implication that all manufacture is intrinsically debased. Human art is mechanical and mimetic, and it is the least impressive kind of creation, according to Hugh's three-fold hierarchy, as it is limited to making copies of natural forms. A builder gets his ideas from mountains, while bark, feathers, and scales all provide inspiration for human clothing.[36] However, although all examples of the mechanical arts are necessarily counterfeit, the work of the fabricator can occasion amazement. "[Necessity] has devised all that you see most excellent in the work of men. From this [necessity] have arisen the infinite varieties of painting, weaving, sculpting, and founding, so that we marvel [*miremur*] not only at Nature but also at the artificer."[37] Human art is by definition mimetic and counterfeit, but it can still evoke wonder.

Magical Mimesis: The Language of Description

The terms used to describe automata and their makers betray the boundary between the work of Nature and the work of the artificer, as they encompass both craft knowledge, such as metalworking, and text-based knowledge, such as astral science. Like the metaphor *Natura artifex*, descriptions of automata and their creators combine artisanal imagery and references to metalworking with allusions to more mysterious intellectual and creative practices.

The language of automata and their creators in twelfth- and early thirteenth-century texts, roughly contemporaneous with the philosophical and didascalic texts discussed above, refers to elements of the human mimetic arts as well as the more transformative arts of Nature. Although automata, especially in twelfth-century texts, are clearly mimetic, their mimesis inheres less in a meticulous reproduction of material appearance (corresponding to human art) and more in principles of operation and behavior. This is a sympathetic mimesis, as it allows objects to tap into and use the power of the original archetype, just as the minted coin takes on something of the power of the sovereign, rather than mere likeness.[38] For example, Hugo's palace, described in the previous chapter, does not resemble the heavens in the same way that an orrery models the celestial spheres, but, rotating around its central axis, the palace in motion resembles the movement of the earth in a fundamental way.

Medieval automata are often characterized in terms that evoke lowly artisanal craft, yet their creators are often described as highly learned men, who are able to draw on extensive natural knowledge. In the *Voyage de Charlemagne*, the two automata that crown Hugo's rotating palace are first described as "two children, cast in copper and metal" and later as "images."[39] *Figure, ymage,* or *ymagete* commonly denote automata throughout the medieval period. "Cast" [*tregeté*], the word used to describe the automata at King Hugo's fictional palace, connects automata to artisanal work (metalworking) and to intellectual (and verbal) endeavor (enchantment). In other texts, objects similar to Hugo's automata are "molded" [*façonez*], "gilded" [*dorez*], and most frequently, "cast in metal" [*tresgetez*].

Yet the depictions of the creators of these automata suggest a more complex picture than an artisan working in a foundry. Automata rest on esoteric knowledge, but instead of artisans (such as the makers of court spectacles and Mystery Plays in the fifteenth century, who guarded their secrets) philosophers, necromancers, and learned men create automata using astral science, enchantment, augury, or even necromancy.[40] The range of possibilities, from studying the *quadrivium* to trafficking with demons, runs the gamut from intellectually legitimate to maximally transgressive. These learned men attain their knowledge after years of studying the liberal arts, including *cumpas*.[41] Astral science was part of the traditional arts education, and was employed in navigation, medicine, and for prediction.[42] Other terms—enchantment, augury, art (skilled human work), and necromancy—go beyond the boundary of the liberal arts, and have in common the study and manipulation of natural phenomena, sometimes called "magic."[43]

Broadly speaking, in the medieval period magic could be considered either natural or demonic. However, these categories overlapped in the twelfth and thirteenth centuries and were often inextricably tangled, both in theory and in practice. Natural magic rested on a naturally occurring sympathy between the celestial and sublunary spheres, and relied on the hidden properties of natural substances or the fundamental structures of the universe.[44] However, demons, disembodied intelligences that could be malevolent, could also manipulate natural laws and create stunning effects.[45] A sorcerer using demonic magic would summon a demon and force it to do his bidding.[46]

The vocabulary for automata and their creators reflects this complicated network of intellectual pursuits and activities. This semantic field indicates that automata embody both the wonder that Hugh of St. Victor allows as well as the inherently fraudulent nature of all mimetic art. Old French words relating to magic, most of which came originally from Latin, were used to describe different ways that natural knowledge could bring about particular effects.[47] The inflected vocabulary of magic testifies to the importance and precision of the categories of magic, at least at a theoretical level. Yet meanings of these words also conflate the mastery of natural knowledge with practices involving demons. For example, *magie* came from the Latin term *magus*, originally meaning a priest, and then came to be identified in the Latin traditions with wisdom, sorcery, astral divination, and demons.[48] The meaning of the verb *enchanter* in this period encompasses singing, seduction, conjuring, and spell casting.[49] *Augure* referred to a pagan priest with specialized and even mystical ability to discern favorable omens by reading bird flight or bird entrails, while *augurerie* was more generally defined as foretelling future events through divination, scrying, or consulting signs (including avian signs).[50] The Latin form of the word *nigromance*—*necromantia*—is defined as either the act of divining through animals or contact with the dead, or more generally magic or sorcery.[51]

Two Latin terms, *ars* and *ingenium*, and their cognates in Old French, encompass a range of objects, activities, and connotations, from the skillful creator, as in *Natura artifex*, to possible demonic involvement in creating moving or speaking statues. *Ars* (Latin) and *art* (Old French) meant the learned ability to do something, such as the art of medicine or the art of poetry. *Art* could also mean the practice of magic or necromancy when it was modified by those terms. Because "art" on its own could refer to many different kinds of learned knowledge, it was frequently modified; for example, William of

Malmesbury said that Gerbert of Aurillac gained access to an underground cache of treasure through "the familiar arts" of necromancy.[52] From this root one also finds the sense of profession or métier in the word *artifex*, usually translated as "artisan," or "artist," and the pejorative connotation with deception in the word *artifice*.[53] In Old French *artifice* has a range of meanings, from admirable skill to sinister fraud: it meant one who worked as an artisan and a creator who copied natural forms with the intention of fooling the senses. Related ideas of skill, fabrication, and fraud inherent in *ars* and *art* in this period are paradoxically also found in its antonym, *ingenium* (*engin* in Old French), which meant in classical and medieval Latin an innate talent or spirit, related to the English "genius." *Engin* was often used to refer to artificial, mimetic, self-moving objects that seemed equally a product of art as of invention. *Engin* also came to mean ruse or trickery, in much the same way as English "ingenious" can sometimes mean "sly" or "crafty." Likewise, words used to denote the creators of automata and the processes used to make them come from the same root—*engeignor* or *gaaignié*. Related words in Old French from the same root (*engignant* and *engignart*) carry meanings of deceit and diabolical trickery, as well as artisanal skill and cunning. The Italian word *ingegnere*, which was introduced into Old French in the late twelfth century and referred to an inventor of siege machinery, reinforced these dual meanings of artisanship and artifice.[54] Both *engin* and *ingenium* were used until the seventeenth century to denote a manmade mechanical device, such as an automaton.[55]

Amphiras's Chariot, Vulcan's Engine

A passage from *Le Roman de Thèbes* (1152–1154), an Old French *roman* composed several decades after Hugh's *Didascalicon*, clearly illustrates the complicated semantic field involving fabrication, magical practices, intellectual ability, and automata. The earliest of the *romans antiques*, a group of Old French poetic texts that took the histories of Greece and Rome as their subject matter, the *roman* is a vernacular retelling of Statius's *Thebaid*, a Latin epic from the first century (ca. 90).[56] The *matière*—the subject—is the story of Oedipus and Thebes, and includes attempted infanticide, parricide, incest, self-mutilation, and ungrateful children. The version of the Oedipus myth given at the beginning of the *Roman de Thèbes* is the first that a non-Latinate audience would have heard.[57]

One major change between Statius's version and that of the *Thèbes*-poet is the addition of Adrastus, king of the Argives and enemy of the Thebans.

His ally, Amphiras, is a "very noble archbishop" and a valued counselor to Adrastus. Knowledgeable in all the secrets of the heavens [*cumpas, augurie*], Amphiras could cast lots and correctly interpret the results, bring the dead back to life, and understand the "Latin" of birds.[58] The commonplace in medieval literature of referring to the language of birds as Latin—the language of scholarship—indicates that the interpretation of avian sounds or signs was considered learned knowledge, rather than vernacular knowledge. The narrator assures the audience that "there is no better sorcerer under heaven."

Amphiras has a magnificent war chariot with two musical automata [*ymages*] on it. Vulcan had made the chariot and the images "with a great deal of thought and over a long period of time."[59] That only Vulcan, a god, could make the chariot and the automata demonstrates that these objects are fundamentally different from other kinds of manufactured objects. As I noted earlier, Vulcan (or Hephaestus, as he is called in the *Iliad*) also made wheeled metal servants to attend to the gods on Mount Olympus and two golden female servants to serve him in his workshop.[60] For Amphiras's chariot, Vulcan wrought a model of the entire cosmos, and placed the nine celestial spheres, along with the constellations, planets, and their movements on the chariot. The central sphere, representing the earth and the sea, was decorated with lifelike paintings of men, beasts, fish, winds, and storms.[61] Vulcan also wrought the seven liberal arts and placed them on the back of the chariot: Grammatica with her divisions, Dialectica with arguments, Rhetorica with judgments, Arithmetica holding an abacus, Musica with the scale, Geometria holding a rod, and Astronomia an astrolabe. The two automata, young men or boys, cast in metal [*tresgetee*], play music: one sounds the horn for the charge of Adrastus's army, the other pipes "clearer than a lute or viol."[62]

The narrator describes the skills needed to make the chariot and the automata on it; both are explicitly linked to metalworking, through Vulcan, as well as to the arts of magic and enchantment. This link is also seen in the term *tresgeter*, which can, like its English counterpart "cast," mean either the casting of objects in metal or the casting of spells, lots, dice, and enchantments.[63] Yet although the chariot and the automata were created in metal by Vulcan, the description of how the chariot and automata are made has less to do with the mechanical, artificial processes of smithing, and much more to do with deliberative and learned knowledge that Vulcan uses. "[He] made [the chariot] with great skill and over a long period of time. After a long time spent in study and deliberation, Vulcan placed the moon and sun on the chariot and, using art and enchantment, cast the entire cosmos in metal."[64] These models of the cosmos and of the terrestrial world are so accurate that they could be used as teaching aids.[65] This mimetic accuracy is represented as due at least as much to the philosophical and magical knowledge of Vulcan as to his metal-working abilities. Twice the author emphasizes the counsel and study that Vulcan undertook while making the chariot; furthermore, the mention of all nine celestial spheres and all seven liberal arts highlights the importance of intellectual endeavor. Vulcan's labor, like Natura's, can be described in artisanal terms, but operates on a more philosophical level. Of course, both learned theoretical knowledge and learned craft knowledge were needed to manipulate natural laws and phenomena. Study in the seven liberal arts, philosophy, and the cosmos was necessary to understand and to control the forces of nature and create automata. Knowing the properties of stones, plants, and metals connects sorcerers to artisans, while knowing how to read the heavens and devise enchantments joins them to philosophers.

How to Make an Automaton

The authors of romance could not and did not give detailed descriptions of how automata are made. Instead, they focused on the astounding and marvelous effects of automata, and described the creators of automata as scholars and magicians. Making an automaton thus required understanding the science of the stars; familiarity with natural objects imbued with marvelous properties as well as confident and intimate knowledge of their powers; or the ability to communicate with and control demons. In the literary texts of the twelfth and thirteenth centuries, learned sages, wise philosophers, and sorcerers created automata using sympathetic magic, celestial forces, esoteric natural knowledge, or demons.

The *Voyage de Charlemagne* contains a description of Hugo's palace, which mimics the earth by harnessing the celestial forces. While the narrator does not state who built the impressive palace, he does mention that it was built using *cumpas*, and as there is no mention of any supernatural involvement, it seems likely that the palace would have been understood to be built either by Hugo himself (as Cosmocrator), or by learned men at his court.[66] The bed in Hugo's palace where Charles spends the night had also been made by *cumpas*; underneath it is the coign for Hugo's spy. Given the moral outrage that Charles and his retinue express upon learning that they had been spied upon, *cumpas* here seems to have a morally negative valence, connoting not just dif-

ficult and highly specialized learning but also trickery and knowledge used
for dishonorable ends.[67] Despite the luxury and rarity of the materials used to
build Hugo's palace, artisanal skill is never mentioned. Both the palace and the
automata are less the result of human craft than the result of the mastery of
recondite and arcane knowledge used in ways not fully understood or morally
sanctioned. The author suggests an ontological distinction between the automata and the palace on the one hand, and the paintings, wall hangings,
and furnishings within the palace on the other; the mimesis of the latter derives from visual likeness to the natural exemplar, while the mimesis of the
former is sympathetic, and copies the original in movement and function.

The movement of the palace and the automata highlights this fundamental difference. If the wind strikes the palace on the western side, the palace
revolves around its central axis (the pillar), while the copper boys blow their
horns very loudly and laugh at each other "so you would swear they were re-
ally alive."[68] The wind also brings a terrible snow squall.[69] Despite the vio-
lence of the storm, the palace rotates smoothly from west to east, just like the
earth, while inside the palace everything remains calm, "as in the summer
month of May when the sun shines."[70] Hugo, "wise, clever, and full of cunning," has tamed elemental and celestial forces. Hugo has created an elaborate illusion of the cosmos: the palace moves, like the spheres, while, inside
the palace, everything appears stationary, like the earth. The automata could
be mistaken for humans or angels. The emphasis on both the corporeal and
the celestial links the automata, and by extension the palace, even more strongly
to natural forms (people) and divine creation (angels).

As the Franks' reaction to the revolving palace and automata demonstrates,
contemporary Western audiences viewed automata and their creators with a
mix of wonder and suspicion. Initially impressed by the splendor of the palace, Charles and his knights become terrified when it begins to move, falling
to the ground and cowering in fear.[71] The situation is comic—even satirical—
and Charles and his knights are the butts of the joke, while Hugo remains
unperturbed by the motion of his palace or the squall that rages outside. The
author describes the spinning palace and the automata in artisanal terms—
wheels and shafts—and part of the comedy may derive from the fact that
Charles and his entourage are taken aback by such mundane technology. Their
terror and confusion, especially compared to Hugo's sangfroid, demonstrate
the disconcerting nature of the automata to those unfamiliar with them. This
anecdote signals both the wonder and the suspicion inherent in automata and
toward the people who make them.

Automata could be created in this period by means other than astral science. The occult, or non-manifest, properties of natural substances (such as a
magnet) might also be used to create automata. Hidden qualities were believed
to inhere in natural substances. These marvelous potencies could involve action at a distance (the lodestone), poison antidotes (the bezoar stone), or pro-
tection from harm (the caladrius bird, which, in its reaction to an ill person,
would convey the prognosis).[72] Gemstones constitute the single largest group
of objects with non-manifest powers. They were used often in medical treatment, and their powers were listed in medieval lapidaries.[73] Mastering the potential abilities and uses of gemstones or any other group of natural objects
required long and careful study of the works of ancient natural philosophers.[74]
These hidden properties occurred naturally, as part of the customary variation
of nature throughout the world. These properties were most often the result of
celestial influences, as when the conjunction of certain planets would give
extra potency to a gemstone. William of Auvergne, writing slightly later in
the early thirteenth century, suggests a link between gems and celestial bodies:

> [the planets] might be collections of lights in parts of heaven itself,
> just as it appears among us in certain gems. For in fact I recollect
> when I saw an emerald, which appeared, in its brilliance, as the most
> luminous of three little stars. And this is true of the stone that is
> called heliotrope, because it is itself a green stone, growing brilliant
> red by means of a star.[75]

The marvelous properties of natural substances could produce astonishing effects when controlled by those who understood their power. In two mid-
twelfth-century *romans antiques*, *Le Roman d'Éneas* (ca. 1160) and *Le Roman
de Troie* (ca. 1165), the cryptic potential of natural substances allows automata
to function. In *Éneas*, a retelling of Vergil's *Aeneid*, the walls of Carthage are
built by *cumpas* (reflecting the amalgamation of knowledge dealing with the
mysterious and powerful) and made of marble and adamant (a very hard substance, either metal or gemstone), in order to withstand fierce attacks. Two
rows of magnets (lodestone) run along the tops of the wall to provide additional defense, presumably by interfering with the iron weapons of enemy
armies.[76] Within the city walls the tomb of Camille the Amazon incorporates
a caladrius bird, carved marble, adamant, a magical mirror, a casket sealed
with mortar made from precious stones crushed and mixed with serpent's blood,
an eternal lamp made from a carbuncle, and an automaton.[77] A golden dove,

on a pillar, holds in its beak a golden chain, one end of which is attached to the carbuncle. Across the room a golden archer stands sentry, bow bent and arrow nocked, ready to let fly its arrow at the dove if the tomb is disturbed.

> The archer could look long and hold the bow bent, but he would not release the arrow unless the noose of a snare (designed for this purpose and that kept the bow always bent) were first disturbed. At a breath all would be lost: if someone blew the snare it would trip the bow immediately, and the archer would shoot at the dove and hit it, breaking the chain and extinguishing the lamp.[78]

Although the description of the mechanism of the automaton seems fairly straightforward, at least to modern readers, its presence in conjunction with the abundance of costly and magical objects in Camille's mausoleum strongly suggests its dependence on or at least association with occult properties. The people responsible for the tomb were clearly learned in natural magic and philosophy, as shown by the many magical substances and objects used: the manipulation of those substances is the work of the scholar, not the artisan. That same knowledge allowed those unknown, unseen philosophers to cast the archer and give it the power of movement.

Benoît de Sainte-Maure's *Roman de Troie* (ca. 1165) contains even more elaborate wonders. The *Roman de Troie* was the first written retelling of the Trojan War in medieval Europe, and was based on two earlier Latin texts, the fourth-century *Ephemeris belli troiani* by Dictys Credensis and the sixth-century *De excidio troiae historia* by Dares Phrygius.[79] The Chambre de Beautés (also called the Alabaster Chamber), where Hector is taken to convalesce after sustaining battle wounds, is a fabulously decorated architectural marvel. The Chamber is made entirely of alabaster but without any kind of mortar or cement, and decorated with gilded doors and golden fixtures.[80]

> In the Alabaster Chamber, where the gold of Arabia sparkles and the twelve gemstones that God established as the most beautiful of all when he named them "precious"—sapphire and sard, topaz, chrysoprase, chrysolite, emerald, beryl, amethyst, jasper, ruby, sardonyx, clear carbuncle and chalcedony—these were to be found in the Chamber in abundance. No other lamp was needed, for the Chamber on the darkest night is brighter than the brightest summer day. The windows are made of green chrysoprase and sard and beautiful almandite, and the

frames are cast from the finest Arabian gold. I do not intend to tell
of the images, sculptures, statues, the paintings, nor of the various
marvels and tricks to be found there at various times, for it would be
tedious to listen to.[81]

Yet the narrator goes on to describe the greatest marvels in the Chamber:
four life-sized human automata, beautiful as angels, made of gold and perched
on columns made of gems. The Chamber itself and all of the decorations, including the human figures, had been made by "three poets, wise teachers, who
were fluent in necromancy."[82] One of the figures, a young maiden, holds up a
mirror so that the inhabitants of the Chamber may see their honest reflection
and "know right away what was unpleasant in their dress; in no time at all
they could put things to rights and arrange their apparel more attractively."[83]
The second maiden, an acrobat, "all day long played and made jests and danced
and gamboled and tumbled and leapt on top of the pillar, so high up it is a
marvel she did not fall."[84] The two other automata are figures of young boys.
One sits on a throne made of obsidian, a stone believed to be beneficial to
health, plays every kind of instrument, and, with the help of two other automata, an eagle and a satyr, scatters fresh flowers on the floor of the Chamber twice a day.[85] The other golden boy carries a censer, made with great
knowledge [grant esciënt], filled with aromatic gums and unguents which burn
but are not consumed, and which have "spiritual qualities, for there is no illness nor pain that is incurable once one has smelled it."[86] Equally important,
the same figure conveys confidentially to each person how his or her behavior is or is not courtly. "Here was proof of the most cunning skill: it was a
marvel that it could exist or how it could have been made," exclaimed the
narrator.[87]

Yet aside from marveling at the skill of these three wise men and the automata they have created, the author of romance can only describe the automata's general appearance, thereby underscoring the fact that these automata
are fundamentally unlike other forms of human art. Instead of analyzing their
operation or causes, the emphasis is on what the automata can do: they can
juggle, or shoot, or play music, or act as perfect courtly servants. This paucity
of detail of the visual description of the automata contrasts with the level of
detail the authors of these romances provided when describing artifacts ordi-
narily made by engineers or artisans. The architecture of Camille's tomb is
detailed over a hundred lines, and is clearly the poet's ekphrastic triumph, an
elaborate compendium of the exotic and the bizarre:

The area was large and was paved with marble. There were four stones, carved in the shape of lions, artfully situated. Above them were two arched vaults, crossed, with a cornice above (like a canopy), completely round. They [the vaults] were joined together in the center with great skill. Above, over the jointure, was placed a beautiful pillar of multi-colored marble. The base, which was set beneath it, was six fathoms high. The base and the pillar were completely worked with flowers, deer, and birds.[88]

Likewise, Benoît gives a vivid description of the censer carried by one of the automata. It was "made from a single large topaz, clear and costly, with finely worked chains woven with golden wire."[89] Yet all the audience can learn of the automata in Camille's tomb or the Chambre de Beautés is that they are made of gold or silver, are as beautiful as angels, and, in the case of the four automata in the Alabaster Chamber, are gendered as male or female.

The descriptions of the automata in the *romans antiques* may reflect the contemporary artistic practices in in Benoit's milieu. The mid-twelfth century saw the beginning of a new and independent visual art style, characterized by an emphasis on natural forms and heightened naturalism, develop in Flanders and northern France, especially in Champagne.[90] This new style flourished in metalwork, especially gold and gilded copper. Large objects, such as monstrances, reliquaries, and coffers, were worked in enameled gold and in-laid with gems, and were embellished with intricate detail.

Illuminated manuscripts of history and romance for the luxury market were produced in France beginning in the fourteenth century, and were most often found in the collections of nobles and courtiers.[91] Because authors did not give clear and exact descriptions of what automata looked like, manuscript painters had license to depict them in different ways. The depictions of the automata in Plates 5 and 6 are from two different northern French manuscripts completed in the second half of the fourteenth century. The automata in the Chamber are shown in two different guises: Plate 5 shows them as human figures on bedposts, while in Plate 6 they are clothed in the same manner as people, yet with wings and halos to emphasize their angelic beauty.

In neither plate do the automata bear any resemblance to machines, demonstrating that they were not thought of in mechanical terms. In Plate 5, each automaton holds or has near it something to identify its purpose in the text: one holds a mirror, one tosses knives, one is pointing, and one scatters flowers, with a bird and satyr nearby. The automata in Plate 5 are very pale, evoking

marble statuary, and they are smaller than the five people in the room. In this
instance, the artist has portrayed the automata as secondary and markedly
different from the people in the image. The painter has also obliquely commented on their striking nature: one of the human figures in the room stares
at the automata, while her companions are focused wholly on Hector. The
automata in Plate 6 are life size, wear clothes, and are represented with hair
and skin that makes them appear to be flesh-and-blood beings. However,
three have wings, and one figure, the musician, has a halo; these mark them
as angelic. The difference between the descriptions of automata and craft objects reflects the differences of status and ontology between the two kinds of
things. The censer carried by one of the automata in *Le Roman de Troie* is an
object of wonder because of the beautiful craftsmanship and the rarity and
size of the stone, while the automaton itself embodies more difficult and extensive knowledge, and is wonderful because of the mystery of its creation.

As I briefly introduced earlier, in addition to natural philosophy and astral science, demonic assistance could also be used to create automata. Demons were believed to be disembodied intelligences that could trick and tempt
Christians into sin. Equipped with superhuman powers, they could not entirely break the rules of nature, but could bend them significantly. Only God
could stop time or cause something to occupy two places at once, but demons
could move extremely quickly or appear to be in several places at once. They
also had foreknowledge and could reveal it to humans under the right circum-
stances.[92] Theoretically, summoning and controlling demons was part of the
ars magia (magical arts), a phrase that referred to controlling the forces of nature to affect future events, but not to *scientia divinationis* (the science of prediction), the knowledge of how to read and interpret signs and commentaries.[93]
Suspicion and condemnation accrued more to practitioners of the former than
of the latter, although both knowing the future and controlling the outcome
of future events negated free will and aped divine prerogative. However, authors of romance, among others, often blurred this conceptual distinction between reading signs of nature and the heavens and changing the future.

Automata, when understood as moved or inhabited by demons, were seen
as strikingly similar to pagan idols. On one hand, the idol-maker is cursed in
Deuteronomy as an abomination, as is the "work of the hands of artificers."[94]
The Hebrew Scriptures explicitly condemn the making of graven images, stating "no man can make a god like to himself."[95] According to St. Augustine,
one of the main authorities on demons throughout the Christian medieval
period, "of course a demon bound to a statue [*simulacro*] by the wicked art of

man is a god for the man who made it, but not for all men."[96] Creators of automata, therefore, were often viewed with suspicion, as they could easily slip into the category of idolators, and their creations could be seen as idols. The link between idols and heretical or un-Christian peoples compounded the suspicion surrounding automata and their creators.

Demonically animated automata appear in some medieval romances and texts, though not in any of the *romans antiques*. In the early thirteenth-century noncyclic Old French prose *Lancelot do lac* (ca. 1220), Lancelot encounters Doloreuse Garde, a forbidding castle guarded by a number of copper knights, including "a gigantic marvelous copper knight made by enchantment" [*chevalier de cuivre grant et merveilleus par anchantement*].[97] After defeating the metal guardians outside the castle, Lancelot goes inside and finds two more copper knights guarding a chamber. He challenges and eventually defeats these automata and enters the room, where he meets a young woman, also made of copper, holding the keys to the enchantments [*anchantemenz*] in her hand. Lancelot uses the keys to open a box nearby; inside it are thirty copper tubes, each of which voices horrible cries. Upon opening the box, a whirlwind appears and a noise so loud that it "seems as if all the devils from hell were there, and *in fact they were devils*."[98] He swoons, he sleeps; upon awakening, he discovers the copper damsel sunk into the ground and the copper knights at the door broken into pieces. Entrapped and controlled by the absent author of the enchantments, the demons are the animating force of the automata. Once their power is broken, the automata can no longer function.[99]

The demonic aspect of the automata appears in several manuscript paintings of *Lancelot do lac* (Plates 7–9): all three are from different French manuscripts from the fifteenth century. In all three paintings, the copper knights have bodies similar to human shape and do not wear any clothing. Their nakedness marks them as less than fully human, as they are uncivilized and have no shame. In Plates 7 and 8, the automata are shown with genitalia, and in Plate 8 they also are depicted with pubic and armpit hair. In Plate 9, the automata have beards and long hair, and look like wild men.[100] It is possible that the artist has chosen to depict the copper knights in this manuscript as wild men in order to allude to Lancelot's several psychotic breaks and his retreat from courtly society to live as a recluse.[101] The facial characteristics are also not human in Plates 7 and 8. In a striking irony, Lancelot, the human hero, is completely covered in metal from head to toe. None of his features are visible, nor does he display any sexual characteristics. Despite their recognizable human form, the automata are not recognizably human.[102] Their nakedness is a sign of debasement; this and their bestial faces mark them as inhuman. Compare these frightening creatures with the automata in the Chambre des Beautés, in which the automata, created by natural magic, have clothes, halos, and wings. In both instances the automata are distinctly different from humans, a difference that could result from both the morally and intellectually illegitimate knowledge of their creators.

The early thirteenth-century prose continuation of Chrétien de Troyes's *Perceval* contains a similar example of a demonic automaton. A cursed castle shelters a copper bull with a demonic oracle trapped inside. Perceval, on arriving, forces the fifteen hundred people in the castle to run the gauntlet between the copper men that guard the door with hammers. Everyone dies, except for thirteen souls who agree to believe in God. Once these thirteen agree to convert, the demon escapes from the bull with a noise like a thunderclap and the bull melts away.[103] The link between automata, demons, and un-Christian belief is evident in this example. The Christian hero breaks the enchantment and saves thirteen people (recalling Jesus and his apostles) who convert to Christianity.

Literary and visual depictions of fictional automata in the twelfth and thirteenth centuries vividly illustrate that they were understood as the products of esoteric, difficult intellectual knowledge, expressed variously as the products of sympathetic, natural, or demonic magic. The descriptions of the men who created them—wise men, fluent in philosophy and necromancy—and the methods they used further show that these creators do not operate in the same manner as the *artifex*. Automata appear in literary forms like the *chanson de geste* and the *roman* as the embodiment of the challenge to Nature's divinely given agenda by philosophers, sorcerers, and poets. They are more troubling and more impressive than other kinds of mimetic art: they can move, speak, perceive, and fight; they can terrify and delight; they can interact with and respond to the human viewer.

Liminal Objects

The automata in the "literature of entertainment" elicit wonder in different ways.[104] They are rare, even singular, objects. They are often highly beautiful or decorated, or are made of precious metals, and appear in exotic settings. They also highlight and confound ontological distinctions, such as natural/artificial, as discussed earlier. In these texts, humanoid automata often perform a disciplinary function. Their ability to surveil, guard, and punish people is as astonishing and marvelous as either their aesthetic value or the mystery of their creation.

The four golden automata in Benoît's Chambre des Beautés enforce aesthetic and behavioral codes of the court. The Chamber contains everyone in Trojan courtly society, and there are strict unspoken social codes of dress and behavior. The automata help the Trojan nobility behave appropriately, and "they were more sure and less anxious because of it. People were hardly ever mocked or accused of behaving foolishly."[105] The first maiden, holding the mirror, allows people to correct their outward appearance, making sure that their hair, brooches, and raiment are all correct and tidy. The second maiden, by performing acrobatic feats and conjuring, captivates the Trojan nobility, and prevents them from leaving the Chamber before the correct time. "It is difficult for anyone to leave the Chamber while the image is conjuring tricks, as it stands on the pillar."[106] One of the young male automata plays music to put the audience in a courtly frame of mind, and to provide privacy for conversation. "When those in the Chamber were talking, sleeping, or keeping watch none could hear the music and remain in low spirits or feel pain. People in the Alabaster Chamber are not gripped by foolish ideas, unpleasant thoughts, or ridiculous desires. The music benefits the listeners, for they can talk aloud, and none can overhear."[107] Last, the inhabitants are forewarned against any other lapses in gesture or deed by the fourth figure.

It would watch over the Chamber and, using signals, demonstrate to each person what he should do and the necessary action: it would make these things known without other people perceiving it. Even if in the Chamber there were seven hundred people, each one would truly know what the figure was showing him he most needed to do. What it showed was completely secret: no one else could know it, not I nor anyone else other than the person it was meant for. Here is proof of the most extraordinary invention: It was a marvel that it could exist and none could tell how it could have been made. None could be in the Chamber any longer than he ought to be; the figure clearly show when it was time to leave, and when it was too soon, and when it was too late; it would often take note of this. It prevented on the part of all in the Chamber, and all who entered or left it, behavior that was boorish, uncouth, or rash. It was not possible to be foolish or rude or irresponsible because the figure skillfully guarded all against uncourtly behavior.[108]

More important, the automaton conveys this to everyone confidentially, so that no one loses face at court.

Automata also enforce boundaries more literally, as in *Lancelot do lac* and the continuation of *Perceval*, in which copper knights patrol the entrances to castles and rooms within castles. Likewise, in *Le Roman d'Alexandre* (ca. 1180) two golden boys garrison a bridge in the Bois des Puceles against Alexander and his army.

> At the other end of the bridge there were, cast in metal, two boys made of fine gold. One was tall and thin, the other short and fat; their limbs were well made, their faces pleasant. When the army approached and [the two boys] heard the cries, each seized a hammer to block the passage. Above them, two inscriptions drawn up by a cleric proclaim that they were made by augury [*augure*] to defend the passage.[109] (Plates 10–11)

In both the manuscript paintings shown here, the figures are armed with hammers. In Plate 10 it is difficult to tell that the guardians are not real people, as they are shown with hair and wearing clothes. The second painting (Plate 11), also from a fourteenth-century manuscript, has a diapered background of red, blue, and gold, against which the automata have been rendered in gold leaf, matching the description in the text. The automata have golden faces and hair and do not wear clothes (there is a barely visible penis on the lower of the two golden figures). In this image, Alexander appears to have already made progress across the bridge, as one automaton is sprawled on the ground. In other instances, automata not only enforce physical boundaries, but also social ones. In the *Continuation de Perceval*, two gold and silver figures safeguard the tent of Alardin, a knight from a distant land. One "holds a spear in his hand and does not allow a churl [*viliain*] to enter." The other figure, holding a harp, bars the entrance to women who are no longer maidens. "If a maiden has been deflowered . . . the harp sounds discordantly and its strings break."[110] In this case, the automata secure a physical boundary (an entrance) and also uphold class distinctions and behavioral standards.

In literary examples in which automata watch over the resting places of the dead, they patrol and enforce spatial and behavioral boundaries.[111] The archer guarding Camille's vault in *Éneas*, mentioned above, is only one example. *Le Roman d'Alexandre* contains a description of the crypt of the "emir of Babylon," which is also protected by two metal automata, copper children in this case. "They both held shields of gold that were very heavy and gave each other great blows with their iron pikes; like two champions they faced each other. After those responsible for the enchantment had departed, nothing and no one alive could enter."[112] By securing spaces consecrated to the dead and enforcing the sanctity of those places, automata ensure that certain moral and religious rules are upheld; for example, that the resting places of the dead not be desecrated, disrupted, or robbed. In the examples from twelfth- and thirteenth-century vernacular literature discussed in this chapter, automata are human-like objects, but they are not human. Yet they interact with people and enforce human social boundaries and norms. It is unsurprising, then, that their creators are not represented as mere artisans, but instead as learned men adept in sorcery, and enchantment.

Ancient Marvels

Automata play a significant role in twelfth- and early thirteenth-century French romance. In some instances, such as the automata at Alardin's tent in *Perceval*, the boys guarding the tomb of the emir of Babylon and Hugo's rotating palace and angelic automata, they reinforce the connection automata have to the world beyond the boundaries of Latin Christendom. In many literary examples, automata are made using foreign knowledge, or are found in foreign lands, where marvels flourished. It is possible that Hugo's palace in *Le Voyage de Charlemagne* was based on contemporary descriptions of the actual Constantinople. Byzantine automata may have already familiar to some Latin Christians from Liudprand's account in the tenth century. Furthermore, twelfth-century Constantinople had a pair of musical statues over the Boukoleon Gate. The central hall of Hugo's fictional palace, with its many windows and rich furnishings, may be based on the Chrystotriclinos (supposedly built by Constantine), and the Triclinos of the Nineteen Beds (attested to in the tenth-century Byzantine handbook to courtly practice, *De ceremoniis*), two banquet halls in Constantinople.[113] In the *romans antiques*—*Le Roman de Thèbes*, *Éneas*, and *Le Roman de Troie*—automata are wonders from the distant past. However, in these settings of antiquity, automata also become part of the classical heritage of the ruling dynasties of Latin Christendom. In the second half of the twelfth century, French and Anglo-Norman writers began to retell ancient texts such as the *Aeneid* and the *Thebaid* in vernacular languages and adapt these myths and epics to foundational stories of France and Anglo-Norman

England.[114] By including automata in these romances, the French and Anglo-Norman authors, and their patrons, could claim automata as part of their cultural patrimony.

The *romans antiques* were composed in an Anglo-Norman milieu, possibly for Henry II Plantagenet.[115] Authors conjoined classical settings and plots with courtly ideals and aesthetics that resonated with the courtly audience of these works. The ancient legends of Thebes, Troy, and Rome were ideally suited to origin myths of nobility and empire. The medieval tendency to claim noble descent from Trojan nobility went back as early as the seventh-century legend that the Franks were descended from Francio, a survivor of the Trojan War.[116] This legend was widely repeated and elaborated upon in the courtly literature of the mid-twelfth century.[117] The *Roman de Thèbes*, the earliest of the *romans antiques*, appears frequently in manuscripts with the *Roman de Troie*. Manuscript evidence demonstrates that medieval writers and audiences understood a causal link between the outcome of the siege of Thebes and the later fall of Troy, and often combined these two narratives into a continuous narrative of Trojan history in manuscript codices.[118] The legends of Troy and Aeneas were similarly yoked, as the *Aeneid* recounts how Aeneas, a Trojan survivor of the conflict, became the legendary founder of Rome. Furthermore, both the poet and his subject matter were inextricably tied to histories of nobility and empire: the *Aeneid* treats of the foundation of the Roman Empire, as told by Vergil, the author of imperial epic.[119] The origin myth of Rome, retold for an Anglo-Norman courtly society in *Éneas*, was significant to the Anglo-Norman lay elite, as Aeneas's great-grandson Brutus was believed to have settled in and founded Britain.[120]

Romans antiques allowed French and Anglo-Norman nobility to claim the cultural, technological, and intellectual achievements of these ancient dynasties. Automata, emblematic of these achievements, figure prominently in these accounts. This historical narrative, which linked Troy and Rome to the ruling dynasties of the medieval Latin West, provided an alternative to the narrative of geographic specificity and natural philosophy outlined in Chapter 1. French and Anglo-Norman writers, such as Benoît, conjoined the *matière* of historical epics with wonder-provoking magical artifacts and automata. By inserting automata into these stories of nation-building, which had been reinvented to reflect the territorial and political aspirations of the French and Anglo-Norman elites, the authors claimed these marvels as culturally legitimate, despite the fact that just how these objects were made could rest on impious knowledge. These automata became part of the Trojan-Roman heritage of the Anglo-Norman and French courts.

Several decades after the *romans antiques* first appeared, French and Anglo-Norman clerics further tightened the bonds between the nobility and automata by inscribing automata into the biography of Vergil. Beginning in the mid-twelfth century, Vergil became a subject of Anglo-Norman clerical writers. These men wrote in Latin, in the genres of natural history and encyclopedia. Both the Latin and vernacular texts about Vergil derived from the Vergilian corpus and commentaries.[121] Contemporaneously with the composition of the *romans antiques*, Vergil's reputation as a magus acquired new dimensions.[122] However, it was not until after the *romans antiques* that he was also credited as an automaton-maker. The earliest medieval version of Vergil as a sorcerer appears in the *Policraticus* (ca. 1159), by John of Salisbury, a bishop, courtier, diplomat, and classicist, and addressed to his patron, Thomas à Becket, the archbishop of Canterbury. According to John, Vergil was the "Mantuan seer" [*uates Mantuanus*]. He created an apotropaic bronze fly that kept real flies away, among other wonderful objects.[123]

There are other accounts of Vergil's legendary magical powers in the decades after the *Policraticus*, but no further mention of automata until Alexander Neckam's *De naturis rerum* (ca. 1190s).[124] Neckam was, like John of Salisbury, an Anglo-Norman cleric. Furthermore, Neckam was even closer to the Plantagenet court than John of Salisbury, as Neckam and Richard I "the Lionheart" of England were foster-brothers.[125] According to Neckam, the best school in the Roman Empire had been Vergil's school at Naples. In a long account of the things Vergil, again referred to as "the Mantuan seer," accomplished with his genius, Neckam includes eliminating poisonous leeches by using a golden leech, similar to the bronze fly mentioned by John of Salisbury; creating a special concoction of herbs at the entrance to the butchers' market that would keep meat fresh for five hundred years; and erecting a bridge made of air which would transport him wherever he wished to go. The most amazing of Vergil's creations, according to Neckam, was the *Salvatio Romae*, an elaborate alarm system for the entire Roman Empire, which operated with multiple automata. Neckam describes the palace Vergil had built in Rome, in which he placed a wooden statue. The statue, representing the empire, held a bell in its hand, and would ring the bell whenever a province threatened revolt. At the same time, a bronze knight on a bronze horse on the roof of the palace would point a spear in the direction of the rebellious province, so that the emperor could send troops to restore the province to order.[126] Neckam does not give further comment on the *Salvatio Romae* or on how it worked. Given Vergil's reputation as the poet who celebrated the foundation of Rome, it is not surprising that Neckam credited him with creating an alarm system to keep the empire intact.

Two decades after Alexander Neckam listed the Vergilian wonders, including the *Salvatio Romae*, Gervase of Tilbury mentioned similar marvels in his *Otia imperialia*. Gervase was, like Neckam, from the Anglo-Norman nobility. Trained as a canon lawyer, he was a courtier at the courts of King Henry II of England; William of Champagne, the archbishop of Rheims; and Otto IV, the Holy Roman Emperor. He repeats John of Salisbury's story of the fly that Vergil made "by mathematical magic" [*arte mathematica*] to keep the flies out of Naples.[127] Gervase also repeats, with slight variations, Neckam's account of Vergil's solution to the problem of rotting meat.[128] He also attributes to Vergil a bronze trumpeter—made by astral science—that kept the noxious vapors and ashes of Mt. Vesuvius from blowing over Naples.

> Also there was a bronze image [*ymago*] holding a trumpet to its mouth. Whenever the south wind opposed it and entered [the trumpet], the breath of the wind reversed immediately. Now what benefit did that reversal of Notus [the wind] convey? Listen. A high mountain borders the city of Naples, next to the sea, overlooking the Terra di Lavoro spread out far and wide below it; in the month of May this mountain belches noxious smoke, and occasionally spits out burnt embers the color of coal and burning cinders; because of this, men assert that a vent of terrestrial hell blows from there. Therefore, when Notus blows, a searing dust scorches the cornfields and all the fruit, and thus the most fertile earth is made barren. Because of this, considering the whole region's loss, Virgil erected the statue with the trumpet on the opposite mountain (as we have said), so that at the first breath of wind the horn sounded and the wind, blowing against that same tube [of the trumpet], entered it; Notus, confused and repulsed, would be beaten back by the strength of astral science [*mathesis*].[129]

It seems that Gervase may have based his account of the trumpeter on a similar one by Conrad of Querfurt, written slightly earlier. In a letter from 1194, Conrad mentions that Vergil had made, among other things, an archer that faced Mt. Vesuvius and kept it from erupting. This device worked until an idiot decided to release the arrow, which then shot into Vesuvius, causing the volcano to begin erupting again.[130] Conrad's archer and Gervase's bugler resemble the trumpeters on King Hugo's palace, as well as other examples of guardian automata, commonly archers or buglers, in twelfth-century Anglo-Norman historical accounts (such as William of Malmesbury), and mid-twelfth-century romances (for example, *Éneas*).[131] In this instance, Vergil creates, through astral science, an automaton that uses the natural power of the wind to confound Nature and safeguard Naples.

It is remarkable that automata were attributed to Vergil only after they appeared in the *romans antiques* of a few decades earlier. Anglo-Norman and French poets and clerics in the twelfth century drew from similar source material, and clerics and courtiers at court would have been familiar with the *romans antiques*. In the *romans antiques* automata are written into the past, as part of the ancient heritage of the nobility, and are credited to men with skills in divination, philosophy, and even poetry (or enchantment). *Romans antiques*, based in part on the *Aeneid*, claim Roman or Trojan lineage for their French and Anglo-Norman noble audiences. The *romans antiques* were staged in a literary past that was heavily inflected by contemporary twelfth-century courtly society. Automata in *romans antiques* are part of the pageantry of the courts from which the French and Anglo-Norman nobility claimed descent. Writers of compendia, encyclopedias, and other nonfictional Latin prose translated automata from the literary *matière*, based on Vergil and recomposed in the *romans antiques*, and reinscribed them into the Vergilian legend and the Roman past, in the way that the authors of vernacular romance had earlier translated Vergil's epic of empire to France and the Anglo-Norman realm.

Vergil's ability to create automata rested, for the twelfth- and thirteenth-century authors, on his reputation as a seer and his knowledge of magic and the *quadrivium*. This echoes the descriptions of automaton-makers in vernacular literature from the same period. Automata, in these texts, are very particular objects. They are often extremely beautiful, and sometimes terrifying. In some instances, they have the power of perception and discernment. In others, they have extraordinary physical capabilities, as warriors, musicians, or entertainers. These objects, although artificial, are very different from other kinds of technology and craftsmanship. These creations appear to be impossible to make by artisanal means only, although they resemble other kinds of artisan-wrought objects in their material, and are presented as resting on a foundation of esoteric knowledge. The metaphor of *Natura artifex* explains the mysterious work of Nature in recognizable terms, in much the same way that Liudprand compared the unfamiliar Throne of Solomon to a familiar wine press. Both the metaphor and Liudprand's comparison are an attempt to grasp the strange and make it known. But descriptions of automata and their creators demonstrate the ontological distinction between golden courtiers and musical statues, on one hand, and a wine press or a mill wheel, on the other. The latter are the work of the artisan, while the former are closer to the work of Nature.

CHAPTER 3

Talking Heads: Astral Science, Divination, and Legends of Medieval Philosophers

Gervase of Tilbury, recording the marvels of Vergil in his *Otia imperialia*, made it clear that they were not the work of God, but were instead due to Vergil's skills in the *quadrivium*:

> We have not written this so that we might favor the sect of the Sadducees, who said that all things were dependent on God and . . . on fate and the accidents of fortune, for all things are ordered by God's will alone, as it is written: "All things are in your power, and there is none that can resist your will," etc.; but instead out of wonder for Virgil's astrological skills [*admirationem artis matematice Virgilii*], we have recorded [these marvels].[1]

Astral science, one subject in the *quadrivium*, was understood to be a way to gain foreknowledge and create automata. Legends that ascribe oracular heads to medieval natural philosophers first appeared in twelfth-century Latin historiography and went on to circulate throughout medieval and early modern Europe in Latin and vernacular texts, in prose and in verse. The most famous version of the legend concerns Roger Bacon's brass head, which first appeared in the Elizabethan drama *Friar Bacon and Friar Bungay* (ca. 1589) by Robert Greene.[2] Roger Bacon's (ca. 1214/1220–1294) interests in experimental science, including alchemy, and astral science, including prediction, during his lifetime caused him to be hailed as a magus and alchemist in the Renaissance; by the Elizabethan period he had a reputation as a sorcerer who used demons to penetrate the mysteries of the universe for personal gain.[3]

Greene's source was a mid-sixteenth-century prose romance entitled *The Fa-mous Historie of Fryer Bacon. Containing the wonderfull things that he did in his Life: Also the manner of his Death; With the Liues and Deaths of the two Conjurers Bungye and Vandermast, Very pleasant and delightfull to be read.* In keeping with the anti-Catholic rhetoric of the new Protestant establishment, Greene used Bacon's status as a Franciscan friar and his close ties with Pope Clement IV to portray Bacon as a sorcerer and practitioner of black magic.[4] The "con-juring friar" proudly boasts that he has "dived into hell / And sought the darkest palaces of fiends," and bound Belcephon, a demon, to his service. After "seven years' tossing nigromantic charms, / Poring upon dark Hecat's princi-ples," Bacon and his demonic servant make "a monstrous head of brass, / That, by th'enchanting forces of the devil, / Shall tell out strange and uncouth apho-risms."[5] The friar boasts, "I have contrived and framed a head of brass / (I made Belcephon hammer out the stuff) / And that by art shall read philosophy."[6]

Alas, the unholy friar's labor brings him no profit. Exhausted from so much sorcery, he orders his servant, Miles, to keep watch on the head while he takes a brief nap. Miles also falls asleep until he is awakened by a great noise. The head speaks, announcing, "Time is. Time was. Time is past," before being destroyed by lightning.[7] Miles, stupefied by the noise and the talking head, does not awaken his master until the head lies in ruins.

The outlines of the legend of Roger Bacon and his brazen head are found in earlier legends about vatic figures made by Gerbert of Aurillac, Robert Grosseteste, and Albertus Magnus. These men, acclaimed for their erudition (particularly erudition in the *quadrivium*—mathematics, geome-try, music, and astral science—and natural philosophy), were, like Bacon, believed to have used their extensive and extraordinary knowledge of celes-tial science to create talking automata. These philosophers are historical counterparts to the fictional learned men, introduced in the previous chap-ter, who used esoteric natural knowledge to make the automata in *Le Roman de Troie* and similar texts. This chapter continues to explore the idea of the philosopher-as-automaton-maker; in particular, the philosopher who makes a specific kind of automaton: the prophetic figure. The legends surrounding the speaking automata attributed to these three philosophers reveal compet-ing ideas about divination and foreknowledge. They also comment on the de-velopment of ideas in natural philosophy that explained the relationship between heavenly bodies and natural phenomena. The introduction of new texts in astral science and other subjects of the *quadrivium* from the Dar al-Islam into Latin Christendom in the twelfth century fostered new possibilities and new anxieties that blossomed in the early and mid-thirteenth century. The promise of astral science—to be able to understand God's design writ in the heavens—was that it held the key to all other forms of natural knowledge. Greater understanding of the heavens could lead to knowledge of future events, and could reveal hidden mysteries of nature. Yet these possibilities raised concerns about how this knowledge might thwart free will. At what point does mastery of the occult mysteries of Nature and natural processes overstep the divinely ordained limits of human intellect? The legendary figures created by astral and demonic magic, ascribed to Gerbert of Aurillac, Robert Grosseteste, and Albertus Magnus, express the excitement and fear that a highly rationalized and rigorous approach to celestial science and astral divination provoked in medieval Latin culture.

The prophetic statues in this chapter differ in important ways from automata in the literature of entertainment discussed in the two previous chapters. Unlike the golden archers, bejeweled animals, and metal knights discussed previously, these automata do not perform specific tasks. The metal people in the Chambre des Beautés and elsewhere do display judgment and perception, but theirs is limited to a specific purview, namely, the enforcement of boundaries and the regulation of behavior. The automata under discussion in this chapter display a different and more powerful kind of sentience: they can foretell the future. Like more conventional automata, these heads are also prestigious objects that evoke wonder, as they were made by men with the ability to harness celestial forces to powerful ends (this includes summoning demons). However, the talking heads and statues of these medieval philosophers are not for public display, but are instead for the private edification and enlightenment of their creators.

From Demonic to Astral Divination: Gerbert of Aurillac

The tale of the oracular head begins with Gerbert of Aurillac, the tenth-century scholar and eventual Pope Sylvester II (999–1003). Gerbert was the leading figure in tenth-century mathematics and astral science in the Latin West, yet he acquired after his death a reputation as a learned man whose erudition encompassed an advanced curriculum in the *quadrivium* that reached beyond the boundaries of permitted Christian knowledge. According to legends that began to circulate a century after his death, Gerbert used either necromantic or astral magic to create an oracular head. Successive versions of this tale, from

the late eleventh through the early twelfth century, illustrate a gradually broad-
ening idea of how foreknowledge could be attained; instead of requiring demonic intervention, divination might rely instead on the legitimate subjects
of the *quadrivium*.[8] This shift parallels the changing intellectual landscape with
regard to the *quadrivium*. Moreover, these legends take up the theme of foreign knowledge and foreign objects I explored in the first chapter. They expose concerns about foreign knowledge, especially in natural philosophy, and
intellectual hubris, which combine in the oracular brazen head.[9] Doctrinal
concerns about foreknowledge and determinism meant that divination, even
if it did not involve demons, was still highly suspect.

William of Malmesbury, monk at Malmesbury Abbey and the most influential English historian since the Venerable Bede (672–735), tells several anecdotes about Gerbert in his *Gesta regum anglorum* (ca. 1125). These stories
emphasize Gerbert's moral turpitude and his intellectual capabilities, especially
his erudition in the *quadrivium*. According to William, Gerbert's immense
learning enabled him to create a metal head that would reveal the future: "After carefully inspecting the stars (that is, at a time when all the planets were
beginning their paths anew), he cast for himself the head of a statue that could
speak, though only if asked a question, and would answer the truth in the
affirmative or the negative."[10]

Gerbert, who died only a few years into his papacy, had a reputation as a
brilliant scholar and teacher that persisted for several decades after his death.
Yet by the last decades of the eleventh century he had a new reputation as a
sorcerer. His infamy was largely due to a polemicist and cleric named Beno
(or Benno), who wrote in support of Holy Roman Emperor Henry IV and
antipope Clement III during the Investiture Controversy.[11] The Investiture Controversy was a struggle between secular leaders, especially the Holy Roman
Emperor, and the papacy, especially Pope Gregory VII (like Gerbert, he was
also known by his birth name, Hildebrand), over whether bishops, abbots,
and others in important positions in the Church served at the pleasure of secular authority, or owed their allegiance to Rome. This ideological struggle co-
alesced around several issues, such as simony and clerical marriage, and, most
important, over who could appoint Church officials. Up through the eleventh
century secular rulers, such as the Holy Roman Emperor, could and did invest bishops with the symbols of their office, and relied on them for administrative purposes. However, beginning in the last decades of the eleventh century
and continuing well into the first decades of the twelfth, the papacy and its
adherents asserted that only the pope had the authority to choose and invest

these high-ranking Church officials. Each side wrote and circulated sermons, letters, and jeremiads that accused the opposing side of all manner of criminal activity, depravity, and licentiousness.[12] Beno, a zealous supporter of the emperor and lay investiture, tried to discredit the papacy and its allies by asserting that previous popes, beginning with Sylvester II (Gerbert), had been necromancers who had defiled the papacy with their impious behavior. In libeling Hildebrand, Beno attacked his education. In his screed, *Contra Gregorium VII et Urbanum II* (ca. 1085), Beno claims Hildebrand had been a student of Benedict IX and Lawrence of Amalfi. Both these men had studied under Gerbert at the school of sorcery in Rome he established during his papacy. Hildebrand learned "the false doctrine of demons" from these teachers, who had learned it from Gerbert.[13] Like his predecessor Gerbert, Hildebrand was accused at the Synod of Brixen in 1080 of teaching sorcery in Rome.[14] "The wicked deeds of Gerbert" included summoning a demon.[15] According to Beno, Gerbert asked the demon about his death, and the demon answered that Gerbert would not die until he had said Mass in Jerusalem. Unfortunately, Gerbert forgot that there was a church in Rome nicknamed "Jerusalem," and he celebrated Mass in it. "Immediately after he died a horrid and miserable death, and in between those dying breaths, he begged his hands and tongue (with which, by offering them to demons, he had dishonored God) to be cut into pieces."[16]

Gerbert was tarred with the brush of sorcery in part because he, like the hated Hildebrand, had a reputation as a reformer. In the early medieval period the papacy was less powerful than it became after the thirteenth century; moreover, some aspects of Church doctrine were honored more in the breach than in the observance. Popes during the early medieval period bought and sold the papacy, solicited bribes, and openly carried on sexual relationships. Some were accused of violent criminal activity, including murder and arson. Thus, the assertion that a pope was in thrall to the dark arts was not as farfetched as one might imagine. Gregory VII's proposed reforms were in part due to the excesses of his predecessors, and included putting an end to secular involvement in Church business, especially ecclesiastical appointments, and to clerical marriage. To those, like Beno, who opposed Gregorian reforms and supported those reforms proposed by the Holy Roman Emperor, the papacy was the root of corruption in the Church. Papal involvement in necromancy and demonic magic recalled details about earlier popes, and was a useful tool for political polemic.

But Gerbert was also a credible target of these accusations because of his reputation for mastering foreign knowledge. Gerbert spent his early years, during the mid-tenth century, as an oblate at the Cluniac monastery of Saint-Géraud of Aurillac, where he received a thorough education in the *trivium* (grammar, logic, and rhetoric) and showed an aptitude for the works of Boethius.[17] According to Richer of Rheims, Gerbert's student and the main source for Gerbert's biography, Gerbert impressed the abbot, Géraud of St.-Céré, with his intelligence and dedication. In 967, the abbot arranged for Gerbert to have the patronage of Count Borrell of Barcelona, a frequent visitor to the monastery. Borrell took Gerbert to Christian Catalonia, and while in Barcelona for the next three years Gerbert studied thoroughly and extensively in the *quadrivium* [*mathesi*] "under the direction of [Atto]," the bishop of Vic.[18]

Gerbert's new situation offered him opportunities to surpass quickly his education at Saint-Géraud. Catalonia was a node of diplomatic, commercial, and religious exchange and a trading zone of scientific knowledge. Borrell was active in diplomacy; as noted above, the count regularly traveled into the Auvergne and other areas north of the Pyrenees, and maintained stable relations with the emirate in Córdoba and the Frankish kings. Atto, Gerbert's new teacher, had a cosmopolitan episcopal court, and diplomats and scholars often traveled between Catalonia and al-Andalus.[19] Gerbert spent some of his time at the monastery of Santa Maria de Ripoll, a ninth-century Benedictine monastery with an extensive library that included scientific treatises indebted to the Arabic tradition.[20]

The three years Gerbert spent in Catalonia allowed him study texts in the subjects of the *quadrivium* that were unavailable elsewhere in the Latin West. Consequently, when he traveled with Count Borrell from Barcelona to Rome in 971 he gained a reputation for erudition that outstripped his contemporaries, as well as many of his predecessors. According to Richer, Pope John XII reported to the king of Italy and later Holy Roman Emperor Otto I, "that such a young man had arrived, one who had perfectly mastered astral science [*mathesis*] and was able to teach it to his men."[21] On the pope's recommendation, Otto engaged Gerbert as a tutor for his son and heir, Otto II. After two years in Rome Gerbert moved to Rheims to teach the *quadrivium* to students at the cathedral school.

Richer credits Gerbert with teaching concepts in "music and astral science that were at that time in Italy completely unknown."[22] Gerbert introduced Arabic numbers and the abacus to the curriculum, and also began instructing students in mathematics and astral science more advanced that what had been previously taught.[23] To help his students master unfamiliar and complicated concepts, he constructed spherical models of the heavens: a solid sphere, a hemisphere, an armillary sphere, and a star sphere. [24] He was an active member of a far-flung intellectual community, writing treatises on spheres and the astrolabe and corresponding with scholars in the Spanish March.[25] There are also some references to an *orologium* and a steam organ he built while in Rheims.[26] He remained there, as master of the school, until 991, when he became archbishop there.

Gerbert maintained his ties to the Ottonian dynasty from 973 to 997, when he left Rheims to become an advisor to Otto III, whose father he had tutored. Otto's court was at Magdeburg, which was, like Rheims, the seat of an archdiocese and the site of a well-established cathedral school.[27] Gerbert was an advisor and tutor to sixteen-year-old Otto, and the two often discussed astronomy and mathematics.[28] While at Otto's court, Gerbert continued his interest in instrument making and celestial observation. A younger contemporary of Gerbert's, writing just a decade after his death (ca. 1015), wrote, "He could observe perfectly the courses of the stars and surpassed all his contemporaries in his understanding of many and varied disciplines, . . . with [Otto] in daily discussion in Magdeburg, [Gerbert] made an *orologium*, positioning it accurately by observing the star that is the mariners' guide [the pole star] through a tube."[29] This *orologium* could have been a sundial, an astrolabe, or a noctur-labe (an instrument operating on the same principle as an astrolabe, but which measured the altitude of a star at night).[30] The viewing-tube was similar to the one Gerbert described in his treatise on the sphere, which Richer also attributed to Gerbert.

Gerbert's patron, Otto III, controlled the papal elections. Given his close relationship with his tutor and advisor, it is unsurprising that he picked Gerbert to become pope in 999.[31] As I noted earlier, Gerbert, like his successor Hildebrand, had a reputation as a reformer. As pope, he urged the moral reform of the clergy, and spoke out against simony and concubinage, both of which were rampant in the Church. He was unpopular in Rome and had to leave the city for a period while the Romans were in open rebellion against him. Gerbert was pope for a short time only; he fell ill in May 1003 while celebrating Mass at the Church of the Holy Cross of Jerusalem and died nine days later.[32] Almost immediately, he won plaudits for his skill as a statesman and scholar. His successors praised him; Sergius IV (1009–1012) said that after Gerbert died "the world darkened and peace disappeared." Just a decade later, Helgaud of Fleury, biographer of the Capetian king Robert the Pious, lauded Gerbert's piety, wisdom, and good works.[33]

Yet, after Beno, Gerbert was known for centuries as a medieval Faust: the wicked pope who sold his soul to the devil in exchange for knowledge. Compare this with the reputation of Fulbert, Gerbert's pupil, the charismatic bishop of Chartres. Fulbert, who founded the school of Chartres in 990, was respected as a learned man, but was never noted for particular expertise in the *quadrivium*. Unlike Gerbert, he had little interest in astral science and mathematics, and was known for his exegetical works. Far from being thought to be in league with the devil, he was believed to have the favor of the Virgin Mary.[34] But Gerbert, due to his education in Spain and his prowess in the *quadrivium*, was a clear target for accusations of necromancy and demonic pacts, even if the accusations were polemical. Despite Gerbert's ties to three generations of the Ottonian dynasty and his attempts at clerical reform, his intellectual legacy to Gregory VII, his alleged sojourn in al-Andalus rather than Barcelona, and his mastery of new and alien knowledge (the abacus, astral science) made it easy to depict him as depraved and iniquitous: exemplary of everything corrupt about the papacy.

Although Beno mentioned Gerbert's association with a demon, there is no mention of an automaton in the form of a prophetic head. It was not until several decades later, in the early twelfth century, that Gerbert's diabolical knowledge became associated with automata. William of Malmesbury devotes several long passages in his *Gesta regum anglorum* to Gerbert's towering intellect and bottomless perfidy, and it is he who first introduces the tale of Gerbert's prophetic brass head and his famous encounter with golden automata.[35] William's account of Gerbert, comprising eight sections of the second book of the *Gesta regum anglorum*, links Gerbert's proficiency in the *quadrivium* with demonic knowledge gained (or stolen) from a foreign source. Yet he notes that Gerbert used his knowledge of celestial science—part of the *quadrivium*— to build a prophetic head.[36] Several texts that repeated some of Beno's assertions about Gerbert also circulated in this period. In his digression on Gerbert, William cites the legends circulating about Gerbert from the previous century, while revealing early twelfth-century ideas about the adoption of astral science into the intellectual environment of early twelfth-century England.

William repeats earlier aspects of Gerbert's biography, especially his education in Spain. Beginning a long digression from the kings of England on Gerbert, William says, "It will not be absurd, in my opinion, if we put in writing those stories which flutter around the mouths of all men."[37] As I shall discuss below, William drew on popular and oral authority for some of this material, but he also took pains to assure his readers of the veracity of his account. Richer had noted that, while in Christian Spain, Gerbert studied the *quadrivium* [*mathesis*], yet Adhémar of Chabannes, the noted fabulist, writing shortly after Gerbert's death, states Gerbert had gone to Córdoba (capital of the caliphate of Córdoba) for the sake of wisdom.[38] Although Adhémar is the only contemporary of Gerbert's who asserts that he studied in al-Andalus, William follows Adhémar's account: "Either bored with monastic life or smitten with a desire for glory, he fled one night to Spain, intending primarily to learn astral science and other arts of this kind from the Saracens [sic]."[39] According to William, Gerbert studied in Seville (rather than Córdoba, but still in al-Andalus), where "those people devote themselves to studying divination and enchantment, as is their customary habit."[40] Gerbert was such an apt pupil that

> there he conquered Ptolemy in knowledge of the astrolabe, Alhandreus in the positions of the stars, Julius Firmicus in astrology. There he learned what the song and flight of birds portended, there to summon ghostly forms from hell; there he learned everything that is either harmful or healthful that has been discovered by human curiosity; but on the legitimate arts, mathematics, music, and astronomy and geometry I need to say nothing. By the way he absorbed them he made them appear to be beneath his ability, and through great effort he recalled to Gaul those subjects that had been long obsolete. He was truly the first to snatch the abacus from the Saracens, and gave the rules for it that abacists, for all their intelligence, hardly understand.[41]

William repeats Richer's pronouncement that Gerbert had introduced heretofore-unknown knowledge to the Latin West. According to William, scholars in al-Andalus pursued subjects unfamiliar in Gerbert's native France, such as astral science [*astronomia*]. Yet they also studied things that were more intellectually and morally problematic, like divination [*diuiniatio*], spells [*incantationes*], and necromancy [*excire tenues ex inferno figuras*]. Furthermore, it is difficult to disentangle the doctrinally acceptable from the impermissible. All the authors William lists were authorities in celestial science: Ptolemy was the leading figure in cosmology, Julius Firmicus was the late antique author of a book on horoscopes (*Mathesis*, ca. 337), and "Alhandreus" refers to a group of texts on the zodiac, astral measurement, and astrological divination known as the *Alchandreana*.[42] Furthermore, William was the first author to assert that Gerbert learned anything from Muslim scholars. This assertion indicates

William's position in the intellectual community of scholars in the West Country of England, which was central to the adoption of Arabic texts on astral science into Latin culture.[43]

William conjoins Gerbert's erudition and the reputation of Muslim Spain as a source of astrology and magic with Gerbert's reputation as a necromancer from sources prior to the 1120s. Beno, who maintains that Gerbert had sold his soul to the devil, is not a lone voice crying in the wilderness. Hugh of Flavigny (ca. 1064–1114), a Benedictine chronicler in France, claimed that Gerbert obtained the see of Rheims "through magic."[44] It is unlikely that William was familiar with Beno's text; however, he was probably familiar with a slightly later text than Beno's: the *Chronicon* of Sigebert of Gembloux (written no later than 1112), which was widely transmitted.[45]

Sigebert (ca. 1035–1112), a Benedictine monk, was, like Beno, a vigorous imperial partisan in the Investiture Controversy. He was certainly familiar with Beno's writings, and referenced them in his own tracts against the papacy, of which the *Chronicon sive Chronographia* was the best known.[46] Writing on Gerbert, Sigebert echoes Beno's account, and repeats it as commonplace.

> Relating to Gerbert and Silvester . . . he shone even among those who were the most brilliant in the books of the sciences . . . . And yet it is said that Silvester did not enter by this door [of proper study], as might be expected of one who is still accused of necromancy. Also, there is something crooked about his death. It is said that he died from a violent beating at the hands of the devil. But we leave off these things in the middle [and] he is apparently excluded from the number of popes.[47]

William, writing only a dozen years after Sigebert, repeats that Gerbert was in league with the devil. In the *Gesta regum anglorum*, Gerbert studied with a "Saracen" philosopher who debated with him and gave him books to copy. Yet there was one book, carefully guarded, "into which [the teacher] had confided all of his art," that Gerbert desired more than the rest.[48] His teacher proved deaf to begging and unmoved by offers of money, so Gerbert tried a ruse. He seduced the man's daughter, "after contriving intimacy with her through constant attention," and enlisted her help in getting the older man drunk.[49] Once the teacher had finally passed out, Gerbert stole the book and escaped. When the teacher awoke and discovered the theft, he pursued his errant pupil, so "[Gerbert] called up the devil with incantations" and entered into a pact with him if the devil would protect him from the revenge of his teacher. "And so it happened," says William, matter-of-factly.[50] In William's version, Gerbert flees his monastery, breaks his vows of obedience and chastity, steals from his teacher, and strikes a bargain with the devil. Over the course of one century, Gerbert changed from a gifted scholar whose aptitude was fostered by powerful secular and ecclesiastical lords to an impious monk whose lust for knowledge was fostered by foreign teachers and the devil.

William also repeats the story of Gerbert's violent death and mutilation, and clearly believed it, as he used that story to give credence to the tales of Gerbert's sacrilege. After detailing the way in which Gerbert trafficked with the devil, William admits that some readers might think that his account of Gerbert no more than a "popular fiction," or an attempt to tarnish the reputation of a learned man.[51] Yet, ultimately he stated his belief in Gerbert's perfidy, saying, "in considering [his] death, it makes me believe the truth of the account of this whispered sacrilege. Because why should a dying man, as I shall tell later, become a butcher, dismembering his own body, unless he had on his conscience some horrible crime?"[52] According to William's logic, because the account of Gerbert's death is true so are the accounts of his pact with the devil and his facility in necromancy, for nothing else could explain his deathbed behavior.

The subjects—licit and illicit—that Gerbert had studied in Seville allowed him to create mechanical marvels and discover ancient automata. William reports that while at Rheims, Gerbert built a clock "using the mechanical arts" and also a pair of hydraulic organs, "which work by hot water violently forcing out air to fill the chest cavity of the instrument in a wonderful manner, and through passages bronze pipes with many holes emit musical sounds."[53] Indeed, William, who almost certainly never traveled abroad, maintains that they could still be seen in the cathedral at Rheims.

The magic Gerbert stole from his teacher in Seville also enabled him to discover Octavian's lost treasure, which included many golden automata. One night while in Rome, Gerbert went to the Field of Mars to examine a metal statue with its arm outstretched and the words "strike here" on its head. "In the past, men had taken this to mean that they would find treasure here, and they had damaged the innocent statue with many blows."[54] Gerbert, cleverer than the others, noted where the shadow of the statue's finger fell at noon.[55] He returned after dark with a servant, and "there, in response to the familiar arts [of necromancy] the earth opened, revealing a broad passage as they entered."[56] Underground, Gerbert and his servant encountered "a golden palace, gold walls, gold ceilings, with everything made of gold; golden knights appeared to be playing with golden dice, and a king and queen of precious metal reclined at a table with their meal before them and servants in attendance; the dishes were of great weight and price, in which human art surpassed nature."[57] The palace was lit by a carbuncle, while in the opposite corner a golden archer aimed an arrow at the carbuncle to deter theft, "for the instant one put out a hand to touch, it appeared as though all those figures leaped forward as though to forestall such effrontery."[58] Fear of retribution stopped Gerbert from taking anything, but his servant, thinking that petty larceny would go unnoticed, tried to steal a knife. "In a moment, truly, all the figures leapt up with a roar and the boy shot his arrow into the carbuncle and plunged everything into darkness. And if the servant, admonished by his master, had not quickly replaced the knife, they both would have paid severe penalties."[59] Gerbert and his servant quickly escaped, with their "insatiable greed" unslaked.[60] William concludes, "the opinion of all the common people is that [Gerbert], contriving through magic, succeeded against his adversaries."[61]

William, writing history at the Abbey of Malmesbury, authenticates his account of Gerbert's marvelous encounter with the testimony of an eyewitness to similar automata. "I have included these words from this Aquitanian, so that a tale about Gerbert which I shall relate will not seem astonishing."[62] When William was a young man the Aquitanian monk told him a similar story, in which he and his cronies searched for the treasure of Octavian. After finding their way into the underground palace, they saw "golden horses with golden riders, and all the other things which have been said of Gerbert's tale."[63] But the automata that the older monk described to William—the golden courtiers and the bronze guardians—are objects that later become included in romances. In the version William heard as a young man, a bronze peasant with a hammer guards the treasure, similar to some of the automata in the romances mentioned in the previous chapter.

William also demonstrates that Gerbert's knowledge from Spain enabled him not only to find automata, but also to create them. As I noted earlier, William reported that "after carefully inspecting the stars (that is, at a time when all the planets were beginning their paths anew), he cast for himself the head of a statue that could speak, though only if asked a question, and could answer the truth in the affirmative or the negative."[64] William repeated Beno's account, in which Gerbert misunderstood the head's equivocal answer to his question, "Shall I die before I sing mass in Jerusalem?" After falling ill in Rome in the church called Jerusalem, he confessed his many nefarious actions to the cardinals, and "went insane and, his reason blunted from the pain, he ordered that he should be cut into small pieces and cast out piece by piece. 'Let him have the service of my members who sought their obedience; my soul never accepted that oath of sacrament, nay, rather, sacrilege.' "[65]

The legends surrounding Gerbert were so well entrenched that they were repeated in later historical texts, and were so compelling that visual artists often illustrated scenes from Gerbert's scandalous biography. A shorter version of William of Malmesbury's account of Gerbert's life appears in an early fourteenth-century French manuscript of a universal chronicle, the *Abrégé des histoires divines*. This chronicle, which is in manuscript M. 751 at the J. Pierpont Morgan Library, is an interpolation of Peter Comestor's *Historia scholastica* (ca. 1175) and Peter of Poitiers's *Compendium Historia in Genealogia Christi* (ca. 1193–1205). These two earlier texts were both abridged versions of the Bible that had been combined with other works of history to create a "universal history" that attempted to synthesize secular and sacred history from the creation of the world up to the time of their completion.[66] While universal chronicles are often based on the *Historia scholastica* and the *Compendium Historia*, they all differ from one another in some particulars.

This version, the *Abrégé des histoires divines*, was written in French and produced in or around Amiens (not far from Rheims), between 1300 and 1310. The manuscript contains two hundred and twenty-eight manuscript paintings, executed in color and gold leaf. The artist or artists have chosen to depict several dramatic moments from Gerbert's life, as well as some of the marvels associated with him (Plates 12–15). In the first miniature, Gerbert is shown in profile stealing the book of necromancy from under the pillow of his tutor (Plate 12). He wears the cloak and garb of a student, and has an intent look on his face as he grasps the book with his left hand (a sign of malevolence), while his teacher, cheeks rosy from too much wine, sleeps in drunken oblivion. On the following folio Gerbert wears episcopal regalia and sits beside a steaming cauldron set beneath organ pipes (Plate 13). The corresponding text on this folio (fol. 100r) notes that King Robert, "the Pious," had deposed the archbishop of Rheims and installed his own teacher, Gerbert, instead. While in Rheims, "[Gerbert] made a marvelous *orologium* and an organ that produced sound from the steam of heated water."[67] A few years later, according to this chronicle, after becoming first archbishop of Ravenna and then pope, Gerbert used "the help of the devil and necromancy" to locate Octavian's treasure in Rome.[68] The next miniature, on the following page (fol. 100v), depicts the moment when Gerbert and his assistant interrupt the golden royals and courtiers in their underground home (Plate 14). Against a vivid blue background framed by an ogee arch, four figures, the table, and the dishes on it are in gold leaf, echoing the textual description and denoting their "art status."[69] The two figures on the left wear crowns; one holds its hands up in an attitude of surprise or shock, and the other stands and looks in dismay at the other crowned figure. Immediately to the right, a servant looks at the two crowned figures and has one hand on the table. Finally, all the way to the right, a golden archer aims his bow and arrow at the carbuncle that hangs just above the second crowned figure, ready to plunge the subterranean palace into darkness.

Gerbert's dramatic death also merited visual representation. The fourth image from the section on Gerbert in M. 751 depicts his dismemberment (Plate 15). Gerbert, again dressed as a bishop, sits while a man with a knife cuts off his right arm. Gerbert, with eyes open, appears to be alive. The visual interest in Gerbert's life continued into the fifteenth century. Another historical chronicle, the *Mare historiarum*, a historical compendium attributed to Giovanni Colonna in the mid-fourteenth century, also repeats the tales of Gerbert's life and death. A fifteenth-century French manuscript contains a painting that vividly illustrates the strangeness and horror of Gerbert's posthumous mutilation (Plate 16). The left side of the painting shows Gerbert, dead, dressed in full papal regalia and attended by several cardinals. The second half shows him naked (but still wearing the papal crown), outside the city walls, with both legs and one arm chopped off, while a man stands above him, wielding an axe.

The Predictive Sciences

Although William repeats prior assertions that Gerbert had made a pact with the devil, he does not present Gerbert's oracular head as the product of demonic magic (recall that in Beno's text Gerbert had summoned a prophetic demon, but did not make a talking head), but rather as the result of astral science. This is evident in the emphasis on the position of the planets ("beginning their paths again"). To William, writing in the early twelfth century, as texts on the science of the stars were introduced into England, prophecy was no longer necessarily linked with demonic magic, but could be the result of newly introduced celestial science.

The use of astral science to create oracular automata, even in legend, is an example of its rise as a predictive science. William of Malmesbury's account of Gerbert's intellectual biography and the self-serving uses to which he put his hardwon knowledge emphasizes both the possibilities new texts in the *quadrivium* presented and corresponding anxiety over the uses to which this knowledge could be put. William's version coincides with the beginning of a flood of new and newly available texts in natural philosophy in Latin. Included in this group were more comprehensive and detailed texts on the science of the stars; these promised new opportunities for prediction and foreknowledge. Twelfth- and thirteenth-century legends about the prophetic statues of learned philosophers illustrate the difficulty of drawing definite boundaries around *scientia divinationis*, defined earlier as the ability to read signs and foretell future events, and *ars magia*, the use of natural knowledge or demons to change the outcome of future events.[70] Although the distinction between foretelling future events and changing them may have been clear to the practitioners of astral divination, it was a distinction without a difference to many medieval writers. Just as terms like augury, necromancy, magic, and enchantment, all of which theoretically referred to different practices, were used interchangeably in twelfth-century vernacular texts to signify morally ambiguous learning, prophecy, whether through reading the stars or creating an oracular head, slid easily from the allowable to the unacceptable, both morally and intellectually.[71]

The legends of medieval sorcerers and their prophetic automata, which emphasize ambition and erudition, reveal intellectual and cultural anxieties surrounding the importation of new natural knowledge, especially in the context of the proper limits of human knowledge.[72] Beginning in Gerbert's lifetime, new texts in the *quadrivium* were introduced into Christian Europe by Christian and Jewish scholars translating Greek and Arabic natural philosophy from Arabic into Latin. Many of these treatises promised the power of divination, power which, up until this period, was often identified with demonic magic, as in Beno's account of Gerbert's prophetic demon. Divination based on astral science did not replace divination based on necromancy and demons. The latter continued for centuries to be viewed as a path to foreknowledge; however, it was no longer the only path. Celestial divination could be legitimate, as it was based on a deep understanding of celestial movements and careful observation of natural phenomena. However, celestial divination enriched and reconfigured Christian concerns about doctrine and orthodoxy, and raised questions about the appropriate limits of foreknowledge. The oracular heads created by philosophers adept in astral science embody these concerns.

Astral science was not uncommon in the early medieval period. As one of the seven liberal arts, it was part of the general curriculum for monastic students. Alcuin (735–804), an Anglo-Saxon scholar, wrote that during his education in York he had been taught the zodiac and natural philosophy alongside Scripture and the subjects of the *trivium*. His education was likely less extensive than the more thorough and programmatic inquiry that a counterpart in the Dar al-Islam would have received.[73] Alcuin traveled to the court of Charlemagne and was tasked in 782 with implementing educational reform throughout the Carolingian empire. During the Carolingian period more broadly, renewed interest in astral science, including prediction, provided the impetus for the circulation of some old texts and the creation of some new ones, despite some ethical and theological objections to this area of study.[74]

Forecasting the outcome of events based on celestial bodies was a sustained focus of astral science. Although this subject became more important in the second half of the Middle Ages, there is compelling textual evidence in favor of ongoing Latin interest in prediction and augury through late antiquity and the early medieval period. Ancient and late antique authors such as Pliny, Macrobius, and Martianus Capella provided information about the planets and their characteristics, as well as the houses of the zodiac.[75] Two Latin texts on horoscopic prediction, *De astronomica* by Marcus Manilius (ca. 9–16 C.E.) and *Mathesis* by Julius Firmicus, which William of Malmesbury mentions as one of the books Gerbert had studied, circulated in monastery and cathedral libraries throughout Europe. By the tenth century, both were fairly well known to men with an interest in the *quadrivium*. Other texts from the eighth through twelfth centuries on lunar divination, the zodiac, and the interpretation of comets survive, as well.[76] But before the introduction of tools to measure the heavens accurately, predictive astronomy was fairly simple, and was based on readily observable astro-meteorological phenomena. Even when celestial divination was not stressed or practiced, rare celestial phenomena were believed to be harbingers, though of what was not always clear.[77] Carolingian emperor and Charlemagne's heir Louis the Pious directed an astronomer at his court to interpret the importance of a comet, and the anonymous chroniclers of the *Anglo-Saxon Chronicle* noted comets, eclipses, and the *aurora borealis*, all believed to portend change or disaster.[78]

Texts on the *quadrivium*, along with astronomical tables, which gave the locations of stars at different latitudes, therefore ensuring more precise predictions, became more widely available in the Latin West in the twelfth century. Arabic texts on celestial science encompassed methods for calculating the position and movements of heavenly bodies with greater accuracy (recorded in astronomical tables), and the proper techniques for using those observations to make more detailed and complicated predictions. Judicial astrology, as this kind of endeavor was often called, could be used to find out information about a particular person based on the location and moment of birth (natal astrology), to ascertain the outcome of a particular event (interrogational astrology), and to establish the best time to undertake a particular activity (electional astrology). Scholars from the Latin Christian West traveled to al-Andalus, North Africa, and the Middle East, where they translated (often with the help of Jewish scholars) texts in natural philosophy, alchemy, and the science of the stars.[79] Scholars and the flow of information went from the Arabic-speaking world to the Latin world, as well. Peter Alfonsi (1062–1110), a Spanish scholar and physician, had an extensive education in mathematics and natural philosophy. In a letter addressed to the "peripatetics of Francia" he deprecated the general ignorance there in the *quadrivium* and offered his services as a tutor, noting that he had the necessary books. He found interested students in England, including Walcher of Lotharingia, the Benedictine prior of Great Malvern (not far from Malmesbury). Walcher, a noted abacist and user of the astrolabe, referred to Peter as "our teacher," and may have helped Peter translate the astronomical tables of al-Khwarizmi into Latin.[80] Walcher also carried out new observations and calculations to predict the dates of each new moon between 1036 and 1111; his calculations were more accurate than Bede's.[81]

In fact, several of the most prolific translators of Arabic scientific texts were from England. Adelard of Bath (fl. 1116–1142) traveled to southern Europe, Asia Minor, and the Latin Kingdom of Jerusalem, and became interested in classical and Arabic texts on the *quadrivium*. In addition to completing the first Latin translation of Euclid's *Elements*, Adelard translated several major works on astral science and the use of talismans, and wrote a treatise on the astrolabe, which he dedicated to his former student, Henry II of England.[82] Robert of Chester, a contemporary of Adelard's, translated Arabic texts on algebra and astral prediction into Latin, and adapted Adelard's version of al-Khwarizmi's astronomical tables to the London meridian.[83] Casting horoscopes could be politically explosive: both Adelard and Robert used their knowledge to cast interrogational horoscopes to divine the outcome of the civil war in England between King Stephen and Empress Matilda, information that was valuable and potentially treasonous[84] (Plate 17).

Yet some theologians believed that astral science and its uses for prediction conflicted with Christian doctrine. The most influential among them was St. Augustine of Hippo. Augustine allowed that some astral science was legitimate, if it helped with timekeeping, navigation, or agriculture. But horoscopes

and other forms of prediction violated free will and called divine omnipo-
tence into question.[85] In *De doctrina Christiana* (ca. 396–427), Augustine clearly
stated that divination, using either demons or horoscopes, was just as un-
Christian as idol worship or augury.[86] Divination and prophecy, even from the
stars, "must be classed among those contracts and agreements made with devils."[87] According to Augustine, writing during a period when paganism was
still widespread, these beliefs and practices are forbidden to Christians. "We
must not omit from this category of deadly superstition the people called *genethliaci* because of their study of natal days, or now in common parlance *mathematici*."[88] *Mathematici*, like *mathesi*, can refer to astral science or mathematics,
or to divination and augury.[89] Moreover, Augustine argued, astral divination
was prone to error. After all, Jacob and Esau had identical natal charts but different destinies. Augustine's views influenced later Christian ideas regarding
astral science, and centuries after Augustine clerical mistrust of divination remained in place. The penalty for pursuing these illicit subjects could be extreme. According to William of Malmesbury, Gerard of Hereford, a scholar of
astral science who later became Archbishop of York, read Julius Firmicus, and
mentioned by William in his account of Gerbert) in private every afternoon.
When he died in 1108 with this "book of curious arts" underneath his pillow,
the canons at York refused to bury him in the minster, and "would hardly suf-
fer a lowly clod of earth to be thrown on the corpse outside the gates."[90]

Nevertheless, celestial divination was common in the eleventh and twelfth
centuries. William the Conqueror consulted with astrologers before setting
the date of his coronation (noon, Christmas Day, 1066).[91] John of Salisbury,
courtier, scholar, and bishop of Chartres, spoke out against divination of all
kinds in his treatise on rulership and ethics, *Policraticus* (1154). Necromancers,
chiromancers, augurers, and astrologers are all mountebanks. "Sometimes they
dupe out of eagerness to deceive, sometimes having been deceived by their
own errors. But they strive constantly to appear privy to all of the future. This
is why they take pains to obscure their prophecies with ambiguous language.
Should they be discovered as lying or deceptive, [one] could regard them with
some pretense of rationality."[92] Despite John's warnings, Becket continued to
consult with diviners even after he became archbishop of Canterbury. In a letter to Becket in 1170, John took the archbishop to task because he had ignored
sensible advice in his political struggle with Henry II. "You cannot say that
you were not told in advance the outcome in these cases: but rather that, as
happens to all those who study the auguries, prophecies not inspired by the
Holy Ghost deceived your wits. I pray that this sick delusion prove not incur-

able . . . . From now on let us renounce prophecies, since on this account mis-
fortunes have fallen on us with greater weight."[93] John maintained that
astrologers purposely exaggerated the influence and power of celestial bodies.
"And finally some arrive at such insanity that they say that it is possible for a
man to create an image which, if formed and guarded under the positions of
certain stars over a period of time and by certain calculated proportions in
the constellations, will receive the breath of life at the nod of the stars and
will reveal to those who consult it the secrets of hidden truth."[94] The idea,
whether one considered it absurd or plausible, was that the planets needed to
be in a certain configuration in order to create—or, according to John, enliven—
the statue.

William explicitly mentioned learned scientific observation and mastery
of abstruse knowledge in his account of Gerbert's prophetic head. The reference to the planets beginning their courses again may mean that the planets
were returning to the positions they had at the moment of creation, with each
planet in its house of exaltation—the position in which its effects on earthly
objects are most potent.[95] However, it might also refer to the precession of the
equinoxes and the Great Year (believed to occur roughly every 26,000, 30,000,
or 36,000 years). Precession refers to the apparent movement of the equinoxes
relative to the fixed stars along the ecliptic, the apparent path the sun traces
through the sky, due to gradual changes in the Earth's rotational axis. Its effects can be viewed easily by observing the North Star. Although the pole star
does not move according to the seasons, as is the case with the constellations
of the zodiac, it traces out an elliptical path, beginning anew at the Great Year.
Imagine a spinning top: even as the top sleeps on its axis, the point on which
it turns moves almost imperceptibly. Pre-Copernican astronomers were able
to calculate rates of precession that were broadly accurate and in keeping with
a geocentric universe.[96] Arabic astronomers were familiar with the writings of
Hipparchus, who based his calculations of precession on Babylonian astronomy, as well as some Indian sources, and incorporated the rate of precession
into their own astronomical tables, which were in turn transmitted to and
adapted for the Latin West.[97]

The explicit reference to the planets and oblique mention of precession is
important for several reasons. Most obviously, it demonstrates that William
was familiar with the concept of equinoctial precession, revealing the extent
to which advanced astronomical concepts were understood by this learned Latin
cleric in England at this time. As a friend of Walcher of Lotharingia, William
may have been introduced to astronomical treatises recently introduced to

England from Spain.[98] William knew that al-Andalus was a source of ancient and Arabic texts on the *quadrivium* and on divination, and linked Gerbert's reputation for having mastered the *quadrivium* with Adhémar's manufactured account of Gerbert's sojourn there. William also understood that astral science was a powerful tool for divination. He concluded that Gerbert's extensive knowledge enabled him to gain foreknowledge. Previous writers, such as Beno and Sigebert, could only understand foreknowledge in the context of demonic intervention. Furthermore, the idea of "the planets beginning their paths anew" was potent for William's audience: the Anglo-Norman court for whom William wrote may not have been deeply educated in the *quadrivium*, but they would have understood that a rare celestial event would have some mysterious power related to prophecy or augury. After all, comets, eclipses, and meteors were believed to portend some future event, such as the appearance of Halley's Comet before the defeat of Harold Godwinson at the Battle of Hastings in 1066. Yet William also stresses that Gerbert learned demonic magic from his foreign teacher. Gerbert's knowledge of astral science and celestial divination came from the same place as his knowledge of the dark arts of necromancy: outside the borders of Latin Christendom.

Beno viewed Gerbert's efforts at divination as the clear result of diabolical magic, while William emphasized that Gerbert's oracular automaton worked due to celestial science. It is no accident that both Gerbert's demonic power and his celestial knowledge are linked to cupidity and intellectual concupiscence; he used the former to unearth pagan treasure and the latter to learn the future.[99] The different versions of the story of Gerbert's oracular head dramatize the difference between demonic magic and celestial science, and also the difficulty of distinguishing between them.

Scholastic Sorcerers

Intellectual innovation per se was not viewed with suspicion; instead, the foreignness of this knowledge raised questions. Legends of Gerbert's abilities and his prophetic head did not end with William of Malmesbury, but were grafted onto other subjects. In the late tenth century, Gerbert had to go to Christian Spain and study ancient and Arabic texts in order to go beyond what was known about the *quadrivium* in the rest of Latin Europe. In the twelfth century, scholars traveled to the Dar al-Islam to gain access to classical and Arabic texts on philosophy, medicine, mathematics, and astral science. Although the twelfth and early thirteenth centuries were a period of rapid intellectual expansion, mostly due to the introduction of ancient and Arabic scientific and philosophical texts, this new knowledge was, in Grosseteste's time—the first half of the thirteenth century—not yet fully assimilated into the intellectual framework of the Latin West and purged of its un-Christian ideas. Robert Grosseteste and Albertus Magnus, both of whom were based in part in universities during the thirteenth century, were familiar with these texts; unlike Gerbert, they did not need to travel very far to gain that knowledge. These two schoolmen and clerics were famous for their erudition during their lifetimes, yet posthumous legends attributed to them the power to create prophetic automata. According to these legends, their extensive knowledge of astral science and natural philosophy (especially from Arabic sources), gave them mysterious and powerful abilities to create automata with demonic or celestial magic.

Robert Grosseteste (ca. 1168–1253), a mathematician, astronomer, theologian, and bishop, was one of the towering intellectual figures of the time. He was an important political figure in the Church as the bishop of Lincoln, the largest see in medieval England, and had a reputation for sanctity. He was first educated at the cathedral school at Hereford, a center for the inquiry of astral science, and he studied there under Roger of Hereford and Alfred of Sareshel, both leading scholars of the science of the stars in England.[100] Grosseteste then read for a few years in Paris, before becoming first chancellor of Oxford and then bishop of Lincoln in 1235, where he remained until his death. His scientific writing includes treatises on computation, comets, spheres, light, and Aristotelian commentary. Grosseteste was also, during the early part of his life, deeply interested in the predictive uses of astral science, and believed that proper education in this field would yield the ability to foretell future events. He argued, "Natural philosophy requires the services of astral science above all other [subjects]," because the position of the planets affects "the planting of crops, the changing of metals, [and] the curing of sickness."[101] In a work on how to forecast the weather, Grosseteste asserted the importance of knowing the natures of the planets and the powers of zodiacal signs.[102] The earliest example of his handwriting is an inscription on a diagram of the conjunctions between Mars and Saturn and Saturn and Jupiter in 1216.

Even though Grosseteste turned his attentions away from astral science and toward theology during his later years, he remained a figure who conjured up the study of the heavens and the potential that it offered. One hundred and fifty years later he became a character in English poet John Gower's

Confessio Amantis (ca. 1386–1393), who used his considerable intellectual talents to create an oracular brass head. This story echoes the legends of Gerbert's talking head, and like that one, derives in large part from Grosseteste's knowledge of astral science. Gower, who wrote the *Confessio Amantis* at the request of King Richard II of England, used a story about Grosseteste to illustrate the pitfalls of *curiositas* and sloth, while also subtly mocking Grosseteste and his erudition in the *quadrivium*.[103] Grosseteste appears as an example in a list of errors and lost opportunities due to procrastination (*lachesse*). Just as Ulysses tarried too long during the Trojan War and risked losing Penelope, Grosseteste spends seven years forging a talking head, only to lose the opportune moment because he is taking a nap.

> For of the grete Clerc Grosseteste
> I rede how besy that he was
> Upon clergie an Hed of bras
> To forge, and make it for to telle
> Of such thinges as befelle.
> And sevene yeres besinesse
> He leyde, bot for the lachesse
> Of half a Minut of an houre,
> For ferst that he began laboure
> He loste all he hadde do.[104]

Grosseteste toils for seven years to make his vatic head, only to miss the crucial moment for animation. Gower draws on the legend of Gerbert's prophetic head, and conjoins it with Grosseteste's reputation as a scholar of celestial science. The reference to "sevene yeres" recalls the seven planets and their influence on the seven metals. Furthermore, the Latin summary in the margin of the text reads, "Note at this point concerning that Astrologer," referring to Grosseteste.[105] Gower also echoes the metaphor of *Natura artifex* employed by Neoplatonist philosophers in the twelfth century, and the conflation of artisanal practice and learned knowledge explored in the previous chapter, when he uses the verb "rede" to indicate that his knowledge of the story comes from a book. "Clergie" means a body of knowledge; thus Gower claims that he read that the head was "forged on book knowledge," such as astral science.[106]

In addition to the similarities to William's tale of Gerbert using the planets to create an oracular automaton, there are a few other clues to Gower's sources. The legend of Grosseteste's talking head is first mentioned in Gower's poem on courtly love, *Confessio Amantis*. However, in 1309, during the trial of the Templars in London, a witness gave evidence that he met a Templar on Cyprus who had a two-faced brazen head that answered anything he asked.[107] The trope of the talking head was still current in Gower's lifetime. Henry Knighton, a chronicler contemporary with Gower, wrote that in 1387, against a backdrop of civil and political unrest due to a struggle between the young King Richard II's supporters and a group of disaffected influential nobles, strange fiery portents had been seen in the skies.[108] A waxen head at Oxford, "the work of necromancy," prophesied, 'First, the head will be cut off. Second, the head will be raised up. Third, the feet will be raised up above the head.'"[109] Gower was familiar with Grosseteste, whose works (especially his *Constitutions*, a treatise on clerical reform, and *Le Chasteau d'Amor*, an Anglo-Norman romance) were influential in Ricardian England.[110]

Grosseteste's position as an intellectual pioneer and his documented interest in astral science made him recognizable to Gower's audience as a scholar who made a prescient head. His mastery of difficult and mysterious knowledge from foreign sources, as well as his interest in astral prediction, translated perfectly to Gower's portrait of the great scholar who toiled for seven years to make an oracular head, only to have his zeal for foreknowledge undone by his "lachesse."[111] Sloth ("lachesse") was a new element in the tradition of the talking automaton, and was later famously dramatized in Greene's play, *Friar Bacon and Friar Bungay*. Grosseteste's labor is undone not by demons or trafficking with illegitimate knowledge (as was implied in the Gerbert story), but by his lachesse, a failing common to wise men, dullards, and servants. Grosseteste, a well-known religious and scholarly figure, cannot even manage to stay awake for the most crucial moment of his elaborate project, like Bacon, thus forfeiting the sought-after foreknowledge the head could impart. Furthermore, Grosseteste's endeavor—to create an oracular head—was tainted with a whiff of the diabolical, thanks to the Gerbert legend.

Like Robert Grosseteste, Albertus Magnus (ca. 1206–1280) was highly regarded during his lifetime and after as a scholar, scientist, and natural philosopher. Like Grosseteste, in his early career Albertus believed the science of the stars to be the key to understanding the natural world, later acquired the reputation of magus, and was credited with creating a talking statue by using celestial magic. Like Grosseteste, he left Paris to become a university chancellor. He settled in Cologne and was named the head of the Dominican order in Germany, and in 1260 he was elevated to the see of Ratisbon. In addition to the *Summa Theologiae*, he wrote numerous commentaries on Aristotle, especially the *libri naturales*. Albertus's intellectual project was to systematize natural knowledge; his emphasis on causality and regularity accordingly diminished the place and purpose of wonder in natural philosophy.[112] The Aristotelian corpus, especially the *libri naturales*, had been long questioned, debated, emended, and corrected by Jewish, Christian, and Muslim scholars in the Dar al-Islam, from the ninth century onward. These texts were translated into Latin over the long twelfth century and were gradually assimilated into the Latin Christian intellectual tradition in the thirteenth, by scholars working within a new kind of institution: the university. Albertus Magnus was vital to the assimilation of Aristotelian natural philosophy into a scholastic university framework.

Within a few years of his death in 1280 written texts, which detailed the many wonders he had created, began to circulate.[113] The earliest mention of Albertus's talking statue is in the moral treatise *Rosaio della Vita* (ca. 1363), just a few years before Gower's *Confessio Amantis*. Very little is known about this treatise and its author, Matteo Corsini; it exists in at least nine extant manuscripts in Florence and Paris.[114] The treatise illustrates various virtues and vices, including kindness, patience, lust, and drunkenness; each virtue or vice begins with a quote (usually from the Bible) that is followed by a story illustrating that attribute, which in turn leads into the next attribute. The legend of Albertus Magnus illustrates the characteristics of wisdom.

I could give you infinite examples of how wisdom must be revered and honored, but in order not to be too prolix, I will briefly tell you only one notable one. We find that one Albert the Great, a member of the Preaching Friars, so perfected his reason that by his sagacity he made a metal statue according to the courses of the planets, and gave it such reason that it spoke. And this was not by diabolical art nor by necromancy, since great intellects take no pleasure in that, because it puts both your soul and body at risk, and since that art is forbidden by the Christian faith. Whence, when a friar called on Brother Albert in his cell when he wasn't there, the statue replied. Believing it to be an idol of evil nature, [the other friar] broke it. When Brother Albert returned he said many bad things to him, and he said that it had taken him thirty years of work to make it, and, "You won't learn that science in the order of the Friars." The friar said, "Forgive me, I did wrong. What? Can't you make another one?"

Brother Albert replied that he could not make another for thirty thousand years, because that planet has made its course and will not return for that length of time.[115]

Corsini, like William of Malmesbury and Gower, explicitly draws attention to the enormous potential of celestial science. The reference in Corsini's tale to the planets beginning their courses and the thirty thousand-year Sidereal Year cycle recalls William's description of how Gerbert relied upon careful celestial observation for the opportune moment to cast his head.[116] Yet Corsini makes the power of this rare celestial event explicit and echoes John of Salisbury: Albertus's statue speaks because the planet that is able to make it do so is in a specific position that will not be repeated for millennia. Corsini also confirms William of Malmesbury's tacit assertion that foreknowledge could be the result of study in the *quadrivium*, rather than mastery of demonic magic. In keeping with Albertus's views on wonder and causality, Corsini admits the possibility that some people—ignorant people—might attribute the abilities of the automaton to demonic powers. This story also dramatizes the boundaries between local and foreign knowledge, as Albertus states that the knowledge he used to create his talking statue comes from outside his order. Retold again in the fifteenth century, the frightened friar is Albertus Magnus's pupil, Thomas Aquinas.[117]

It is possible that the source of this fantastic legend may be the description of a device called an aeophile or fire-blower in Albertus's work *De meteoris*. Originally described by Vitruvius, an aeophile is a hollow metal vessel that is filled with water and then heated. A small tube inside the vessel sends steam and water out of a small hole and onto a fire, making the flames flare up. Albertus claimed these were usually made in human form, with steam and water spraying out of the mouth or genitals.[118] This connection may have contributed to the legends of Albertus, but, as I have demonstrated earlier in this chapter, the story of the learned man and the speaking figure had antecedents closer to hand.

Albertus was, like Grosseteste and Gerbert, extremely interested in astral science, and his familiarity with it meant that he was a credible figure to have created a talking head in accordance with the stars. Albertus wrote the *Speculum astronomiae* (ca. 1260) to defend astral prediction as a Christian science against detractors who argued that it negated free will.[119] Albertus claimed, from a position grounded in Aristotelian natural philosophy, that understanding the heavens and the movement of celestial bodies might allow humans to perfect free will (rather than thwarting it), since all celestial influence began with God. Although even before this period there was a belief that things in the sublunary world were influenced by celestial bodies (such as the action of the moon on the tides), Aristotelian natural philosophy provided a specific rationality for this belief.[120] Aristotle argued, in *De generatione et corruptione* and elsewhere, that change on earth (specifically, corruption and generation) is caused by a change in the heavens, and that celestial bodies are included in a causal chain of influence which begins with the *primum mobile* and ends with earth.[121] Sometimes celestial influence gave natural objects marvelous properties, which were part of the specific form of a substance. These formal properties (such as the fire-retardant properties of salamander skin) were termed "occult" because they were hidden from immediate observation, unlike the "manifest" properties—size, color, and shape.[122] Aristotelian doctrine also accounted for a common element of medical practice; namely, the belief that plants had different healing properties depending on when on the lunar or zodiacal cycle they were harvested. Scholars and philosophers in the twelfth century objected to horary and natal astrology, but readily accepted its utility in medicine and agriculture. By the end of the thirteenth century, concerns over Aristotelian philosophy in the universities led to a reassessment of astral prediction. Yet it remained an important subject in the university curriculum for arts students, as well as students in the advanced faculties, such as medicine; in fact, the first university chair in astrology was founded at Bologna in this period.[123]

Yet even as the belief in celestial influences on earthly things was widely taught, and mundane astral science—predicting the weather, interpreting comets or eclipses—was widely used, the influence of stars and planets upon humankind and human events was debated. Natal astrology could reveal a person's attributes, but also the person's future, including the time and manner of death. Patristic authors, such as Augustine, objected to the determinism implied by all kinds of divination, as well as its links to paganism and heresy. Augustine's condemnation of celestial divination, especially natal charts, retained its potency in the fourteenth century. Charles V of France (r. 1364–1380) was particularly interested in astral science and its practical applications, and had at his court a personal astronomer, alchemist, and physician. His astronomer's daughter, Christine de Pizan (1364–1430), debated the validity of astrology with Nicole Oresme (ca. 1325–1382), an Aristotelian philosopher and counselor to Charles V. Christine maintained that astral science was the study of the motion of the spheres, and that it was a mathematical and speculative practice that could bring one closer to God. Oresme, though in agreement with Christine's definition, included geomancy, chiromancy, and necromancy as part of this branch of knowledge, thereby affirming Augustine's position that astral divination was, like all other forms of divination, morally bankrupt and inherently fraudulent.[124]

Furthermore, the belief that astrologers could and did summon demons remained common in the fourteenth century. In the *Omne Bonum*, a midfourteenth-century compendium of law, theology, and general knowledge by Englishman James le Palmer, astral prediction was deemed allowable when it helped farmers or physicians, but was condemned as impermissible when it involved celestial bodies to summon spirits[125] (Plate 18). In the image illustrating astral science [*constellacio*], a scholar consults an astronomical table and the stars with his right hand while pointing with his left hand to a demon, which he has summoned and circumscribed in a circle. The scholar's legs are crossed, signaling his malevolent intent. An almost identical image illustrates divination [*divinatio*] (Plate 19). In this instance, the sorcerer, dressed identically to the scholar in the preceding image, has both his hands and legs crossed. He sits in front of an open book (which looks very similar to the astrologer's book) and looks upward at a demon; to the right is another demon, also circumscribed inside a circle. Both images beautifully illustrate Augustine's assertion that astral divination involves demons.

All four men—Bacon, Gerbert, Grosseteste, and Albertus Magnus—were known for the breadth and depth of their knowledge in natural philosophy and the *quadrivium*, including astral science. Furthermore, they were all pioneers in these fields during their lifetimes, venturing outside the conventional intellectual avenues, mainly to pursue knowledge from Arabic and ancient sources. Their willingness to go outside the boundaries of familiar or doctrinally acceptable natural knowledge enabled them (according to legend) to create prophetic automata. These legends also extend the association between moving, mimetic objects and foreign places outlined in the first two chapters. Stories of philosophers and their talking heads dramatize concerns about the introduction of new natural knowledge, its power, un-Christian origins, and the desires and abilities of those who sought it.

CHAPTER 4

The Quick and the Dead: Corpses, Memorial Statues, and Automata

As in *The Iliad*, in the mid-twelfth-century Old French *roman antique*, *Le Roman de Troie*, Achilles kills Hector in combat and afterward denies Hector's body the traditional funeral rites. Hector's father, King Priam, negotiates with Achilles to return the body, which is then carefully embalmed, richly dressed, and paraded through Troy on a litter.[1] Three gifted artificers (*engeigneor*) design and build a mausoleum, "rich, and strange, and marvelous," in the shape of a tabernacle. The structure is an elaborate version of what could be found in a medieval church: an altar supported by columns, covered with a carved canopy (baldaquin), which also rested on pillars, and ornamented with sculptures, paintings, and carved marble.[2] Figures of two young men and two old men, all rendered in gold and seated on golden lions, support the tabernacle.[3] Each statue holds a pillar in one hand, which holds an arrangement of arches to support the altar; this in turn supports columns made of gold and gems, on top of which rests the marble baldaquin.[4] A golden throne rests on the altar, in place of a pyx or a monstrance for the Eucharist or relics. "What shall I tell you of the throne?" asks Benoît. It defies description, and in his view, the rulers of Germany or Spain would be unable to construct its equal.[5] The three artificers illuminate the tabernacle with eternal lamps and place at the apex of the tabernacle a golden statue of Hector brandishing a sword. They also devise a way to preserve Hector's body so that it could be displayed out in the open, under the marble canopy. They place Hector's feet inside two basins that are filled with balm and other rare and fragrant substances. Alongside his feet, they install "two golden tubes, very beautiful and well-made . . . [that] reached up to Hector's nose. In this way the essence and odor of the perfume permeated the entire body."[6] According to Priam's wishes, Hector's preserved corpse, made incorruptible by the embalming process and the vessels of fluid at his feet, remains visible to the subjects of Troy.

Hector's hybrid body fulfills the same function of demarcating different categories as the automata in the Chambre de Beautés earlier in the *Roman de Troie*. In this instance, the categories cohere around definitions of alive and dead. Hector's body, though unmoving and unresponsive, rests in a strange in-between state that suggests a strong conceptual affinity between moving figures and specially preserved corpses. Similar language describes the makers of both Hector's marvelous tomb and other kinds of automata. Although the human figures at Hector's tomb do not move, they do recall the four golden automata in the Chambre de Beautés, as well as other moving statues of animals, such as the lions flanking the Throne of Solomon in Liudprand's tenth-century *itinerarium*. The corpse rhymes visually with more conventional funerary statuary, and its surroundings recall saints' reliquaries. Hector's strange corpse, suspended between life and death, vividly articulates the boundary work that medieval automata undertake. Earlier chapters explored the ways that automata mark and also efface boundaries between opposing categories such as local/foreign and noble/common. This chapter takes up medieval definitions of life.

Automata are frequently found at gravesites, mausoleums, and memorials in medieval literature. A spectrum of automata appears in literary accounts from the twelfth to the fifteenth century. In some cases, automata memorialize human beings; in others, they guard the dead against the effects of death. Memorial automata often look human, and they can be eerily lifelike copies of individuals. This group of automata shares certain characteristics, embodying several themes. First, descriptions of memorial automata emphasize verisimilitude, especially when the automata are intended to be exact copies of the people they recall. None of the golden courtiers or prophetic statues in the previous chapters is an individual with a name and a unique identity. In contrast, the automata under discussion in this chapter are either copies of individuals or embalmed bodies of important people. Automata, as lifelike proxies for individuals, call identity into question. Is a perfect copy of someone the same as the exemplar? Second, sepulchral automata interrogate what makes a living body. Some automata mimic natural processes like breathing, while others halt natural processes like corruption. In related examples, embalmed bodies, such as Hector's, do not appear dead but are not fully alive. The lifelikeness of these bodies illuminates a continuum between life and death,

rather than strictly bounded definitions of life and death. Embalmed bodies
are clearly natural objects, but are also the product of artificial intervention.
The efforts to duplicate exactly particular people or to keep them from putrefaction result in automata that are simultaneously impressive and monstrous,
and produce a frisson of the uncanny.[7]

In the final section, I examine the two previous themes in conjunction
with evidence of changes in the technological imagination from the late twelfth
century to the early fifteenth century. Three iterations of the Troy story
illustrate the transition from magical to mechanical automata at the site of
Hector's memorial. Over the chronological trajectory of this chapter, human automata increasingly resemble real people and appear as naturalistic
hybrids of natural substances and human artifice.

Replicating the Un-Dead

In many examples from twelfth-century literature, automata guard tombs in
much the same way they patrol other liminal places, such as the bridge in *Le
Roman d'Alexandre*.[8] In other instances, memorial automata replace the departed, often in an attempt to deceive or defraud the beholder. Two twelfth-
century romances, *Le Conte de Floire et Blancheflor* (ca. 1150–1170) and Thomas
of Britain's *Tristran* (ca. 1160–1180), both roughly contemporaneous with *Le Roman de Troie*, demonstrate the way that automata symbolize these related concepts of liminality and fraud.[9] Additionally, the strikingly lifelike automata
that replace living people in these romances are paradoxical: they memorialize people who are not dead; they comfort the bereaved with delusion and fantasy.[10] Their discrepant nature reveals that the distinction between alive and
dead is not always clear or easily characterized.

The ability of automata to engender amazement and to deceive is evident
in *Le Conte de Floire et Blancheflor*. Moving, speaking statues of the epony-
mous lovers grace the tomb of Blancheflor, the daughter of the Christian hand-
maiden to the emir's wife.[11] The two women, one Christian, one Muslim, had
given birth the same day to a girl and a boy respectively. Their children, Blancheflor and Floire, grow up as playmates and eventually fall in love, despite their
differences in religion and social status. King Fenix, Floire's father, becomes
concerned about the attachment and sends Blancheflor away to serve the emir
of Babylon, but tells Floire she has died. To give weight to this lie the king
constructs a mausoleum for Blancheflor. The fake memorial is erected by en-

chantment and artifice and is decorated with elements that are often found in connection with automata: elaborate paintings of animals, precious stones, enamel, a carbuncle, and crystal.[12] Marble statues of the two young lovers, uncannily like the real pair, grace the top of the mausoleum. The figure of Floire "resembled him so closely that none could have improved on it;" the statue of Blancheflor was equally like her.[13]

> When wind touched the children they kissed and embraced one another and they would speak by magic [*ingremance*] of all their love and their childhood memories. Floire said to Blancheflor, "Kiss me, my beautiful, my love." Blancheflor said, while kissing him, "I love you more than any living thing." When air touched them the figures embraced and kissed each other, but when the wind stopped the figures ceased to speak.[14]

Opening the door and entering the mausoleum causes the figures to move and talk. Once the door is shut, the statues are quiet and still.

The automata on the tomb mimic the lovers in speech and action and also commemorate the love between Blancheflor (supposedly dead) and Floire (still alive). The tomb is a realistic and intentionally deceptive representation of the two lovers and their undying love. In a stunning instance of verbal irony, the statues refer to themselves as alive. In a further layer of dramatic irony, at this point in the narrative only Floire's father and the audience know that Blancheflor is still alive. Floire, broken-hearted and convinced of his lover's death, uses the memorial as a proxy to relive his affair with Blancheflor, and watches the statues perform his love affair and listens to them rehearse his own feelings. However, to the audience of the romance, the statues are obviously copies; since neither Floire nor Blancheflor is actually dead, the automata are clearly not the preserved, moving bodies of the two lovers. The statues, while beautiful, marvelous, and poignant, are clearly fakes. King Fenix, wealthy and powerful, uses his wealth and the knowledge available to him to deceive his son about Blancheflor's death. The embodiments of this duplicity, the automata, expose the association of esoteric foreign knowledge, mimesis, and trickery. They also comment ironically on their own status as fakes, allowing the audience to appreciate them but then dismiss them an instant later. The lifelike statues recall the dead as they were when alive, illustrating a fiction of life, even as the memorial, to a person not actually dead, offers the fiction of death.

A similar irony illustrates the tension between verisimilitude and artifice in Thomas of Britain's Anglo-Norman *Tristran*. Thomas's tale exists in only ten fragments, two of which are no longer extant. The episode in the Hall of Statues is in the now-lost Turin fragment. However, there is an Old Norse translation of Thomas's *Tristran*, called the *Tristansage*, which dates from 1226. Textual scholars note that this Old Norse translation is the best translation of Thomas's entire work. The chapters relating to the Hall of Statues exist completely in the Old Norse *Tristrams Saga ok Ísondar* and partially in the Turin fragment of Thomas's *Tristran*.[15]

In the Hall of Statues, as in *Floire et Blancheflor*, automata replace people who are not dead. The descriptions of the automata highlight simultaneously mimetic perfection and fraud. Tristran, alone and cast out, commands a vanquished giant to build an elaborate monument to his beloved Queen Ysolt, containing numerous automata. Ysolt is still alive, but far beyond Tristran's grasp. Still under the influence of the love potion that inspired his feelings, yet unable to continue his affair with Ysolt, Tristran cannot live without seeing his lover. So he designs a private diorama, where he will be able to reminisce and indulge his imagination. He hires artisans and goldsmiths from foreign lands to craft lifelike statues of Ysolt and her dog, Petitcru; her serving-maid, Brangvein; and the dwarf that denounced the guilty pair to Ysolt's husband, Mark. He keeps these golden images, along with several additional animals, in a private vault that is guarded by moving statues of the giant on one side and a lion on the other. The lion is "cast of copper and constructed so cunningly that no one who saw it would have thought otherwise than it was alive. It stood on its four feet and lashed its tail."[16] Tristran visits the statues often and uses the diorama as a space where he can reenact and continue his affair with Ysolt. "He made that image because he wanted to tell it his heart's feelings, his good thoughts, his foolish acts, his grief, and his joy of love, because he did not know to whom to reveal his desire and yearning."[17] The copy of Ysolt is "so artistic in regard to face and form that no one who looked at it could think otherwise than there was life in all its limbs."[18] In one hand, she holds a scepter on which a golden bird beats its wings. In the other, she grasps a ring inscribed with the last words Ysolt had spoken to Tristran. Inside her breast is a coffer "filled with the sweetest gold-mingled herbs in the whole world." The scent of the herbs travels through tubes to her mouth, so that she exhales perfumed air, "as if all the most precious herbs were inside it. . . . In regard to shape, beauty, and size this figure was so much like Queen Ysolt as though she herself were standing there, and lifelike as though it were actually alive."[19] Beside it, a statue of her dog Petitcru, "very artfully made," shakes its head and jingles its collar.

There are two different types of automata in this passage. The more conventional forms, such as Petitcru and the bird, are similar to those described by Liudprand and Robert of Clari. The statue of Ysolt is a different kind of automaton, as it mimics human physiology. The figure has inside its chest a coffer filled with fragrant herbs and precious substances; tubes carry the perfumed air to her mouth, whence it issues forth, like breath. This emphasis on air and breath is also present in *Floire et Blancheflor*. However, in that text, the movement of air refers to the circulation of air within the mausoleum, which causes the statues to move and speak. In *Tristran*, the breath emanates from the substitute's heart and is crucial to maintaining the appearance of life. The Ysolt figure echoes contemporary physiological theory, which placed the heart at the center of respiration and insisted on the importance of *spiritus* (breath) for life. *Spiritus* was a physical substance made in the heart and transmitted to the rest of the body via the arteries.[20] This moving, breathing artificial figure of Ysolt is the midpoint between the automata in the Chambre des Beautés and Hector's embalmed body.

The tale of Tristran and his statue evokes the story of Pygmalion, albeit with some significant changes. In Ovid's *Metamorphoses*, Pygmalion, a goldsmith, spurns the love of real women after seeing how they have been reduced to prostitution, a punishment for failing to worship Venus appropriately. He carves out of ivory a woman so beautiful that, as William of Malmesbury noted of the golden people in Octavian's underground palace, his art surpasses nature.[21] He eventually falls in love with his own creation and prays to Venus to bring his statue to life. Returning to his workshop, he kisses and caresses the ivory figure and feels her come alive beneath his touch.[22] The tale is a parable about the power of mimetic creation, the ability of humans to confuse the artificial with the natural, and the potential for artificial objects to become naturalized. The story of Pygmalion was told many times and in many guises throughout the Middle Ages, and was sometimes glossed as a cautionary tale about the pitfalls of idolatry.[23]

The Tristran story is an inversion of the Pygmalion tale. Pygmalion made a statue of a woman, but she did not become an individual until she came to life. Tristran made an exact copy of an individual, a woman with a unique identity and past. For Tristran, the artificial copy replaces the human individual. In both Pygmalion's story and Tristran's, mimetic art is nearly indistinguishable from natural creation. The audience knows that Tristran has been driven mad by love, grief, and desire, and that this is what has inspired him to create the Hall of Statues. Yet Tristran and the audience both know that the statue of Ysolt is an elaborate ruse; Ysolt is merely separated from Tristran, not dead. The subtle mimesis undermines Ysolt's individuality, and the way that Tristran treats his substitute as the "real" Ysolt glosses the morally dubious nature of this kind of art. Both stories have in common more than a hint of sex. Before he prayed to Venus to bring his creation to life, Pygmalion wooed the figure with kisses, caresses, and gifts, before finally having intercourse with it. And in every version Tristran and Ysolt's affair was torrid. As I noted earlier, Tristran spent much of his time kissing and holding the Ysolt-figure, and for him, this *was* Ysolt. The golden proxy acts as an extension of Tristran's imagination and psychological state, and is the passive subject of his fantasies and delusions.

Between Life and Death

At tombs, automata problematize the boundary between the living and the dead. The automata in *Floire et Blancheflor* and *Tristran* are memorials to people far out of reach (though not dead) and love affairs that are believed to be over. They are replacements for living individuals that deceive the beholder, either willfully or unwittingly. The statues of Floire, Blancheflor, Ysolt, and the others are so lifelike—they move, speak, and breathe—that they complicate the distinction between a living body and an artificial one. In the mid-twelfth-century *roman antique, Le Roman d'Éneas* (ca. 1160), the golden archer guarding Camille's tomb exposes and obscures the distinction between life and death. Camille's elaborate entombment and mausoleum, introduced in the second chapter, are described over three hundred lines in the text.[24] Her preserved corpse and the archer that guards her body are marvels that emphasize her liminal status in different ways.

Camille is a warrior, and after she dies in battle she is given a hero's rest. Camille's tomb is genuine, like Hector's, built by her countrymen both as a resting place for her body and as a memorial to her life and death. Indeed, Camille's tomb may have been the basis for Benoît's description of Hector's embalming and mausoleum.[25] Because she has died in battle, her corpse first has to be prepared for a long journey home.[26] Her attendants "wash off the blood from her with rose-perfumed water, cut her hair, and embalm her with balm and myrrh, and they prepare the body well."[27] As mentioned earlier, her mausoleum is an architectural marvel, and is also decorated with many powerful natural objects, including the feathers of a caladrius bird, a magical mirror, and a carbuncle (a precious stone that emitted light). Her casket is sealed with mortar made of serpent's blood mixed with crushed gemstones.[28] Once her casket has been placed inside the mausoleum, her attendants surround her with vessels filled with aromatic unguents to "refresh her with their scent."[29]

The costly aromatics like balm, myrrh, and rose water that keep Camille's body preserved from the ravages of corruption are similar to the balm that bathes Hector's corpse and the coffer of herbs inside the statue of Ysolt, both from texts later than *Éneas*. The emphasis on lovely smells links these bodies (whether artificial or preserved) to divine scents, especially the glorious smells of heaven.[30] Balm [*basme*] was an aromatic resinous substance, prized for its beautiful fragrance, therapeutic abilities, and rarity. The word is derived from the Latin *balsamum*, denoting a shrub from the genus *Commiphora*.[31] The resin of this plant has a number of specific attributes; however, in the medieval period, any revitalizing sap or ointment could be called balm or balsam, and oils or unguents that were used to preserve corpses were also called balm [*basme*] or balsam.[32] Balm was also in the medieval period thought to be vital to processes of rejuvenation, and could confer superhuman longevity on a person.[33] In *Éneas* it is used alongside other magical and rare objects to safeguard Camille's body from the ravages of death.

Yet unlike Hector's body, which is preserved and displayed in the same manner as an early modern saint or a twentieth-century tyrant, Camille's corpse is sealed in a coffin, which is in turn kept in a guarded vault. An automaton— an archer—stands sentry, ready to shoot an arrow at the carbuncle should Camille's rest be disturbed.[34] The carbuncle provides light inside the crypt and will shine forever unless it is dislodged. It is kept in place by a golden dove with a chain in its beak, at the end of which hangs the lamp. The archer is stationed across the room, ready to loose an arrow at the dove if the tomb is disturbed.

> The archer may look long and hold the bow bent, but he would not loose the arrow unless first the noose of a snare (designed for this purpose and which held the bow always bent) was disturbed. At a breath all was lost: if someone blew the snare it would trip the bow immediately, and the archer would shoot at the dove and hit it, which would break the chain and snuff out the lamp.[35]

"At a breath all was lost." The slightest current of air activates the archer, which, in turn, plunges Camille's tomb into darkness. As with the statues of Floire and Blancheflor, the automaton relies on a breath of air to come to life. Yet, in this instance, the movement of air inside the tomb also exposes Camille's in-between status: although she is no longer completely alive, the artifacts in her tomb signify that she is not completely dead, either. The carbuncle, with its endogenous illumination, symbolizes the radiant human spirit, according to the Christian tradition of *lux et vita*.[36] Furthermore, in ancient and medieval physiology, the life force was often compared to a lamp. Just as a reservoir of oil keeps a lamp burning, radical moisture [*humidum radicale*] was thought to be the intrinsic substance necessary to sustain life. When this finite amount of moisture dried up, vitality flickered, dimmed, and guttered out.[37] The eternally radiant carbuncle symbolizes Camille's eternal soul, while the balm replaces her radical moisture (as is the case with Hector), and keeps her body from drying out. Camille is preserved in a tomb illuminated by a light that symbolizes her human spirit. Yet the moment that a living person, metonymically referred to as "breath," enters her mausoleum, the archer springs into action, plunging the space into darkness and extinguishing the signifier of Camille's eternal spirit.[38] The moving statue shatters the illusion that Camille's body and spirit are unchanged in death.

Camille is an in-between figure in death and in life. She is a dedicated, competent, and chivalric warrior; a ruler in her own right; a beautiful woman; and a virgin. She exists outside the social structure that viewed women, especially noblewomen, as political and military spoils, whose role was to forge new alliances and dynasties through marriage and childbirth. Her marginal nature marks her as abject, "as she stands on the border of culture, threatening the terms that structure it."[39] Camille is not the only fallen warrior in *Éneas* who is embalmed. Pallas, a boon companion to Aeneas, dies earlier in the sequence of events. Already somewhat changed by death, he is washed (like Camille and Hector) in wine steeped with herbs, and anointed with balsam.[40] Unlike Camille, Pallas is not a monstrous or hybrid figure—he is a warrior and a hero. Although, like Camille, he dies without issue, his death exemplifies the tragic waste of life that attends warfare. His rotting corpse receives the treatment accorded to noble heroes and is then locked in a magnificent tomb. Because he was unambiguous in life, he remains easily categorized in death.

Pallas's corpse has begun to putrefy before it is washed and anointed, and Hector's corpse, in the *Roman de Troie*, has been dragged behind Achilles's chariot and left as carrion. The care taken to erase or at least halt the decay of their bodies reflects contemporary practices surrounding the preparation of important dead bodies. Jacques de Vitry, writing slightly later than the authors of the *romans antiques*, recalled the appearance of Pope Innocent III just after his death. Arriving in Perugia to be consecrated as bishop of Acre the day after the pope's death (July 16, 1216), Jacques encountered the body of Innocent on display in the cathedral of Perugia. He found that thieves had stripped the corpse of its clothes, and that the corpse was already decaying [*fetidum*].[41] Camille's and Hector's bodies are carefully washed, repaired, and preserved for eternity, unlike actual embalming practices, even of popes, that were intended to work only in the short term. Although papal funeral arrangements were not rigidly codified until the fifteenth century, there were established customs for burial that began at least as far back as the early twelfth century, several decades before the completion of *Éneas* and *Le Roman de Troie*.[42] In the mid-fourteenth century Pierre Ameil, a courtier of Pope Urban V (1362–70), recorded the established practice for preparing the papal body for burial. Initially, the pope's corpse was prepared and embalmed in the papal chamber. The corpse was washed in cold water with herbs, shaved, washed again in white wine with herbs, and then rubbed with balsam. Ameil went into further detail about the embalming procedure:

> Once the pope is dead and his body washed and his hair cut and beard shaved, then the apothecary of the aforementioned friars of the *Bulla* will close all his orifices securely with wool or flax; the anus, mouth, nostrils, and ears with myrrh, incense, and aloe (if it can be procured). His body should then again be washed with white wine, steeped with fragrant herbs and good vernaccia . . . . Then his throat should be filled with aromatics and with wool in particular and the nostrils with musk. Finally, his whole body, even his hands, should be rubbed down and anointed with good balsam.[43]

The level of care and ceremony, the emphasis on the ritual washing and preparation of the body, the use of costly ingredients such as myrrh, aloe, and balsam, and especially the attention to filling the nose and mouth with sweet-smelling aromatics recall the preparation of the bodies of both Hector and Camille. Camille's hair is cut, her body washed and then prepared with myrrh and balm, though she is not eviscerated. Hector's corpse is washed with white wine steeped with herbs, and his nose and mouth filled with

sweet-smelling liquids (by the tubes). However, the careful embalming of even
a pope or ruler was only intended to last for a fairly short period of time (nine
days in the case of popes), while Camille and Hector are preserved from putrefaction forever. Eternal preservation was (and is) beyond human ability, and it
appears in these texts as a wonder that is very similar to that of automata.

Two fifteenth-century paintings of embalming depict the process and reinforce that it was for high-status individuals (Plates 20 and 21). Both images
show the embalming of Alexander the Great, who was, according to historical legend, eviscerated and embalmed after his death, and placed in a gold
sarcophagus in Memphis. Both paintings clearly demonstrate influence from
contemporary medical illustrations. In the first (Plate 20), the procedure takes
place in Alexander's bedroom, as surgeons and physicians surround his opened
body. One holds a vessel of embalming fluid. In the next vignette, a golden
replica of his body is displayed above a sarcophagus, with his helmet, tunic,
and standard hanging above like relics. The courtiers in the second half of
the painting echo the physicians and surgeons in the first half. It is not clear
if the golden figure of Alexander is a memorial statue or his actual body. However, the ambiguity further demonstrates the lack of clear distinction between
embalmed bodies and funerary statues: both gold and the wondrously embalmed bodies of Camille and Hector resist corruption. In the second painting (Plate 21), Alexander's body is embalmed by evisceration (like Hector's).
His body has been opened up, with the organs visible. At his feet is a large
basin for viscera, and on the right is a figure with several jars for storing organs and smaller vessels of fluid, details related to the iconography of dissection. As in Plate 20, a crowd of people observe the process.

The sweet unguents, which keep these dead bodies from decomposing,
recall saintly bodies and the divine intervention that halts those very special
dead bodies from decay. While evidence of holiness was sometimes found on
the body itself (for example, in the appearance of the stigmata or an image of
the crucified Jesus impressed onto the heart), further evidence of their holiness was that the bodies of some saints did not decompose. Their bodies became filled with sweet-smelling liquor rather than the noxious deliquescence
of decay.[44]

These signs of sanctity—perfect or near-perfect preservation of the body,
and a strong, sweet smell—were known to many, and could be employed to
suggest that a dead person was also a devout person who enjoyed divine favor.
At Pentecost in the year 1000, Holy Roman Emperor Otto III (the student
of Gerbert), visited Charlemagne's tomb in Aachen. Two contemporary ac-

counts, one from Thietmar of Merseburg (who also wrote about Gerbert's scientific conferences with Otto), who often traveled in Otto's court, and one based on a possible eyewitness account and later recorded in the *Chronicon Novaliciense* (ca. 1027–1050), describe the emperor visiting the tomb of his symbolic ancestor, whom he revered as a holy man. In both accounts, Otto removes several relics from the tomb—a tooth, a gold cross, a bit of clothing—but in the slightly later account he and his companions find themselves with absolute evidence of Charlemagne's sanctity. According to Count Otto of Lomello, they entered the tomb, immediately smelled a strong fragrance, and saw Charlemagne sitting on a throne, perfectly preserved except for the tip of his nose.[45] Otto III stood to gain political and religious authority by reemerging from Charlemagne's tomb at the start of the new millennium as that holy emperor's heir. And legends of Charlemagne's saintliness multiplied and circulated even after Otto III's early death two years later.[46] The preserved corpses of Hector and Camille are artificial marvels that mimic supernatural ones (i.e., miracles) and are displayed in lavish settings that resemble reliquaries. Yet for all the wonder that these bodies summon they are doubly false: they are neither alive nor sanctified.

Preservation, Putrefaction, and Rejuvenation

Hector's perfectly preserved corpse appears in successive versions of the Trojan War from the mid-twelfth to the early fifteenth century. While all three versions have several aspects in common, the changes from one to the next reveal different ideas about the nature of marvels, the space between life and death, and the increasing potential of human technology to match or surpass Nature. The first example, which I discussed at the opening of this chapter, is from Benoît de Sainte-Maure's mid-twelfth-century Old French romance, *Le Roman de Troie* as classical history was retold in vernacular verse for an elite, courtly audience. This text is based on two earlier accounts of the Trojan War: the *Ephemeris belli Troiani* by Dictys Credensis (fourth century), and the *De excidio Troiae historia* (sixth century) by Dares Phrygius.[47] The *Ephemeris* was believed to be the diary of a Cretan soldier, Dictys, during the conflict, and the *De excidio* was attributed to Dares, a Trojan participant in events. Both narratives circulated widely throughout medieval Europe in texts, redactions, and compilations due to their status as true histories of the Trojan War.[48] Yet despite the historical *matière*, the *Roman de Troie*, like other romances, is more fully imaginary and less tethered to time than historiography. Benoît expanded significantly on his source material, and included people, plots, and marvels of his own invention.

Many of these additions are deemphasized, dropped, or questioned in the *Historia destructionis Troiae* by Guido delle Colonne (ca. 1272–1287), the second example.[49] In Latin prose, Guido names only Dares and Dictys as his sources; yet he actually relies most heavily on Benoît de Sainte-Maure's *Roman de Troie*, although he does not mention it by name. Guido would likely have been familiar with Benoît's work, which was widely copied for courtly audiences. As a young man, Guido was a poet at the Sicilian court of Frederick II, and was part of a court culture that was polyglot and cosmopolitan.[50] Later in his life he became a judge, and he wrote the *Historia* at the end of his life for his patron, the Archbishop of Salerno, Matteo da Porta.[51] Guido rationalizes Benoît's version of Hector's memorial and uses the marvel to highlight concerns about fraud. His version also indicates contemporary Aristotelian ideas about the physics of corruption and decay. The *Historia destructionis Troiae* was accepted as history almost immediately and proved especially influential in late medieval England, where it was translated into English three times between 1400 and 1426.[52] One of these translations and the third example, John Lydgate's *Troy Book*, presents Hector's body and memorial as a natural-artificial hybrid marvel.

In the *Roman de Troie*, Hector's corpse is a marvel because it is preserved forever. This extraordinary result seems to be due to the care taken with Hector's body and the rare, expensive natural substances that keep him protected from corruption. The preparations of Hector's corpse, the construction of his tomb, and his funeral unfold over three hundred and fifty-five lines in the *Roman de Troie*, but are absent from Benoît's source material.[53] After Priam persuades Achilles to return Hector's body, he conveys it back to Troy. Attendants there remove his armor and then gently wash him "seven times in white wine steeped with rare herbs. Before his body is wrapped in its shroud, his stomach, intestines, liver, lungs, and the rest of his entrails are gently removed, and his corpse is filled with aromatic substances. The body is embalmed—completely filled with balm, inside and out."[54] Embalming by evisceration was reserved for the wealthy, the powerful, or the holy, and its use to preserve Hector reflects his high status.[55]

After Hector's body is washed, eviscerated, and replenished with balsam, it is dressed in rich garments, installed at a memorial, and displayed in the open. The liquor necessary to keep corruption at bay flows through Hector's body by two tubes that run from each nostril to basins of balsam at his feet.

A painting from a late thirteenth- or early fourteenth-century manuscript of *Le Roman de Troie* illustrates this marvel (Plate 22). The artist has made some changes from the text: the four golden figures no longer hold the tabernacle; instead, their arms are extended in a dramatic gesture. Furthermore, there is no golden statue of Hector; rather, Hector himself brandishes the sword. The image of Hector, however, closely hews to the text in *Le Roman de Troie*. He is seated, wearing luxurious fabric, and his face, hair, and hands are completely visible. His feet rest in two green bowls; golden tubes extend from these bowls up to his nostrils. Except for his lowered eyelids, he looks as alive as the interested onlookers on either side of him. The observers' facial expressions and gestures clearly register the marvel before them. Several of the figures have wide-open eyes and open mouths; a few are pointing at Hector. The artist has taken pains to convey the extraordinary nature of this marvel; many of the figures express surprise or delight, and virtually all of them are looking directly at Hector.

The embalming fluid moving through Hector's corpse makes it possible to hide the truth of his condition. It replaces his blood and humors, just as the perfumed air that fills his body and exits through his nose replaces his *spiritus*. There were, in the twelfth century, several ideas about the importance and potential of balsam. Natural philosophical texts, including Isidore of Seville's *Etymologiae*, Hildegard of Bingen's *Physica*, and several encyclopediae identified balsam as having intrinsic qualities that allowed it to halt corruption and preserve youth.[56] In *Le Roman de Troie* the wonderful, revitalizing substance of balm recalls the miraculous evidence of sainthood, discussed above, as well as the potential for natural knowledge to simulate miracles.

In the late twelfth and thirteenth centuries the story of the Trojan War circulated in several versions: Benoît's *Roman de Troie*, and the histories of Dares and Dictys. The latter two works, although characterized by Curtius as "prose romances," were written in Latin prose and were taken to be credible accounts of the events of the Trojan War; indeed, their claims to credibility rested on the eyewitness testimony they supposedly conveyed.[57] Guido's stated aim was to combine those two accounts into one seamless historical chronicle, and in this he was successful, as the *Historia* was taken to be the authentic history of the Trojan War.[58] The astonishing marvel of Hector's body remains in the *Historia*, but in this instance it embodies late thirteenth-century natural philosophical ideas about corruption, as well as Guido's meditation on the artifice and deceit of poetry.

Guido especially emphasized the dangers of putrefaction and Priam's desire to display Hector's body in the open:

because the body of Hector had become a corpse, such is human weakness, and could not be kept above ground without corruption for long, King Priam, in consultation with many learned men, closely investigated if the body could always appear in the guise of a man, perceived falsely as though alive (though without the horrible odors of a dead body) without being in a sealed tomb.[59]

These men, "who were very skilled and ingenious [*ualde artificiose*]," constructed an elaborate tomb.[60] The four golden men on pillars in *Le Roman de Troie* are in the *Historia* four golden angels. The ingenious inventors make an apotropaic golden likeness of Hector and place it on top of the tabernacle. Thanks to their "mastery and skill [*magisterii eorum artificio*]," they find a way to place Hector's body on a throne in the middle of the tabernacle, "and there it sat as though alive [*quasi viuum*]."

> For, in a wondrously wrought [*artificioso*] aperture in his head they placed a vase, full of pure and precious balsam, into which were mixed compounds that had the power to sustain life. This liquid, of balsam and other things, flowed first to the front of the forehead, through the insides, then to the eyes and nose, and then, descending in a straight course through the inner parts, reached the cheeks, through which it preserved the gums and teeth, so that his entire face with its quantity of hair bloomed in its keeping. Then this liquid, descending through his throat and neck, ran to his chest, and through the inner bones of his arms permeated to his hands and even to the fingertips. And so this liquid, running copiously, flowing down each side, preserved each side [of his body] in such condition that they appeared to be living [flanks]. By this continuous application the liquid spread to the contents of his chest and through them reached the legs, and by continuing this course it pervaded the feet. At his feet there was another vase full of pure balsam. And so through these applications the corpse of Hector was presented like the body of a live man, safeguarded by many precautions for longevity.[61]

The mechanisms for Hector's preservation are similar to those in *Tristran* and *Le Roman de Troie*: vessels of balm and unguent that course throughout the body. Guido rationalizes the flow of fluid from the head to the feet, instead of the reverse in *Le Roman de Troie*. A painting of Hector's body and tabernacle in a fourteenth-century Venetian manuscript of the *Historia destructionis Troiae*, done by illuminator Guistino da Forli, concentrates mainly on the marvel of lifelikeness and the application of balsam from the head down to the feet (Plate 23).[62] The image depicts Hector on a golden throne, holding a sword in a threatening manner. Four angels hold golden pillars (the two front pillars are visible), which in turn support the throne. The angels are rendered in grisaille, evoking marble statuary, and recall the painting of the automata in the Chambre de Beautés from a late fourteenth- or early fifteenth-century French manuscript of *Le Roman de Troie* (Plate 5) discussed in the second chapter. Several figures to the left of the tabernacle gaze and point at the figure of Hector, the focal point. The mixture of balsam and other substances pours on to his head from a golden vase, bathing his entire head and body in moisture. Hector's face and hands are clearly visible, and have been rendered in the same pigments as the faces and hands of the visitors gazing on him. His eyes are open, and look to the right, away from his subjects, at something outside the frame of the image. His facial expression and gaze are animated. The stark contrast between the pale angelic figures and the human ones places Hector's corpse squarely in the same category as the living people in the image.

The balsam cascading over Hector's head and face in Plate 23 is crucial to maintaining his lively appearance, as it staves off corruption. Guido stresses the importance of keeping Hector's corpse from decomposing, and goes a step further by actually mentioning the "horrible" smell of putrid flesh as a concern.[63] Achilles had violated Hector's body by dragging it behind his chariot like garbage, and without Priam's intervention would have left him to be eaten as carrion. By carefully embalming Hector's body and halting corruption, the Trojans can erase the evidence of Achilles's abuse and restore Hector's body to a pristine condition. Guido's audience of educated courtiers may have viewed Hector's decomposing body as a health concern. Putrid bodies were in this period viewed as possible sources of contagion, and the physics of corruption and possibility of rejuvenation were in late thirteenth-century Italy a preoccupation of popes and scholars.[64]

Theories of change and decomposition were in this period strongly influenced by Aristotelian texts, which had become part of the university curriculum a few decades before Guido began composing his history. According to Aristotle, generation is the manner by which a thing comes into being; destruction is the manner by which a thing passes out of existence.[65] Corruption—one kind of destruction—occurs when a body loses its moisture and heat as it ages, part of a long process of decay that begins before death.[66] The balsam that keeps Hector and Camille fresh and vibrant was believed to be intrinsically hot and moist and therefore replaces their bodies' intrinsic heat and moisture.[67] The process of decay occurs more quickly when a body is in a warm environment, such as Pope Innocent III's corpse in the stifling July heat.[68] Therefore, decomposition could be slowed or halted by keeping a body's innate heat and moisture replenished, and by keeping that body in a cool and dry environment. Several examples of automata at tombs or mausoleums act to protect dead bodies from the corrupting influences of warm or humid air. The archer guarding Camille's tomb is there to ensure not only that her tomb is not looted, but also that dampness from outside is kept out. Likewise, two copper boys that watch over the tomb of the emir of Babylon in *Le Roman d'Alexandre* do so to make sure that "nothing living was to penetrate the tomb."[69] By keeping his tomb sealed against air that could contaminate the corpse, the automata slow the emir's inevitable decay.

Guido repeatedly describes Hector's corpse in terms that draw attention to its artificiality and its deceptive nature. Guido includes this marvel to establish his own credibility as a chronicler and to critique his immediate source material, the *Roman de Troie*. The *Historia destructionis Troiae* was immensely popular throughout the Middle Ages, and it was also immediately accepted as history.[70] This is due in part to the fact that Guido was careful to cite Dares and Dictys as his sources, disdaining the work of "certain persons" [i.e., Benoît] who had already transcribed much of this material and dealt with it "lightly, as poets do," filling the tale with fanciful inventions.[71] Hector's body is an implicit metaphor that equates verse with artificiality and fraud: just as the marvel of Hector's lifelike body confuses the viewer into thinking something false is actually true, poets obscure the truth of past events with embellishments and lies. Guido not only reveals how Hector's body is preserved, but also reiterates its fraudulent effect. Guido repeats the phrase "as though alive" [*quasi viuum*] four times and the word "falsely" [*ficticie*] twice in his description of this artificial marvel. Hector is lifelike in appearance, but he is not alive. By repeating the account of Hector's embalmed body while highlighting the fraud and artifice, Guido comments on the untrustworthiness of poetry. He does not approve of artifice and invention (at least in relation to historical subjects), and suggests that the artificiality of Benoît's romance, like the artificiality of Hector's body, constitutes trickery and deceit.

Just over a century later, John Lydgate translated Guido's *Historia* into English verse. Lydgate's *Troy Book* was one of three Middle English translations to appear in the first quarter of the fifteenth century; the author tells us that he began the work in 1412 and finished it in 1420. Lydgate's patron, Prince Hal, later King Henry V, commissioned Lydgate, a monk at Bury St. Edmunds, to write the history of Troy, the greatest story of chivalric warfare in antiquity, "y-written as wel in oure langage / As in latyn and in frensche it is."[72] Lydgate amplifies and embellishes the events and descriptions in the *Historia*; nevertheless, he retains a commitment to historical truth.[73] Just as Guido, writing just over a hundred years after Benoît, expands upon the description of Hector's tomb, Lydgate, writing for a warrior-prince over a hundred years after Guido, elaborates on the method of Hector's preservation. Lydgate does not emphasize the fraudulent nature of this marvel, but he does echo Guido's concern with corruption. In the *Troy Book* Lydgate presents Hector's astonishing lifelikeness as the result of superior craft knowledge. As in Guido's version, in Lydgate's version King Priam wanted Hector's corpse to remain uncorrupted and aboveground. He summoned "the craftiest maisteres of the toun, / Swiche as hadde most discrecioun / To parforme his axynge coriously."[74] Priam's wishes were

> To preserue it hool fro thinges tweyne;
> From odour and abomynacioun,
> And ther-with eke, by crafty operacioun,
> þat it in sight be not founde horrible,
> But þat it be lifly and visible
> To þe eye, as be apparence,
> Like as it were quyk in existence . . .[75]

These skilled men keep Hector looking alive [*quyk*] by even more elaborately explained mechanical means than in Guido's *Historia*. Hector's lifelikeness is in large part due to his radiant complexion and skin-sheen; this is achieved by placing a golden urn at his head "þat was filde with bawme natural / þat ran through pipes artificial, Þoruз nekke & hede in-to many place, Penytrable by veynes of þe face."[76] The balm trickled through "smale pipes wrouзt and made of gold" to render him "lifly of colour, Fresche of hewe, quyke, & no þinge pale."[77] Hector appears completely organic and lifelike, with no change in his complexion or the texture of his skin, just as in Plates 22 and 23. The "licour" that is partly responsible for this marvel has halted—and perhaps reversed—the natural process of corruption.[78] In Lydgate's telling, natural body parts are replaced by mechanical processes that move vital fluids through the body.

The wondrous mixture of fluids that preserves Hector's body from decay may possibly be due to interest in alchemy and its potential in late medieval England, although the text and historical context are far from clear. Alchemy was concerned primarily with the nature of change: how one substance can change into another, and how changes in nature could be halted or reversed. Mixing, decocting, and distilling liquids were central to this intellectual undertaking. Roger Bacon (believed that rejuvenation (the ability to halt or reverse decay) could be aided by the study of experimental sciences (optics, astronomy, and alchemy).[79] Several alchemical texts that argued in favor of the possibility of this kind of transformational art, such as the *Breve breviarum* and the *Summa perfectionis*, circulated widely throughout the fourteenth century, especially in England. Both Edward III and Richard II favored alchemical imagery and symbolism.[80] However, Henry IV, Richard II's successor, was less enthusiastic about the promise of alchemy, and went so far as to issue an edict in 1404 banning it. Henry V, who became king in 1413 (shortly after Lydgate began the *Troy Book*), had a more relaxed and pragmatic attitude toward alchemy than his father, though not as enthusiastic as Richard II. There is no strong tie between Lydgate or his monastery, Bury St. Edmunds, and alchemical texts or practices. However, Lydgate's description of the vial of aromatic gums and spices at Hector's feet—the scent of which would grow stronger each day by means of a "processe"—may possibly evoke alchemy.[81] In Middle English, "proces" refers to a specific sequence of steps over a period of time, perhaps an oblique reference to the creation of the Philosopher's Stone. However, the same term can refer to events over time, in the ordinary course of nature.[82] The gold in this marvel is likewise ambiguous with regard to alchemy. Gold was considered perfect (as the only element that did not oxidize) and was thought to be central to rejuvenation. For example, it was believed by some that the proper ingestion of gold would restore bodily humors to their perfect equilibrium, and could arrest aging and corruption.[83] However, the gold pipes and tubes likely reference contemporary practice: gold could easily be hammered into a thin sheet, then rolled to make a tube.

The language of craft in this passage refers to the highly skilled labor of the master craftsman. However, the terms can also connote intentional fraud and deception, of the kind intended to trick the senses.[84] The "avys and subtylite" in the work of making Hector appear alive reinforces these overlapping meanings of cleverness and trickery.[85] The references to the "maisteres" who build the structure and are responsible for Hector's preservation oscillate between notions of mechanical manufacture and intellectual endeavor, as the word can mean a man who has attained the professional rank of master-craftsman or a man with a university degree.[86] The apposition of "bawme natural" and "pipes artificial" glosses the wonderful concoction of liquor and the contrived system of tubes that carry it. In Lydgate's Troy, natural substances collude with human artifice to keep Hector lifelike. Lydgate clearly outlines how this effect is achieved through mechanical and artificial methods, resulting in a dead body that appears alive.

By the early fifteenth century in England and elsewhere in the Latin West, automata had moved from bookish fantasy to fact, and the men who created actual automata were skilled and ingenious craftsmen working with their hands to apply mechanical principles. The artifice that produces the marvel of Hector's corpse appears more clearly, and is more easily explained, than in the twelfth-century *Roman de Troie*. The detailed description of Hector's body in the *Troy Book*, with emphasis on tubes, smithing, and hydraulics reflects actual developments in mechanical technology and the creation of mechanical automata in the fifteenth century. This shift from magical to mechanical mirrors technological developments that began in the early fourteenth century, which allowed for the creation of more complex machines, including automata. Although the automata that were created in the fourteenth and fifteenth centuries were not nearly as astonishing or capable as the magical dancing courtiers or prophetic brass heads from twelfth and thirteenth century texts, they nevertheless evoked wonder. The following chapter takes up how automata changed from golden courtiers, created by magic, in the twelfth-century *Roman de Troie* to Hector's body, preserved by an elaborate system of tubes and wires, in the fifteenth century.

CHAPTER 5

From Texts to Technology: Mechanical
Marvels in Courtly and Public Pageantry

The increasingly elaborate artifice behind Hector's preserved corpse, from the twelfth through the fifteenth centuries, generally mirrors the development of increasingly complex machines during the same period in the Latin West. As we have seen, automata were known in Latin Christendom from the Carolingian period onward, and were understood for much of the medieval period as foreign objects whose creation and operation rested on an understanding of Nature that ascribed hidden abilities to natural objects, the movement of celestial bodies, and demons. Furthermore, the existing hierarchies of knowledge that privileged text-based learning over artisanal know-how insisted on the mastery of textual knowledge as the only route to creating prophetic heads or artificial servants. Automata began to lose their association with exoticism in the middle of the thirteenth century. By 1430, contemporary with Lydgate's *Troy Book*, automata were designed and built throughout the Latin West. As artisans there began to build more complex machines, automata became gradually decoupled from their foreign origins and some attendant disquieting valences.

From the late thirteenth century onward mechanical automata became increasingly complex and more commonly fabricated. A fixture in courts and central to public pageantry, automata were mechanical marvels that retained an aura of mystery and evoked surprise, delight, and sometimes terror. Yet as automata changed from textual to material objects, the methods and materials of their fabrication became more pedestrian: instead of being rare objects that were created or operated with magical power, they were constructed with wood, ropes, pipes, and screws. Likewise, the creators of automata changed from the philosophers and magicians (in twelfth- and thirteenth-century romances) to artisans skilled in craft knowledge. Yet automata themselves were not mundane, as they appeared in opulent settings, such as at court or in lavish public displays. They included ecclesiastical objects, artificial birds, elaborate fountains, mechanical beasts, and clockwork automata. The first recorded instance of automata that were built, rather than designed, in the Latin West appeared in Artois (now part of France), in the park of the chateau of Hesdin, at the turn of the fourteenth century. By the late fourteenth century, mechanical automata proliferated as a result of new inventions in mechanical technology; and these new inventions flourished in the courtly settings that fostered innovation in mechanical engineering and design. By the second quarter of the fifteenth century, automata were increasingly elaborate.

The chronology of the rediscovery of mechanism in Latin Christian Europe in the late medieval period exposes two themes. The first is the form and fabrication of these automata, and the important differences between earlier textual examples and foreign objects. Descriptions of textual automata prioritize the learned men who made them, and the costly materials they used, as in *Le Roman de Troie*. In contrast, actual automata were made of iron, rope, and wood by artisans. Some courtly automata, like their more literary counterparts, conveyed a sense of grandeur and evoked amazement; others, however, were intended for mockery and play. Yet, unlike the courtly setting of automata in so many of the romances, *chansons*, chronicles, and travel accounts discussed earlier, far more automata in the late medieval period were found in public or semi-public contexts. Mechanism, as marvel and model, abounded in multiple spaces and in multiple registers.

The second theme is the relationship between late medieval mechanical automata and earlier foreign examples. Crucially, some of the automata that were created in this period are similar to the foreign automata encountered in literary sources. Water fountains and mechanical birds in courtly settings recall exotic gardens in romances and *chansons*. These initial similarities suggest that foreign automata, such as the examples in the first chapter, were exemplars for the earliest automata built in the Latin West, at Hesdin. Despite the concerns that foreign automata evoked, discussed in earlier chapters, Latin Christians looked to these objects as models for their own initial attempts at creating similar objects. Yet by the end of the fourteenth century, Western automata often took distinctive forms, varied settings, and alternative purposes from their foreign exemplars. These changes indicate the process of indigenizing that took place with actual objects. This process began earlier with textual objects, in the twelfth-century *romans antiques*, which posited that these objects belonged to the cultural heritage of the ruling elites in Latin Christian Europe. The rediscovery of mechanical engineering allowed Latin Christians to build complex automata and eventually to make those objects familiar.

Early Mechanical Automata in Europe

The first examples of historical automata from the Latin West appear in the middle of the thirteenth century. Villard de Honnecourt (fl. 1225–1250), a Picardien, was a draftsman and engineer who recorded a number of mechanical objects, including automata.[1] His notebook, in the Bibliothèque nationale in Paris, comprises thirty-three parchment folios and over sixty drawings. Based on his drawings of the cathedral at Rheims, as well as his geometric studies, Villard has been hailed a master builder, and thus a member of a high-status group of professionals whose work conferred privileges and significant income.[2] While it is true that Villard flourished during a period of intense architectural innovation, especially in northern France, he was also interested in smaller objects, and included in his notebook drawings of sculptural figures, designs for a crossbow and a trebuchet, an ingenious hand-warmer, a perpetual-motion machine, and several mechanical automata.[3] Given this evidence of his interests beyond cathedrals, it is possible that he was a highly skilled journeyman artisan and engineer and that his notebook may have been used as a portfolio to show potential employers.

Villard's drawings of automata are based on recognizable mechanical technology, relying on ropes, pulleys, levers, and weight-driven movement. One of these, a Tantalus cup (also called a "chantepleure") is similar to those found in earlier sources in Greek and Arabic, such as the work of Hero of Alexandria and al-Jazari, an engineer at the Urtuqid court in Diyar Bakr at the turn of the thirteenth century (Plate 24). However, there is no evidence that Villard had access to these texts (al-Jazari's work was not available in Latin or French in the early thirteenth century, and only part of Hero's work, *Pneumatics*, had been translated into Latin), and it is more likely that he either saw an object like this or had it described to him.[4] The bird appears to drink the liquid in the goblet, and makes a bubbling noise. The cup has a hollow base, with a concealed tube rising up through the central tower or battlement, which terminates just below the rim of the basin. Hidden holes in the bottom of the battlement allow liquid to flow into it. When the level of the liquid (wine, water, or something else) rises in the cup, it overflows into the tower through the concealed holes to let the wine slowly drip into the hollow base of the cup. This forces air up into the bird, which then tips forward, letting air escape from its beak, and produces a bubbling or "drinking" sound. Once the level of liquid has equalized, the head of the bird rises.[5] The Tantalus cup embodies the development of hydraulic and pneumatic mechanical principles and is a portable object over which to exclaim and wonder.[6] The mobilization of hydraulic and pneumatic engineering places it in the same category as the automata in the previous chapter, especially the figure of Hector.

Two of Villard's designs for automata—a mechanical angel and an eagle—appear on the same page as designs for a crossbow and a hydraulic-powered saw (Plate 25). The crossbow is, of course, a mechanical weapon, and the hydraulic-powered saw was found in connection with mills and the workshops of woodworkers.[7] However, the angel and eagle are intended for a church, and reflect Villard's experience with religious buildings. The mechanism for the angel is located directly below the drawing of the hydraulic-powered saw (the angel itself is in drypoint on the parchment, and thus invisible in most light and in reproductions). The text under the drawing explains, "How to make an angel point its finger always toward the sun."[8] Placed in a church or chapel, the angel slowly traces the direction of the sun, its hand and finger always extended. It is not entirely clear from this drawing exactly how the automaton would work, except that it involved weight-driven rotational movement. The mechanism has a system of ropes and pulleys with weights, which are in turn wound around an axle and a wheel. The mechanical eagle, at the bottom of the same page, was designed according to the same principle of weight-driven movement as the angel. The bird had inside a system of weights, ropes, and pulleys; these would make the eagle turn its head toward the deacon during the Gospel lesson. The eagle is likely a part of a design for a lectern that appears on a different folio.[9] Both the rotating angel and the nodding eagle appear, at least from the drawings, to be fairly rudimentary. It is not at all clear in the drawing how the weight-driven rope and pulley system would have turned the head of the eagle. The abbreviated nature of these technical drawings is especially remarkable in comparison to the relative specificity of the design for the hydraulic saw, which appears on the same folio. Given the brevity of the captions and the style of drawing, these two mechanical designs in Villard's sketchbook appear notional: they resemble thought-experiments more than detailed designs. Yet they also represent thought-experiments toward replicating natural processes via mechanism (the movement of an eagle) and the representation of celestial motion (the sun moving in the sky), broadly similar to much earlier Hellenistic automata, as well as the automata from the early medieval Byzantine Empire and the 'Abbasid caliphate.

By the time Villard made his drawings, the principles of hydraulics, as well as mechanics involving weights and leverage, were commonly used for several different kinds of machines, such as mills and water clocks. Water mills, used extensively throughout the Roman Empire, had been made more powerful and efficient in the eleventh century and were widely used to grind grain for flour and mash for ale.[10] Windmills began to appear in Europe just over a century later, especially in those areas where there was a dearth of fast-flowing streams or where rivers would freeze during the winter months. As water- and windmills became more common throughout the Latin West, builders began to use the power they generated to do more than mill grain. The cam, an eccentric wheel that works as a lever, first appeared in the Latin West in the early thirteenth century, contemporary with Villard. A cam can make something move up and down in a pattern; for this reason cams were introduced to fulling mills in the thirteenth century. They were attached to wooden hammers to beat or "full" wool cloth, thus replacing human labor.[11] This innovation helped to spur an economic boom in England's textile industry; more broadly, it signals the use of hydraulic and pneumatic engineering in conjunction with other mechanical principles. These more complex machines could, using one source of power, begin to carry out more than one operation. Complex machinery was used for constructing very large buildings, like cathedrals, castles, and towers. (Plate 26) In the image depicting the construction of the Tower of Babel in the Crusader Bible of Louis IX (ca. 1250), masons and builders employ machinery identical to that which appears in Villard's drawings. This Bible was made in northern France just a few decades after Villard compiled his notebook, and the tools shown in the image of the Tower of Babel echo Villard's familiarity with building design and construction. A large crane, attached to a system of ropes and pulleys and powered by human locomotion, hoists heavy building materials. The rotational movement of the wheel on the crane is converted to vertical motion by pulleys and weights. Both Villard's designs and the depiction of the construction of the Tower of Babel depict developments in mechanical technology in the thirteenth century, especially in dynamics (the movement of energy through systems). Although the mechanisms in Villard's angel and eagle are weight-driven, they both use one kind of kinetic energy and transfer that energy to motion carried out in another direction, as do the crane in the Morgan Bible illumination and fulling hammers at water mills. The falling weight in the angel's mechanism appears to turn a wheel and two axles, eventually moving the angel laterally as well as vertically, following the direction of the sun.

Villard's automata contrast sharply with those in narrative sources. The automata at tombs, in the Chambre des Beautés, on top of Hugo's palace, and in the underground treasure-chamber of Octavian, to name just a few examples, are all made of precious stones and metal, such as marble, gold, or bronze. Rare and costly objects, many of which contain hidden powers, often surround these automata. In these texts philosophers, necromancers, and men with access to foreign and occult knowledge make automata using processes and knowledge that can never be described accurately or depicted visually. Yet Villard's automata operate in a different register: they use pulleys, ropes, straps, and weights to move. They work according to sensible materials rather than insensible celestial, natural, or demonic forces. Despite the fact that Villard's designs may not have been entirely accurate, they still reflect an understanding of mechanical principles in harmony with contemporary technology, as well as the idea that quotidian construction materials, instead of precious metals and esoteric knowledge, could be used to make automata.

Some of Villard's designs, particularly the Tantalus cup and the perpetual motion wheel, are very similar to designs from the Dar al-Islam. However, Villard's angel and eagle are far less elaborate, and less elaborately drawn, than contemporary automata designed by Arabic engineer Badi'al-Zaman Abu al-'Izz ibn Isma'il ibn al-Razaz al-Jazari (1136–1206/AH 531–603), more commonly known in the West as al-Jazari. His early thirteenth-century mechanical engineering treatise, *The Book of Ingenious Mechanical Devices*, contains detailed plans for fifty different mechanical devices, including pumps, fountains, and clocks, ornamented with moving figures of elephants, musicians, dancing slave girls, and servants on them.[12] Al-Jazari was, like Villard, a craftsman first and an author second, yet his figures display much more complex and intricate technology than Villard's.[13] One automaton designed by al-Jazari (likely built by him and copied by later artisans) is a female wine servant (Plate 27). The cupbearer wears colorful clothing, a spotted veil, and gold bracelets. A domed reservoir above her head holds the wine, which trickles through a small opening into a basin. The basin, when full, tilts and discharges the wine into a glass goblet. This, in turn, causes the figure, mounted on wheels, to roll down an inclined plane toward the drinker, while lowering and extending the arm holding the wineglass. In her left hand, the servant holds a napkin embellished with a red and gold border to wipe the drinker's mouth. Arabic text to the right of the figure gives a detailed description of the automaton and how to make it.[14] The design calls for copper, glass, cast bronze, iron, and, for the figure itself, paper and gesso. The skills needed to make this object encompass fine metalworking, sculpture, and painting, and the expectation is that more than one artisan would be involved in the construction of such an object.

As discussed earlier, al-Jazari's work, as well as that of his predecessors, the Banu Musa, was based in part on older texts, such as the *Pneumatics* of Hero of Alexandria.[15] However, the works of the Alexandrian school were not fully translated into Latin until the sixteenth century. Furthermore, there was no direct transmission of al-Jazari to the Latin West.[16] Thus, where Villard learned of these designs remains an open question. There is not enough historical evidence to hazard more than a suggestion. Although Villard was based mainly in northern France, he did travel to Hungary.[17] It is possible that, either while in Hungary or on his voyages to and from there he was exposed to mechanical principles or their applications (either from other artisans or from material objects) and found them noteworthy or interesting. Other scholars have postulated that Western artisans generally learned of Arabic automata and mechanical technology through contact between tradesmen and travel accounts.[18] Recall that William of Rubruck, in his 1255 account of his mission to China, notes the elaborate fountain with automata at the khan's court, and states that a Parisian goldsmith named William Buchier had built it for the khan. In addition to his trade as goldsmith, Buchier was a courtier and had frequent contact with Latin travelers to the Mongol Empire. Furthermore, Master William (as Rubruck calls him) was married to a woman whose family had ties in Lorraine, but who had herself been born in Hungary.[19] Hungary and the Balkans, long part of the Byzantine Empire and attacked by the Mongols, may have been sites where artisans from the Latin West became acquainted with Eastern craft, including automaton making.

Hesdin: Automata at Court

Fifty years after the death of Villard, automata for a private courtly setting first appeared at the chateau of Hesdin, in Artois, near the modern border between the Netherlands and France. Initially introduced in the late thirteenth century and expanded in the fourteenth and fifteenth centuries, the automata at Hesdin included trick fountains, a timekeeping device, artificial monkeys and birds, and android automata. In 1300 Hesdin, with its gardens and automata, resembled the pleasure gardens found in the distant courts of the Islamicate world and in the fictional world of romance. Just over a century later, under the Burgundian dukes, the automata were even more elaborate and well known, yet they were markedly different stylistically from both earlier automata at Hesdin and those in romances. Household accounts detail the methods and materials used to construct the automata at Hesdin and point to other substantial differences between textual automata and the material automata in the fourteenth and fifteenth centuries: They were built by artisans who, like Villard, used mechanical designs. The mechanisms or *engiens* in the park at Hesdin reflect the development of clockwork technology, particularly cranks and gear trains in conjunction with existing mill technology, as well as the combination of mechanical technology with fine craftsmanship.

The lush fountains and automata in the park at Hesdin provide the earliest example of automata built in Europe. They were built at the behest of Robert II (1250–1302), Count of Artois, and recall the elaborate gardens of the Eastern caliphs, such as those in the *chanson Aymeri de Narbonne*, explored in the first chapter. Count Robert was a member of the Capetian royal family, which ruled France and the Kingdom of Sicily, and he spent much of his life serving his family's interests, including as regent for the monarchy in Sicily from 1285–92. The count returned to Hesdin in 1292 with an entourage that included his Sicilian physician and two men from Apulia: John, whose expertise was tree-grafting, and Renaud Coignet (also called Rinaldo Cognetti), who was the chief administrator for major renovations to the chateau and surrounding estate.[20] Acting under Robert's direction, Coignet enlarged the park to 2200 acres, directed the construction of new walls around it, and oversaw construction of the buildings in the park.[21] The estate supported several species of cultivated wildlife, including fallow deer, rabbits, and heron for hunting, and carp for stocking the ponds (and the kitchens).[22] The animal species were introduced to the estate and their habitats were carefully managed as part of Robert's display of power over the natural landscape. Like the caliphs of Baghdad and other Muslim rulers, Robert used civil engineering, irrigation technology, animal husbandry, and mechanical devices to shape his environment to accommodate his pleasures and to demonstrate his power. For example, the Canche and Ternoise rivers ran through the estate and provided water for the fountains and the hydraulic automata, as well as marshland for the herons and ponds for the carp. The area called the *Marès* (marsh) included an artificial pond, a small manor, and the *pavillon du Marès*.[23] This "pavilion complex," located deep in the park, included a bridge adorned with six groups of mechanical monkeys covered in badger fur, mechanized fountains, a large sundial supported by lions and leopards, and a bellows-operated organ.[24] In 1300 the *orloges* needed repair.[25] It is not entirely clear what is meant by *orloges*, given that mechanical clocks were in their infancy in 1300, but it could refer to the sundial, a water clock or, possibly, part of a mechanical timekeeper. Hesdin also included a room or suite of rooms called a *gloriette* near the main hall of the chateau. The *gloriette* included large windows, high ceilings, statues, paintings, an indoor fountain, and automata, such as artificial birds, as well as captive songbirds.[26] These objects required significant maintenance from the outset. Accounts in 1299 and 1300 mention that the *engiens* required repairs, and that the lead pipes needed to be resoldered.[27]

Robert II died in 1302, but his daughter and heir, Mahaut, upheld her father's legacy of the "engines of amusement" at Hesdin until her death in 1329.[28] Mahaut (also called Matilda) was married to Odo IV, count of Burgundy in 1285, and became countess of Artois on her father's death.[29] She became one of the few women of her time to hold land and title *suo jure* rather than through her husband.

Hesdin was Mahaut's favorite residence. She preserved her father's legacy and built on it. The mechanical monkeys in the marsh pavilion complex, out in the open and exposed to the elements, needed to be refurbished every year or two. In 1304, for example, there is a bill for 300 nails to re-cover the monkeys.[30] In 1304 the mechanical birds in the *gloriette* received a new cage, and in 1308 extensive work was done on the lions and leopards that held the sundial (*miedi*) and on the automata (*ymages*) in the *gloriette*.[31] In 1312 the monkeys were re-covered and horns were added, giving the monkeys the appearance of satyrs or demons.[32] Given the elaborate fountains and mechanical birds also at Hesdin, it seems likely that the monkey figures were operated by some kind of weight-driven mechanical device, although it is not obvious from the accounts. The mechanized fountains required regular upkeep and plumbing, and no expense was spared. In 1314 the mechanical birds in the *gloriette* were repaired and regilded with over four hundredweight of gold.[33] The following year the countess installed a mechanical king on a throne.[34] Records of this moving figure do not describe the exact mechanism in detail; however, given its proximity to the hydraulic-powered birds, one may assume that king-automaton may also have been moved by water power in conjunction with moving weights.

For the rest of Mahaut's tenure as countess, the household accounts for Hesdin reveal extensive spending on repainting, gilding, plastering, and repairing the fountains, water-jets, sundial, monkeys, and other figures in the chateau and the park. The repeated mention of regular maintenance and work on the automata at Hesdin—repelting the monkeys, refurbishing the fountains, and later, renovating the entire park—highlights the mechanical nature of these objects, and, by extension, the difference between the magical automata and the mechanical ones. Ropes snapped, pipes rusted, fur dried out and became moth-eaten, unlike the incorruptible automata found at tombs, distant courts, or guarding treasure in the leaves of romance and legend.

The Duke of Burgundy, Odo IV, Mahaut's successor, retained the diversions at Hesdin and added to them, even during the instability brought on by the Hundred Years War. In 1344 a new fountain was installed in the *gloriette* (also called the *gaiole*): the fountain resembled a tree, and was gilded. Like the earlier indoor fountain in the *gloriette*, this one also included mechanical birds that sprayed water from their beaks.[35] The Hundred Years' War gave rise to periodic attacks on Hesdin, and work on the machinery in the park was sometimes interrupted. But in general, the dukes of Burgundy continued work on Hesdin in latter half of the fourteenth century, perfecting the existing *engiens*, and installing new automata.

The automata at Hesdin are the product of several layers of cultural mediation. The park, from its inception at the close of the thirteenth century until the middle of the fourteenth, with fountains, moving statues, and mechanical birds, was very similar to gardens and parks found in the Dar al-Islam, introduced in the first chapter. Robert II spent several years, on different occasions, in the Kingdom of Naples and Sicily, which, as I discussed earlier, was an important trading zone of scientific ideas.[36] He accompanied his uncle, King Louis IX, on crusade in 1270. After Louis died later that year, Robert accompanied his body from Tunis and spent several weeks in Palermo, where the king's heart was removed and left behind (intentionally). Zisa Palace (also called "El Aziz," or, in French "Le Glorieux") in Palermo was known for its spectacular garden features, including automata, and Robert's *gloriette* at Hesdin strongly resembles Zisa Palace. Both were adjacent to a lush, aggressively cultivated outdoor garden; both had indoor fountains; both were richly decorated with paintings, sculptures, and textiles; and both contained automata.[37] It is also possible that Robert had been inspired by his sojourn in Apulia, 1285–1292, where he may have heard about the mechanical marvels that belonged to Emperor Frederick II (1194–1250), the former ruler of southern Italy. Frederick had received two automata as gifts from Muslim rulers, an astrological clepsydra from the sultan of Damascus, and a metal tree with artificial songbirds on its branches.[38] Renaud Coignet may also have been familiar with Islamic gardens and fountains; Renaud was from cosmopolitan Barletta, the second largest city in the Kingdom of Naples and an important Adriatic port.

The *gloriette* at Hesdin also resembles the description of a *gloriette* in a late twelfth-century French *chanson de geste*, *Prise d'Orange*, and, as I demonstrate below, many other examples of gardens and pleasances in twelfth- and thirteenth-century French literature. It is also possible that Robert and, later, Mahaut were equally influenced by literary accounts of automata in foreign places.[39] There are no Arabic books on automaton making (such as al-Jazari's) in the library inventories for the castle. One scholar has noted that Robert II was an enthusiastic manuscript collector, and has suggested that he was inspired by literary descriptions of strange, moving inanimate objects, such as the magic horse in *Cléomades*.[40] In many medieval romances, the gardens and palaces of caliphs, emirs, and kings contained beautiful metal statues of animals, soothing fountains, and mechanical animals, such as the caliph of Baghdad's tree in *Aymeri de Narbonne*, with its jeweled, singing birds.[41] Likewise, in *Floire et Blancheflor*, Blancheflor is imprisoned by the emir of Babylon in a garden. Surrounded by a high wall painted in blue and gold, the garden contains bronze birds. When the wind blows, they sing melodiously, more sweetly than anyone has ever heard.

> When the wind blew stronger the birds sang even more sweetly. And so in good weather the birds sang beautifully there—the fake ones and the real birds. Thus the blackbirds, skylarks, jaybirds, starlings, nightingales, finches, orioles and others which flocked to the park in high spirits, on hearing the beautiful birdsong, were quite unhappy if they did not find their partner![42]

In this instance, the mechanical birds sing so realistically that they fool real birds into thinking they could find a mate among them. From the same period (ca. 1160), *Éneas* contains a description of a similar object in the city of Carthage. Ten thousand "golden birds, large and small, and greatly wondrous," sit on a golden grapevine.[43] The grapevine is hollow, and when the wind blows the birds sing and flutter their wings.[44] Hidden human agency in conjunction with pneumatic technology gives voice to the mechanical birds in the Dutch version of the story of Gawain, *Le Roman van Walewein* (ca. 1230–1260). Ysabele, a captive of her father, King Assentijn, in India, lives in a pleasance with aromatic plants and flowers, a fountain, and a golden tree with golden birds.[45] Under the tree is a chamber for sixteen men working eight bellows that force air up through the tree roots. "And when the little birds were moved by the wind they stood up straight and twitched as if they were alive; then each bird sings its song six and seven in chorus."[46] These fictional automata are based on examples of elaborate fountains and mechanical animals and people in gardens in the Islamicate world.[47] The automata at Hesdin were based on descriptions of those found in palaces—either actual or literary—in the Islamicate world, as well.

The naturalistic monkeys in the landscape in the *pavillon du Marès* and the combination of artificial and live songbirds in the *gloriette* indicate the significant overlap between categories of natural and artificial. The mechanical monkeys on the bridge are covered in badger skin so that they resemble real monkeys more strongly, and they are outdoors in order to evoke them in their natural habitat. However, the monkeys are part of a landscape that, although naturalistic, is wholly the product of human art.[48] The records of Hesdin are silent on the topic of the artificial birds in the *gloriette*. It is not clear if they were enameled, gilded wood, or covered in feathers.[49] Yet the juxtaposition of both real and fake birds suggests a desire to confound and delight visitors with the slow realization that not all the birds in the *gloriette* are real, perhaps in the same way that elite visitors to the estate would have slowly realized that the landscape and animals in it had been painstakingly managed for Count Robert's pleasure.

Hesdin was familiar to the French royal court in the late thirteenth and fourteenth centuries: Robert, as I have said, was a member of the Capetian ruling dynasty, and his daughter and granddaughters were linked to the royal family through blood and marriage. It is quite possible that the automata at Hesdin may have piqued royal interest in similar objects. Mahaut's younger daughter, Blanche, married Charles, a younger son of King Philip IV, at Hesdin in 1308.[50] Mahaut's elder daughter, Jeanne, queen of France and wife of Philip V, inherited her mother's title in 1329, but outlived her mother by only one year. Beginning around 1320, French royals began to collect elaborate table fountains and water clocks. This collection grew under the Valois dynasty that replaced the Capetians in 1328, and one of the earliest extant examples of a musical table fountain dates from the 1320s (Plate 28). In 1330 Mahaut's granddaughter, Jeanne (III), inherited the title of Countess of Artois in her own right, and also held the title of Duchess of Burgundy through her marriage to Odo IV, duke of Burgundy; it was at this point that Artois became part of Burgundy. During Jeanne and Odo's lifetimes (they died in 1349 and 1350 respectively), members of the Valois dynasty continued to visit Hesdin and enjoy the automata there. While it is certainly possible that the French court became enamored with automata from accounts of them in travelers' tales, romances, and histories, no doubt the automata at Hesdin, expanded under the conservatorship of Mahaut and her heirs, provided them with material examples of objects that, a few decades prior, could be encountered only in texts or by traveling outside France.

Royal familiarity with Hesdin was certainly responsible for its appearance in one of the most famous fourteenth-century love lyrics, *Le Remede de Fortune* by the courtier, composer, and poet Guillaume de Machaut (ca. 1340). Guillaume was secretary to John, king of Bohemia and count of Luxembourg, and later a protégé of John's daughter, Bonne (also known as Jutta of Luxembourg). Bonne married the dauphin of France, John (later King John II "the Good"), although she died before her husband's coronation. The French royal family frequently visited Hesdin when it was under the rule of Jeanne III and Odo IV of Artois and Burgundy, and it is likely that Guillaume had been to Hesdin on at least one occasion.[51] In *Le Remede de Fortune*, which Guillaume composed for Bonne, the Lover loves his Lady in silence and from afar, and writes anonymous lais about her beauty and compassion.[52] The Lover's verses circulate around the court, and the Lady, after hearing one, asks the Lover who wrote it. The Lover, unable to confess his love for fear of rejection and equally unable to lie to his beloved, flees without answering. "Forlorn, lost in thought, and sighing," he seeks refuge in a hidden place where he can regain his composure. He wanders around in a daze until he reaches "a very beautiful garden called the Park of Hesdin."[53] "And I could never describe the marvels, the delights, the inventions, the engines, the contrivances, the water-courses, the strange things that were enclosed there."[54] Inspired by the beauty and genius surrounding him in the park, the Lover composes a complaint to Fortuna, one of the many lyrics in the poem.

Given the elaborate and extraordinary nature of the automata at Hesdin, it is surprising that Guillaume, as a casual visitor, did not describe them in more detail. Instead, the Lover says only that he could not possibly describe them all. The indescribable is a literary trope, but it also may be a factual claim due to the hidden mechanisms of the automata. The machinery of the automata, though visible in the account books, was concealed from visitors to produce the illusion of life, similar to the hidden tubes and wires in Hector's preserved body in the *Troy Book*.[55] However, in contrast to his lack of description of the *engiens* at Hesdin in the text, Guillaume does allude to the complexity of the mechanical automata in a manuscript painting from a presentation copy of *Le Remede de Fortune* that illustrates this scene. Guillaume directed the production of the manuscript in 1350 to honor his patroness Bonne just after her death, and he also oversaw the production of the thirty-four manuscript paintings.[56] One illumination depicts the Lover as he composes his complaint to Fortune in the park at Hesdin; automata are nowhere in evidence. Directly underneath this vignette, Fortuna wears a blindfold and turns her wheel. Fortuna's wheel is a complex mechanism, rendered in gold leaf, comprising a crank that rotates an axle around which a gear wheel turns a larger wheel, this one with the usual figures representing the reigning favorite of Fortuna, the one without reign, and the one who will reign again (Plate 29).

The appearance of a crank in conjunction with meshed gears in this painting is significant. A crank transmits reciprocal motion into rotational motion, like the pedals of a bicycle, while a gear is a toothed wheel that engages with another toothed wheel to change the speed or direction of the transmitted motion. The crank was an important invention and was known in the Latin West as early as the ninth century.[57] However, despite this knowledge, cranks were not incorporated into machines in Europe until the fourteenth century.[58] They do appear in earlier European drawings of Fortuna's wheel, but without a clear understanding (at least on the part of the illustrator) of how a crank works (Plate 30). In the twelfth-century drawing of Fortuna, added to a tenth-century manuscript of Gregory the Great's sermon on the Book of Job, Fortuna holds in her left hand a crank attached with a lynchpin to the center of her wheel. However, there are no gears in this illustration, and it would be impossible for the crank to rotate the wheel. Even the later drawings in Villard's notebook do not have the specificity of Fortuna's wheel in the fourteenth-century painting from *Le Remede de Fortune*. In that manuscript painting Fortuna turns a crank that is clearly connected to an axle in the center of the gear wheel. The motion from the crank turns the axle, which then rotates the gear counterclockwise. The teeth on the gear interlock with teeth in Fortuna's wheel, turning it clockwise. Perhaps Guillaume, having seen the engines and automata at Hesdin, wanted to refer to them visually by having the elaborate mechanism of Fortuna's wheel represent the *engiens* at Hesdin. The visual tradition of depicting Fortuna turning a wheel with a crank is here conjoined to the scene in which the Lover seeks refuge among the mechanical diversions of Hesdin. Perhaps Guillaume described some of the automata to the artist who painted the miniature; perhaps the artist was already familiar with such machinery. Either way, the artist was able to create a clear picture of a fairly complex system of gear-wheels and a crank, indicating that in 1350 mechanical knowledge encompassed not only the use of this kind of machinery in settings like Hesdin, but also was understood well enough so that it could be rendered accurately.

The two images of Fortuna's wheel also testify to the increasing prominence of mechanical technology from the twelfth to the fourteenth century, and the power of mechanism as a metaphor. In the later image, Fortuna's wheel is a beautiful, complex machine, far more complex than the twelfth-century drawing or Villard's sketches. In the earlier drawing, Fortuna, a powerful figure on the right, is almost as large as her wheel, and she looms over the hapless figures that cling to it. In the fourteenth-century miniature, she is much smaller—only slightly larger than the figures on the wheel—and she is completely dwarfed by the elaborate machinery of her wheel. By 1350, when the miniature in *Le Remede de Fortune* was produced, machines were large and complex, and could be used to depict the rise and fall of kings and the vicissitudes of Fortune.

Hesdin in the Fifteenth Century

The automata at Hesdin fell into disrepair in the 1380s and remained in a state of decrepitude for half a century. Philip the Good, duke of Burgundy, renovated the *engiens* at great expense in the 1430s, and the castle and its amusements became even more famous than they had been in the previous century. Hesdin was one of Philip's five principal residences, and he maintained it until his death in 1467.[59] Elaborate and amazing, the mechanical automata were a statement about the duke's wealth and his access to marvels, just as they were a statement about Robert's wealth and position at the turn of the fourteenth century. Philip had exotic animals in his menageries, beautifully illuminated books in his libraries, and potent relics in his churches. At Hesdin, one of his favorite castles, he had a full complement of technological marvels—the place was a massive mechanical *Wunderkammer*. The moving figures and mechanized fountains at Hesdin under Philip's rule no longer demonstrated the interpenetration of the natural and the artificial, as they had done at Hesdin under Robert. Yet these objects were still remarkable and evoked wonder. The automata at Hesdin indicate that by the mid-fifteenth-century developments in technological engineering enabled the construction of even more complex artificial marvels, and that these objects operated within a framework of sci-

entific understanding that no longer looked first to the non-manifest powers
of natural objects or demons to explain how they worked. In yet another break
with earlier examples of automata, these fifteenth-century automata and the
functions they performed were raucous and disruptive, like elaborate practical jokes rather than the strange and serious prophetic heads, incorruptible
guardians, preserved bodies, and models of courtly behavior found in literary
texts, or even the naturalistic monkeys and pleasing mechanical songbirds
found at Hesdin in earlier centuries.

The most vivid description of the newly renovated automata and *engiens*
at Hesdin is in a bill from 1433 in the ducal accounts. Detailed and bizarre, it
deserves to be quoted at length.

To Colard le Voleur, *valet-de-chambre* and painter of my lord duke,
the sum of 1000 pounds at 40 groats per pounds/pound currency of
Flanders, for the following work which he has carried out at Hesdin
castle. For painting the gallery of the said castle in the same manner
and design as before, very ornately and with the finest painting materials possible. Item: for having, making, or renovating the legends
and painting the three figures that squirt water and wet people at
will. And at the entrance to the gallery there is a device [*engien*] for
soaking ladies when they tread on it; and a mirror in which one sees
many deceptions; and with it he [Colard] also made a machine
[*engien*] at the entrance to the said gallery; which, when the knobs
are touched, strikes those who are underneath in the face and covers
them with black or white, and also there is a fountain in that gallery,
and which spouts water when one wishes and always when ladies
come before it. Item: at the exit of this gallery there is another machine [*engien*] that will strike and cuff all who pass through on their
heads and shoulders. Item: in the room before the hermit, a machine
makes it rain everywhere . . . , and also thunder and snow and lightning, too, as if one were looking at the sky. Item: next to [that] room
there is a wooden hermit that speaks to people when they enter . . . .
And also for paving the place where people go to avoid the showers,
where they then fall from on high down onto a sack filled with feathers. . . . Item: He built in addition . . . a bridge that, at will, makes
people who walk on it fall into the water. Item: There are machines
[*engiens*] in several places, and when one touches the knobs one causes a
great quantity of water to fall on people. Item: In the gallery there

are six more figures than there were before, which soak people in
different manners. Item: At the entrance to the gallery [there are]
eight pipes for soaking ladies from below and three pipes which,
when people stop in front of them, [cause them to be] whitened and
covered with flour. Item: There is a window and when people wish
to open it a figure in front of it wets people and closes the window
on them. Item: There is a lectern with a book of ballads on it and
when people try to read it they are all covered with soot, and, as soon
as they look inside they can be sprayed with water. And there is another mirror where people are sent to look at themselves after they
are ruined, and when they stand before it they are once more all covered with flour, and made all white. Item: There is a wooden figure
that appears above a bench in the middle of the gallery, and it tricks
people and can speak by a machine [*engien*] and make a cry on behalf of my lord the duke that everybody should go out of the gallery;
And those who go because of that cry will be beaten by large figures
like idiots . . . and they will fall into the water at the entrance to the
bridge; and those who do not want to leave will be so completely
soaked that they will not know where to go to escape from the water.
A box is suspended in one window, and above the box is a figure that
makes faces at people and replies to their questions, and one can both
hear and see the voice in this box. . . . After all this was completed,
my lord duke ordered [Colard] to make conduits and necessary devices low down, all along the walls of the gallery, to squirt water in so
many places that nobody in the gallery could possibly prevent themselves from getting soaked, and many other conduits and devices
everywhere under the pavement to wet the ladies from below.[60]

The gallery was lavishly decorated with "beautiful oil paints, gold leaf,
and azure," and the ceiling was covered in golden stars, recalling the central
hall in Hugo's palace in *Le Voyage de Charlemagne*. Gilded angels and beautifully painted automata (*ymaiges*) moved, spoke, and watched over the courtiers in gallery, similar to the Alabaster Chamber in *Le Roman de Troie*.[61] Yet
the *engiens* are very different from the golden automata in the Alabaster Chamber. Those astounding figures model and enforce courtly behavior in all its
aspects—dress, thought, speech, and gesture. They excite, playing music and
performing feats of acrobatics and conjuring; and they soothe, helping to sup-
press uncourtly thoughts or actions, and banishing illness and pain. In con-

trast, the Burgundian automata at Hesdin purposely inflicted pain and misery; they ruined clothing, hair, and make-up; they stripped their subjects of dignity and comfort. The speaking wooden hermit and the "figure" in the window box that answered questions do recall the prophetic heads attributed to Gerbert, Grosseteste, and Albertus Magnus. Yet they lack the gravitas associated with those earlier oracular heads. One of the duke's automata made faces at the courtiers, and was part of an overall setting designed to discomfit and amuse, rather than edify and instruct.

Part of the difference between these Burgundian automata and earlier textual examples in courtly settings can be attributed to changes in courtly mores and fashions. In the twelfth century the notion of a courtier as a refined noble councilor, skilled in the nuances of ceremony and deportment, was still novel. The automata in the Chambre des Beautés demonstrate the importance of proper courtly behavior, both to the inhabitants of the Chamber and to the audience of the romance. The narrative functions of the automata in the *Roman de Troie* betray anxiety on the part of the audience (and the writer) about appropriate behavior, speech, and dress. The automata enact perfect courtly etiquette and surveil the inhabitants of the Chamber, disciplining those who need it.

By the fifteenth century courtly society was more ritualized, and reached its zenith under Philip III, "The Good," of Burgundy. He was part of the Valois family, and was the great-grandson of John II "The Good" and Bonne of Luxembourg, patrons of Guillaume de Machaut. The Burgundian territories were extremely prosperous, and the dukes were the wealthiest rulers in Europe, monarchs in all but name.[62] Because the duchy comprised several distinct geographic territories in the Low Countries, Flanders, and eastern France it lacked a common language. Philip employed public spectacle and an imposing and ostentatious court as a way to join together the disparate territories under his rule and create a sense of unity and shared aristocratic culture.[63] Building on the legacies of his father, John the Fearless, and grandfather, Philip the Bold, Philip was a noted patron of the arts, with many painters, sculptors, architects, musicians, poets, historians, and jewelers in his employ. He kept an extravagant and formal court, especially in matters of dress. Philip often dressed in black—the most expensive color to produce—and the ornate, colorful clothing of his courtiers drew attention to the subtle luxe of his costume. Meals, masques, tournaments, hunts, and all other activities were painstakingly choreographed and marked by lavish display and consumption; all were performances designed to highlight his extraordinary wealth and nobility. Philip founded the Order of the Golden Fleece, a chivalric order based on the heroic deeds of Jason of Troy, and he wore the golden collar of his order at all times.[64] He also frequently employed mechanical fountains and automata at feasts and public occasions, such as at his wedding to Isabelle of Portugal in 1430. On that occasion, a statue of a lion, representing Philip, holding a stone, representing his new chivalric order of the Golden Fleece, was erected outside the outer wall of the ducal palace in Bruges. Red and white wine gushed from the stone into a basin below for the duration of the wedding feast (over a week). Inside the palace walls, figures of a deer and a unicorn spouted hippocras and rose water, respectively.[65] The wine fountains—especially the ones that overtly invoked the duke through heraldic devices—proclaimed that the duke, rather than Nature, was the "unreciprocated giver of an indeterminate amount of wine."[66]

The automata at Hesdin underscored the formality and strictures of the ducal court by disrupting it in a controlled setting. If you were a courtier or a guest of the duke and hurried, in the gallery, to obey the figure that gave orders on the duke's behalf to leave, you would be beaten with rods and pushed into the water. Yet if you tried to avoid this, you would be soaked all the same. Some of the devices seem to have been designed to overturn or perhaps mock normative courtly behavior, such as the lectern and the book of ballads. Reading poetry and singing lyrics were common pastimes in fifteenth-century courtly culture, especially in the Burgundian court.[67] But if you tried to read the book in the gallery you would be covered in soot and soaked with water. Guests and courtiers of the duke were expected to adhere to high standards of brilliant and luxurious dress. Yet, within the topsy-turvy space of the gallery, one mirror would reflect a distorted image, while another would reveal the true extent of your sodden appearance and ruined clothing. Adding insult to injury, the mirror would also spray you with flour as you stood before it. These mirrors reflect the inversion of courtly norms; the mirror held by the automaton in the Chambre des Beautés helps to uphold those norms. Yet ultimately, the rambunctious pleasures and emphasis on ruined dress throw the formality and standards of normative courtly conduct into sharper relief. You had only to leave the gallery, change into another costly outfit (thereby demonstrating your wealth and ability to participate in the ducal court), and return to the more usual pastimes of hunting, feasting, or dancing. The automata at Hesdin are a particularly vivid example of elaborate display and artistic endeavor, and they had their roots, as I discussed earlier, in accounts of automata from earlier centuries.

Exposing the gap between high and low culture, the automata at Hesdin stripped away the carapace of formality and fancy dress, leaving behind confusion, disarray, and even terror, as people were beaten, soiled, mocked, and soaked. As with all marvels, reaction to the devices depended on perspective. If one, such as the duke, was in on the tricks, then the automata were not terrifying, but amusing and entertaining. In this way the "engines" at Hesdin are very similar to the Throne of Solomon encountered by Liudprand of Cremona. As discussed earlier, Liudprand made sure to note that he had consulted with people who knew about courtly ceremony, and thus he was neither awed nor terrified when he saw the throne. At least some of the devices in Philip's gallery were built to the duke's specifications, such as the jets of water along the walls below eye level, and the "many other conduits and devices everywhere under the pavement to wet the ladies from underneath."[68] The surprise, terror, dismay, or delight of the guests in the gallery were part of the spectacle for those who were more knowledgeable or experienced. Networks of pleasure and privilege cohered around knowledge, even knowledge of jokes or tricks. Knowing the joke signaled inclusion into an elite group. Being the butt of the joke signified exclusion from the group, but the experience could also initiate courtiers into the elite court, by providing them with a way of gaining the knowledge that would lead to inclusion. And for the courtiers, their surprise and humiliation came not only from physical pain or social embarrassment, but also from something deeper: the uncanny feeling of being confronted with something (the automata) that they could not anticipate and did not understand.

The duke of Burgundy was not the first to imagine that automata could be used to provoke terror or humiliation and demarcate networks of knowledge. At a feast to celebrate the coronation of the wife of Ferdinand I of Aragon in 1414, theatrical machinery was used as part of the entertainment. A cloud (also called a pomegranate) descended from the ceiling to the amazement of the guests. This kind of theatrical machine worked by means of hidden mechanisms, and was used in stagecraft to convey the appearance of God, angels, or demons.[69] During the feast, Death appeared in the cloud and captured a jester named Borra.

When Death came in his cloud in front of the table, Borra began to scream, and the Duke led him up; Death threw down a rope, they tied it around Borra, and Death hanged him. You would not believe the racket Borra made, weeping, expressing his terror, and as he was pulled up, he urinated into his underclothes, and the urine fell on the heads of those below. He was quite convinced he was being carried off to Hell. The king marveled at this and was greatly amused, as were all the others.[70]

Usually these kinds of theatrical devices were used to create wondrous effects, especially in religious drama. In this instance, the technology was used for entertainment and humiliation. The king, at the very least, knew that the figure of Death was an actor, and the cloud was a man-made device to provide entertainment during the feast. Borra, however, was clearly terrified, because he was not in on the joke, nor was he being initiated into elite knowingness.[71] Likewise, at Hesdin the duke and a few experienced courtiers knew that the marvels in the gallery were mechanical, rather than demonic, and that there was no way to escape with dignity and dress intact.

Yet by the late fourteenth century, automata had also become a part of sober public spectacle and elite courtly pageantry throughout Europe. These automata had, in contrast to those at Hesdin, a more serious function. As part of public pageantry they embodied the majesty of royal and noble courts, and proclaimed the power and wealth of the prince. In particular, the court of Richard II of England, as well as the courts of Savoy and France, relied on the public display of opulence and wealth to communicate majesty and might.[72] In 1377, the Worshipful Company of London Goldsmiths created a mechanical angel used at the coronation pageant of Richard II. The angel, which crowned the king during the public pageant the day before his religious anointing at Westminster, not only demonstrated the importance of the goldsmiths' guild to London politics, but also indicated the glory of the new king, and set a precedent for the importance of elaborate public spectacle in Richard's reign. The Valois kings of France also used mechanical *mirabilia*, including automata, in public fêtes for symbolic purposes. In 1389, King Charles VI of France (and cousin to the duke of Burgundy) commanded a grand spectacle for the entry of Queen Isabel of Bavaria into Paris. According to the chronicler Juvenal des Ursins, the royal entry included numerous *tableaux vivants* and fountains throughout Paris dispensing wine, milk, and water. A small man, dressed as an angel, descended "by means of some well-constructed machinery" from one of the towers of Notre-Dame, placed a crown on the queen's head, and then ascended "by the same means, and thus appeared as if he were returning to the skies of his own accord." In front of the Grand Chastelet there was an artificial white stag—signifying purity—with gilt horns and a golden crown around its neck. "It was so ingeniously constructed that its eyes, horns, mouth, and all its limbs, were put in motion by a man who was secreted within its body." Around its neck, in addition to the crown, hung the royal arms, and when the queen passed, the stag held out a sword in its right forefoot, symbolizing royal justice and prerogative.[73] Philip III of Burgundy also included automata that were not disruptive in courtly entertainments and spectacles. After the conquest of Constantinople by Sultan Mehmet in 1453, Philip pledged (after some delays) to support a crusade to defeat the Turk. He celebrated his pledge with a massive banquet, the Feast of the Pheasant (Banquet du Voeu du Phaisan), on February 17, 1454, in Lille. According to two eyewitness accounts, by Olivier de la Marche and Mathieu d'Escouchy, the sumptuous feast included numerous symbolic tableaux and automata, including table fountains in the shape of women and animals, mechanical birds, and a lion.[74]

Artisans and the Creation of Mechanical Automata

There was, of course, another group that would not have been terrified or surprised by the automata at Hesdin and elsewhere: the people who made them. The skilled artisans responsible for the fountains and *engiens* at Hesdin came from a variety of trades, thus exposing the wide range of techniques and materials used to make and repair mechanical, hydraulic, and pneumatic automata. The accounts from Hesdin provide a clear picture of fine technology and mechanical engineering in later medieval Europe. By around 1310, the mechanical works at Hesdin required someone to oversee their maintenance, and Jacques de Boulogne, trained as a painter, was appointed "master of the engines of the castle and the paintings."[75] He was part of a family of painters that appears regularly in the archival accounts for Hesdin, beginning in the last years of the thirteenth century. By around 1310, Jacques, who from this point onward is mentioned more than anyone else in his family, was occupied more with the *engiens* than with other work. In accordance with Mahaut's wishes, he received, between 1310 and 1312, two sous tournois per day and a rent of ten pounds parisis per year for his work as overseer of the *engiens*, a wage that reflected the high labor value of this kind of skilled work. His family worked on the automata at Hesdin for the next five generations.[76] Likewise, Colard le Voleur, paid a thousand pounds for his work on the gallery in 1433, was trained as a painter, and was also in charge of the renovations and maintenance of the "engiens" at Hesdin.

The appointment of painters as the masters of the automata at Hesdin is striking. It is perhaps due to the fact that many of these devices were decorated or painted, and only painters had access to the necessary pigments and the ability to turn them into paints. Or it is possible that painters, especially in the fifteenth century, had an elevated status, akin to architects or military engineers, and were used to overseeing large groups of artisans and laborers.[77] Jacques and his successors oversaw the work on the automata, the fountains, and the decorations, and coordinated with the many other kinds of artisans whose expertise was also required.[78] Household accounts from the years 1294–1295 detail payment to laborers for their work on the park of Hesdin, including work on plumbing for the fountains.[79] Metalsmiths were paid for work done to the bridge of the pavilion in the park, for a mechanized boar's head on the wall of the pavilion, and for work done to the *ymaginetes*.[80] Records from the early fourteenth century mention locksmiths [*serrurie*] and blacksmiths responsible for, respectively, the iron rods for the glass panes in the *gloriette* and iron for the *orloge*.[81] Tanners were responsible for regularly repelting the monkeys in badger skin.[82] Plumbers built and maintained the fountains and dealt with laying lead pipe and hydraulic engineering. Fine metalsmiths were in charge of gilding the mechanical birds in 1315, and carpenters made the wooden hermit and other wooden figures.[83]

The nature of the devices meant that different kinds of artisans often had to work in collaboration. A plumber may have built the elaborate fountain and mechanical birds, but a goldsmith was responsible for gilding the birds. Likewise, the mechanized boars' heads were made by the *tailleurs de coutel*, but were then decorated by a painter, like Jacques de Boulougne.

Craft knowledge was recognized as part of the foundation of a community, and artisans, and more specifically, the guilds into which they were organized, began to exercise more economic power in the late medieval period.[84] The rise of urbanism and elaborate urban courts in the early fourteenth century led to an expansion of artisanal trades. Craftsmen began to organize into guilds in this period (although the relationship between craft guild and town varied widely), and gained economic, social, and even political power. Artisan guilds often produced pageants that contained machinery to produce effects similar to those at Hesdin. The golden angel that crowned the boy king in London in 1377 was a material example of the goldsmiths' political and economic power in London.[85] Artisans and craftsmen in England also staged religious Mystery plays based on Bible stories. Wooden ships rocked on mechanical seas; giant mechanical beasts guarding the Hellmouth opened their jaws to admit sinners to fiery depths; and angels, demons, the Virgin, and even God descended from the clouds above using devices similar to the one that fooled Borra.[86] Collaboration was the norm, as weavers', carpenters', or painters' guilds had to be consulted and paid for their expertise.[87] The artisans responsible for these theatrical effects were mystery-makers, using secret, carefully guarded knowledge to produce stunning effects.[88] By the fifteenth century, secular and episcopal courts required painters, weavers, carpenters, and metal smiths to create and stage public pageants, and to make objects that reflected the glory of those courts. The expanded interest in courtly and public pageantry led to an increase in status and salary for certain groups of artisans, including painters, architects, and fine metalsmiths.

As craft guilds became more established, they protected the transmission of their knowledge in increasingly aggressive and sophisticated ways. With regard to automata, this resulted in the uncoupling of secret knowledge from morally problematic knowledge; however, automata remained emblematic of esoteric knowledge, just of a different kind. Until the thirteenth century there is evidence of the sharing and exchange of mechanical knowledge.[89] As guilds became more powerful in the fourteenth century, artisans began to view craft processes and inventions as separate from material objects and labor. Craft secrecy—limiting craft knowledge to guild members only—also developed in this period.[90]

As automata shifted from textual to material objects, they underwent a dual shift in perception and prestige value. As discussed earlier, authors of textual descriptions of automata use terms for them that are both specific and maddeningly vague. According to these writers, these objects are usually made from metals, such as gold, copper, or brass; they are found in conjunction with other objects of immense value and power, such as gemstones, carbuncles, and even precious herbs and spices. They can foretell the secrets of fate; perform music, magic, and acrobatics; discern friend from foe; identify threats and halt intruders. Yet how they do this remains mysterious. Writers can say only that learned men used esoteric knowledge, diabolical practices, or natural or celestial magic to create these objects, they cannot say with any specificity how these objects are made. The power of these textual automata inheres in their material opulence and the mystery of their creation and operation. Descriptions of literary or textual automata tantalize audiences with the unknown, the strange, and the forbidden.

Mechanical automata, in contrast, are the product of different processes and materials. Some elaborate fountains, such as those found first at foreign courts and later in the Latin West, were made of gold and decorated with precious gems. And the duke of Burgundy certainly spared no expense renovating the gallery and the *engiens* at Hesdin, paying for costly materials such as azure and cloth of gold. Yet the hermit was made of wood, as were the monkeys, the boar's heads, and Villard's eagle and angel. Pipes for the spouting jets and fountains were made from lead; ropes, pulleys, and iron and wooden gears helped to move the automata. Despite these more humble materials, mechanical automata could be seen, experienced, and wondered at. Their material reality was at the root of their allure, as that which had previously only been known through words and description gradually became physical and sensible. By the late medieval period, automata existed because of artisans, not magicians or sorcerers. The register of their creation shifted from the mysteries of nature and esoteric knowledge to a more egalitarian understanding of natural forces, employed by craftsmen who created with their hands.

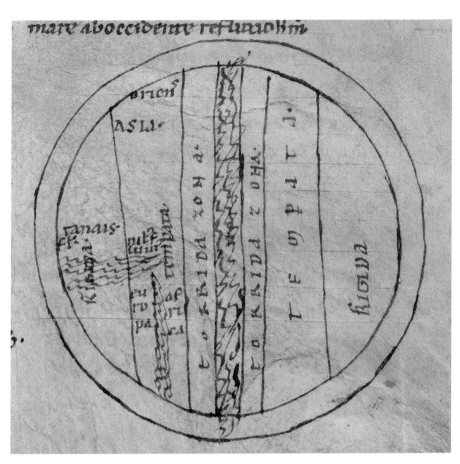

Plate 1. Macrobian zone map, oriented to the East, like a *mappamundi*. William of Conches, *De philosophia mundi*, Lotharingia, ca. 1150. Philadelphia, University of Pennsylvania Library, LJS 384, fol. 15a.

Plate 2. Table fountain at the khan's court in Karakorum. From a French version of the travels of Marco Polo, entitled *Livres du Grant Caam*. France, ca. 1400. Oxford, The Bodleian Libraries, University of Oxford, MS Bodley 264, fol. 239v.

Plate 3. The false paradise of the Old Man in the Mountain, called Aloadin in *MT* and Gathonolabes in Marco Polo's *Devisament du monde*. A fortress leads to an enclosed garden, in which beautiful women play music and pass the time in conversation. One maiden, in red, picks fruit from one of the many trees in the garden. The Old Man, in white beard and red hat, leads a youth into his paradise. In the center of the garden stands a tree raised up on a plinth. From this base flow the milk and honey of this false paradise. From the French translation of Marco Polo, *Livres du Grant Caam*. France, ca. 1400. Oxford, The Bodleian Libraries, University of Oxford, MS Bodley 264, fol. 226v.

Plate 4. *Natura artifex.* Natura, using hammer, anvil, and forge, makes people out of body parts. *Roman de la Rose*, France, fifteenth century. New Haven, Conn., Yale University, MS 418, fol. 282v. Courtesy of the Yale University Library.

Plate 5. Automata on golden pillars surround Hector's sickbed in the Chambre de Beautés. An eagle and a satyr hover around the automaton in the far right corner with the flowers. One of the female figures holds up a mirror while the other one juggles. This artist has followed the text very closely. Yet this image is not from the *Roman de Troie*, but from the *Histoire ancienne jusqu'à César*. France, late fifteenth century. Paris, BnF, MS Fr. 301, fol. 94r.

Plate 6. Four automata in the Chambre de Beautés. Here, the painter followed the description of the automata less exactly: there are two musicians, and a third figure holding the censer. In the far left a fourth figure makes hand signals, to tell courtiers how to adjust their behavior. *Roman de Troie*, France, fourteenth century. Paris, BnF, MS Fr. 60, fol. 141.

Plate 7. Copper knights guarding Doloreuse Garde. Note the demonic facial features and the exaggerated physique and genitalia. *Histoire du saint graal*, France, fifteenth century. Paris, BnF, MS Fr. 113, fol. 1.

Plate 8. Lancelot battles the copper knights just before finding the box that contains the enchantments over the castle. These figures are naked, with chest and armpit hair, as well as genitalia. Lancelot, a human knight wearing a metal suit, is completely covered. *Lancelot do lac*, France, ca. 1470. Paris, BnF, MS Fr. 112, fol. 78.

Plate 9. Lancelot battles the automata to enter Doloreuse Garde. Again, Lancelot is covered in metal, with no distinguishing physical characteristics. The automata have human faces and fairly undefined bodies. *Lancelot do lac*, France, fifteenth century. Paris, BnF, MS Fr. 118, fol. 200v.

Plate 10. Two youths guard the bridge in the *Roman d'Alexandre*. Alexander and his army approach from the left. The rubricated text reads: "Comment alixendre e la gent furent au bois as pucelles faees." *Le Roman d'Alexandre*, Paris, fourteenth century. Paris, BnF, MS Fr. 791, fol. 58v.

Plate 11. Alexander encounters two golden automata guarding the bridge to the Bois des Puceles. The rubricated text reads: "Comment alexandre trovea le pont ouer .ii. ymages dor et tres beel." *Le Roman d'Alexandre*, French, illuminated by the Flemish painter Jehan de Grise and his school, ca. 1338–1344. Oxford, The Bodleian Libraries, University of Oxford, MS Bodley 264, fol. 70v.

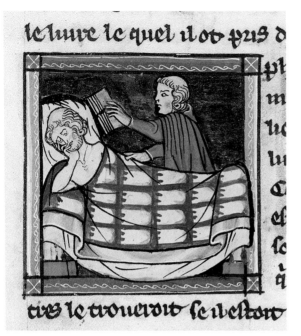

Plate 12. Gerbert steals a book of magic from his teacher, who is passed out, drunk. *Abrégé des histoires divines*, France, ca. 1300. New York, Pierpont Morgan Library, MS M. 751, fol. 99v.

Plate 13. According to legend Gerbert, while bishop, made a steam organ, shown here. *Abrégé des histoires divines*, French, ca. 1300. New York, Pierpont Morgan Library, MS M. 751, fol. 100r.

Plate 14. The underground palace with golden automata. These four figures are described in William of Malmesbury's account of Gerbert's discovery of a Roman treasure hoard. In accordance with the text, all the figures, the table, and all the furnishings are golden. There are two crowned figures, and an archer aiming an arrow at the carbuncle. The crowned figures appear surprised or dismayed. *Abrégé des histories divines*, France, ca. 1300. New York, Pierpont Morgan Library, MS M. 751, fol. 100v.

Plate 15. Sylvester and the executioner. *Abrégé des histories divines*, France, ca. 1300. New York, Pierpont Morgan Library, MS M. 751, fol. 101r.

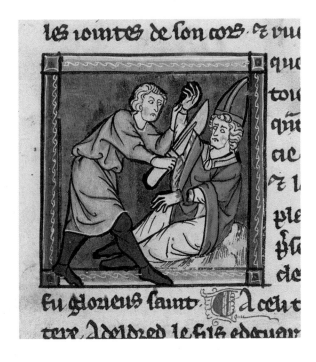

Plate 16. The death and dismemberment of Sylvester II (Gerbert). The left-hand image shows him in his papal vestments and with cardinals in attendance. The right-hand image shows him naked except for the papal crown, and is in the process of being dismembered by a man wielding an axe. An arm and a leg are in the foreground, and to the right is a wheeled cart. From the *Mare historiarum* by Johannes de Columna. Painting by the master of Jouvenel des Ursins. Anjou, ca. 1447-1455. Paris, BnF, MS Lat. 4915, fol. 335.

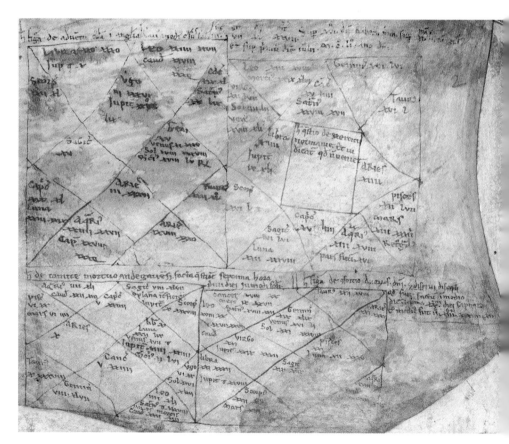

Plate 17. Anglo-Norman horoscope (1151) attributed to both Adelard of Bath and Robert of Chester. The horoscope forecast developments relating to the civil war between King Stephen and Empress Matilda. London, BL, Royal App. 85, fol. 2. © The British Library Board.

Plate 18. The historiated initial C (for *constellacione*) provides a warning about astral science. *Omne Bonum*, ca. 1350, England. London, BL, Royal MS E VI, fol. 396v. © The British Library Board.

Plate 19. D, for *divination*, shows that divination is practiced using demons. *Omne Bonum*, ca. 1350, England. London, BL, MS Royal E VI, fol. 535v. © The British Library Board.

Plate 20. Alexander the Great being embalmed after his death. His body is opened by physicians and surgeons in his bedroom. One holds a jar of balm. The body is then displayed in gold, with his helmet, standard, and tunic hung above, like relics. *Historia Alexandri magni,* by Quintus Curtius, trans. Vasque de Lucène, France, fifteenth century. Paris, BnF, MS Fr. 711, fol. 41v.

Plate 21. Alexander is eviscerated and embalmed. *Historia Alexandri magni*, by Quintus Curtius, trans. Vasque de Lucène, Flanders, fifteenth century. Paris, BnF, MS Fr. 20311, fol. 301.

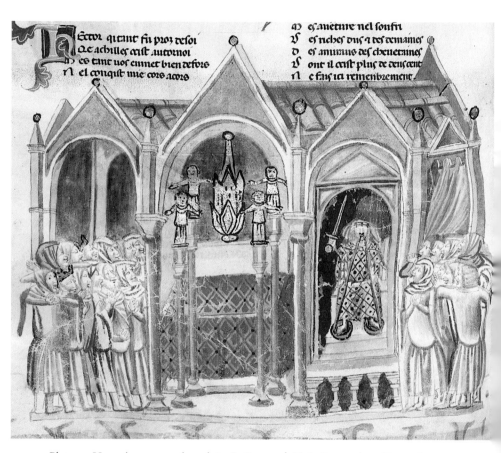

Plate 22. Hector's corpse and tomb in *Le Roman de Troie*, France, late thirteenth or early fourteenth century. Venice, Biblioteca Marciana, MS Fr. Z. 17 (230), fol. 131v.

Plate 23. Hector's embalmed and lifelike body at his mausoleum. A vase of balm pours elixir over his head. Guido delle Colonna, *Historia destructionis troiae*, Italy, fourteenth century. Cologny, Switzerland, Fondation Martin Bodmer, Cod. Bodmer 78, fol, 58r.

Plate 24. A "chantepleure," or Tantalus cup. The chantepleure is an oversized basin resting on a pedestal, with a tube or column reaching down to the bottom of the basin. When the basin was full, the bird, perched atop a crenellate battlement, would lower its beak into the liquid and drink. Once the bird drank enough, it would raise its beak, and the liquid would drain from the bird through the perch and tube, and back into the basin. This device in particular is reminiscent of Arabic and ancient automata. Villard de Honnecourt, France, ca. 1230. Paris, BnF, MS Fr. 19093, fol. 9r.

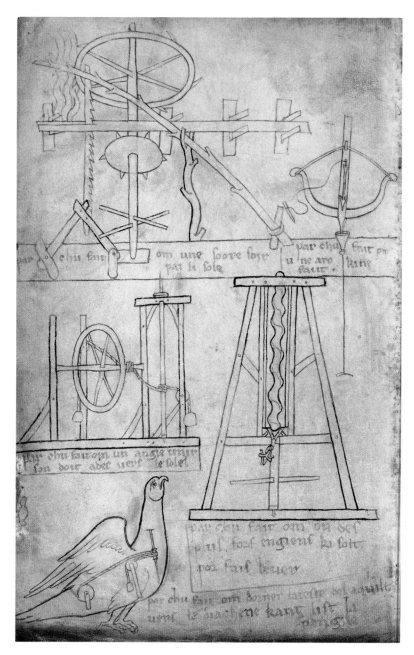

Plate 25. A hydraulic saw and crossbow appear at the top of the folio, in the bottom left is a mechanical eagle, and directly above it a system of ropes and pulleys, which power a mechanical angel (etched in drypoint on the parchment). The angel would point its finger towards the sun, while the eagle would turn its head toward the reader at the church lectern. Villard de Honnecourt, France, ca. 1230. Paris, BnF, MS Fr. 19093, fol. 22v.

Plate 26. Building the Tower of Babel. From the Morgan Picture Bible of Louis IX, France, ca. 1250. New York, Pierpont Morgan Library, MS M. 638, fol. 3r.

Plate 27. A mechanical cupbearer. This image is from a copy of the illustration of this object from an early copy of the 1206 al-Jazari manuscript. Al-Jazari, *Book of Ingenious Mechanical Devices*, Turkey, fourteenth century. Cambridge, Massachusetts, Harvard Art Museums/Arthur M. Sackler Museum, bequest of Hervey E. Wetzel, 1919.138. Photo: Imaging Department © President and Fellows of Harvard College.

Plate 28. Silver-gilt table fountain for the royal court. Paris, ca. 1320. Cleveland, Cleveland Art Museum.

Plate 29. The Lover composes his complaint to Fortuna while, below, she turns
her wheel. The inscription across the top in blue reads, "Comment lamant fait
une complainte de fortune et de sa roe" (How the Lover made a complaint against
Fortuna and her wheel). Guillaume de Machaut, *Remede de Fortune*, northern
France, ca. 1350–1356. Paris, BnF, MS Fr. 1586, fol. 30v.

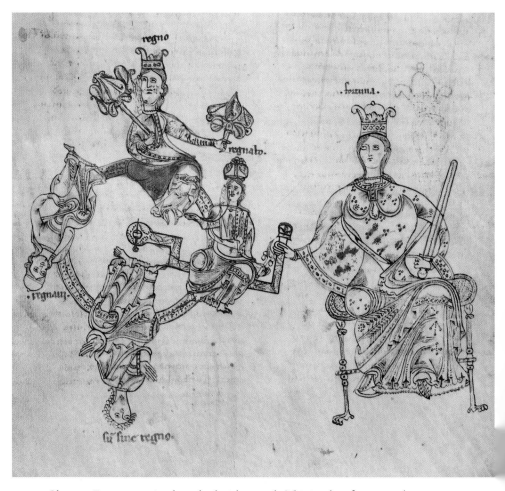

Plate 30. Fortuna turning her wheel with a crank. This is taken from a tenth-century manuscript, although the added drawing is from the twelfth century. St. Gregory, *Moralia in Iob*, Spain, 914. Manchester, John Rylands Library, University of Manchester, MS. Lat. 83, fol. 214r.

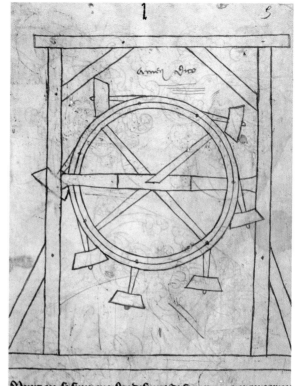

Plate 31. A perpetual motion wheel. The weights on the outside of the wheel are to be filled with mercury. The legend underneath the drawing reads, "On a number of occasions, learned men have discussed how to make a wheel which turns of its own accord; here you can see how one may be constructed with an odd number of 'hammers' filled with mercury." Paris, BnF, MS Fr. 19093, fol. 5r.

Plate 32. A water clock in a miniature from a French *Bible moralisée*. The central clock-wheel has teeth that interlock with a bell-striking mechanism at the top left of the wheel; another bell-striking mechanism is on the bottom right of the wheel. The water drips into a basin below the wheel. Paris, ca. 1250. Oxford, The Bodleian Libraries, University of Oxford, MS Bodley 270, fol. 183v.

Plate 33. Al-Jazari's castle clock from the *Book of Ingenious Mechanical Devices* (ca. 1206). This clock displays the signs of the zodiac and the phases of the moon. Two mechanical birds sound the hours, along with two drummers, two trumpeters, and a cymbalist. Persia, thirteenth century. Boston, Museum of Fine Arts, 14.533. Photograph: © Museum of Fine Arts, Boston.

Plate 34. Harun al-Rashid's envoys present the clock as a gift to Charlemagne's envoys. There are two golden objects, which could be goblets or possibly portable fountains. In between these two items sits the clock, which the main ambassador points to with an outstretched hand. The painter has painted a mechanical rather than a water clock, reflecting the technological reality of the fifteenth rather than the ninth century. *Grandes chroniques de France*, France, third quarter of the fifteenth century. Paris, BnF, MS Fr. 2610, fol. 110.

Plate 35. Detail of the clock. The gear wheels and escapement are visible. Paris, BnF, MS Fr. 2610, fol. 110.

Plate 36. Nineteenth-century engraving of the monumental clock at the Cathedral of Notre-Dame, Strasbourg.

CHAPTER 6

The Clockwork Universe:
Keeping Sacred and Secular Time

The wheels and gears of Fortuna's wheel in the painting from *Le Remede de Fortune* relate to developments in fine technology—especially the development of mechanical timekeepers—in the late medieval period. After the appearance of mechanical clocks at the cusp of the fourteenth century, clocks and automata were often found together. The Arabic tradition conjoined automata and water clocks as early as the ninth century, as seen on Harun al-Rashid's gift to Charlemagne. Although the historical record testifies to water clocks in the Latin West as early as the late tenth century, there is no evidence of automata alongside them. It was not until the development of the mechanical escapement and the consequent ability to build large, complex astronomical clocks in the late thirteenth and fourteenth centuries that automata and clocks were yoked together in the Latin tradition. From the fourteenth century onward throughout the Latin West, in monastery churches, cathedrals, and public squares, gigantic mechanical clocks measured out the hours of the day. The moving figures on them performed the passage of time: secular time, as bell-ringing clock-jacks struck the hours, or sacred time, as religious figures reenacted scenes of salvation and sacrifice. As monumental clocks proliferated throughout the Latin West, the automata on them became visible to an audience larger and more heterogeneous than the courtiers privy to the delights of Hesdin. These automata also took on religious significance and were designed to dramatize divine creation and human salvation.

Monastic Timekeeping

Timekeeping was important to religious institutions throughout the medieval period, both to mark the correct hours for prayer and to ascertain the correct timing for Easter.[1] Medieval monasteries, which might differ in their interpretations of poverty or manual labor, followed various of practices related to daily prayer and devotion based on those set down by Benedict of Nursia in his *Rule for Monasteries* (ca. 530–545). Benedict's intention was to provide religious communities with a set of practices that would order the community and structure the calendar, in accordance with Christian prayer and contemplation. The Rule included praying eight times a day, comprising the Divine Office: Matins (sometimes called Vigil or Nocturne), Laud, Prime, Terce, Sext, None, Vespers, Compline.[2] The shifting amount of available daylight at different times of year (and at different latitudes) meant that timing the services could be somewhat difficult. (Indeed, Benedict accounted for this in his *Rule*, stating that Matins should be shorter in the summer because the nights were shorter.)[3] Churchmen tried to find ways to tell time correctly, in order to observe the Divine Office. Gregory of Tours (ca. 538–593) codified a method of nighttime timekeeping for his brethren in charge of assembling the community for the nighttime offices. According to the time of year, one would sing a varying number of psalms depending on when a particular star appeared on the horizon.[4] A century later, in northern England, the Venerable Bede (672–735) wrote a treatise on the computus, the set of calculations involved in setting the correct date for Easter. This work, *On the Reckoning of Time*, remained in widespread use throughout the Latin West for centuries.[5]

Other methods of timekeeping, such as sundials and water clocks, appear in the historical record at monasteries as early as the late tenth century.[6] The Catalonian monastery of Santa Maria de Ripoll, former home and library of Gerbert of Aurillac, apparently used a clepsydra that does not appear to have been a gift from a foreign court. As established earlier, at that time the monastery was noted for its extensive library in texts on the *quadrivium*, and as a trading zone of scientific information from the neighboring courts of Barcelona and al-Andalus.[7] Water clocks work by regulating the flow of water from one chamber into another over a set period of time. The Santa Maria de Ripoll clepsydra had this kind of hydraulic drive coupled with a cam-and-wheel system that released weights at regular intervals; the weights in turn caused iron arms to move and strike the bell every hour.[8] The aural component of a clepsydra was what marked the passage of time, thus water clocks were often attached to bell-striking mechanisms. These bells gave us the word "clock"; the Latin word for bell is *cloca*. The water clock at Santa Maria de Ripoll was far less elaborate than Harun al-Rashid's gift to Charlemagne, which not only used water power to make an audible signal (dropping metal balls into a metal basin), but also made small metal figures of horsemen move in and out of different apertures.[9] A century after the appearance of the Santa Maria de Ripoll clepsydra and several hundred miles to the north, Jocelin of Brakelond, at the monastery of Bury St. Edmunds, noted that in 1198 a fire began "that same hour the clock struck before the hours of Matins," and the monks, thinking quickly, used the water from the clock to help quench the fire.[10] However widespread clepsydrae were at monasteries, they had limited practical utility. The water in them froze during the winter and evaporated in the summer heat.[11] Sundials were more accurate and less prone to failure, but could only be used during daylight hours. Villard's angel may have been a variation on a sundial, as the angel's finger followed the sun and could been used as a gnomon.[12]

Villard did not include any other timekeeping devices in his book of drawings, but he did offer a design of a perpetual motion wheel that strongly echoes contemporary visual designs of clepsydrae. In his sketch, hammers "trip" compartments filled with mercury, which would, in turn, propel the wheel another notch, ad infinitum (Plate 31). In the accompanying text, Villard mentioned that learned men had turned their talents to designing a similar device, thus illustrating the extent to which others had begun to envision the ways in which mechanical principles could use new sources of energy to replace human and animal power.[13] This general design idea, a wheel made to rotate regularly by using a flow of water or mercury, appears just a few decades later in the *Libros del Saber de Astronomia* (ca. 1276), compiled at the request of King Alfonso X of Castile and Leon, for the purpose of making Arabic knowledge available in Castilian.[14] Just as mechanical engineering was understood well enough by the mid-fourteenth century that the artist who illuminated Fortuna's complicated wheel in *Le Remede de Fortune* could do so with startling accuracy, hydraulic clocks were understood well enough in the mid-thirteenth century that an artist working for the royal French court could depict one clearly. A small manuscript painting in a French *Bible moralisée* (ca. 1250) made for the French royal court illustrates the story of Hezekiah, the terminally ill king of Judah (Plate 32). God, acting through the prophet Isaiah, extended Hezekiah's life by fifteen years.[15] The clepsydra, representing the importance of time and God's power over it, is clearly operational. Water flows beneath the main toothed wheel, causing it to rotate.[16] A bell-striking mechanism at the lower right corner of the main wheel complements the toothed bell-wheel at the opposite corner of the main wheel. It is possible that this painting shows a clock similar to one that may have been in use at the royal palace in Paris in the same period.[17]

None of these Latin examples of water clocks fuse hydraulic technology with automata, unlike examples from the Dar al-Islam. There, water clocks were often built with elaborate automata, due in part to the inheritance of an older Syrian tradition that predated the Islamic conquest.[18] The clepsydra with the metal horsemen, Harun al-Rashid's gift to Charlemagne, is only one example. In the mid-twelfth century the emir of Damascus, Nur al-Din ibn Zangi (1118–1174/511–569 AH), commissioned a massive clepsydra at the Gate of Bab Jayrun, the eastern gate entrance to the Great Mosque of Damascus.[19] The clock face contained twelve doors, with an opening at either end, through which a bird appeared above a basin. The bird sounded the hours by dropping a weight into the vessel below. Above the doors was a series of discs, representing the sun in the zodiac and the lunar cycle.[20] Before the construction of the Bab Jayrun clock most clepsydrae and automata were found only in courtly settings, and were not seen by large or diverse audiences. But the construction of massive clocks for public display dramatically widened the audience for automata. Benjamin of Tudela (1130–1173), the Navarrese Jewish traveler and writer, described the Bab Jayrun clepsydra in his account of his travels to Asia. "Here is a wall of crystal glass of magic workmanship, with apertures according to the days of the year, and as the sun's rays enter each of them in daily succession the hours of the day can be told by a graduated dial."[21] His description "suggests, for many in the medieval world, east and west, the boundaries between technology, theatre, and magic were not clearly defined; the scientific tradition of automata to which the surviving treatises on the subject testify is paralleled by a body of popular lore concerning moving figures, magical statues and cosmological architecture."[22]

Many of these features are similar to those found in al-Jazari's treatise on ingenious mechanical devices. One of these, the Castle Clock, was eleven feet high (Plate 33). The image, taken from an early fourteenth-century copy of al-Jazari's treatise, shows the similarities among Harun al-Rashid's gift, Nur al-Din's commission in Damascus, and al-Jazari's design. The Frankish chronicler described the 'Abbasid caliph's gift and noted that "in this clock there were the same number of horsemen, which would, through twelve windows, come forth at the end of the hours. With the force of their exit they would close the proper number of windows, which had before been open."[23] In the illustration of al-Jazari's design, there are twelve apertures underneath the zodiacal wheel. The first window is open, with a small human figure inside it. Al-Jazari's clock is far more elaborate than the one given to Charlemagne, at least according to the Frankish chronicler's testimony. It resembles the Bab Jayrun clepsydra: in addition to the twelve windows with figures behind them, the castle clock contained mechanical falcons that dropped balls into glass bowls to sound the hours; the signs of the zodiac; a golden orb to mark the position of the sun, and a glass orb to denote the phases of the moon.[24] The lunar and solar indicators are immediately beneath the zodiac disc. The twelve golden circles, over the archway and between the falcons, may be the balls they dropped into the bowls. The clock also contains several musical figures: two drummers, two trumpeters, and a cymbalist who made music after the sixth, ninth, and twelfth hours. Certainly it appears that certain elements of Arabic clockwork design remained constant from the ninth through the thirteenth centuries. One element—birds dropping weights into basins—dates back to the Hellenistic period and the designs of Hero of Alexandria, and clearly enjoyed a widespread popularity in the medieval Dar al-Islam.[25]

How Clocks Became Clockworks

In medieval Europe, automata remained separate from clockwork until the development of the mechanical escapement and, thus, the appearance of the first mechanical clocks, in the late thirteenth century. Many monasteries in the late thirteenth century had large tower clocks, but as the word used to denote a clock (*horologium*) refers only to a timekeeper, not to the technology involved, it is difficult to pinpoint the earliest example of a mechanical clock.[26] By the first quarter of the fourteenth century, mechanical clocks were widespread, especially at cathedral churches and wealthy monasteries, both of which had the necessary texts in physics and geometry as well as the funds to employ skilled artisans to cast, carve, and construct the parts for mechanical clocks.[27] And mechanical clocks had an advantage over water clocks: though they were no more reliable (at least in the early decades), they could be used year-round.

Mechanical clocks are so called because they employ a mechanical escapement to mark the incremental passage of time. The details surrounding the invention of the escapement are known only partially, but it is likely that the alarm, or bell-striking devices on water clocks (such as the one at Santa

Maria de Ripoll), were gradually adapted into something different.[28] The mechanical escapement allows the energy, generated from a falling weight or a spring and stored in the drive, to be released slowly and in regular increments. The earliest version of this mechanism, called verge-and-foliot or crown wheel escapement, consists of a toothed gear wheel (the crown), oriented horizontally, with the teeth sticking up. Across the crown, oriented on the same plane as the wheel, is a rod (the verge), with two metal plates (the pallets), mounted perpendicular to the verge. The pallets are oriented at an angle, so that only one of the pallets catches one of the teeth on the crown at a time. The other end of the verge was connected to the balance wheel (later, the pendulum). This mechanism worked to turn the rotational movement of the crown wheel into the oscillation of the verge (similar to a metronome), and meant that timekeeping could shift from a continuous process (the movement of water) to a repetitive process (the back-and-forth of the verge).[29] The energy from the mainspring or falling weight drive was transmitted to the escapement by a system of gear wheels, called the "going train;" the gears turned the crown wheel, which engaged first one and then the other of the pallets, and caused the verge to move back and forth.[30]

A late medieval manuscript painting of Harun al-Rashid's clock illustrates the proliferation of mechanical clocks after the invention of the mechanical escapement at the turn of the fourteenth century (Plates 34–35). This image, from a fifteenth-century French chronicle, depicts Harun al-Rashid's ambassadors presenting gifts to Charlemagne's representatives. The centerpiece of this diplomatic largesse is a large table clock rendered in gold leaf. According to the Carolingian *Annales*, Harun al-Rashid's clock was a clepsydra with automata, yet here the artist has shown the clock without any automata but with the gear train and escapement clearly visible. This is a mechanical clock. Indeed, mechanical clocks were known widely enough by the middle of the fourteenth century that a courtly Flemish chronicler, Jean Froissart (ca. 1337–1405), could use the mechanical escapement as the comparand to the human heart in an extended metaphor of love. In the allegorical poem *L'Horloge amoureuse* (ca. 1368), Froissart compares a lover's heart to a clock case, and the emotions "inside the heart" to the verge-and-foliot escapement. Desire, the crown wheel, gets its power from Beauty and Pleasaunce (the falling weight and the cord that holds it respectively), but is checked by Temperance, the balance wheel. The escapement is Fear and the balance is Courage, and the person who tends the clock is Remembrance.[31] The poem dates from only a few decades after

Guillaume de Machaut's presentation copy of *Le Remede de Fortune*. Frois-sart's extended metaphor demonstrates confident understanding of mechani-cal horology, just as the painting of Fortuna's wheel in MS Fr. 1586 (Plate 30) demonstrates masterful knowledge (on the part of either the artist or Guil-laume) of gear wheels and cranks. The audience for *L'Horloge amoureuse*, wealthy elites connected to the English court of King Edward III and Philippa of Hain-ault, was also familiar with mechanical marvels, including clocks, for, by the this time, aristocratic courts often included automata and other marvels of fine engineering as part of spectacle and pageantry.

The falling weight drives and mechanical escapements on monumental clocks offered the possibility to create large and heavy automata. One of the most common automata on large civic or religious clocks in the late medieval period is the *jacquemart*, or clock-jack. These were large figures, most often of men, who struck a bell to sound the hours.[32] Technological developments that allowed clocks to ring bells at shorter intervals enabled the creation of new automata in addition to the *jacquemart*. As large mechanical clocks were initially most often found in religious buildings, many early mechani-cal clocks had religious-themed automata.[33] The earliest example of automata on a monumental astronomical clock is from the Norwich cathedral clock (ca. 1321–1325).[34] According to the Sacrists' Rolls from the cathedral priory, the clock cost fifty-two pounds and had fifty-nine automata, including a procession of choir monks and figures representing the days of the month, lunar and solar models, and an astronomical dial.[35] A similar clock, with automata and an or-gan, was installed in the same period at Glastonbury Abbey, according to a local chronicle.[36] By 1324 large and complex clocks were common enough in En-gland that the treasurer of Lincoln Cathedral offered a donation toward a new clock, because "the cathedral was destitute of what other cathedrals, churches, and convents almost everywhere in the world are generally known to possess."[37]

Heavenly Automata

Aside from the administrative purpose of notification and signaling the tim-ing of services and public events, mechanical clocks most importantly mod-eled the movement of celestial bodies, the grandest example of divine power and ingenuity. To a Latin Christian intellectual, to contemplate the heavens was to look at a perfectly organized system, created by God, and also repeated

in a smaller scale on earth. Nicole Oresme (ca. 1320–1382), the scholastic philosopher and theologian, used the mechanical clock that his patron, King
Charles V of France, had erected in his palace in 1362 as the vehicle for a metaphor of cosmological design and movement. In his *Book of the Heavens and the
World* (1377) Oresme compared the regular, predictable movement of the clock
to planetary motion, and, anticipating Robert Boyle (1627–1691) by three
hundred years, implicitly compared God to a clockmaker. He wrote that the
regularity of celestial motion "is similar to when a person has made an *horloge*
and sets it in motion, and it then moves by itself."[38]

Astronomical clocks were themselves automata. Richard of Wallingford,
abbot of St. Albans, designed two astronomical timepieces just a few years
after the treasurer of Lincoln Cathedral donated money to build one there.
Richard was the son of a blacksmith, and it is possible that his familiarity with
metal work, combined with his education in the *quadrivium*, enabled him to
design an astronomical clock and an astronomical calculator.[39] He detailed
his design in the *Tractatus horologii astronomicii* (1327), which contains the earliest description of a mechanical escapement, though in this case it is not a
verge escapement, but rather something called a "strob" escapement. Richard's design used a pair of toothed wheels mounted on the same axle and separated by a verge. The verge had a crosspiece mounted on it, which flipped back
and forth between the teeth on either wheel.[40] It is possible that this design
predated the verge-and-foliot escapement, or that it was a synchronous variant. The other device that he designed and built was an equatorium, or astronomical calculating device, which Richard named "Albion." According to his
Tractatus Albionis, it was a different form of timekeeper from the horloge. It
showed the position of the sun, the phases and eclipses of the moon, the position of the planets, and the tides at London Bridge.[41] Richard described the
Albion as follows:

> The Albion applies directly to the individual motions of the nine
> spheres, since it corresponds exactly to the appearance of the planets
> in every position and at all times. By its means and by means of the
> fixed stars it shows all the properties of diurnal motion. The *armil-
> lae*, the *rectangulus*, and the *turkatum* certainly confirm the parame-
> ters of all the stars. The almanac and several calculated tables confirm
> the various motions of the planets. The astrolabe, quadrant, horloge,
> and saphea make known the movements of times and hours.[42]

The "Albion" was a three-dimensional, moving artifact that modeled the motions of the planets and stars, conceptually similar to Hugo's revolving palace. In *Le Voyage de Charlemagne*, the Byzantine emperor used *cumpas* to make his palace a revolving automaton. Using sympathetic magic, and relying on the movement of the spheres to make his palace rotate, Hugo created a model of the world with himself as Pantocrator in the center. The mechanical horologe at St. Albans, like other astronomical clocks, likewise revealed the movement of the cosmos and the rotation of the earth. Astronomical clocks of the fourteenth century, such as those Richard designed (and perhaps built), relied on astral science in order to calculate accurately the varying rates of rotation to correspond to different planets, the sun, and the moon. This knowledge overlaps significantly with the computus (or *cumpas*).

Astronomical clocks showed the glory of the macrocosm; the automata on them embodied the microcosm, often with religious undertones. Clocks and their human automata displayed cyclical time (days, weeks, months) alongside linear time (toward the reappearance of Christ and salvation). This is most apparent in the cathedral clock at Notre-Dame de Strasbourg, the most famous example from the medieval and early modern periods. Built between 1352 and 1354, it symbolized microcosm and macrocosm, demonstrated the glory of God's creation, and dramatized the timeline of salvation. Figures of the Blessed Virgin, the newborn Jesus, and the three Magi gave the clock its nickname: the "Horloge des Trois Mages" or "Die Dreikönigsuhr." The clock also had a mechanical astrolabe, a perpetual calendar, a carillon, tables that indicated proper times for phlebotomy, and a mechanical rooster that flapped its wings and crowed every hour.[43] The perpetual calendar and mechanical astrolabe reflected the divinely ordered macrocosm. The tables for bloodletting indicated the harmonies between the macrocosm and the microcosm. The characters in the hourly pageant (Virgin, infant Jesus, Magi, and rooster) enacted a moving memorial to Jesus's sacrifice for humankind. The rooster symbolizes Peter's denial of Jesus and his repentance, as well as papal vigilance, as Peter later became head of the Church. The rooster's morning cry reminds Christians to be prepared to accept the sudden second coming of Jesus, along with the resurrection of the dead and the final judgment.[44] On the Strasbourg clock the rooster, taken together with the appearance of Mary and Jesus, performed a double reminder for the community of Strasbourg: to remain ready for Jesus's return and to remember his first appearance and what it portended for humanity. The cock and the clock appear to have played a part in religious pageantry, as the clock was also known as the Leidensuhr (the Clock of the Passion), and Passion plays given in the cathedral were coordinated with the movements of the automata.[45]

"L'Horloge des Trois Mages" broke around 1500 and was not renovated until 1571, when Conrad Dasypodius, professor of mathematics at the Strasbourg Academy, was appointed by the Senate of Strasbourg to repair and renovate the timekeeper. The clock visible today is a nineteenth-century refurbishment of the sixteenth-century machine (Plate 36). The sixteenth-century astronomical horologe stands sixty-five feet high by twenty-five feet wide, taller and narrower than the fourteenth-century original. The clock depicts cosmological, Christological, biological, diurnal, and horological time. A portrait of Copernicus and paintings of scenes from myth and history decorate the case. An astrolabe reveals the positions of the planets, a lunar dial marks the phases of the moon, a calendar indicates the days of the month, and a numerical dial shows the time of day. The clock tower houses a descending weight drive that powers four principal trains of automata, all of which dramatize timekeeping. Roman gods in chariots chase each other through the week. The four stages of man (infant, youth, adult, old man) come out every three hours, illustrating the life cycle each day and night. Every hour figures of Death and Christ do battle, and Death wins every hour except the last. A mechanical angel turns an hourglass every fifteen minutes. Dasypodius made sure that the rooster, which had by then fallen into disrepair, was cleaned and restored to the clock. "This poultry cock itself was skillfully made two hundred years ago and placed on the old clock, and since at that time it was customary to commemorate the Passion of the Christ in the Christian church, this cock by its crowing warned men of the denial of Peter."[46] At the bottom of the clock a celestial sphere supported by a pelican conveys the conjunction of divine creation and Jesus's sacrifice for humanity. Dasypodius designed the overall clock and worked closely with a painter, Tobias Stimmer, and two horologists, Isaac and Josias Habrecht, on aspects of the design. Once the plans had been agreed upon, Dasypodius left all of the work to artisans, except for the celestial sphere, which he fabricated.[47] After the renovation was complete, in 1574, Dasypodius wrote a treatise for the Senate of Strasbourg and his colleagues at the university explaining his design in technical and symbolic terms. "But we have attached this Pelican so that it should be in the place of Atlas and represent a symbol of eternity, or even of our Redeemer and Savior."[48] The gear trains of the clock also powered a second clock on the outside of the church that faced the public square, demonstrating that timekeeping was not the only or primary function of the clock inside the cathedral.[49]

The clock illustrated the meaning of both secular and sacred time in a Christian context. The pelican signified Christ's death; the celestial orb, lunar dial, and moving astrolabe pointed to the magnificence of God's universe. The paintings, legends, vignettes, and automata all had a specific meaning relating to the passage of time. "For all and individual details were so ordered and arranged by us that they have a definite meaning and one worthy of note, taken either from things sacred to the pagans, or the stories of the poets, or writings of the historians and annalists."[50] Although the hours, days, and weeks were elsewhere indicated on the clock, the automata enacted the passage of time "for the sake of delight and wonderment, not however without a certain particular significance."[51] The figures of humankind, Christ, and Death allegorize the linear span of a human lifetime and the ultimate triumph of Christian resurrection. The automata, along with the dials, complications, and decorations, model the totality of time, in every context.

> And on this clock we exhibit eternity, the century, the orbits of the planets, the yearly and monthly revolutions of the sun and moon, the divisions of the week, days, hours, parts of hours, minutes; all these I say, we exhibit to be seen. We have added also, for the sake of adornment, splendor, admiration, various contrivances, pneumatic, sphaeropoetic, and automatic, everything from history and the tales of the poets, and also from sacred and profane writings in which there is or can be some delineation of time.[52]

The clock at the cathedral of Notre-Dame de Strasbourg celebrates divine creation and memorializes Jesus's sacrifice for humankind, exposes the links between the macrocosm and the microcosm, and rests on mechanical principle and skilled labor.

> There is a very great variety of arts and sciences, not only those of a theoretical sort, but also those that contrive and accomplish something. Among those needed in doing and making mechanics does not hold the last place. Those who in former times especially mastered this art were reckoned among the philosophers. For just as the philosophers examine by observing the nature, force, and effect of things, so do mechanicians bring about with the work of their hands,

their industry, talent, and skill those things which are either necessary for life, or made for pleasure or benefit daily use.[53]

The work of the "mechanicians" who worked on the clock was, in the past,
the work of philosophers. Conrad's statement about the work and dignity of
artisans reflects the shift in the creation of automata. Initially believed to be
the result of natural philosophy or demonic magic wielded by sorcerers and
philosophers, automata were, by the sixteenth century, moved by mechanical
engineering and crafted by artisans.

Once the new clock was completed, it was the most technologically advanced piece of machinery in Europe. In the decades after its completion, René
Descartes and other natural philosophers looked to the clock as they posited
divinely created mechanisms, too small to be sensible, inside humans and the
cosmos alike. Descartes (1596–1650) explained that natural processes are no different from mechanical ones, thereby explaining the human body in mechanical terms. Thomas Hobbes (1588–1679), in the introduction to *Leviathan*,
described the "artificial life" of mechanical things, like watches, and the mechanical nature of living things, like nerves. Robert Boyle used the Strasbourg
horloge as his referent when he compared the world to a giant clock, establish-
ing a fundamental similarity between the two.[54] Although the world and a
massive clock both appear to be single organisms, each is a collection of discrete
machines, hidden from the observer, who can interpret only the effects. This
intellectual problem—how to distinguish the cause from observing its effect—
was also, as I have demonstrated, central to the Latin Middle Ages, and was
illustrated by automata that could move from a variety of causes. The early modern heuristic of mechanistic philosophy contradicted a central tenet of the supposedly long-entrenched Aristotelian view of an absolute distinction between
natural and artificial. Yet, as I have shown, early modern natural philosophers
were beholden to their medieval predecessors, who used automata to challenge
binary concepts of living/dead and natural/artificial.

Despite this cultural and intellectual debt, the renovated Strasbourg clock
and its automata herald a narrowing of the capacious category of medieval
automata, which included preserved bodies, prophetic metal figures, and
eerie copies of living people. The Strasbourg clock is intimately related to the
magical, fantastic, strange, and unsettling automata from the medieval period.
The cathedral horloge and its automata initially emerged during a period in
the Latin West in which moving, singing, speaking figures—human, animal, and astronomical—appeared in multiple guises and multiple registers,

and as a result of multiple causes. The rediscovery of mechanism in the Latin West that began in the late thirteenth century developed alongside a natural philosophical framework that included magical explanations for artificial birds, golden knights, and moving models of the cosmos. Actual fourteenth- and fifteenth-century automata mimicked natural forms and relied on hidden mechanical operations, at the same time that textual accounts of conceptually similar objects, such as the speaking figure created by Albertus Magnus, ascribed their operation to the science of the stars and the power of celestial bodies. Even as automata, including clocks, became more commonly fabricated in the Latin West, they retained their luster as marvels, stunning examples of human art and the ability to understand and surpass Nature. Medieval robots pose enduring questions about the limits of knowledge and creation; about the relationship between people and technology; and about identity, subjectivity, and the definition of life.

NOTES

INTRODUCTION. THE PERSISTENCE OF ROBOTS:
AN ARCHAEOLOGY OF AUTOMATA

1. Scholars often define the Scientific Revolution, at least in part, by the success of mechanical philosophy and the use of mechanical metaphors to explain the natural world. For example, Steven Shapin, *The Scientific Revolution* (Chicago: University of Chicago Press, 1996), 13; Peter Dear, *Revolutionizing the Sciences: European Knowledge and Its Ambitions, 1500–1700*, 2nd ed. (Princeton, N.J.: Princeton University Press, 2009), 79–99; H. Floris Cohen, *How Modern Science Came into the World: Four Civilizations, One 17th-Century Breakthrough* (Amsterdam: Amsterdam University Press, 2011), 241–42.

2. The word first appears in English in 1611. Rabelais defined these objects as "c'est à dire soy mouvens eulx mesmes." See *Dictionnaire étymologique de la langue française*, ed. Gilles Ménage, 2 vols. (Geneva: Slatkine, 1973) s.v. "automate"; *Dictionnaire historique de la langue française*, ed. Alain Rye, 2 vols. (Paris: Robert, 1992), s.v. "automate"; *OED*, s.v. "automaton." "Robot" comes from the Czech word for forced labor, *robota*, and first appeared in Karel Čapek's 1920 play, *Rossum's Universal Robots*, or *R.U.R.* Čapek used the word to refer to machines that strongly resembled humans and were designed to replace human labor and carry out tasks automatically. Now "robot" refers to a larger category of humanoid or anthropomorphized machines, such as the Cylons in the rebooted television series *Battlestar Galactica* (2004–2009), R2D2 and C-3PO in *Star Wars* (Lucas, 1977), or *WALL*E* (Stanton, 2008). "Android," from the Greek *andro-eides* ("like a man"), also refers to humanoid automata, while "cyborg," a contraction of "cybernetic organism," refers to human-machine hybrids such as RoboCop or The Borg in the television series *Star Trek: The Next Generation* (1987–1994). Yet robots do not always have to resemble human, or even natural forms; indeed, many robots that are commonly used to replace or augment human labor, from Roombas® to minesweepers, do not look like natural objects. See *OED*, s.v. "robot."

3. Sylvia Berryman, "Ancient Automata and Mechanical Explanation," *Phronesis* 48 (2003): 344–69; Berryman, "The Imitation of Life in Ancient Greek Philosophy," in *Genesis Redux: Essays in the History of Philosophy and Artificial Life*, ed. Jessica Riskin (Chicago: University of Chicago Press, 2007). For recent work on automata in the early modern period and the Enlightenment, see Adelheid Voskuhl, *Androids in the Enlightenment:*

Mechanics, Artisans, and Cultures of the Self (Chicago: University of Chicago Press, 2013); Kevin LaGrandeur, *Androids and Intelligent Networks in Early Modern Literature and Culture: Artificial Slaves* (New York: Routledge, 2013); Wendy Hyman, ed., *The Automaton in English Renaissance Literature* (Surrey: Ashgate, 2011); Minsoo Kang, *Sublime Dreams of Living Machines: The Automaton in the European Imagination* (Cambridge, Mass.: Harvard University Press, 2011); Jessica Riskin, "The Defecating Duck, Or, The Ambiguous Origins of Artificial Life," *Critical Inquiry* 29 (2003): 599–633; Riskin, "Le canard, l'homme, et le robot," *Le Recherche* (2002): 36–40. See also Daniel Schultness, "Zur Infinitisierung der Automaten: Descartes und Leibniz," in *Androïden: zur Poetologie der Automaten*, ed. Jürgen Söring (Frankfurt: P. Lang, 1997); Marc Vanden Berghe, "Technique et utopie au siècle des lumières: Les androïdes Jaquet-Droz dans l'Encyclopédie d'Yverdon," in ibid. Victoria Nelson, *The Secret Life of Puppets* (Cambridge, Mass.: Harvard University Press, 2001) concentrates on the psychological valences of automata, dolls, and puppets from the eighteenth through the twentieth century. Recent works on automata for a more general audience include Gaby Wood, *Edison's Eve: A Magical History of the Quest for Mechanical Life* (New York: Knopf, 2002); Tom Standage, *The Turk: The True Story of the Chess-Playing Machine That Fooled the World* (London: Penguin, 2002), and *Hugo* (Scorcese, 2010).

4. Scott Lightsey, *Manmade Marvels in Medieval Culture and Literature* (New York: Palgrave Macmillan, 2007); Lorraine Daston and Katharine Park, *Wonders and the Order of Nature* (New York: Zone, 1998); Huguette Legros, "Connaissance, réception, et perceptions des automates orientaux au XIIe siècle," in *Le merveilleux et la magie dans la littérature*, ed. Gérard Chandès (Amsterdam: Rodopi, 1992); Patricia Trannoy, "De la technique à la magie: Enjeux des automates dans *Le Voyage de Charlemagne à Jérusalem et à Constantinople*," in ibid.; Mary Baine Campbell, *Wonder and Science: Imagining Worlds in Early Modern Europe* (Ithaca, N.Y.: Cornell University Press, 1999); Suzanne Conklin Akbari, *Idols in the East: European Representations of Islam and the Orient, 1100–1450* (Ithaca, N.Y.: Cornell University Press, 2009).

5. Homer, *The Iliad*, 18: 373–77, trans. Michael Reck (New York: HarperCollins, 1994), 343.

6. Ibid., 417–20, 344.

7. R. E. Langer, "Alexandria: Shrine of Mathematics," *American Mathematical Monthly* 48 (1941): 109–25, esp. 121–22.

8. The source for Ktesibios comes from Vitruvius, in Book 10, chapter 4 of the *Ten Books on Architecture*. Although Vitruvius claimed to have read the book on mechanics that Ktesibios wrote, the original text is lost. "Plures et variis generibus ab eo liquoris pressionibus coacto spiritu efferre ab natura mutatos effectus ostenditur, uti merularum aquae motu voces," Vitruvius, *De architectura libri decem*, 10.7.4, ed. Curt Fensterbusch (Darmstadt: Wissenschaftliche Buchegesellschaft, 1976). There is some disagreement about the exact dates for Ktesibios, and if the works attributed to him came from the pen of one author or two. See A. G. Drachmann, *Ktesibios, Philon, and Heron: A Study in Ancient Pneumatics* (Copenhagen: Munksgaard, 1948); Drachmann, *The Mechanical Technology of Greek and Roman Antiquity* (Copenhagen: Munksgaard, 1963).

9. Drachmann, *Ktesibios, Philon, and Heron*, 68–72; D. E. L. Haynes, "Philo of Byzantium and the Colossus of Rhodes," *Journal of Hellenic Studies* 77 (1957): 311–12.

10. Susan Murphy, "Heron of Alexandria's *On Automaton-Making*," *History of Technology* 17 (1995): 1–45, 3. This article contains an entire translation of Hero's treatise on automata. See also Marie Boas, "Hero's *Pneumatica*: A Study of Its Transmission and Influence," *Isis* 40 (1949): 38–48.

11. Heron, in Murphy, "Heron of Alexandria's *On Automaton-Making*," 11.

12. Karin Tybjerg, "Wonder-Making and Philosophical Wonder in Hero of Alexandria," *Studies in History and Philosophy of Science* 34 (2003): 443–66. Tybjerg claims that Hero used wonder and wonder-making to promote mechanics above manual work and to give it an elevated status on par with philosophy, and she makes an excellent point about the historiography of these mechanical *mirabilia* as mere toys. See also R. S. Brumbaugh, *Ancient Greek Gadgets and Machines* (New York: Cromwell, 1966).

13. Tony Freeth, Alexander Jones, John M. Steele, and Yanis Bitsakis, "Calendars with Olympiad Display and Eclipse Prediction on the Antikythera Mechanism," *Nature* 454 (31 July 2008): 614–17; Michael T. Wright, "Epicyclic Gearing and the Antikythera Mechanism, part 1," *Antiquarian Horology* 27 (2003): 270–79; Wright, "Epicyclic Gearing and the Antikythera Mechanism, part 2," *Antiquarian Horology* 29 (2005): 54–60; Derek J. de Solla Price, "Gears from the Greeks. The Antikythera Mechanism: A Calendar Computer from ca. 80 B.C." *TAPS* 64 (1974): 1–70.

14. Edward Grant, "Henricus Aristippus, William of Moerbeke, and Two Alleged Mediaeval Translations of Hero's *Pneumatica*," *Speculum* 46 (1971): 656–69.

15. See Nancy F. Partner, *Serious Entertainments: The Writing of History in Twelfth-Century England* (Chicago: University of Chicago Press, 1977), 187; Jean Blacker, *The Faces of Time: Portrayal of the Past in Old French and Latin Historical Narrative of the Anglo-Norman Regnum* (Austin: University of Texas Press, 1994), xiii.

16. Isidore of Seville, *Etymologiarum sive originum libri XX*, ed. W. M. Lindsay, 2 vols. (Oxford: Clarendon, 1911), 1.40.1: "Fabulas . . . quia non sunt res factae, sed tantum loquendo fictae"; 1.41.1: "Historia est narratio rei gestae."

17. "Fabulas poetae quasdam delectandi causa finxerunt quasdam ad naturam rerum, nonnullas ad mores hominum interpretati sunt. Delectandi causa fictas, ut eas, quas vulgo dicunt," Isidore of Seville, *Etymologiarum*, 1.40.3.

18. "Item inter historiam et argumentum et fabulam interesse. Nam historiae res verae quae factae sunt; argumenta sunt quae etsi facta non sunt, fieri tamen possunt; fabulae vero sunt quae nec factae sunt nec fieri possunt, quia contra naturam sunt," Isidore of Seville, *Etymologiarum*, 1.44.5.

19. See the discussions of William of Malmesbury and Guido delle Colonna, in Chapters 3 and 4 respectively.

20. Thomas of Britain's *Tristran* is an exception, although Thomas was probably Anglo-Norman, and therefore at least familiar with the French tradition. There is a tree with artificial birds in Lamprecht's late twelfth-century *Alexanderlied* and some examples of

magical automata in the thirteenth-century German *Heldenbuch*. See Gerard Brett, "The Automata in the Byzantine 'Throne of Solomon,'" *Speculum* 29 (1954): 477–87, 485.

CHAPTER I. RARE DEVICES: GEOGRAPHY AND TECHNOLOGY

1. The poem survived in a single manuscript, no longer extant, as an Anglo-Norman translation of a French poem. Scholars have proposed dates of composition that range from 1075 to 1175. Two editors of *Le Voyage de Charlemagne*, Aebischer and Burgess, have proposed 1112 and ca. 1150 respectively. See *Le Voyage de Charlemagne à Jérusalem et à Constantinople*, ed. Paul Aebischer (Geneva: Droz, 1965), 29; *Le Pèlerinage de Charlemagne*, ed. and trans. Glyn S. Burgess, intro. Anne Elizabeth Cobby (New York: Garland, 1988), 3.

2. "Tutes creatures," *Le Pèlerinage de Charlemagne*, ed. Burgess, l. 346, 46. All subsequent references are to this edition. Unless otherwise noted, all translations are my own.

3. "Cumme roe de char," *Le Pèlerinage de Charlemagne*, l. 357, 46.

4. "De quivre e de metal tregeté douz enfanz: / Cascun tient en sa buche un corn d'ivorie blanc," *Le Pèlerinage de Charlemagne*, ll. 352–361, 46. "Douz" means twelve, "deuz" and "dous" mean two. However, the statues are later compared and described as "one . . . the other," suggesting that they were a pair, rather than a dozen. See also ll. 373, 375.

5. "Li uns esgardet le altre ensement cum en riant, / Que ço vus fust viarie que tut fussent vivant," *Le Pèlerinage de Charlemagne*, ll. 360–361, 46.

6. "Cum arbre de mulin. / E celes imagines cornent, l'une a l'altre surrist, / Que ceo vus fust viarie que il fussent tuz vis. / L'un halt, li altre cler, mult feit bel a oir; / Ceo est avis, qu'l'ascute, qu'il seit in parais, / La u li angle chantent suef e seriz." *Le Pèlerinage de Charlemagne*, ll. 372–377, 46.

7. "E fu fait par cumpas e serét noblement," *Le Pèlerinage de Charlemagne*, l. 348, 46.

8. *Dictionnaire historique de la langue française*, ed. Rye, s.v. "cumpas." Cf. *OED*, s.v. "computus."

9. "Mult fut grés li orages e hidus e costis," *Le Pèlerinage de Charlemagne*, l. 384, 46.

10. "Karles vit le paleis turner e fremir; / Il ne sout que ceo fud, ne l'out de luign apris. / Ne pout ester sur pez, sur le marbre s'assist. / Franceis sunt tuz versét, ne se poent tenir, / E coverirent lur chés e adenz e suvin." *Le Pèlerinage de Charlemagne*, ll. 385–389, 46–48.

11. These boasts, or *gabs*, are a generic convention.

12. *Le Pèlerinage de Charlemagne*, ll. 448–617, 50–56.

13. "Enter en la citez e emplir les celers, / La gent lu rei Hugun e moiller e guaer, / En la plus halte tur li reis s'en fuid a ped," *Le Pèlerinage de Charlemagne*, ll. 777–779, 66.

14. *Le Pèlerinage de Charlemagne*, ll. 774–792, 66.

15. The foundational text on the theory that heavenly bodies act on earth via cosmic rays was Al-Kindi's *De radiis*. Al-Kindi was himself influenced by Aristotle's *libri naturales*, especially *De meteorologica* and *De generatione et corruptione*. For how this theory was interpreted and understood in the medieval period, see Marie-Thérèse Alverny and Franchise Hudry, "Al-Kindi, *De Radiis*," *Archives d'Histoire Doctrinale et Littéraire du Moyen*

Âge 61 (1974): 139–259; Katharine Park, "The Meaning of Natural Diversity: Marco Polo on the 'Division' of the World," in *Texts and Contexts in Medieval Science: Studies on the Occasion of John E. Murdoch's Seventieth Birthday*, ed. Edith Sylla and Michael McVaugh (Leiden: Brill, 1997), 134–47, 140–42; Daston and Park, *Wonders*, 109–33.

16. Daston and Park, *Wonders*, 13.

17. Caroline Bynum, "Wonder," *AHR* 102 (1997): 1–26, 6.

18. "Nam propter admirari homines et nunc et primum inceperunt philosophari . . . ." Aristotle, *Metaphysica* 1.2, in *Metaphysica Lib. I–XIV: Recensio et translatio Guillelmi de Moerbeka*, ed. Gudrun Vuillemin-Diem (Leiden: Brill, 1939), 16, trans. Jonathan Barnes, *The Complete Works of Aristotle: The Revised Oxford Translation*, 2 vols. (Princeton, N.J.: Princeton University Press, 1984), 2: 1554.

19. "Que inaudita percipiuntur amplectimur, tum ex mutatione cursus naturalis quam admiramur, tum ex ignorancia cause cuius ratio nobis est imperscrutabilis," Gervase of Tilbury, *Otia imperialia: Recreation for an Emperor*, ed. and trans. S. E. Banks and J. W. Binns (Oxford: Clarendon, 2002), book 3, preface, 558, translation my own. According to some medieval writers, "wonder was the natural emotional response to the natural diversity of the world." Park, "The Meaning of Natural Diversity," 136.

20. Some literary scholars have said the opposite; namely, that these texts were not particularly interested in providing explanations for marvels. See Helen Cooper, "Magic that Does Not Work," *Medievalia et Humanistica* 7 (1976): 131–46; Michelle Karnes, "Wonder, Marvels, and Metaphor in *The Squire's Tale*," *English Literary History* 82 (2015), forthcoming.

21. See Herodotus, *The Histories*, 3.106; Hippocrates, *Airs, Waters, Places*; James Romm, *The Edges of the Earth in Ancient Thought* (Princeton, N.J.: Princeton University Press, 1992), 34–37, 82–108.

22. Evelyn Edson, "The Medieval World View: Contemplating the Mappamundi," *History Compass* 8/6 (2010): 503–17, 505.

23. Akbari, *Idols in the East*, 28.

24. Shem=Asia, Japheth=Europe, Ham=Africa. The idea of the simultaneous centripetal and centrifugal nature of the T-O map comes from Akbari, *Idols*, 24, 51.

25. William of Conches, *De philosophia mundi*, Philadelphia, University of Pennsylvania Library, LJS 384.

26. Eastern-oriented *mappaemundi* were more common in the medieval period until the fourteenth century. Akbari, *Idols*, 22.

27. "Sicut enim orientales plagae propriis quibusdam et sibi innatis praeeminent et praecellunt ostentis, sic et occidentales circumferentiae suis naturae miraculis illustrantur. Quoties quippe, tanquam seriis et veris fatigata negotiis, paululum secedit et excedit, remotis in partibus, quasi verecundis et occultis natura ludit excessibus." Gerald of Wales, Preface, *Topographia Hiberniae*, in *Opera*, 8 vols., ed. James Dimock, RS 21 (Weisbaden: Kraus, 1964), 5: 20–21. Translation in Gerald of Wales, *History and Topography of Ireland*, trans. John J. O'Meara (Harmondsworth: Penguin, 1982), 31.

28. "Quod mundi extremitates novis semper quibusdam prodigiis pollent; ac si natura licentius ludat in privato et remoto, quam in propatulo et propinquo." Ranulf Higden,

Polychronicon 1.34, in *Polychronicon Ranulphi Higden monachi cestrensis, together with the English Translation of John Trevisa and an unknown Writer of the Fifteenth Century,* 9 vols., ed. Churchill Babington, RS 41 (London, 1865–86), 1: 360.

29. John Block Friedman, *The Monstrous Races in Medieval Art and Thought,* 2nd ed. (Syracuse, N.Y.: Syracuse University Press, 2000), 45–54; Akbari, *Idols,* 68; Daston and Park, *Wonders,* 25.

30. *Epistola Alexandri Macedonis ad Aristotelem magistrum suum de itinere suo et de situ Indiae.* For a good introduction to this text, see Lloyd L. Gunderson's introduction in *Epistola Alexandri Macedonis ad Aristotelem magistrum suum de itinere suo et de situ Indiae,* trans. and ed. Lloyd L. Gunderson (Meisenheim am Glan: Verlag, 1980), 1–133, esp. 34–47. See also Mary Baine Campbell, *The Witness and the Other World: Exotic European Travel Writing, 400–1600* (Ithaca, N.Y.: Cornell University Press, 1988), 48; George Cary, *The Medieval Alexander* (Cambridge: Cambridge University Press, 1956), 15. On the marginal nature of England itself, see Kathy Lavezzo, *Angels on the Edge of the World: Geography, Literature, and English Community, 1000–1534* (Ithaca, N.Y.: Cornell University Press, 2006).

31. *Epistola Alexandri Macedonis ad Aristotelem magistrum suum de itinere suo et de situ Indiae,* ed. W. Walther Boer, Beiträge zur Klassischen Philologie (Meisenheim am Glan: Verlag, 1980), 4–5, 13–18, 32–33 (hereafter cited as *Epistola Alexandri*).

32. See Daston and Park, *Wonders* on the *Tractatus monstrorum* and *Liber monstrorum,* two early medieval texts on the monstrous peoples of the East, 26; Friedman, *The Monstrous Races,* 149–53.

33. On interest in India, see Akbari, *Idols,* 67–111.

34. "In partibus autem Indiae et caeteris illis adjacentibus copia rerum huiusmodi magna est, et propter hoc magica naturalis potissimum ibi viguit, et viget quam de causam sunt ibi super experimentatores multi, et rerum mirabilium per huiusmodi peritiam effectores." William of Auvergne, *De universo,* 2.3.23, in *Opera omnia,* ed. Peter Aubouin, 2 vols. (Paris: Aureliae, 1674), 1: 1065, col. 1.

35. For example, automata appear in the following tenth- and eleventh-century romances: *Yasastilakacampu,* ed. P. Sivadatta and Kasinath Pandurang Parab (Bombay: Tukaram Javaji, 1901); *Srngaramanjarikatha,* ed. and trans. K. M. Munshi (Bombay: Bharatiya Vidya Bhavan, 1959; and in a didactic work attributed to King Bhoja of Dara (ca. 1000–55); V. Raghavan, "Somadeva and King Bhoja," *Journal of the University of Gauhati* 3 (1952): 35–38. On the importance of fountains and gardens in medieval Indian courtly culture, see Daud Ali, "Gardens in Early Indian Court Life," *Studies in History* 19 (2003): 221–52. I am grateful to Daud Ali for alerting me to the literature on and of the Indian tradition.

36. Edson, "The Medieval World View," 506; Alessandro Scafi, *Mapping Paradise: A History of Heaven on Earth* (Chicago: University of Chicago Press, 2006), 88; Jean Delumeau, *Une histoire du Paradis,* 2 vols. (Paris: Fayard, 1992), 1: 59–60.

37. Akbari, *Idols,* 37–38, 249.

38. Edson, "The Medieval World View," 507; Campbell, *Witness and the Other World,* 18. For example, balsam was believed to be specific to the Holy Land and a direct result

of a Christian miracle. See E. R. Truitt, "The Virtues of Balm," *Early Science and Medicine* 14 (2009): 711–36.

39. On automata found in medieval Arabic sources, particularly texts concerning the kings of ancient Egypt, see Ursula Sezgin, "Pharaonische Wunderwerke bei Ibn Wasif As-Sabi' und Al-Mas'udi: einige Remineszenzen an Ägyptens vergangene Grösse und an Meisterwerke der Alexandrinischen Gelehrten in arabischen Texten des 10. Jahrhunderts n. Chr. Teil I–V," Published in five parts in *Zeitschrift für Geschichte der Arabisch-Islamischen Wissenschaften*: I, 9 (1994): 229–91; II, 11 (1997): 189–250; III, 14 (2001): 217–56; IV, 15 (2002/03): 281–312; V, 16 (2004/05): 149–209. The last two parts, IV and V, contain numerous descriptions of medieval Arabic automata. Sezgin notes the similarities between these automata and those in medieval Latin literature.

40. Daston and Park, *Wonders and the Order of Nature*, 32.

41. Grant, "Henricus Aristippus,William of Moerbeke and Two Alleged Mediaeval Translations of Hero's *Pneumatica*," 656–69; Boas, "Hero's *Pneumatica*," 38–40.

42. Dimitri Gutas, *Greek Thought, Arabic Culture: The Graeco-Arabic Translation Movement in Baghdad and Early 'Abbasid Society (2nd–4th/8th–10th Centuries)* (Abingdon: Routledge, 1998), 23.

43. Ibid., 57.

44. Ibid., 58, 111.

45. Donald Hill, "Medieval Arabic Mechanical Technology," in *Proceedings of the First International Symposium for the History of Arabic Science, Aleppo, April 5–12, 1976* (Aleppo: Institute for the History of Arabic Science, 1979), rep. in Hill, *Studies in Medieval Islamic Technology: From Philo to al-Jazari—from Alexandria to Diyar Bakr*, ed. David A. King (Aldershot: Ashgate, 1998), 222–37, 226–27. See also Gutas, *Greek Thought, Arabic Culture*, 133, 138.

46. Gutas, *Greek Thought, Arabic Culture*, 125.

47. See Murphy, "Heron of Alexandria's *On Automaton-Making*," 1–45; Merriam Sherwood, "Magic and Mechanics in Medieval Fiction," *Studies in Philology* 44 (1947): 567–92, 580.

48. D. Fairchild Ruggles, *Islamic Gardens and Landscapes* (Philadelphia: University of Pennsylvania Press, 2008), 78–79; Suzanne Méjean, "A propos de l'arbre aux oiseaux dans *Yvain*," *Romania* 91 (1970): 392–99, esp. 393–94; Georges Salmon, *Introduction topographique à l'histoire de Bagdad d'Abou Bakr Ahmad ibn Thabit al-Kathib al-Bagdadi* (Paris: Bouillon, 1904), 135, 138–39.

49. Ruggles, *Islamic Gardens and Landscapes*, 75.

50. Fredegarius, *Chronicarum quae dicuntur Fredegarii Scholastici continuationes*, 5.51, *Fredegarii et aliorum chronica: Vitae sanctorum*, 2 vols., MGH, SS. rer. Mer., ed. Bruno Krusch (Hanover: Hahn, 1888), 2: 191–92.

51. "Necnon et horologium ex auricalco arte mechanica mirifice compositum, in quo duodecim horarum cursus ad clepsidram vertebatur, cum totidem aereis pilulis, quae ad completionem horarum decidebant, et casu suo subiectum sibi cimbalum tinnire faciebant additis in eodem eiusdem numeri equitibus, qui per duodecim fenestras completis

horis exiebant, et inpulsu egressionis suae totidem fenestras, quae prius erant apertae claudebant." *Annales regni Francorum*, ann. 807, *MGH, SS. rer. Ger.*, ed. F. Kurze (Hanover: Hahn, 1895), 123–24.

52. See Finbarr Barry Flood, *The Great Mosque of Damascus* (Leiden: Brill, 2001), 115–18; Alfred Chapuis and Edmond Droz, *Les automates, figures artificielles d'hommes et d'animaux* (Neuchatel: Griffon, 1949). On clocks in the Byzantine Empire, see Benjamin Anderson, "Public clocks in Late Antique and Early Medieval Constantinople," *Jahrbuch der Österreichischen Byzantinistik* 64 (2014): 24–32; Derek J. de Solla Price, "Automata and the Origins of Mechanism and Mechanistic Philosophy," *Technology and Culture* 5 (1964): 9–23.

53. Gerhard Dohrn-Van Rossum, *The History of the Hour: Clocks and Modern Temporal Orders*, trans. Thomas Dunlap (Chicago: University of Chicago Press, 1996), 31–37; Derek J. de Solla Price, "Clockwork Before the Clock and Timekeepers Before Timekeeping" in *The Study of Time II: Proceedings of the Second Conference of the International Society for the Study of Time, Lake Yamanaka—Japan*, ed. J. T. Fraser and N. Lawrence (Berlin: Springer-Verlag, 1975), 367–80; Katharine Park, "Observation in the Margins," in *Histories of Scientific Observation*, ed. Lorraine Daston and Elizabeth Lunbeck (Chicago: University of Chicago Press, 2011), 15–44, esp. 22–24.

54. See Elspeth Whitney, *Paradise Restored: The Mechanical Arts from Antiquity Through the Thirteenth Century*, TAPS 80 (1990): 1–169, 57–73.

55. "Misit Constantinus imperator regi Pippino cum aliis donis organum, qui in Franciam usque pervenit," *Annales regni Francorum*, ann. 757, *MGH, SS. rer. Ger.*, 14; "Constantinus imperator misit Pippino regi multa munera, inter quae et organum," *Annales qui dicuntur Einhardi*, ann. 757, *MGH, SS. rer. Ger.*, ed. F. Kurze and G. H. Pertz (Hanover: Hahn, 1895), 15.

56. James Trilling, "Daedalus and the Nightingale: Art and Technology in the Myth of the Byzantine Court," in *Byzantine Court Culture from 829–1204*, ed. Henry Maguire (Washington, D.C.: Dumbarton Oaks, 1997), 217–30, 222.

57. Trilling, "Daedalus and the Nightingale," 225.

58. Romanos I Lekapenos ruled as Byzantine emperor from 920 until his deposition in 944, and was the father-in-law of Constantine VII Porphyrogennetos, author of *De ceremoniis*, emperor during Liudprand's visit.

59. "Aerea sed daurata quaedam arbor ante imperatoris sedile stabat, cuius ramos itidem aereae diversi generis deaurateque aves replebant, quae secundum species suas diversarum avium voces emittebant. Imperatoris vero solium huiusmodi erat arte compositum, ut in momemto humile, exelsius modo, quam mox videretur sublime; quod inmensae magnitudinis, incertum utrum aerei an lignei, verum auro tecti leones quasi custodiebant, qui cauda terram percutientes, aperto ore, linguisque mobilibus rugitum emittebant . . . . Cumque in adventu meo rugitum leones emitterent, aves secundum species suas perstreperent, nullo sum terrore, nulla admiratione commotus, quoniam quidem ex his omnibus eos qui bene noverant fueram percontatus. Tercio itaque pronus imperatorem adorans, caput sustuli, et quem prius moderata mensura a terra elevatum sederi vidi, nox aliis indutum vestibus poenes domus laeuear sedere prospexi; quod qualiter fieret, cogitare non

potui, nisi forte eo sit subvectus argalio, quo torcularium arbores subvehuntur." Liudprand of Cremona, *Antapodosis*, 6.5, *Liudprandi Episcopi Cremonensis Opera Omnia, MGH, SS. rer. Ger.*, ed. J. Becker (Hanover: Hahn, 1915), 154–55; trans. in *The Embassy to Constantinople and Other Writings*, trans. F. A. Wright, ed. John Julius Norwich (London: Dent, 1993), 153. Liudprand later became bishop of Cremona and was sent back to Constantinople nineteen years later, as an envoy of Holy Roman Emperor Otto I.

60. It is possible Liudprand is referring here to a capstan. See Trilling, "Daedalus and the Nightingale," 228–29. Trilling posits that Liudprand's expression of ignorance of the technology on which the throne relied is linked to Latin ignorance and fear of Greek fire.

61. Averil Cameron, "The Construction of Court Ritual: The Byzantine *Book of Ceremonies*," in *Rituals of Royalty: Power and Ceremonial in Traditional Societies*, ed. David Cannadine and Simon Price (Cambridge: Cambridge University Press, 1987), 106–36.

62. Constantine VII, *The Book of Ceremonies*, 2.15, trans. Anne Moffat and Maxeme Tall, 2 vols., (Canberra: Australian Association for Byzantine Studies, 2012), 2: 569.

63. Brett, "The Automata in the Byzantine 'Throne of Solomon'," 478.

64. I am grateful to Katherine Richard for this interpretation.

65. Nor were they the first. Holy Roman Emperor Otto II (967–83) was married to Theophanu, a niece of Eastern Roman Emperor John I Tzimisces.

66. Hubert Houben, *Roger II: A Ruler Between East and West*, trans. Graham A. Loud and Diane Milburn (Cambridge: Cambridge University Press, 2002); Pierre Aubé, *Roger II de Sicile* (Paris: Payot et Rivages, 2001).

67. On the satirical nature of *Le Voyage de Charlemagne* see John L. Grigsby, "A Note on the Genre of the *Voyage de Charlemagne*," in *Essays in Early French Literature Presented to Barbara M. Craig*, ed. Norris J. Lacy and Jerry C. Nash (New York: French Literature Publications, 1982), 1–8; Paul Brians, "Paul Aebischer and the 'Gab d'Olivier,'" *Romance Notes* 15 (1973–74): 164–71.

68. John Julius Norwich, *Byzantium: The Decline and Fall*, (1995; rep. London: Folio Society, 2003), 169–70.

69. Jonathan Phillips, *The Fourth Crusade and the Sack of Constantinople* (New York: Viking, 2004), 127–41.

70. It survives in one late thirteenth- or early fourteenth-century manuscript, Royal Library of Copenhagen, MS 487.

71. On these two contemporary crusade narratives, see Alfred J. Andrea, "Essay on Primary Sources," in *The Fourth Crusade: The Conquest of Constantinople*, ed. Donald E. Queller and Thomas F. Madden (Philadelphia: University of Pennsylvania Press, 1993): 299–313, 303; Suzanne Fleischman, "On the Representation of History and Fiction in the Middle Ages," *History and Theory* 22 (1983): 278–310, 297; Sharon Kinoshita, *Medieval Boundaries: Rethinking Difference in Old French Literature* (Philadelphia: University of Pennsylvania Press, 2006), 139–75.

72. "Si avoit il ymages d'omnes et de femmes et de chevaus et de bués et de cameus et de ors et de lions, et de molt de manieres de bestes getees de coivre, qui si estoient bien faites et si natureument formees qu'il n'a si boin maistre en paienisme ne en crestienté qui

seust mie pourtraire ne si bien former ymages comme chil ymage estoient formé; et soloient cha en arriere giuer par encantement, mais ne juoient mais nient; et ches jus l'empereeur esgarderent li Franchois a mervelle, quant il les virent." Robert of Clari, *La conquête de Constantinople*, ed. Philippe Lauer (Paris: Champion, 1924), § 90, 88.

73. Jonathan Bardill, "Monuments and decoration of the Hippodrome," in *Hippodrome/Atmeydanı*, ed. Brigitte Pitarakis (Istanbul: Pera Müzesi, 2010), 149–84.

74. As Pamela O. Long has pointed out, societies adapt and adopt technologies as they are suited to their own cultural requirements. Long, *Technology and Society in the Medieval Centuries: Byzantium, Islam, and the West, 500–1300* (Washington, D.C.: Society for the History of Technology and the American Historical Association, 2003), 101.

75. Michel Zink, *Medieval French Literature: an Introduction*, trans. Jeff Rider (Binghamton, N.Y.: MRTS, 1995), 18–20.

76. "Paiens unt tort et chrestïens unt dreit," *La Chanson de Roland*, ed. Luis Cortès (Paris: Nizet, 1994), l. 1015, 242.

77. See *Aymeri of Narbonne: A French Epic Romance*, trans. Michael A. H. Newth (New York: Italica Press, 2005), ix. On the portrayal of Muslims in Western medieval literature, see Lynn Tarte Ramey, *Christian, Saracen, and Genre in Medieval French Literature* (New York: Routledge, 2001); Norman Daniel, *Heroes and Saracens: An Interpretation of the Chansons de Geste* (Edinburgh: Edinburgh University Press 1984); George F. Jones, *The Ethos of the Song of Roland* (Baltimore: Johns Hopkins University Press, 1963).

78. Burgess, *Le Pèlerinage de Charlemagne*, x. See also Eugene Vance, "Semiotics and Power: Relics, Icons, and the *Voyage de Charlemagne à Jérusalem et à Constantinople*," *Romanic Review* 79 (1988): 164–83, rep. in *The New Medievalism*, ed. Marina S. Brownlee (Baltimore: Johns Hopkins University Press, 1991), 226–49; Martin Gosman, "La propagande politique dans *Le Voyage de Charlemagne à Jérusalem et à Constantinople*," *Zeitschrift für Romanische Philologie* 102 (1986): 53–66.

79. *Le Pèlerinage de Charlemagne*, ll. 129–139, 36.

80. Ibid., ll. 193–197, 38.

81. Ibid., l. 262, 42.

82. "E treis mile puceles a orfreis relusant, / Vestues sunt de pailes e ount les cors avenanz, / E tenant lur amis, si se vunt deportant." *Le Pèlerinage de Charlemagne* ll. 267–274, 42.

83. "Si a cundut sun arêt tant adreceement, / Si fait dreite sa rei cum line que tent. / Atant est vus Carlun sur un mul amblant!" *Le Pèlerinage de Charlemagne*, ll. 283–298, 42.

84. " 'Car la tenise en France e Berteram si i fusset, / A peals e a marteals sereit esconsue.' " *Le Pèlerinage de Charlemagne*, ll. 327–328, 44.

85. Karl Leyser, "*Theophanu divina gratia imperatrix augusta*: Western and Eastern Emperorship in the Later Tenth Century," in *The Empress Theophano: Byzantium and the West at the Turn of the First Millennium*, ed. Adelbert Davis (Cambridge: Cambridge University Press, 1995), 1–27.

86. The language stressing the lifelikeness of the automata appears first at l. 361 ("Que ço vus fust viarie que tut fussent vivant") and shortly afterward at l. 374 ("Que ceo vus fust viarie que il fussent tuz vis"). See Trannoy, "De la technique à la magie," 227–52, 239.

87. "Atant ast vus un angele qui Deus i aparut, / E vint a Carlemaine, si l'ad relevéd sus: / 'Carlemaine, ne t'esmaer, ço te mandet Jhesus / Des gas que ersair desistes, grant folie fud; / Ne gabez mes hume, ço te cumandet Cristus. / Va, si fas cumencer, ja n'en faldras uns.'" *Le Pèlerinage de Charlemagne*, ll. 672–677, 62.

88. *Le Pèlerinage de Charlemagne*, ll. 774–792, 66.

89. Peter Brown, *The Cult of the Saints: Its Rise and Function in Latin Christianity* (Chicago: University of Chicago Press, 1981); Bynum, "Wonder"; Daston and Park, *Wonders*, 69–70.

90. See *Le Pèlerinage de Charlemagne*, l. 357, 46; l. 372, 46; Trannoy, "De la technique à la magie," 230.

91. *Le Pèlerinage de Charlemagne*, ll. 375–378, 46. That said, Trannoy points out that the horn was sometimes seen as a sign of the devil, meaning that the pipers are both wondrous and suspect. See Trannoy, "De la technique à la magie," 231.

92. Zink, *Medieval French Literature*, 32.

93. See Newth, *Aymeri of Narbonne*, i–xxxiii.

94. *Aymeri de Narbonne*, ed. Louis Demaison, SATF, 2 vols. (Paris: Firmin Didot, 1887), ll. 162–189, 2: 8–9 for the description of Narbonne. All references to *Aymeri de Narbonne* are from the 1887 Demaison edition. I have used my own translation.

95. *Aymeri de Narbonne*, ll. 190–204, 2: 9.

96. Leo Henkin, "The Carbuncle in the Adder's Head," *Modern Language Notes* 58 (1943): 34–39. See also Theodore Ziolkowski, *Varieties of Literary Thematics* (Princeton, N.J.: Princeton University Press, 1983), 54–55.

97. "Si merveillex com vos m'orroiz conter." *Aymeri de Narbonne*, l. 3506, 2: 148.

98. "Par nigromance i fait le vent entrer, / Encontremont par le tuel monter; / Qant li vanz sofle, les oisiax fet chanter, / En lor maniere, seriement et cler," *Aymeri de Narbonne*, ll. 3520–3523, 2: 148–49.

99. "Soz ciel n'a home qu s'en puist saouler;/ S'il est iriez, por coi l'oie soner,/ Tout maintenant li fet sire oublier." *Aymeri de Narbonne*, ll. 3524–3526, 2: 149.

100. "Li vif deable lor donent tel oré / Qu'an .xv. jorz sont deça arivé. / Voient la terre de la crestienté," *Aymeri de Narbonne*, ll. 3617–3619, 2: 152.

101. See *Dictionnaire de l'ancienne langue française et tous ses dialects du IXe au XVe siècle*, ed. Frédéric Godefroy, 8 vols. (Geneva: Slatkine, 1982), s.v. "nigromance"; *Novum glossarium mediae Latinitatis, 350–1250*, ed. Franz Blatt et al. (Copenhagen: Munksgaard, 1957–69), s.v. "necromantia." For a more comprehensive discussion of the definition of "necromancy" and related concepts, see Chapter 2.

102. Indeed, this was a fairly common example of automata in medieval texts. See Brett, "The Automata in the Byzantine 'Throne of Solomon.'"

103. See, for example, Matthew Paris's description in *Chronica Majora*, "They are inhuman and bestial, better called monsters rather than men, thirsting for and drinking blood, tearing and devouring the flesh of dogs and men. . . . They are without human laws, know no comforts, and are more ferocious than lions or bears." Matthew Paris, *Chronica Majora*, ann. 1240, ed. Henry Richard Luard, 7 vols. (London: Longman, 1877), 4: 76–77.

"Viri sunt enim inhumani et bestiales, potius monstra dicendi quam homines, sanguinem sitientes et bibentes, carnes caninas et humanas laniantes et devorantes . . . . humanis legibus carentes, nescii mansuetudinis, leonibus aut ursis truculentiores." On Latin Christian ideas about the Mongols, see Campbell, *Witness and the Other World*, 112–21; Daston and Park, *Wonders and the Order of Nature*, 63–64, 92–93.

104. Akbari, *Idols in the East*, 112–18.

105. Park, "The Meaning of Natural Diversity," 138.

106. *The Journey of William of Rubruck to the Eastern Parts of the World*, ed. and trans. William Woodville Rockhill (London: Hakluyt Society, 1900), 151–52, 156, 187, 239–40.

107. This comparison could be read as evidence of defensiveness on William's part.

108. Elsewhere in the text his name is given as William Buchier.

109. Rubruck, *Journey of William of Rubruck*, ed. Rockhill, 208.

110. Daston and Park, *Wonders*, 111–12; Bynum, "Wonder," 7–9.

111. "Nec sistit inquisitio quousque perveniatur ad primam causam . . . .Prima autem omnium causa Deus est. Est igitur ultimus finis hominis cognoscere Deum." Thomas Aquinas, *Summa contra Gentiles* 3.25.11, Leonine ed. (Rome: Marietti, 1961), 67 Chaucer later took up the issue of wonder and Eastern marvels in *The Squire's Tale*, in which he discusses the Mongol court's reaction to a flying brass horse that was a gift from the ruler of India to the Mongol ruler Cambyuskan. Chaucer, *The Squire's Tale* in *The Riverside Chaucer*, 3rd ed., ed. Larry Benson (Boston: Houghton Mifflin, 1987). See Patricia Ingham, "Little Nothings: The Squire's Tale and the Ambition of Gadgets," *SAC* 31 (2009): 53–80, esp. 59; Scott Lightsey, "Chaucer's Secular Marvels and the Medieval Economy of Wonder," *SAC* 23 (2001): 289–316, esp. 309–11; Karnes, "Wonder, Marvels, and Metaphors in *The Squire's Tale*."

112. Daston and Park, *Wonders*, 33.

113. *The Book of Ser Marco Polo the Venetian, Concerning the Kingdoms and Marvels of the East*, 2.13, ed. and trans. Henry Yule, 2 vols. (London: Murray, 1875), 1: 369. *The Book of Ser Marco Polo* emphasizes natural diversity and variation and presents them as cause for delight. Park, "The Meaning of Natural Diversity," 137.

114. *The Book of Ser Marco Polo*, 2.13, 1: 369.

115. "In ipso etiam palatio sunt multi pavones de auro. Cum aliquis tartarus festum aliquod vult facere domino, tunc sic illic sunt percucientes ad invicem manus suas, tunc hii pavones alas suas emittunt, et ipsi tripudiare videntur. Hoc autem fit vel arte diabolica vel ingenio quod sub terra sit," Odoric of Pordenone, *Relatio* in *Sinica franscicana*, vol. 1, *Itinera et relationes fratrum Minorum saeculi XIII et IV* (Florence: Quaracchi, 1929): 413–95, 426, 473.

116. Lightsey, *Manmade Marvels*, 144.

117. Iain MacLeod Higgins, *Writing East: The "Travels" of Sir John Mandeville* (Philadelphia: University of Pennsylvania Press, 1997), 6–8.

118. Mandeville, *The Book of John Mandeville, with Related Texts*, ed. Iain MacLeod Higgins (Indianapolis: Hackett, 2011), xiv–xvi; Christian Deluz, *Le Livre de Jehan de Mandeville: Une "géographie" au XIVe siècle* (Louvain-La-Neuve: Institut d'Études Médiévales de l'Université Catholique de Louvain, 1988), 370–82. On the relationship between Odoric's text and *Mandeville's Travels* see Lightsey, *Mandmade Marvels*, 143–51; Campbell, *Witness and the*

Other World, 154–59. Higgins's 2011 translation of *TBJM* is excellent. However, I use *Mandeville's Travels*, ed. M. C. Seymour (Oxford: Clarendon, 1967, an edition of the Middle English translation (the Cotton version, ca. 1400) closest to the original French. See Higgins, *TBJM*, 199.

119. *MT*, 155, *Middle English Dictionary*, ed. Hans Kurath, Sherman Kuhn, et al. (Ann Arbor: University of Michigan Press, 1951–2001), s.v. "mountour."

120. *MT*, 157.

121. Ibid.

122. Campbell, *Witness and the Other World*, 156.

123. *MT*, 157.

124. Daston and Park, *Wonders*, 93.

125. The Old Man in the Mountain is variously identified with Hasan i Sabbah, founder of the Assassins (d. 1124), and Ala-eddin and his son Rukn-eddin ben Ala-eddin, Ismaili princes killed by the Moghuls. See respectively *MT*, 290; *The Book of Ser Marco Polo*, 146–47 n1.

126. *The Book of Ser Marco Polo*, 1.23, 1: 145–46. See also Daston and Park, *Wonders*, 32–34; Campbell, *Witness and the Other World*, 106–12.

127. The tale of the Old Man in the Mountain is found in *MT*, 200–202. See Lightsey, *Manmade Marvels*, 151–55. Although many authors have written extensively about the natural marvels found in *Mandeville's Travels*, Lightsey is the first to specifically address manmade or mechanical marvels. On skepticism and belief of accounts of wonders, especially in travel narrative, see Daston and Park, *Wonders*, 61–66.

128. Higgins, *Writing East*, 193–94.

129. *MT*, 201.

130. Ibid.

131. Ibid.: "I will give to you a land flowing with milk and honey." This is an imitation of Leviticus 20:24: "Vobis autem loquor possidete terram eorum quam dabo vobis in hereditatem terram fluentem lacte et melle ego Dominus Deus vester qui separavi vos a ceteris populis. [But I say to you: Possess their land that I will give to you for an inheritance, a land flowing in milk and honey. I am the Lord your God, who has separated you from other people.], Vulgate Bible. The biblical reference is discussed by Lightsey, *Manmade Marvels*, 154.

132. In some cases, the un-Christian beliefs and practices of these people render them morally or politically weak. However, in the case of *Mandeville's Travels*, the Muslims who yearn for paradise and are susceptible to Gatholonabes's predation are part of a depiction of Muslims as more pious and ethical in their faith than Latin Christians.

CHAPTER 2. BETWEEN ART AND NATURE: *NATURA ARTIFEX,*
NEOPLATONISM, AND LITERARY AUTOMATA

1. For example, William of Conches, who studied and taught at Chartres, was also engaged as tutor to Henry II Plantagenet in the mid-twelfth century. Writing was generally

not included with the "mechanical arts" of painting, sculpture, or architecture, and medieval writers tried to claim for themselves the status of philosopher or sorcerer. See E. R. Truitt, "'*Trei poëte, sages dotors, qui mout sorent di nigromance*': Knowledge and Automata in Twelfth-Century French Literature," *Configurations* 12 (2004): 167–93.

2. These authors all were deeply familiar with Platonic theory, but equally were influenced by Aristotelian concepts. John Marenbon, "Twelfth-Century Platonism: Old Paths and New Directions," in *Aristotelian Logic, Platonism, and the Context of Early Medieval Philosophy in the West* (Aldershot: Ashgate, 2000), 1–21; Marenbon, *Early Medieval Philosophy* (London: Routledge, 1983), 1–39, 80–90; Marie-Dominique Chenu, *Nature, Man, and Society in the Twelfth Century*, trans. Jerome Taylor and Lester K. Little (Chicago: University of Chicago Press, 1968), 49–50.

3. C. S. Lewis, *The Discarded Image: An Introduction to Medieval and Renaissance Literature* (Cambridge: Cambridge University Press, 1964), 43.

4. Plato, *Timaeus*, 31b–c, 34c, translation from Lewis, *Discarded Image*, 43. See also George Economou, *The Goddess Natura in the Medieval Literature* (Cambridge, Mass.: Harvard University Press, 1972), 10.

5. "Omnia enim quae sunt uel dei opera uel naturae uel naturam imitantis hominis artificis," Chalcidius, *Timaeus: A Calcidio translatus commentarioque instructus*, ed. J. H. Waszink, *Plato Latinus: Corpus Platonicum Medii Aevi*, ed. Raymond Klibansky, vol. 4 (London: Warburg, 1962), 330.324–25, 23.73–74. See also Economou, *Goddess Natura*, 16–24.

6. See *Commentarius in Somnium Scipionis*, ed. Franz Eyssenhardt (Leipzig: Teubner, 1868), 529; *Macrobius' Commentary*, trans. William Harris Stahl (New York: Columbia University Press, 1952) 1.14.8, 43–144.

7. For an overview of the Victorine School and Hugh's influence, see Patrice Sicard, *Hugues de Saint-Victor et son école: Introduction, choix de texte, traduction et commentaires* (Turnhout: Brepols, 1991); Roger Barron, *Science et sagesse chez Hugues de Saint-Victor* (Paris: Lethielleux, 1957); Jerome Taylor, *The Origin and Early Life of Hugh of St. Victor: An Evaluation of the Tradition* (South Bend, Ind.: Press of the Medieval Institute, University of Notre Dame, 1957).

8. Hugh of St. Victor, *Didascalicon: A Medieval Guide to the Arts*, trans. and intro. Jerome Taylor (New York: Columbia University Press, 1961), 4.

9. Edgar de Bruyne, *Études d'esthétique médiévale*, 3 vols. (Bruges: De Tempel, 1946), 2: 204; Wladyslaw Tatarkiewicz, *History of Aesthetics*, 3 vols. (The Hague: Mouton, 1970), 2: 112–13. For more on the aesthetics of the Victorines, see de Bruyne, 2: 203–54; for Hugh specifically, 2: 205–49.

10. Whitney, *Paradise Restored*, 58–63; Richard McKeon, "Poetry and Philosophy in the Twelfth Century: The Renaissance of Rhetoric," *Modern Philology* 43 (1945–46): 217–34.

11. Hugh of St. Victor, *Didascalicon*, ed. Charles Henry Buttimer (Washington, D.C.: Catholic University of America Press, 1939), 2.20, 23–47. Later, in Chapter 23, *navigatio* is defined to mean anything having to do with commerce and trade, local and long distance ("Navigatio continet omnem in emendis, vendendis, mutandis, domesticis sive peregrinis mercibus negotiationem.") I will be citing both the Latin edition of the *Didascalicon* and

Taylor's translation with its valuable notes and introductions, and differentiate the two by using Taylor to indicate his edition and simply *Didascalicon* for Buttimer's Latin edition, as I have made some changes to Taylor's translation of the Latin. The idea of a hierarchy among the arts is an innovation of Hugh's. See Tatarkiewicz, *History of Aesthetics*, 2:113.

12. *Didascalicon*, 1.6, 12–13. The distinctions among these three categories (eternal, perpetual, and temporal) appear at the same time in William of Conches's commentary on *De consolatione philosophiae*, III, m. ix; see Joseph-Marie Parent, *La doctrine de la création dans l'École de Chartres* (Paris: J. Vrin, 1938), 125–36. Taylor asserts that these distinctions appear to be original to William; Taylor, *Didascalicon*, 185.

13. "Cuius causa et effectus diversa non sunt, quod non aliunde sed a semetipso subsistere habet, ut est solus naturae genitor et artifex." *Didascalicon*, 1.6, 13.

14. *Didascalicon*, 1.6, 13.

15. "Tertia pars rerum est quae principium et finem habent, et per se ad esse non veniunt, sed sunt opera naturae," *Didascalicon*, 1.6, 13.

16. "Id est, opus Dei, opus naturae, opus artificis imitantis naturam," *Didascalicon*, 1.9, 16.

17. "Quae oriuntur super terram sub lunari globo, movente igne artifice, qui vi quadam descendit in res sensibiles procreandas," *Didascalicon*, 1.6, 13.

18. "Opus artificis est disgregata coniungere vel coniuncta segregare . . . .Neque enim potuit vel terra caelum creare, vel homo herbam producere, qui nec palmum ad staturam suam addere potest," *Didascalicon*, 1.9, 16.

19. "In his tribus operibus convenienter opus humanum, quod natura non est sed imitatur naturam, mechanicum, id est, adulterinum nominatur, quemadmodum et clavis subintroducta mechanica dicitur," *Didascalicon*, 1.9, 16. Taylor translates "clavis subintroducta" as "skeleton key." Hugh conflates "mechanical" with "adulterate" just a few sentences earlier, at the end of 1.8, 15.

20. John J. Contreni, *The Cathedral School of Laon, 850–930: Its Manuscripts and Masters* (Munich: Arbeo-Gesellschaft, 1978), 55–58, 67–70, 114; Berenice M. Kaczynski, "Some St. Gall Glosses on Greek Philanthropic Nomenclature," *Speculum* 58 (1983): 1008–17, 1009. Contreni argues that Martin was likely not the author of the *Scholica*.

21. Taylor, *Didascalicon*, 191, n. 64. Cf. Martin of Laon, *Scholica graecarum glossarum*, *Bulletin of the John Rylands Library* 7 (1922–23): 421–56, 439. This association between mechanical and adulterate, or counterfeit, is also found in French. See *Dictionnaire de l'ancienne langue française*, ed. Godefroy, s.v. "mécanique."

22. "Uerum semine semel intra formandi hominis monetam locato hoc primum artifex natura molitur ut die septimo folliculum genuinum circumdet," Macrobius, *Commentarius in Somnium Scipionis*, ed. Eyssenhardt, 1.6.63, 509: *Macrobius' Commentary*, trans. Stahl, 1.6.63, 112.

23. *Didascalicon*, 1.1, 5–6.

24. Economou, *The Goddess Natura*, 58–59; Paul Dutton, ed., *The Glossae super Platonem of Bernard of Chartres* (Toronto: PIMS, 1991), 32–33.

25. Bernard Silvestris, *Cosmographia*, 1.4.32, trans. Winthrop Wetherbee (New York: Columbia University Press, 1973), 90; Economou, *The Goddess Natura*, 64.

26. Bernard Silvestris, *Cosmographia*, trans. Wetherbee, 15–17; Economou, *The Goddess Natura*, 68.

27. Economou, *The Goddess Natura*, 72; Winthrop Wetherbee, "The Function of Poetry," *Traditio* 25 (1969): 85–125; R. H. Green, "Alan of Lille's *De planctu naturae*," *Speculum* 31 (1956): 649–74.

28. "Ex his materiam ductam Natura monetat in speciem," Alan of Lille, *Anticlaudianus*, 7.34, ed. Thomas Wright, *The Anglo-Latin Satirical Poets and Epigrammatists*, RS 59 (Wiesbaden: Kraus, 1964), 2: 383.

29. See Jan M. Ziolkowski, *Alan of Lille's Grammar of Sex: The Meaning of Grammar to a Twelfth-Century Intellectual* (Cambridge, Mass.: Medieval Academy, 1985), 27–30.

30. "Me igitur sui vicariam, rerum generibus sigillandis monetariam destinavit, ut ego in propriis incudibus rerum effigies commonetans, ab incudis forma conformatum, deviare non sinerem, sed mei operante solertia, ab exemplaris vultu, naturarum nullarum dotibus defraudata exemplatis facies deviaret," Alain de Lille, *De planctu naturae*, ed. Wright, 2: 469. See also Mechtild Modersohn, *Natura als Göttin im Mittelalter: Ikonographische Studien zur Darstellung der personifizierten Natur* (Berlin: Akademie Verlag, 1997), 29–38

31. Guillaume de Lorris wrote *Le Roman de la Rose* around 1230; Jean de Meun composed his continuation, roughly three times the length of Guillaume's original, around 1270–85.

32. "Mais Nature douce e piteuse, / Quant el veit que Mort l'envieuse, / Entre li e Corrupcion, / Vienent metre a destruccion / Quanqu'eus treuvent dedenz sa forge, / Toujourz martele, toujourz forge, / Toujourz ses pieces renouvele / Par generacion nouvele . . . / Don Art faisait ses essemplaires, / Qu ne fait pas fourmes si veires," Guillaume de Lorris and Jean de Meun, *Roman de la Rose*, ed. Ernest Langlois, 5 vols., SATF (Paris: Firmin-Didot, 1914), ll. 16005–16018, 4: 128–29. See also Modersohn, *Natura als Göttin im Mittelalter*, 73–90.

33. "Cum arbre de mulin," *Le Pèlerinage de Charlemagne*, l. 372, 46.

34. "Opus artificis est disgregata coniungere vel coniuncta segregare," *Didascalicon*, 1.9, 16.

35. *Dictionnaire de l'ancienne langue française*, ed. Godefroy, s.v. "forge"; cf. *OED*, "forge."

36. *Didascalicon*, 1.9, 16–17.

37. "Hac equidem ratione illa quae nunc excellentissima in studiis hominum vides, reperta sunt. Hac eadem pingendi, texendi, sculpendi, fundendi, infinita genera exorta sunt, ut iam cum natura ipsum miremur artificem," *Didascalicon*, 1.9, 17.

38. This is similar to, though earlier than, Ficino's sympathetic magic. Brian Copenhaver, "Scholastic Philosophy and Renaissance Magic in the *De vita* of Marsilio Ficino," *Renaissance Quarterly* 37 (1984): 523–54; Richard Kieckhefer, "The Specific Rationality of Medieval Magic," *AHR* 99 (1994): 813–36.

39. "De quivre e de metal tregeté douz enfanz," *Le Pèlerinage de Charlemagne*, l. 352, 46; "E celes imagines cornent," l. 373, 46.

40. Truitt, "'*Trei poëte, sages dotors,*'" 168.

41. "Fu fait par cumpas e serét noblement," *Le Pèlerinage de Charlemagne*, l. 348, 44. See Chapter 1, n 8.

42. E. R. Truitt, "Celestial Divination and Arabic Science in Twelfth-Century England: The History of Gerbert of Aurillac's Talking Head," *Journal of the History of Ideas* 73 (2012): 201–22.

43. Kieckhefer, "The Specific Rationality of Medieval Magic"; Lynn Thorndike, *The Place of Magic in the Intellectual History of Europe* (New York: Columbia University Press, 1905), 1–32.

44. See Stuart Clark, *Thinking with Demons* (Oxford: Oxford University Press, 1997), 214–32.

45. Demons were not necessarily threatening to humans. For example, William of Conches, in his *De philosophia mundi* (ca. 1130), posited two kinds of good demons (*kalodaemones*); these dwelt in the aethereal and aerial atmospheres. However, there was a third kind of demon that was evil (*kakodaemon*) and inhabited the humid atmosphere closer to earth. William of Conches, *De philosophia mundi*, cited in Lynn Thorndike, *The History of Magic and Experimental Science*, 8 vols. (New York: Columbia University Press, 1923–58), 2: 55.

46. See Clark, *Thinking with Demons*, 233–50.

47. Robert-Leon Wagner, *"Sorcier"et "magicien": Contribution à l'histoire du vocabularies de la magie* (Paris: Droz, 1939), 133.

48. *Dictionnaire historique de la langue française*, s.v. "magie"; *Dictionnaire de l'ancienne langue française*, ed. Godefroy, s.v. "magique." For Latin, see *Novum glossarium mediae Latinitatis, 350–1200*, ed. Franz Blatt et al. (Copenhagen: Munksgaard, 1957–69), s.v. "magus."

49. *Dictionnaire historique de la langue française*, s.v. "enchanter"; *Dictionnaire de l'ancienne langue française*, s.v. "enchant"; *Dictionnaire etymologique de la langue française*, s.v. "enchanter." On charm magic, see Lea Olsan, "Latin Charms of Medieval England: Verbal Healing in a Christian Oral Tradition," *Oral Tradition* 7 (1992): 116–42; Olsan, "The Inscription of Charms in Anglo-Saxon Manuscripts," *Oral Tradition* 14 (1999): 401–19.

50. *Dictionnaire historique de la langue française*, s.v. "augure"; *Dictionary of Old French*, ed. Hindley, Langley, and Levy (Cambridge: Cambridge University Press, 2000), s.v. "augure"; *Dictionnaire de l'ancienne langue française*, ed. Godefroy, s.v. "augurement," "augureor," and "augurerie."

51. *Novum glossarium mediae Latinitatis*, ed. Blatt, s.v. "necromantia." The French follows the Latin closely; see *Dictionnaire de l'ancienne langue française*, s.v. "nigromance."

52. "Ibi terra solitis artibus," William of Malmesbury, *De gestis regum Anglorum libri quinque*, 2.169, ed. and trans. R. A. B. Mynors, completed by R. M. Thomson and M. Winterbottom, 2 vols. (Oxford: Clarendon, 1998), 1: 284. See Chapter 3 for a longer discussion of William's account of automata. Later, by the fourteenth century, "art" can also refer to alchemical practice.

53. *Dictionnaire historique de la langue française*, s.v. "art"; *Dictionnaire de l'ancienne langue française*, ed. Godefroy, s.v. "artificier."

54. See *Dictionnaire historique de la langue française*, s.v. "ingénieur"; *Dictionnaire de l'ancienne langue française*, ed. Godefroy, s.v. "engignart," "engigne," "engigneor."

55. *Dictionnaire historique de la langue française*, s.v. "engin"; *Dictionnaire etymologique de la langue française*, ed. Ménage, s. v. "engin"; *Dictionnaire de l'ancienne langue française*, ed. Godefroy, s.v. "engin"; *Glossarum mediae et infimae latinitatis*, ed. Charles DuCange, 10 vols. (Paris: Librairie des Sciences et des Arts, 1937–38), s.v. "ingenium." Cf. *OED*, s.v. "engine."

56. *Roman de Thèbes*, ed. Léopold Constans, 2 vols. (Paris: Firmin Didot, 1890); Statius, P. Papinius, *Thebaid*, I–VII, ed. and trans. D. R. Shackleton Bailey, Loeb Classical Library (Cambridge, Mass.: Harvard University Press, 2003).

57. *Roman de Thèbes*, ll. 19–20; ll. 33–36, 1: 2–3; Renate Blumenfeld-Kosinski, *Reading Myth: Classical Mythology and Its Interpretations in Medieval French Literature* (Palo Alto, Calif.: Stanford University Press, 1997), 19; Daniel Poirion, "Eddypus et l'enigme du roman medieval" in *L'enfant du Moyen Age*, Senefiance 9 (Aix-en-Provence, 1980), 287–99.

58. "Amphiaras manda li reis, / Un arcevesque mout corteis: / Cil esteit maistre de lor lei, / De ciel saveit tot le secrei; / Il prent respons et giéte sorz / Et revivre fait homes morz / De toz oiseaus sot le latin, / Soz ciel n'aveit meillor devin," *Roman de Thèbes*, ll. 2025–2033, 1: 103.

59. "Vulcans le fist par grant porpens / Et a lui faire mist grant tens," *Roman de Thèbes*, ll. 4715–4716, 1: 230.

60. Homer, *Iliad*, 18.373–377, 343; 18.417–420, 44.

61. "La nuefeme assist in mé le monde: / Ço est la terre et mer parfonde. / En terre peinst homes et bestes, / En mer peissons, venz et tempestes," *Roman de Thèbes*, ll. 4725–4728, 1: 231.

62. "Une image i ot tresgetee, / Que vait cornant a la menee; / Une autre, que toz tens frestèle / Plus clér que rote ne vïèle," *Roman de Thèbes*, ll. 4765–4768, 233; for a description of the chariot see ll. 4731–4778, 1: 231–33.

63. *Dictionnaire historique de la langue française*, s.v. "tresgeter"; cf. *OED*, s.v. "cast."

64. "Vulcan le fist par grant porpens / et a lui faire mist grant tens. / Par estuide et par grant conseil, / I mist la lune et le soleil, / Et tregeta le firmament / Par art et par enchantement," *Roman de Thèbes*, ll. 4715–4720, 1: 230.

65. "Qui de fisique sot entendre, / Es peintures pot mout apprendre," *Roman de Thèbes*i, ll. 4729–4730, 1: 231. In other mss, this line is rendered: "Qu des set arz rien entendre, / Iluec em puet assez aprendre." See *Le Roman de Thèbes*, ed. Guy Raynaud de Lage (Paris: Champion, 1966, 1968), vol. 2, ll. 4968–4969. In a neat irony, the description of Amphiras's chariot was so striking that later authors used it as a model for ekphrastic description of the personification of the liberal arts and the cosmos. See Edmond Faral, "Le merveilleux et ses sources dans les descriptions des romans français du XIIe siècle," in his *Recherches sur les sources latines des contes et romans courtois du Moyen Age* (Paris: Champion, 1913), 314.

66. See Chapter 1, n. 7.

67. "Li trezimes enmi est taillez a cumpas," *Voyage de Charlemagne*, ll. 428–441, 48–50.

68. "Si galerne ist de mer, bise ne altre vent, / Ki ferent al paleis devers occident, / Il le funt turner e menut e suvent, / Cumme roe de char qu a tere decent; / Cil corn sunent e buglent e tunent ensement / Cumme taburs u toneires u grant cloches qui pent. / Li uns esgardet le altre ensement cum en riant. / Que ço vus fust viarie que tut fussent vivant," *Voyage de Charlemagne*, ll. 354–361, 46.

69. "Mult fud grand li orages, la neif e li gresilz, / E li vent durs e forz, qui tant bruit e fremist," *Voyage de Charlemagne*, ll. 378–379, 46.

70. "Cumme en mai en estét, quant soleil esclarist," *Voyage de Charlemagne*, l. 383, 46.

71. *Voyage de Charlemagne*, ll. 387–391, 46–48.

72. On occult qualities and natural philosophy, see Daston and Park, *Wonders*, 109–34; Brian P. Copenhaver, "Natural Magic, Hermetism, and Occultism in Early Modern Science," in *Reappraisals of the Scientific Revolution*, ed. David C. Lindberg and Robert S. Westman (Cambridge: Cambridge University Press, 1990), 261–301; John Henry, "Occult Qualities and the Experimental Philosophy," *History of Science* 24 (1986): 335–81; Keith Hutchinson, "What Happened to Occult Qualities in the Scientific Revolution?" *Isis* 73 (1982): 233–53; Kieckhefer, "The Specific Rationality of Medieval Magic."

73. On gemstones and their occult powers, see Christel Meier, *Gemma Spiritalis* (Munich: Verlag, 1977), 361–459.

74. For the sheer amount of knowledge a natural magician had to master, see William Eamon, *Science and the Secrets of Nature: Books of Secrets in Medieval and Early Modern Culture* (Princeton, N.J.: Princeton University Press, 1994), 38–90.

75. "An sint aggregationes luminum in partibus ipsius coeli, sicut apparet apud nos in quibusdam gemmis. Memini enim me vidisse smaragdum, in cujus splendore apparebant tres stellulae lucidissimae. Et certum est de lapide, qui dicitur heliotropius, quia ipse est lapis viridis, stellis rubeis stellatus," William of Auvergne, *De universo*, 1.1.42, in *Opera Omnia*, 1: 642, col. 1. See also Chapter 1, n. 44.

76. *Éneas*, ed. J. -J. Salverda de Grave (Geneva: Slatkine, 1975 [1891]), ll. 422–440, 18–19. For magic in courtly literature in this period, see Richard Kieckhefer, *Magic in the Middle Ages* (Cambridge: Cambridge University Press, 1989), 116–75; Kieckhefer, *Forbidden Rites: A Necromancer's Manual of the Fifteenth Century* (University Park: Pennsylvania State University Press, 1997), 1–21; Wagner, *"Sorcier" et "Magicien"*, 46–78.

77. *Éneas*, ll. 7430–7724, 276–87 for a description of the tomb.

78. "Li archiers pot longues viser / et toz tens mes l'arc anteser, / mais ja li boldons n'i trairoit, / se primes l'arc ne destandoit / le laz d'une regeteore / qui aparoilliez ert desore, / qui tenoit l'arc toz tens tendu. / A un sofle fust tot perdu: / qui soflast la regeteore, / et al destandist anislore / et li archiers idonc traisist / droit au colon, se l'abatist, / dunc fust la chaene rompue / et la lampe tote espandue," *Eneas*, ll. 7705–7718, 287.

79. See Chapter 4 for a thorough introduction to the source material for *Le Roman de Troie*.

80. Benoît de Sainte-Maure, *Le Roman de Troie*, ed. Léopold Constans, 6 vols. (Paris: Firmin Didot, 1904–12), ll. 14919–14936, 2: 392–93. For a complete translation of the section on the Alabaster Chamber, see Penny Sullivan, "Medieval Automata: The 'Chambre de Beautés' in Benoît de Sainte-Maure's *Roman de Troie*," *Romance Studies* 6 (1985): 1–20; translation begins on 13. I have used my own translation.

81. "En la Chambre de Labastrie, / Ou l'ors d'Araibe reflambie, / E les doze pieres gemeles / Que Deus en eslist as plus beles, / Quant precioses les noma, / Ço fu safirs e sardina, / Topace, prasme, crisolite, / Maraude, beriz, ametiste, / Jaspe, rubis chiere sardoine, / Charbocles clers e calcedoine, / D'icestes ot de lonc, de lé, / En la Chambre mout grant plenté. / N'i coveneit autre clarté, / Quar toz li plus beaus jorz d'esté / Ne reluist sin'a tel mesure / Come el faseit par nuit oscure. / De prasmes verz e de sardines / E de bones alemandines / Sont les vitres, e li chassis / D'or Araibe tresgeteïz. / Des entailles ne des figures / Ne des forms ne des peintures / Ne des merveilles ne des gieus, / Dont mout i ot par plusors lieus, / Ne quier retraire ne parler, / Qu'enuiz sereit de l'escouter," *Roman de Troie*, ed. Constans, ll. 14631–14656, 2: 374–76.

82. "Trei poëte, sages dotors, / Qui mout sorent de nigromance," *Roman de Troie*, ll. 14668–14669, 2: 377.

83. "Lor semblances i esguardoënt: / Bien conoisseient maintenant / Ço que sor eus n'ert avenant; / Sempres l'aveient afaitié / E gentement apareillié," *Roman de Troie*, ll. 14692–14696, 2: 378.

84. "L'autre danzele ert mout corteise, / Quar tote jor joë e enveise / E bale e tresche e tombe e saut, / Desus le piler, si en haut / Que c'est merveille qu'el ne chiet," *Roman de Troie*, ll. 14711–14715, 2: 379.

85. *Roman de Troie*, ll. 14759–14862, 2: 382–88.

86. "Esperital en est l'olor, / Quar il nen est maus ne dolor / Que n'en guarisse, qui la sent,"*Roman de Troie*, ll. 14911–14913, 2: 391.

87. "Ici ot sen trop engeignons: / Merveille fu com ço pot estre / Ne come rien de ço fu maistre," *Roman de Troie*, ll. 14878–14880, 2: 389.

88. "La place esteit large dedenz, / de marbre esteit li pavemenz. / Il i aveit quatre perrons, / tailliez a guises de lions, / molt maistrement i furent mis; / de desus ot deus ars asis, / en cros estient vols amont, / a aguilles taillié reont; / dreit en mi furent asenblé, / par maistrie furent soldé. / Desus sor la jointure dreit / uns granz pilers asis esteit, / de marbre de mainte color; / granz set teises ot de haltor; / la base ki seeit desoz / et li pilers fu tailliez toz / a flors, a biches, a oisels, et ensement li chapitels," *Éneas*, ll. 7537–7560, 280–81. See Faral, *Recherches*, 81–82; Otto Söhring, "Werke bildender Kunst in altfranzösischen Epen," *Romanische Forshungen* 12 (1900): 491–640; 507.

89. "D'un grant topace cler e chier / Tint en sa main un encensier, / O caeines bien entailles / E de fil d'or menu treciees," *Le Roman de Troie*, ll. 14895–14898, 2: 390–91.

90. See Thierry Magnier, ed., *Une renaissance: L'art entre Flandre et Champagne de 1150–1250* (Paris: Réunion des Musées Nationaux, 2013).

91. Brigitte Buettner, "Profane Illuminations, Secular Illusions: Manuscripts in Late Medieval Courtly Society," *Art Bulletin* 74 (1992): 75–90.

92. Clark, *Thinking with Demons*, parts 1 and 2.

93. Wagner, *"Sorcier" et "Magicien"*, 134.

94. "Opus manuum artificum," Deuteronomy 27.15.

95. "Nemo enim sibi similem homo poterit deum fingere," Wisdom 15.17. On the complicated history between idolatry and mimesis, see Michael Camille, *The Gothic Idol: Ideology and Image Making in Medieval Art* (Cambridge: Cambridge University Press, 1989), 27–72, 244–57.

96. "Daemon quippe simulacro arte impia conligatus ab homine factus est deus, se tali homini, non omni homini," Augustine, *De civitate Dei*, 8.24, in *The City of God Against the Pagans*, trans. David S. Wiesen, Loeb Classical Library, 7 vols. (Cambridge, Mass.: Harvard University Press, 1918), 3: 126. Translation mine.

97. *Lancelot do Lac: The Non-Cyclic Old French Prose Romance*, ed. Elspeth Kennedy, 2 vols. (Oxford: Clarendon, 1980), 1: 183.

98. "Et com il l'ot overt, si an sailli uns granz estorbeillons et une si granz noisse que il li fu avis que tuit li deiable d'anfer i fuissient; et por voir si estoient il, *que deiable estoient ce*," *Lancelot do lac*, 1: 250. Emphasis mine.

99. For a discussion of the intellectual genealogy of demonic speech, as well as the link between the destruction of demonically animated automata and conversion narratives in medieval literature, see Arthur Dickson, *Valentin and Orson: A Study in Late Medieval Romance* (New York: Columbia University Press, 1929), 191–200.

100. The darker pigmentation of the automata might indicate racial difference, or it could be that a brown pigment was used to signify a copper tone.

101. On the medieval romantic hero as wild man, see Richard Bernheimer, *Wild Men in the Middle Ages: A Study in Art, Sentiment, and Demonology* (New York: Octagon, 1970), 14–15.

102. It is possible that the painter of Plate 8 (and possibly Plates 6 and 7 as well) has replaced the automata with demons or wild men. However, there are other examples of naked automata in manuscript paintings; see Plate 10.

103. *Perceval le Gallois, ou le conte du Graal*, ed. Charles Potvin, 6 vols. (1866–71; Geneva: Slatkine, 1977), 1: 202–4.

104. Bynum, "Wonder," 13–15.

105. "Plus seürement s'en estoënt / E mout meins assez en dotoënt. / N'i esteit om guaries repris / De fol semblant ne de fol ris," *Roman de Troie*, ll. 14703–14706, 2: 379.

106. "A peine s'en puet rien partir / Ne de la Chambre fors eissir, / Tant com l'image ses gieus fait, / Que desus le piler s'estait," *Le Roman de Troie*, ll. 14755–14758, 2: 382.

107. "Quant cil de la Chambre conseillent, / A l'endormir e quant veillent, / Sone e note tant doucement, / Ne trait dolor ne mal ne sent / Quil puet oïr ne escouter. / Fol corage ne mal penser / N'i prent as gens, ne fous talanz. / Mout fait grant bien as escoutanz, / Quar auques haut pueent parler: / Nes puet om pas si scouter," *Le Roman de Troie*, ll. 14791–14800, 2: 384.

108. "La quarte image reserveit / D'une chose que mout valeit; / Quar ceus de la Chambre esguardot / E par signes lor demostrot / Que c'ert que il deveient faire / E que plus lor

ert necessaire: / A conoistre le lor faseit / Si qu'autre ne l'aperceveit. / S'en la Chambre fussent set cent, / Si seüst chascunt veirement / Que l'image li demonstrast / Iço que plus li besoignast. / Ço qu'uil mostrot ert bien segrei: / Nel coneüst ja rien fors sei, / Ne jo ne nus, fors il toz sous. / Ici ot sen trop engeignos: / Merveille fu com ço pot ester / Ne come rien de ço fu maistre. / Ja en la Chambre n'esteüst / Nus hom, fors tant com il deüst: / L'image saveit bien monstrer / Quant termes esteit de l'aler, / E quant trop tost, e quant trop tart; / Sovent preneit de ço reguart. / Bien guardot ceus d'estre enoios, / D'estre vilains, d'estre coitos, / Qui dedenz la Chambre veneient, / Qui entroënt ne qui eisseient: / Nus n'i poëit ester obliëz / Fous ne vilains ne esguarez, / Quar l'image, par grant maistrie, / Les guardot toz de vilanie," *Le Roman de Troie*, ll. 14863–14894, 2: 388–390. On Benoît's use of the first person singular in *Le Roman de Troie*, see Penny Eley, "Author and Audience in the *Roman de Troie*," *Courtly Literature: Culture and Context. Selected papers from the 5th Triennial Congress of the International Courtly Literature Society, Dalfsen, The Netherlands, 9–16 August, 1986*, ed. Keith Busby and Erik Kooper (Amsterdam: Benjamins, 1990), 179–90; Eley, "Translation and Adaption in the *Roman de Troie*," in *The Spirit of the Court: Selected Proceedings of the Fourth Congress of the International Courtly Literature Society (Toronto, 1983)*, ed. Glyn S. Burgess and Robert A. Taylor (Woodbridge: Brewer, 1985), 350–59. "Maistrie" can mean a clever ruse, or trick, and also great wisdom or skill. *Dictionnaire de l'ancienne langue française*, ed. Godefroy, s.v. "maistrie."

109. "De l'autre part du pont ot un tresgeteïs, / Deus enfans de fin or fais en molle fontis; / Li uns fu lons et grailles, l'autre gros et petis, / Menbres orent bien fais, vis formés et traitis. / Si com l'os aprisma et il oënt les cris, / Chascuns saisist un mail, li pas et contredis. / Des or aus ot deus bries, que uns clers ot escris, / Qui les fait par augure deffendre au passeïs," Alexandre de Paris, *Le Roman d'Alexandre* (Paris: Livre de Poche, 1994), ll. 3393–3400, 508.

110. "L'autre ymage del autre part / Ens en sa main tenoit un dart, / Ja n'i véist entre villain / . . . Pucièle ne s'i puet céler / Qu'ensi se face apiéler / Por oee que soit despucelée, / Tantos come vient à l'entrée, / La harpe sone la descorde, / De la harpe ront une corde," *Perceval le Gallois*, ed. Potvin, "Livre de Karados," ll. 13352–13372, 3: 149.

111. See Chapter 4 for a more complete discussion of this kind of automaton.

112. *Le Roman d'Alexandre*, ll. 7176–7182, 700: "Chascuns tint un escu d'or et fort et pesant, / A deus bastons de fer se vont grant caus donant, / Comme autre champion se vont escremissant. / Puis que cil s'en issirent qui firent cest enchant, / Ni vit on puis entre nisune riens vivant."

113. Gaston Paris, "La chanson du pèlerinage de Charlemagne," *Romania* 9 (1880): 1–50; Margaret Schlauch, "The Palace of Hugon de Constantinople," *Speculum* 7 (1932): 500–514; Lucie Polak, "Charlemagne and the Marvels of Constantinople," in *The Medieval Alexander Legend and Romance Epic: Essays in Honour of David J. A. Ross*, ed. Peter Noble, Lucie Polak, and Claire Isoz (London: Kraus, 1982), 159–72.

114. Aimé Petit, *L'anachronisme dans les romans antiques du XIIème siècle: Le Roman de Thèbes, le Roman d'Énéas, le Roman de Troie, et le Roman d'Alexandre* (Paris: Champion, 2002); Blumenfeld-Kosinski, *Reading Myth*, 2–5. On *translatio*, the act of literal trans-

lation of or reinterpretation and retelling of texts, see Michelle Freeman, "Problems in Romance Composition: Ovid, Chrétien de Troyes, and the *Romance of the Rose*," *Romance Philology* 30 (1976): 158–68.

115. Blumenfeld-Kosinski, *Reading Myth*, 17. On the Anglo-Norman interest in *romans antiques* see Lee Patterson, *Negotiating the Past: The Historical Understanding of Medieval Literature* (Madison: University of Wisconsin Press, 1987), 157–95.

116. Richard Waswo, "Our Ancestors, the Trojans: Inventing Cultural Identity in the Middle Ages," *Exemplaria* 7 (1995): 269–90.

117. Colette Beaune, "L'utilisation politique du mythe des origines troyennes en France à la fin du moyen âge," in *Lectures médiévales de Virgile: Actes du colloque organisé par l'École Française de Rome (Rome, 25–28 octobre 1982)* (Rome: École Française de Rome, 1985), 331–55; Frederic N. Clark, "Authenticity, Antiquity, and Authority: Dares Phrygius in Early Modern Europe," *Journal of the History of Ideas* 72 (2011): 183–207; Domenico Comparetti, *Vergil in the Middle Ages*, trans. E. F. M. Benecke, intro. Jan M. Ziolkowski (Princeton, N.J.: Princeton University Press, 1997), 244–46.

118. Dominique Battles, "Trojan Elements in the Old French *Roman de Thèbes*," *Neophilologus* 85 (2001): 163–76, 163–65.

119. See Jan M. Ziolkowski's introduction to Comparetti, *Vergil in the Middle Ages*, vii–xxxviii. In his introduction, Ziolkowski also explains the reason for the variant spelling of Vergil (Virgil).

120. Daniel Poirion, "De l'*Eneide* à l'*Éneas*: Mythologie et moralisation," *CCM* 19 (1976): 213–29.

121. Ziolkowski, "Introduction," in Comparetti, *Vergil in the Middle Ages*, vii–vii.

122. Vergil's reputation as a seer stems from his fourth *Eclogue*, which can be read as a prophecy of the coming of Christ. Additionally, there may have been a late antique practice called "sortes Vergilianae," in which one opened at random a volume of Vergil. *The Virgilian Tradition*, ed. Jan M. Ziolkowski and Michael C. J. Putnam (New Haven, Conn.: Yale University Press, 2008), 829–30.

123. "Fertur uates Mantuanus interrogasse Marcellum, cum depopulationi auium vehementius operam daret, an auem mallet instrui in capturam auium, an muscam informari in exterminationem muscarum. Cum uero quaestionem ad auunculum retulisset Augustum, consilio eius preelegitut fieret musca, quae ab Eneapoli muscas abigeret, et ciuitatem a peste insanabili libaret," John of Salisbury, *Policraticus, sive nugis curialium et vestigiis philosophorum, libri VIII*, 1.4, ed. Charles Webb, 2 vols. (Oxford: Clarendon, 1909), 1: 26.

124. Conrad of Querfurt recorded several Vergilian legends in a letter dated ca. 1196, including one legend in which Vergil created, by magical incantations, a bronze horse which, while it remained intact, allowed other horses to carry immensely heavy loads without injury. *Epistula Conradi cancellari*, ll. 25–30, in Arnold of Lübeck, *Chronica Slavorum*, *MGH, SS. rer. Ger.*, ed. Lappenberg (Hanover: Hahn, 1868), 194, cited and translated in *The Virgilian Tradition*, 848–49.

125. On Neckam's biography and *De naturis rerum*, see Thorndike, *A History of Magic and Experimental Science*, 2: 188–204.

126. "Romae item construxuit nobile palatium, in quo cujuslibet regionis imago lignea campanulam manu tenebat. Quotiens ver aliqua regio majestati Romani imperii insidias moliri ausa est incontinenti prodictricis icona campanulam pulsare coepit. Miles vero aeneus, equo insidens aneo, in summitate fastigii praedicti palatii hastam vibrans, in illam se vertit partem quae regionem illam respiciebat," Alexander Neckam, *De naturis rerum*, 2.174, ed. Thomas Wright, RS 34 (London: Longman, Green, 1863), 310. See also *The Virgilian Tradition*, 855–57; John Webster Spargo, *Virgil the Necromancer* (Cambridge, Mass: Harvard University Press, 1934), 11–13; Comparetti, *Vergil in the Middle Ages*, 296.

127. Gervase of Tilbury, *Otia imperialia*, 3.10, 576, translation mine. See also *The Virgilian Tradition*, 851–55. For a discussion of the definition of *arte mathematica* see Chapter 3.

128. Gervase of Tilbury, *Otia imperialia*, 3.12, 576–83, translation mine.

129. "In eodem erat ymago enea bucinam ad os tenens, quam quotiens auster ex obiecto subintrabat, statim ipsius uenti flatus conuertebatur. Quid autem conuersio ista Nothi commodi portabat? Audite. Est in confinio ciuitatis Neapolitane mons excelsus, mari infixus, subiectam sibi Terram Laboris spatiose prospectans; hic mense Madio fumum teterrimum eructuat et interdum cum cinere ardenissimo ligna proicit exusta in carbonis colorem, unde illic quoddam inferni terreni spiraculum asserunt ebulire. Flante igitur Notho, puluis calidus segetes omnesque fructus exurit, sicque terra in se feracissima ad sterilitatem ducitur. Ob hoc, tante regionis illius dampno consulens, Virgilius in opposito monte statuam, ut diximus, cum tuba erexit, ut ad primum uentilati cornu sonitum et in ipsa tuba flatus subintrantis impulsum, Nothus repulsus ui mathesis quassaretur," Gervase of Tilbury, *Otia imperialia*, 3.13, 582–85.

130. Conrad of Querfurt, *Epistula Conradi cancellarii*, ll. 24–28, in *Chronica Slavorum, MGH, SS. rer. Ger.*, ed. Lappenberg, 196, cited and translated in *The Virgilian Tradition*, 850–51. See also Spargo, *Virgil the Necromancer*, 13–15; Comparetti, *Vergil in the Middle Ages*, 257–59.

131. For automata in William of Malmesbury's *Gesta regum anglorum*, see Chapter 3.

CHAPTER 3. TALKING HEADS: ASTRAL SCIENCE, DIVINATION, AND LEGENDS OF MEDIEVAL PHILOSOPHERS

1. "Non tamen hec scripsimus quasi Saduceorum sectam comprobemus, qui omnia dicebant in Deo . . . consistere, hoc est in fato et casu fortune, cum omnia in sola uoluntate Dei sint posita, secundum illud: 'In uoluntate tua omnia sunt posita, et non est qui possit resistere uoluntati tue,' etc.; sed istud ad admirationem artis matematice Vergilii memorauimus," Gervase of Tilbury, *Otia imperialia*, 3.12, 582, translation mine.

2. Dickson, *Valentine and Orson* remains the most comprehensive on oracular brazen heads in medieval literature and culture, especially 194–216. Minsoo Kang shared some of his early research on oracular heads with me as I began to think about this topic. See Kang, *Sublime Dreams of Living Machines*, 69–79. The most recent account of the

context behind Greene's play and Bacon's head can be found in LaGrandeur, *Androids and Intelligent Networks*, 91–102.

3. On Bacon's interest in alchemy, see William R. Newman, "An Overview of Roger Bacon's Alchemy," in *Roger Bacon and the Sciences*, ed. Jeremiah Hackett (Leiden: Brill, 1997): 317–36; on astral and experimental science see Jeremiah Hackett, "Roger Bacon on Astronomy-Astrology: The Sources of the *Scientia experimentalis*," in ibid., 175–99. However, Bacon specifically addressed the impossibility of demonic magic and viewed wonder as an indication of underlying ignorance. Roger Bacon, *Epistola de secretis operibus artis et naturae, et de nullitate magiae*, ed. J. S. Brewer, RS 15 (1859; Wiesbaden: Kraus, 1965), 521–51. See also Daston and Park, *Wonders*, 94.

4. Robert Greene, *Friar Bacon and Friar Bungay*, ed. Daniel Seltzer (Lincoln: University of Nebraska Press, 1963), xii–xiii.

5. Ibid., xi, ll. 14–19; Seltzer, 73. On Greene's demonization of manual labor and technology, see Todd Andrew Borlik, "'More Than Art': Clockwork Automata, the Extemporizing Actor, and the Brazen Head in *Friar Bacon and Friar Bungay*," in *The Automaton in English Renaissance Literature*, ed. Wendy Hyman (Farnham: Ashgate, 2011), 129–44.

6. Greene, *Friar Bacon and Friar Bungay*, ii, ll. 6–8.

7. Ibid., xi, ll. 53, 63, 73. LaGrandeur notes that the story of the brass head conveys the point that "people should attend carefully to the duties of their own station . . . , Much of what the head signifies is the improper devolution of power to servants or agents that results when desire prompts a person to neglect the duties of his station in life. Bacon's android . . . is designed to lecture on philosophy, something that is a primary duty of his own." LaGrandeur, *Androids and Intelligent Networks*, 96.

8. Truitt, "Celestial Divination and Arabic Science in Twelfth-Century England," 201–22.

9. See also Kevin LaGrandeur, "The Talking Brass Head as a Symbol of Dangerous Knowledge in *Friar Bacon* and in *Alphonsus, King of Aragon*," *English Studies* 5 (1999): 408–22; and Sarah Lynn Higley, "The Legend of the Learned Man's Android," in *Retelling Tales: Essays in Honor of Russell Peck*, ed. Thomas Hahn and Alan Lupack (Rochester, N.Y.: Brewer, 1997), 127–60.

10. "Fudisse sibi statuae caput certa inspectione siderum, cum uidelicet omnes planetae exordia cursus sui meditarentur, quod non nisi interrogatum loqueretur, sed uerum uel affirmatiue uel negatiue pronuntiaret," William of Malmesbury, *De gestis regum Anglorum libri quinque*, 2.172, 1: 292–94 (henceforth *GRA*). Translation mine.

11. Benno, a German, was the cardinal of Osnabruck; Beno, an Italian, was a cardinal-priest of the Church of SS. Marino and Silvestro in Rome. See Pierre Riché, *Gerbert d'Aurillac: Le pape de l'an mil* (Paris: Fayard, 1987), 10; I. S. Robinson, *Authority and Resistance in the Investiture Contest: The Polemical Literature of the Late Eleventh Century* (New York: Holmes and Meier, 1978), 45; Anna Marie Flusche, *The Life and Legend of Gerbert of Aurillac: The Organ-Builder Who Became Pope Sylvester II* (Lampeter: Edwin Mellen, 2005), 82, n. 17.

12. Robinson, *Authority and Resistance*, 156–78.

13. "Erroris doctrinis demoniorum quas accepit Hildebrandus magister eorum a magistris suis . . . ," Beno, *Benonis aliorumque cardialium schismaticorum contra Gregorium VII et Urbanum II*, 2.3, *MGH, Libelli de lite imperatorum et pontificum saeculi XI*, ed. K. Francke (Hanover: Hahn, 1892), 376.

14. Johann Joseph Döllinger, *Die Pabst-fabeln des Mittelalters* (Munich: Cotta, 1863), 151–59. It is possible that the accusations against Gerbert and Hildebrand were part of a longer rhetorical tradition that began in the seventh century. See Edward Peters, *The Magician, the Witch, and the Law* (Philadelphia: University of Pennsylvania Press, 1978), 28.

15. "His maleficiis Gerbertus ille," Beno, *Contra Gregorium VII et Urbanum II* 2.4, 377.

16. "Hic responsum a suo demone acceperat se non moriturum, nisi prius in Ierusalem missa ab eo celebrata. Hac ambage, hac nominis equivocatione delusus, dum civitatem Ierusalem sibi predictam credit, Romae in aecclesia, quae vocatur Ierusalem, missam faciens in die stacionis, ibidem miserabili et horrida morte preventus, inter ipsas mortis angustias supplicat manus et linguam sibi abscidi, per quas sacrificando demonibus Deum inhonoravit," Beno, *Contra Gregorium VII et Urbanum II* 2.4, 377. Massimo Oldoni makes the interesting point that Gerbert is always known by his secular name, Gerbert, rather than his papal name, Sylvester, suggesting that his wickedness is somehow intrinsic to his nature. See Oldoni, "Gerberto e la sua storia," I, *Studi Medievali* 18 (1977): 629–704, 670.

17. Richer, *Historiarum Libri Quatuor MGH SS. Rer. Ger.*, 3.43, ed. G. Waitz (Hanover: Hahn, 1877), 192; François Picavet, *Gerbert: Un pape philosophe, d'après la légende* (Paris: Leroux, 1897), 27–37; Riché, *Gerbert d'Aurillac*, 21, 279.

18. "Apud quem etiam in mathesi plurimum et efficaciter studuit." Also, "atque Hattoni . . . [sic] episcopo instruendum commisit. Richer, *Historiarum* 3.43, 100. See Rudolf Beer, "Die Handschriften des Klosters Santa Maria de Ripoll," *Sitzungsberichte der Akademie der Wissenschaften, Philosophisch-historische Klasse* 155 (1908), Abhandlung III.

19. Philippe Sénac, "Note sur les relations diplomatiques entre les comtes de Barcelone et le califat de Cordoue au Xe siècle," *Histoire et archéologie des terres catalanes au Moyen Âge*, ed. Philippe Sénac, Centre de recherche sur les problèmes de la frontière (Perpignan: Presses Unitaires de Perpignan, 1995), 87–101; Marco Zuccato, "Gerbert of Aurillac and a Tenth-Century Jewish Channel for the Transmission of Arabic Science to the West," *Speculum* 80 (2005): 742–63, esp. 752–55; David Juste, *Les Alchandreana primitifs: Études sur les plus anciens traits astrologiques latins d'origine arabe, Xᵉ siècle* (Leiden: Brill, 2007), 234–35. The concept of the "trading zone" in scientific and intellectual culture comes from Peter Galison, *Image and Logic: A Material Culture of Microphysics* (Chicago: University of Chicago Press, 1997).

20. See Picavet, *Gerbert*, 30; Duc de la Salle de Rochemaure, *Gerbert. Silvestre II. Le savant, le "faiseur de rois," le pontife* (Paris: Émile-Paul Frères, 1914), 53; Miquel dels Sants Gros i Pujol, "La vila de Vic i el monestir de Ripoll en els anys 967–970," in *Actes del Congrés internacional Gerbert d'Orlhac i el seu temps: Catalunya i Europa a la fi del 1r milleni. Vic-Ripoll, 10–13 de novembre de 1999* (Vic: Eumo, 1999), 747–61; Juste, *Alchandreana*, 235. The earliest Arabic manuscripts at the library at Santa Maria de Ripoll are from the very early eleventh century, thus, a few decades after Gerbert's time there.

21. "Indicavit illuc hujusmodi advenisse juvenem, qui mathesim optime nosset, suosque strenue docere valeret," Richer, *Historiarum* 3.44, 192–93.

22. "Et quia musica et astronomia in Italia tunc penitus ignorabantur," Richer, *Historiarum*, 3.44, 100. See Oscar Darlington, "Gerbert, the Teacher," *AHR* 52 (1947): 456–76, 461.

23. Although he apparently used the abacus wrongly, his name became associated with it, as the words "gerbercist" and "abacist" were used interchangeably in the eleventh and twelfth centuries. Flusche, *The Life and Legend of Gerbert of Aurillac*, 24.

24. He explained the principles of making a sphere in a treatise to pupil Constantin, dated between 972 and 982. This is sometimes included as a letter, and sometimes as a larger work, entitled "Sphera, mi frater." See *Gerbert d'Aurillac: Correspondance*, ed. Pierre Riché and J. P. Callu, 2 vols. (Paris: Belles Lettres, 1993), 2: 680–86. On the four types of spheres, see Richer, *Historiarum*, 3.50, 195: "Sperae solidae compositio"; 3.51, 196: "Intellectilium circulorum comprehensio"; 3.52, 197: "Sperae compositio planetis cognoscendis aptissima"; 3.53, 197: "Aliae sperae compositio signis cognoscendis idonea." See also Richer, *Historiarum* 3.50–3.54, 102–4; Darlington, "Gerbert, the Teacher," 467. Gerbert's armillary sphere may have been the first in northern Europe; see Zuccato, "Gerbert of Aurillac," 758–59; Uta Lindgren, *Gerbert von Aurillac und das Quadrivium: Untersuchungen zur Bildung im Zeitalter der Ottonen*, Sudhoffs Archiv 18 (Weisbaden: Steiner, 1976), 28–32; Emmanuel Poulle, "L'astronomie de Gerbert," in *Gerberto: Scienza, storia e mito, Atti del Gerberti Symposium, Bobbio 25–27 Iuglio 1983. Archivium Bobiense II*, ed. M. Tosi (Piacenza: Archivi Storici Bobiense, 1985), 597–617.

25. In 984, Gerbert wrote to Miró Bonfill, bishop of Gerone, for a copy of *De multiplicatione et divisione numerorum*, which had been edited by Joseph the Wise (also known as Joseph of Spain), and which may have been a treatise on the abacus. Gerbert, *Lettres de Gerbert*, ed. Julien Havet, Librairie des Archives Nationales et de la Société de l'École des Chartres (Paris, 1889), letter 24. See also Zuccato, "Gerbert of Aurillac," 754–55. In late 988 or early 989, Gerbert wrote to the monk Remi about a difficult treatise on spheres; see ep. 148 in *Gerbert d'Aurillac: Correspondance*, 2: 362. See also Richer, 3.50–3.54, cited above; Darlington, "Gerbert, the Teacher," 467. On Gerbert's other astronomical texts, see Charles Burnett, "King Ptolemy and Alchandreus the Philosopher: The Earliest Texts on the Astrolabe and Arabic Astrology at Fleury, Micy and Chartres," *Annals of Science* 55 (1998): 329–68; Zuccato, "Gerbert of Aurillac," 743; Jean-Patrice Boudet, *Entre science et nigromance: Astrologie, divination et magie dans l'Occident médiéval (XIIe–XVe siècle)* (Paris: Publications de la Sorbonne, 2006), 51.

26. Havet, letter 153. William of Malmesbury mentions several kinds of instruments, including the *orologium* and a steam-powered organ. *GRA*, 2.168.

27. C. Stephen Jaeger, *The Envy of Angels: Cathedral Schools and Social Ideas in Medieval Europe, 950–1200* (Philadelphia: University of Pennsylvania Press, 2000), 47–48.

28. Gerbert spent much time discussing philosophy and mathematics with the emperor, and recalls this time in the preface of his book *De rationali et ratione uti*, PL 139, col. 158–68. Quoted in French in Riché, *Gerbert d'Aurillac*, 182–83.

29. "Optime callebat astrorum cursus discernere et contemporales suos variae artis noticia superare . . . .Et cum eo diu conversatus in Magadaburg orologium fecit, illud recte constituens, considerata per fistulam quadam stella nautarum duce," Thietmar of Merseburg, *Thietmari Merseburgensis Episcopi Chronicon*, 7.40, ed. F. Kurze (Hanover: Hahn, 1889), 191. For a brief biography of Thietmar, see David A. Warner, *Ottonian Germany: The Chronicon of Thietmar of Merseburg* (Manchester: Manchester University Press, 2001), 49–63.

30. See Gerbert, *Correspondance*, 2: 682–84. Richer also describes this apparatus; see Richer 3.50, 3.53. See Poulle, "L'astronomie de Gerbert," 599 . Poulle is of the opinion that Thietmar was referring to a nocturlabe, or *horologium noctis*, while other sources say the instrument may have been a sundial or an astrolabe. See Silvio A. Bedini, "Sylvester II, Pope," *Dictionary of the Middle Ages*, ed. Joseph Strayer, 12 vols. (New York: Scribner, 1982–89), 11: 553. However, this debate is in turn influenced by the mixed scholarly opinion of Gerbert's use of the astrolabe. For a detailed account of the historiography surrounding this instrument, see Patrick Gautier Dalché, "Le 'Tuyau' de Gerbert, ou la légende savante de l'astronome: origines, thèmes, échos contemporains (avec un appendice critique), *Micrologus* 21 (2013): 243–76.

31. On the relationship between Emperor Otto III and Pope Sylvester II, see Gerd Althoff, *Otto III*, trans. Phyllis G. Jestice (University Park: Pennsylvania State University Press, 2003), 65–89.

32. Riché, *Gerbert d'Aurillac*, 232.

33. See Olivier Guyotjeannin and Emmanuel Poulle, *Autour de Gerbert d'Aurillac, le Pape de l'an mil*, École des Chartres (Paris: Champion, 1996), 337; Oldoni, "Gerberto e la sua storia, I," 666–67 citing Sergius IV; Helgaud of Fleury, *Vie de Robert le Pieux*, ed. Robert-Henri Bautier (Paris: CNRS, 1965), 60: "Is quippe Girbertus, pro maximo sue sapiente merito que toto radiabat in mundo . . . .multa in eo virtutum operatus est insignia et precipue in elemosyna sancta, quam fortiter tenuit, dum fideliter vixit." According to William of Malmesbury, Robert the Pious was a student of Gerbert's. *GRA*, 2.168, 1: 284. Certainly Gerbert had been instrumental in elevating Hugh Capet to king, thus effectively ending the Carolingian rulership of the Franks.

34. R. W. Southern, *The Making of the Middle Ages* (New Haven, Conn.: Yale University Press, 1953), 201.

35. The most complete introductions to William of Malmesbury as an historian are as follows: William Stubbs's introductions to both volumes of William of Malmesbury, *Gesta regum anglorum*, ed. Stubbs (Wiesbaden: Kraus, 1964); D. H. Farmer, "William of Malmesbury's Life and Works," *Journal of Ecclesiastical History* 13 (1962): 39–54; Antonia Gransden, *Historical Writing in England c. 550 to c. 1307* (Ithaca, N.Y.: Cornell University Press, 1974), 166–89; Rodney M. Thomson, *William of Malmesbury* (Woodbridge: Boydell, 2003), 3–39.

36. *GRA*, 2.167–72, 1: 278–94.

37. "Qui et Gerbertus dictus est, non absurdum erit, ut opinor, si litteris mandemus quae per omnium ora uolitant," *GRA*, 2.167, 1: 278–80. On the importance of oral culture

in clerical writing and historiography in medieval England, see Rachel Koopmans, *Wonderful to Relate: Miracle Stories and Miracle Collecting in High Medieval England* (Philadelphia: University of Pennsylvania Press, 2011), 9–46; Catherine Cubitt, "Folklore and Historiography: Oral Stories and the Writing of Anglo-Saxon History," in *Narrative and History in the Early Medieval West*, ed. Elizabeth M. Tyler and Ross Balzaretti (Turnhout: Brepols, 2006): 189–223.

38. "Apud quem etiam in mathesi plurimum et efficaciter studuit," Richer, *Historiarum*, 3.43, 100. Again, "mathesis" can mean astral science, mathematics, or divination. Cf. "Gerbertus vero natione Aquitanus monacus . . . , causa sophiae primo Franciam, deinde Cordobam lustrans . . . ," Adhémar of Chabannes, *Historiarum libre tres*, PL 141, cols. 19–80, at col. 49. After 1002, al-Andalus splintered into a number of local lordships called *taifas*, no longer under the political control of a single leader.

39. "Seu tedio monachatus seu gloriae cupiditate captus, nocte profugit Hispaniam, animo precipue intendens ut astrologiam et ceteras id genus artes a Saracenis edisceret," *GRA*, 2.167, 1: 280. Jules Chavanon, an editor of Adhémar's texts, noted that Adhémar is the only contemporary of Gerbert's who reported that he studied in Córdoba. See *Adémar de Chabannes: Chronique*, ed. Jules Chavanon (Paris: Picard, 1897), 154 n. 2. However, Adhémar's testimony has been repeated numerous times, well into the twentieth century. See, for example, E. M. Butler, *The Myth of the Magus* (Cambridge: Cambridge University Press, 1948), 95; Higley, "The Legend of the Learned Man's Android," 138; LaGrandeur, "The Talking Brass Head," 412–13. Yet most scholars agree this is a complete fabrication. Picavet, *Gerbert*, 34–37; Rochemaure, *Gerbert*, 55; Flusche, *The Life and Legend of Gerbert of Aurillac*, 115.

40. "Sibiliam uulgariter uocant, caput regni habent, diuinationibus et incantationibus more gentis familiari studentes," *GRA*, 2.167, 1: 280. By the time William wrote his account of the events of Gerbert's life, both Seville and Córdoba were part of the Almoravid dynasty, based in Marrakech.

41. "Ibi uicis scientia Pthlomeum in astrolabio, Alhandreum in astrorum interstitio, Iulium Firmicum in fato. Ibi quid cantus et uolatus auium portendat didicit, ibi excire tenues ex inferno figuras, ibi postremo quicquid uel noxium uel salubre curiositas humana deprehendit; nam de licitis artibus, arithmetica musica et astronomia et geometria, nichil attinet dicere, quas ita ebibit ut inferiores ingenio suo ostenderet, et magna industria reuocaret in Galliam omnio ibi iam pridem obsoletas. Abacum certe primas a Saracenis rapiens, regulas dedit quae a sudantibus abacistis uix intelliguntur," *GRA*, 2.167, 1: 280.

42. Juste, *Alchandreana*, 9, 24. William's account strikingly echoes the contents of a manuscript from the mid-eleventh century, MS Munich, BSB, Clm 560. Juste, *Alchandreana*, 254, 340–41.

43. Professor Charles Burnett asserts that William is the earliest writer to credit Gerbert with importing Islamic science. Cited as a personal communication in Mynors, Thomson, and Winterbottom, *GRA*, 2: 151. See also Truitt, "Celestial Divination and Arabic Science."

44. Hugh of Flavigny, *Chronicon, PL* 154: 196 "quibusdam praestgiis." Patrick Healy, *The Chronicle of Hugh of Flavigny: Reform and the Investiture Contest in the Late Eleventh Century* (Aldershot: Ashgate, 2006), 76–101, 228–41.

45. For William's familiarity with Sigebert's *Chronologium*, see Thomson, *William of Malmesbury*, 123–24. For William's sources more generally, see Monika Otter, *Inventiones: Fiction and Referentiality in Twelfth-Century Historical Writing* (Chapel Hill: University of North Carolina Press), 96–102; Stubbs, vol. 2, preface, in William of Malmesbury, *Gesta regum anglorum*; Thomson, *William of Malmesbury*, 40–75, 119–36.

46. On Sigebert's life, writing, and part in the Investiture Contest, see Mireille Chazan, *L'empire et l'histoire universelle de Sigebert de Gembloux à Jean de Saint-Victor* (Paris: Champion, 1999), 33–59, 80–92, 253–310; Jutta Beumann, *Sigebert von Gembloux und der Traktat de investitura episcoporum* (Sigmaringen: Jan Thorbecke, 1976), 7–14.

47. "A.D. 995: Gerbertus qui et Silvester . . . qui et ipse inter scientia litterarum claros egregie claruit . . . is enim Silvester non per ostium intrasse dicitur;—quippe qui a quibusdam etiam nichromantiae arguitur; de morte quoque ejus non recte tractatur; a diabolo enim percussus dicitur obisse, quam rem nos in medio relinquimus;—a numero paparum exclusus videtur," Sigebert of Gembloux, *Chronologium, PL* 160, cols. 196–97. Orderic Vitalis, whom William also probably met, repeated the same story in muted terms; see William of Malmesbury, *Gesta regum anglorum*, ed. Mynors, Thomson, and Winterbottom, 2: 150–51; Stubbs, 2: lxix.

48. "Vnus erat codex totius artis," *GRA* 2.167, 1: 280.

49. "Cum qua assiduitas familiaritatem parauerat,"*GRA*, 2.167, 1: 282.

50. "Ibi per incantationes diabolo accersito, perpetuum paciscitur hominium si se ab illo qui denuo insequebatur defensatum ultra pelagus eueheret. Et factum est," *GRA*, 2.168, 1: 282.

51. "Sed haec uulgariter ficta crediderit aliquis, quod soleat populus litteratorum famam ledere," *GRA*, 2.167, 1: 282.

52. "Michi uero fidem facit de istius sacrilegio inaudita mortis excogitatio. Cur enim se moriens, ut postea dicemus, excarnificaret ipse sui corporis horrendus lanista, nisi noui sceleris conscius esset?" *GRA*, 2.167, 1: 282.

53. "Extant apud illam aecclesiam doctrinae ipsius documenta, horologium arte mechanica compositum, organa hidraulica ubi mirum in modum per aquae calefactae uiolentiam uentus emergens implet concauitatem barbiti, et per multiforatiles tractus aerae fistulae modulatos clamores emittunt," *GRA* 2.169, 1: 284. As noted above, Gerbert did build an *orologium* while in Magdeburg at the court of Otto III, but this is the first account of his construction of musical organs, and it appears to be groundless. Musical organs were not unknown in Europe at this time; indeed, representatives from the Byzantine court of Constantine V sent one to Pepin the Short in 757. See Chapter 1, n. 55.

54. "Quod superioris aeui homines ita intelligendum rati quasi ibi thesaurum inuenierent, multis securium ictibus innocentem statuam laniuerant," *GRA*, 2.169, 1: 284.

55. It is possible that William here made a connection to Gerbert's construction of an *orologium* (which can refer to a sundial), and that the outstretched arm and pointing finger of the statue were recognizable to Gerbert as a kind of gnomon.

56. "Ibi terra solitis artibus dehiscens latum ingredientibus patefecit introitum," *GRA*, 2.169, 1: 284.

57. "Conspicantur ingentem regiam, aureos parietes, aurea lacunaria, aurea omnia; milites aureos aureis tesseris quasi animum oblectantes; regem metallicum cum regina discumbentes, apposita obsonia, astantes ministros, pateras multi ponderis et pretii, ubi naturam uincebat opus." *GRA*, 2.169, 1: 286.

58. "Continuo enim ut quis manum ad contingendum aptaret, uidebantur omnes illae imagines prosilire et impetum in presumptorem facere," *GRA*, 2.169, 1: 286.

59. "Verum mox omnibus imaginibus cum fremitu exsurgentibus, puer quoque emissa harundine in carbunculum tenebras induxit, et nisi ille monitu domini cultellum reciere accelerasset, graues ambo penas dedissent," *GRA*, 2.169, 1:286.

60. "Sic insatiata cupiditatis uoragine laterna gressus ducente dicessum." *GRA*, 2.169, 1: 286.

61. "Talia illum aduersis prestigiis machinatum fuisse constans uulgi est opinio." *GRA*, 2.169, 1: 286. "Prestigiis," the word William uses, is the same as "praestigiis," used by Hugh of Flavigny, see n. 44 above. See also David Rollo, *Glamorous Sorcery: Magic and Literacy in the High Middle Ages* (Minneapolis: University of Minnesota Press, 2000), 1–31.

62. "Haec Aquitanici uerba ideo inserui, ne cui mirum uideatur quod de Gerberto fama dispersit," *GRA*, 2.172, 1: 292.

63. "Visebantur mirae magnitudinis equi aurei cum assessoribus aeque aureis, et cetera quae de Gerberto dicta sunt," *GRA*, 2.170, 1: 288; "producens rusticum aereum cum aereo malleo," *GRA*, 2.170, 1: 290.

64. See n. 10, above.

65. "Ille insaniens et pro dolore ratione hebetata minutatim se dilaniari et membratim foras proici iussit, 'Habeat,' inquiens 'membrorum offitium qui eorum quesiuit hominium; namque animus meus numquam illud admauit sacramentum, immo sacrilegium," *GRA*, 2.172, 1: 294. Stubbs argued that William seems to have confused Gerbert with one of his predecessors, John XVI, who was in fact mutilated by his rival's supporters. Stubbs goes on to say that this "fatal mistake" of William's is "the most unfortunate blunder in the whole of the works of William of Malmesbury." See Stubbs, 1: li; 2: lxxiii–iv. Rollo argues that William did not make a mistake, but rather that he intended this as a challenge to his reader, for his plea for dismemberment stems from Gerbert's fear of eternal damnation. Thus, if William knew this was false, then "there is no reason to presume [Gerbert] ever traded his soul to the devil." See Rollo, *Glamorous Sorcery*, 11–12. Yet Rollo does not take into account William's mention of Gerbert summoning the devil to protect him from his angry Saracen teacher; and neither Stubbs nor Rollo account for Beno's and Sigebert's mentions of Gerbert's pact with the devil and his violent death.

66. Mary Carruthers, *The Book of Memory: A Study of Memory in Medieval Culture*, 2nd ed. (Cambridge: Cambridge University Press, 2008), 328; Camille, *The Gothic Idol*, 253–54; Laura Alidori, "Il Plut. 20.56 della Laurenziana. Appunti sull'iconografia dei manoscritti della *Genealogia* di Petrus Pictaviensis," *Rivista di Storia della Miniatura* 6–7 (2001–2002): 157–70, 167.

67. "Robert chapet qui puis fu rois de france et othes fils del empereour othe. Et le dit Robert qunt il fu rois desposa larcevesque de Rheims et i fist arcevesque Gerbert son mestre. Il i fist .i. orloge merveilleusment et orghes qui sonoient de la fume qui vient saillaint deaue chaude,"*Abrégé des histories divines*, New York, Morgan Library, M. 751, fol. 100r.

68. "Il volt par laide dou dyable et par nigromance," Ibid.

69. Camille, *The Gothic Idol*, 254.

70. See Wagner, *"Sorcier" et "Magicien"*, 133–41. See also Chapter 2.

71. For a more detailed account of how these terms were collapsed and interpenetrated, see Truitt, "*Trei poëte, sages dotors*," 176–79.

72. On foreknowledge and the limits of human understanding, see Daston and Park, *Wonders*, 127–28; Lois Sturlese, "Saints et magiciens: Albert le Grand en face d'Hermes Trismégiste," *Archives de Philosophie* 43 (1980): 615–41, 627–29; Paola Zambelli, "Scholastic and Humanist Views of Hermeticism and Witchcraft," in *Hermeticism and the Renaissance: Intellectual History and the Occult in Early Modern Europe*, ed. Ingrid Merkel and Allen G. Debus (Washington, D.C.: Folger Shakespeare Library, 1988), 125–35.

73. David Pingree, "Astrology," in *Religion, Learning, and Science in the 'Abbasid Period*, ed. M. J. L. Young, J. D. Latham, and R. B. Serjeant (Cambridge: Cambridge University Press, 1990), 290–300.

74. Bruce Eastwood, "Astronomy in Christian Latin Europe, c. 500–c. 1150," *Journal for the History of Astronomy* 28 (1997): 235–58; Riché, *Gerbert d'Aurillac*, 35–56, 80–82; Riché, "Fulbert de Chartres et son école," in *Le temps de Fulbert: Actes de l'Université d'été du 8 au 10 juillet 1996* (Chartres: Société archéologique d'Eure-et-Loire, 1996), 27–32; Juste, *Alchandreana*, 24–25.

75. Juste, *Alchandreana*, 18; Eastwood, "The Astronomies of Pliny, Martianus Capella, and Isidore of Seville in the Carolingian World," in *Science in Western and Eastern Civilization in Carolingian Times*, ed. P. L. Butzer and D. Lohrmann (Basel: Verlag AG, 1993), 161–80. For the opposite view, see Valerie Flint, *The Rise of Magic in Early Medieval Europe* (Princeton, N.J.: Princeton University Press, 1991); Tamsyn Barton, *Ancient Astrology* (London: Routledge, 1994).

76. Gerbert wrote to Rainaud of Bobbio in 988 for a copy of Manilius's *De astrologia*, and around the year 1000 an English monk, Leofnoth, transcribed the first four books of Firmicus at Fleury. Havet, ep. 130; Juste, *Alchandreana*, 20–24.

77. This concept is brilliantly illustrated in the opening episode of the second season of "Game of Thrones" titled "The North Remembers" (2012).

78. Stephen C. McCluskey, *Astronomies and Cultures in Early Medieval Europe* (Cambridge: Cambridge University Press, 1997), 145–49; *Anglo-Saxon Chronicle*, trans. and ed. M. J. Swanton (New York: Routledge, 1998), ann. 1, 664, 678, 729, 800, et passim.

79. David Lindberg, "The Transmission of Greek and Arabic Learning to the West," in *Science in the Middle Ages*, ed. David C. Lindberg (Chicago: University of Chicago Press, 1980), 62–67; Thorndike, *The History of Magic and Experimental Science*, 2: 14–59; 2: 66–98; et passim.

80. Charles Burnett, *The Introduction of Arabic Learning into England* (London: British Library, 1997), 38–39; Ellen McCaffery, *Astrology: Its History and Influence in the Western World* (New York: Scribner's, 1942), 192–93.

81. Walcher, *De experientia scriptoris*, Oxford University, Bodleian Library, MS Auct. F. I. 9, fols. 86r–99r, partially edited in Charles Homer Haskins, "The Reception of Arabic Science in England," *English Historical Review* 30 (1915): 56–69, 57; McCluskey, *Astronomies and Cultures in Early Medieval Europe*, 180–84.

82. See Charles Burnett, "Adelard, Music, and the Quadrivium," in Burnett, ed., *Adelard of Bath: An English Scientist and Arabist of the Early Twelfth Century* (London: Warburg, 1987), 69–86; Burnett, "Adelard, Ergaphalau, and the Science of the Stars," in same, 133–45; Marie-Thérèse Alverny, *La transmission des textes philosophiques et scientifiques au moyen age* (Aldershot: Variorum, 1994); Louise Cochrane, *Adelard of Bath: The first English Scientist* (London: British Museum, 1994), esp. 62–108; Charles Haskins, *Studies in the History of Medieval Science* (Cambridge, Mass.: Harvard University Press, 1924), 20–33; Raymond Mercier, "Astronomical Tables in the Twelfth Century," in Burnett, ed. *Adelard of Bath*, 87–118; Emmanuel Poulle, "Le Traité de l'astrolabe d'Adélard de Bath," in ibid., 119–32.

83. Lindberg, "The Transmission of Greek and Arabic Learning to the West," in Lindberg, ed. *Science in the Middle Ages*, 63–64; Olaf Pedersen, "Astronomy," in ibid., 313.

84. See Burnett, *Introduction of Arabic Learning into England*, 58 n. 116; Sophie Page, *Astrology in Medieval Manuscripts* (London: British Library, 2002), 11.

85. McCluskey, *Astronomies and Cultures*, 32–33, 38–40; Juste, *Alchandreana*, 16–17.

86. Augustine, *De doctrina Christiana*, ed. and trans. R. P. H. Green (Oxford: Clarendon, 1995), 2.20.30–32, 90–93. I have used this edition (hereafter *Doctr. Chr.*) for both the Latin text and the English translation.

87. "Quare istae quoque opinionis quibusdam rerum signis humana praesumptione institutis ad eadem illa quasi quaedam cum daemonibus pacta et conventa referendae sunt," Augustine, *Doctr. Chr.*, 2.22.33–34, 94–97.

88. "Neque illi ab hoc genere perniciosae superstitionis segregandi sunt qui genethliaci propter natalium dierum considerationes, nunc autem vulgo mathematici vocantur," Augustine, *Doctr. Chr.*, 2.22.32, 92–93.

89. *Novum glossarium mediae Latinitatis*, ed. Blatt et al., s.v. "mathesis." Cf. Richer, *Historiarum*, 3.43, 192.

90. "Vix ignobilem cespitem cadaueri pras foribus inici passi," William of Malmesbury, *Gesta pontificum anglorum*, 3.118, ed. and trans. Michael Winterbottom and Rodney M. Thomson, 2 vols. (Oxford: Clarendon, 2007), 1: 394. Gerard of Hereford, before he became archbishop of York, was part of a community of scholars in the West Country that also included Walcher of Lotharingia. See Charles Burnett, "Mathematics and Astronomy in Hereford and Its Region in the Twelfth Century," in *Hereford: Medieval Art, Architecture, and Archaeology*, ed. David Whitehead, British Archaeological Association Conference Transactions (Leeds: Maney, 1995): 50–59, 50, n. 1; Roger French, "Foretelling the Future: Arabic Astrology and English Medicine in the Late Twelfth Century," *Isis* 87 (1996): 453–80, 458.

91. McCaffery, *Astrology*, 188.

92. "Fallunt autem interdum studio fallendi, interdum cecitatis suae errore decepti; id tamen agunt assidue ut futurorum conscii per omnia uideantur. Inde est quid ambiguitate uerborum obnubilare student oracula ut, cum mendaces aut fallaces inuenti fuerint, aliquo rationis uelamento suam queant tueri fallaciam," John of Salisbury, *Policraticus*, 1: 144.

93. John of Salisbury, ep. 301, ann. 1170: "Nec dixeritis quae prouenerunt uobis non fuisse praedicta, sed potius quod, onmium auspicantium more, subtilitatem uestram uaticinia, quae non erant a Spiritu, deluserunt. Vtinam non sit deceptionis huius morbus irreparabilis . . . .Vaticiniis ergo reuntiemus in posterum, quia nos in hac parte grauius infortunia perculerunt," in *The Letters of John of Salisbury*, ed. W. J. Millor and C. N. L. Brooke, trans. Brooke, 2 vols. (Oxford: Clarendon, 1979), 2: 708–11.

94. "Ad tantam denique quidam peruenere uesaniam, ut ex diuersis stellarum positionibus dicant imaginem ab homine posse formari, quae si per interualla temporum et quadam ratione proportionum in constellatione seruata formetur, stellarum nutu recipiet spiritum uitae, et consulentibus occultae ueritatis manifestabit archana," John of Salisbury, *Policraticus*, 2.19, ed. Webb, 1: 112.

95. J. D. North, "Medieval Concepts of Celestial Influence: A Survey," in *Astrology, Science and Society, Historical Essays*, ed. Patrick Curry (Woodbridge: Boydell, 1987), 5–18.

96. Raymond Mercier, "Studies in the Medieval Conception of Precession," in Mercier, *Studies on the Transmission of Medieval Mathematical Astronomy* (Aldershot: Ashgate, 2004), 197–220, 197.

97. Ibid., 199–209.

98. On the link between William and Walcher of Malvern, see Stubbs, 2: lxx. Thomson does not mention any scientific books in his account of the library at Malmesbury, or in William's reading, leading me to believe William must have become familiar with these scientific texts (or at least with their existence) through Walcher. See Thomson, *William of Malmesbury*, 202–14.

99. See Dickson, *Valentine and Orson*, 207; Riché, *Gerbert d'Aurillac*, 10–12; Thorndike, *History of Magic and Experimental Science*, 1: 697. On *curiositas* see also Oldoni, " 'A fantasia dictiur fantasma,' " 167–245. Oldoni argues that this legend illustrates twelfth-century *mentalité*. Gerbert, the millennial pope, symbolizes the shift toward *curiositas* as the major ethical problem from the end of the tenth century.

100. See Southern, *Medieval Humanism and Other Studies* (Oxford: Blackwell, 1970), 168–71; Southern, *Robert Grosseteste: The Growth of an English Mind in Medieval Europe* (Oxford: Clarendon, 1986), 103–7. On Robert Grosseteste's biography, see James McEvoy, *Robert Grosseteste* (Oxford: Oxford University Press, 2000), 19–30; Southern, *Robert Grosseteste*, 63–82; Thorndike, *History of Magic*, 2: 436–53.

101. "Astronomiae ministerio plus ceteris eget philosophia naturalis: nulla enim aut rara est operatio, quae naturae sit et nostra, utpote vegetabilium plantatio, mineralium transmutatio, aegritudinum curatio, quae possit ab astronomiae officio excusari," Robert Grosseteste, *De artibus liberalibus*, in Ludwig Baur, *Die philosophischen Werke des Robert Grosseteste, Bischofs von Lincoln*, BGPM (Munster: Aschendorff, 1912), 1–7, 5.

102. Grosseteste, *De impressionibus aeris seu de prognosticatione*, in Baur, 42–51. Grosseteste noted that the planets' houses of exaltation are as follows: Sun in Aries, Moon in Taurus, Saturn in Libra, Jupiter in Cancer, Mars in Capricorn, Venus in Pisces, and Mercury in Virgo, 43. MS Savile 21, Oxford University, Bodleian Library, fol. 158.

103. On Gower, see Robert F. Yeager, *John Gower's Poetic: The Search for a New Arion* (Rochester, N.Y.: Brewer, 1990); John Fisher, *John Gower: Moral Philosopher and Friend of Chaucer* (New York: New York University Press, 1964).

104. John Gower, *Confessio Amantis*, 4, ll. 234–249, ed. G. C. Macaulay, 2 vols. EETS (London: Oxford University Press, 1969), 2: 307.

105. "Nota adhuc super eodem de quodam Astrologo," Gower, *Confessio Amantis*, ed. Macaulay, 2: 307. On the use of Latin summaries in the margins of different manuscripts, see Macaulay, 2: cxxxviii–clxv. Many but not all manuscripts include marginal Latin summaries.

106. I am grateful to Scott Lightsey for his reading of the Grosseteste passage in the *Confessio Amantis*, personal communication with the author.

107. "Frater Henricus Tanet Hibernus dicit . . . .Item deponit, quod quidam Templarius habebat quoddam caput aeneum bifrons in custodia, et dicebat, quod illud respondebat ad omnia interrogata," D. Wilkins, *Concilia Magnae Britanniae et Hiberniae*, 2 vols. (London, 1737), *Acta contra Templaros in regnis Angliae, Scotiae, et Hiberniae*, 2: 329–92, 358. The accusations of sorcery against the Templars are a well-known example of sorcery as political denunciation. See W. R. Jones, "The Political Uses of Sorcery in Medieval Europe," *The Historian* 34 (1972): 670–87.

108. Henry Knighton, *Chronicon Henrici Knighton*, ed. J. R. Lumby, RS 92, 2: 257.

109. "In praecedenti quadragesima factum est quoddam caput de cera opere nigromantico ut dicebatur . . . .Ista sunt verba: Primo, caput decidetur. Secundo, caput elevabitur. Tertio, pedes elevabuntur super caput," *Chronicon Henrici Knighton*, 2: 258.

110. On Gower's use of Grosseteste in the *Confessio Amantis* 4, ll. 234–243, see George G. Fox, *The Medieval Sciences in the Works of John Gower* (Princeton, N.J.: Princeton University Press, 1931), 154–55.

111. As with Gerbert, tales of Grosseteste's brazen head did not end with Gower. Richard of Bardney, a monk, writing in 1503, in his *Vita Roberti Grosthead Episcopi Lincolniensis*, says that Grosseteste made a head "tempore Saturni loquitur Saturnia proles." It broke during an accident, and is apparently preserved in the vault at Lincoln, although I have not seen it. See Henry Wharton, *Anglia Sacra* (London, 1691), 333.

112. Daston and Park, *Wonders*, 117–18.

113. See the account by Jacob van Maerlant (ca. 1235–1300), a Flemish poet, in *Merlin's Book* (*Boec van Merlant*). It contains a description of a meeting between count William II of Holland and Albertus Magnus in 1249, and attributes to Albertus a magical garden. Cited in Fritz van Oostrom, *Maerlants Wereld* (Amsterdam: Prometheus, 1996), 184–85. On Albertus's reputation for omniscience in natural philosophy see also Agostino Paravincini-Bagliani, "La légende médiévale d'Albert le Grand (1270–1435): Prèmieres recherches," *Micrologus* 21 (2013): 295–368; D. J. Collins, "Albertus, 'Magnus' or Magus? Magic, natural

philosophy, and religious reform in the late Middle Ages," *Renaissance Quarterly* 63 (2010): 1–44.

114. Matteo Corsini, *Rosaio della Vita*, ed. Filippo Luigi Polidori (Florence: Societá Poligrafica Italiana, 1845), introduction. The list of manuscripts given in the Polidori edition is not exhaustive, and Polidori made only a good guess at the author, possibly a cleric. Four of the manuscripts in Florence, Riccardiano, MSS 656, 1159, 1735, 1736, are between moderately and very fine, with examples of rubrication and decorated initials, and decorated pages (esp. MSS Ricc. 656). MSS 1159, 1735, and 1736 appear to be commonplace books, with Corsini's text copied in alongside other short verses or texts. All are written in extremely legible and regular fifteenth-century humanistic script, suggesting that these books all belonged to educated men of at least moderate wealth.

115. "Troviamo che uno Alberto Magno, el quale fu de' Frati Predicatori, venne a tanta perfezione di senno, che per la sua grande sapienza fe' una statua di metallo a sì fatti corse di pianeti, e colsela sì di ragione, ch'ella favellava: e non fu per arte diabiolica nè per negromanzia; però che gli grandi intelletti non si dilettano di ciòe, perchè è cosa da perdere l'anima e'l corpo; che è vietata tale arte dalla fede di Cristo. Onde uno frate, chiamando frate Alberto alla sua cella, egli non essendogli, la statua rispose. Costui, credendo che fosse idolo di mala ragione, la guastò. Tornando frate Alberto, gli disse molto male, e disse che trenta anni ci avea durata fatica, e: Non imparai questa scienza nell'ordine de' frati. El frate dicea: Male ho fatto; perdonami; come! Non ne potrai fare un'altra? Rispose frate Alberto, di qui a trenta migliaia d'ani non se potrebbe fare un'altra per lui; però che quello pianeto ha fatto suo corso, e non ritornerà mai più per infine a detto tempo," Corsini, *Rosaio della Vita*, 12. Translated from the Italian by Katharine Park.

116. "Certa inspectione siderum," *GRA*, 2.172, 1: 292.

117. Bishop Alonso Tostado (1400?–1455) *Commentary on the Numbers*, cap. 21, qu. 19, cited in Dickson, *Valentine and Orson*, 214, n. 147. Dickson writes, "I have not been able to consult this, but rely on the accounts of R. de Yepes, *Historia de la muerte y martyrio del S. Innocente de la Guardia* (Madrid, 1583), fol. 60 ff."

118. Lynn White, Jr., *Medieval Technology and Social Change* (Oxford: Oxford University Press, 1962), 90–91. White also notes that Albertus was familiar with the writings of Vitruvius. See also Camille, *The Gothic Idol*, 245–46.

119. There has been some disagreement among scholars over the authorship of the *Speculum astronomiae*; however, most scholars now accept that this is a genuine work of Albertus Magnus. See Paola Zambelli, *The Speculum Astronomiae and Its Enigma: Astrology, Theology, and Science in Albertus Magnus and His Contemporaries* (Dordrecht: Kluwer, 1992). Nicolas Weill-Parot gives a concise account of the arguments both for and against Albertus as the author of the *Speculum astronomiae*. See Weill-Parot, *Les "images astrologiques" au moyen âge et à la renaissance* (Paris: Champion, 2002), 78–80.

120. See North, "Medieval Concepts of Celestial Influence: A Survey," 5–18.

121. See, for example, Aristotle, *De generatione et corruptione*, 2.10; *De meteorologica*, 1.4–8. Al-Kindi was influenced by these Aristotelian ideas and engaged with them in *De*

radiis (ninth century); his text was also influential on later Latin scholars. See Alverny and Hudry, "Al-Kindi, *De Radiis*," cited in Chapter 1.

122. See Copenhaver, "Natural Magic, Hermetism, and Occultism in Early Modern Science," 261–301, esp. 273–77.

123. Pedersen, "Astronomy," 304.

124. Joan Cadden, "Charles V, Nicole Oresme, and Christine de Pizan: Unities and Uses of Knowledge in Fourteenth-Century France," in *Texts and Contexts in Ancient and Medieval Science: Studies on the Occasion of John E. Murdoch's Seventieth Birthday*, ed. Sylla and McVaugh, 208–44.

125. Lucy Freeman Sandler, *Omne Bonum: A Fourteenth-Century Encyclopedia of Universal Knowledge* (London: Harvey Miller, 1996); Sophie Page, *Magic in Medieval Manuscripts* (London: British Library, 2002), 59–60.

CHAPTER 4. THE QUICK AND THE DEAD: CORPSES,
MEMORIAL STATUES, AND AUTOMATA

1. *Le Roman de Troie*, ll. 16503–16517, 3: 89. For the entire description of Hector's embalming and entombment see ll. 16503–16858, 3: 89–108.

2. "Firent trei sage engigneor / Un tabernacle precios, / Riche e estrange e merveillos," *Roman de Troie*, ll. 16650–16652, 3: 96–97.

3. *Roman de Troie*, ll. 16640–16659, 3: 96.

4. *Roman de Troie*, ll. 16665–16736, 3: 97–102. The stunning and complicated architecture of Hector's tomb here recalls Camille's tomb in *Éneas*.

5. "De la chaeire que direie? / Ja tant ne m'en porpensereie / Qu'ele fust ja par mei retraite / Quel ert ne coment estoit faite; / Mais l'emperere d'Alemaigne, / Al mien cuidier, e cil d'Espaigne, / Co vos puis dire senz mentir. / Ne la porreient tel bastir," *Roman de Troie*, ll. 16737–16744, 3: 102. On the trope of eulogizing or outdoing in medieval literature, see Ernst Robert Curtius, *European Literature and the Latin Middle Ages*, trans. Willard R. Trask, Bollingen Series 36 (Princeton, N.J.: Princeton University Press, 1953), 162.

6. "Li sages maistres e li dotors / Ont pris le cors, jo n'en sai plus; / Enz en la voute de desus / L'ont gentement posé e mis / E dedenz la chaeire asis. / Dous vaisseaus ont apareilliez / D'esmeraudes bien entaillez, / Toz pleins de basme e d'aloès; / Sor un bufet de gargantès / Les ont asis en tel endreit / Que ses dous piez dedenz teneit. / Del basme grant plentè i ot: / Jusqu'as chevilles i entrot. / Dui tuëleet d'or geteïz, / Merveilles bel e bien faitiz, / Desci qu'al nes li ataigneient / De dedenz les vaisseaus estient, / Si que la grant force e l'odor / De vert basme e de la licor / Li entroënt par mi le cors," *Roman de Troie*, ll. 16764–16783, 3: 103–4.

7. Sigmund Freud, "The Uncanny," in *The Uncanny*, trans. David McLintock (New York: Penguin, 2003), 121–98.

8. *Le Roman d'Alexandre*, ll. 3396–3400, 508.

9. See also *Le Roman d'Alexandre* (ca. 1180), in which the tomb of the emir of Babylon was guarded by two copper youths made by magicians. *Le Roman d'Alexandre*, ll. 7176–7182, 700.

10. E. R. Truitt, "Fictions of Life and Death: Tomb Automata in Medieval Romance," *postmedieval* 1 (2010): 194–98.

11. *Le Conte de Floire et Blancheflor*, ed. Jean-Luc Leclanche (Paris: Champion, 1980).

12. *Floire et Blancheflor*, ll. 543–642, 32–36.

13. "Li uns des deus Flore sanloit / plus que riens nule qui ja soit. L'autre ymage ert ensi mollee / comme Blanceflor ert formee," *Floire et Blancheflor*, ll. 568–569, 32.

14. "Quant li vens les enfans toucoit, / l'un baisoit l'autre et acoloit / si disoient par ingremance / trestout lor bon et lor enfance. / Ce dit Flores a Blancheflor: / 'Baisié moi, bele, par amour.' / Blancheflor respont en baisant: / 'Je vos aim plus que rien vivant.' / Tant con li vent les atoucoient, / et li enfant s'entrebaisoient. / Et quant il laissent le venter, / dont se reposent a parler," *Floire et Blancheflor*, ll. 589–600, 34.

15. Thomas of Britain, *Tristran*, ed. and trans. Stewart Gregory (New York: Garland, 1991), ix–xi. See Joseph Bédier, ed., *Le Roman de Tristan par Thomas, poème du XIIème siècle*, SATF, 2 vols. (Paris: Firmin-Didot, 1902–5), vol. 2; *Gottfried von Strassburg: Tristan, with the Surviving Fragments of the Tristran of Thomas*, ed. and trans. A. T. Hatto (New York: Penguin, 1960; *Die nordische Version der Tristan Sage*, ed. and trans. Eugen Kölbing (Hildesheim: Georg Olms, 1978; Thomas of Britain, *The Romance of Tristram and Ysolt by Thomas of Britain, Translated from the Old French and the Old Norse*, trans. Roger Loomis (New York: Columbia University Press, 1931); *The Saga of Tristram and Ísönd*, ed. and trans. Paul Schach (Lincoln: University of Nebraska Press, 1973). It is possible that the Norse translator amplified elements of the Hall of Statues from Thomas of Britain's original.

16. *The Saga of Tristram and Ísönd*, trans. Schach, 122. The lion recalls the lions guarding the Throne of Solomon in Liudprand of Cremona's account of his embassy to Constantinople.

17. "Por iço fist il ceste image / Que dire li volt son corage, / Son bon penser, sa fole errur, / Sa paigne, sa joie d'amor, / Car ne sot vers cui descovrir / Ne son voler ne son desir," Thomas of Britain, *Tristran*, ed. and trans. Gregory, ll. 985–991, 52. I have used my own translation.

18. *The Saga of Tristram and Ísönd*, trans. Schach, 120.

19. *The Saga of Tristram and Ísönd*, trans. Schach, 120–21.

20. Nancy G. Siraisi, *Medieval and Early Renaissance Medicine* (Chicago: University of Chicago Press, 1990), 101–8.

21. See Chapter 2.

22. Ovid, *Metamorphoses*, 10.243–97.

23. See Paul Franklin Baum, "The Young Man Betrothed to a Statue," *PMLA* 34 (1919): 523–79.

24. *Éneas*, ll. 7409–7718, 2: 275–87.

25. Guillemette Bolens, "La momification dans la littérature médiévale: L'embaument d'Hector chez Benoît de Sainte-Maure, Guido delle Colonne, et John Lydgate," *Micrologus* 13 (2005): 213–31, 217.

26. *Éneas*, l. 7516, 2: 280.

27. "Ele esteit tote ensanglentee, / d'eue rosade l'ont lavee, / sa bele crinë ont trenchiee, / et puis l'ont aromatisiee. / Et basme et mirre i ot plenté, / le cors en ont bien conreé," *Éneas*, ll. 7433–7438, 2: 276–77.

28. *Éneas*, ll. 7430–7724, 2: 276–87 for a description of the tomb.

29. "Veissiaus ot asis lez lo cors, / plains de basme, d'autre licors / por refreschir la des odors," *Éneas*, ll. 7648–7650, 2: 285.

30. Clifford Davidson, "Heaven's Fragrance," in Clifford Davidson, ed., *The Iconography of Heaven* (Kalamazoo, Mich.: Medieval Institute, 1994), 110–27, especially 112–16.

31. The plant is now classified as *Commiphora opobalsamum* (L.) Engl. In both the French and English traditions, balm (or balsam) can mean the plant itself, the resin it secretes, or an unguent made from this fragrant substance.

32. Truitt, "The Virtues of Balm," 714–16; Andrew Dalby, *Dangerous Tastes: The Story of Spices* (London: British Museum, 2000), 33–35; Nigel Groom, *Frankincense and Myrrh: A Study of the Arabian Incense Trade* (London: Longman, 1981), 126–31. The use of balm for this purpose is reflected in the word "embalm" [*embasmé, enbaumer, baumen*]. See *Dictionnaire historique de la langue française*, s.v. "baume." For the Middle English *baume*, see the *Middle English Dictionary*, , s. v. "baume;" *OED*, s. vv. "balm," "balsam."

33. Jean-Pierre Albert, *Odeurs de sainteté: La mythologie chrétienne des aromates* (Paris: Éditions de l'École des Hautes Études en Sciences Sociales, 1990), 117–22.

34. For an account of Camille's tomb and the magical substances in it, see Chapter 2.

35. "Li archiers pot longues viser / et toz tens mes l'arc anteser, / mais ja li boldons n'i trairoit, / se primes l'arc ne destandoit / le laz d'une regeteore / qui aparoilliez ert desore, / qui tenoit l'arc toz tens tendu. / A un sofle fust tot perdu: / qui soflast la regeteore, / et al destandist anislore / et li archiers idonc traisist / droit au colon, se l'abatist, / dunc fust la chaene rompue / et la lampe tote espandue," *Éneas*, ll. 7705–7718, 2: 287.

36. See Theodore Ziolkowski, *Varieties of Literary Thematics* (Princeton, N. J.: Princeton University Press, 1983) 54–55.

37. Peter H. Niebyl, "Old Age, Fever, and the Lamp Metaphor," *Journal of the History of Medicine and the Allied Sciences* 26 (1971): 351–68; Michael McVaugh, "The 'Humidum Radicale' in Thirteenth-Century Medicine," *Traditio* 30 (1974): 259–83.

38. Truitt, "Fictions of Life and Death," 195.

39. Wendy Chapman Peek, "King by Day, Queen by Night: The Virgin Camille in the *Roman d'Éneas*," in *Menacing Virgins: Representing Virginity in the Middle Ages and the Renaissance*, ed. Kathleen Coyne Kelly and Marina Leslie (London: Associated University Presses, 1999), 71–82, 73.

40. *Éneas*, ll. 6444–6451, 2: 249.

41. "Post hoc veni in civitatem quandam que Perusium nuncupatur in qua papam Innocentium inveni mortuum, sed nundum sepultum, quem de nocte quidam furtive vestimentis preciosis, cum quibus scilicet sepeliendus erat, spoliaverunt; corpus autem eius fere nudum et fetidum in ecclesia relinquerunt. Ego autem ecclesiam intravi et oculata fide cognovi quam brevis sit et vana huius seculi fallax gloria," Jacques de Vitry, *Lettres de Jacques de Vitry*, ed. R. B. C. Huygens, 2 vols. (Leiden: Brill, 1960), 1: 73–74.

42. The earliest historical evidence is for Pope Paschal II (d. 1118).

43. Marc Dykmans, *Le cérémonial papal de la fin du Moyen Age à la Renaissance*, 4 vols. (Brussels: Institut Historique Belge de Rome, 1977–85), 4: 219, no. 969, as cited in Agostino Paravicini-Bagliani, *The Pope's Body*, trans. David S. Peterson (Chicago: University of Chicago Press, 2000), 134. There is no mention of evisceration, although Katharine Park notes this practice was likely standard for popes by the fourteenth century. Personal communication.

44. On medieval sainthood and signs of sanctity, see Brown, *The Cult of the Saints*; Thomas Head, *Hagiography and the Cult of Saints: The Diocese of Orleans, 800–1200* (Cambridge: Cambridge University Press, 1990).

45. See Thietmar of Merseburg, *Chronicon* 4:47; *Chronicon Novaliciense, MGH SS. rer. Ger*, ed. G. H. Pertz (Hanover: Hahn, 1846), 55–56.

46. On Otto III's religious and political motives for his visit to Aachen, see Knut Görich, "Otto III öffnet das Karlsgrab in Aachen," in *Herrschaftsrepräsentation im ottonischen Sachsen*, ed. Gerd Althoff and Ernst Schubert (Sigmaringen: Jan Thorbecke, 1998), 381–430; Matthew Gabriele, "Otto III, Charlemagne, and Pentecost A.D. 1000: A Reconsideration Using Diplomatic Evidence," in *The Year 1000: Religious and Social Response to the Turning of the First Millennium*, ed. Michael Frassetto (New York: Palgrave, 2003), 111–32.

47. Dictys Cretensis, *Ephemeris belli troiani*, ed. F. Meister (Leipzig: Teubner, 1872); Dares Phrygius, *De excidio troiae historia*, ed. F. Meister (Leipzig: Teubner, 1873). See Aimé Petit, *Naissances du roman: Les techniques littéraires dans les romans antiques du XIIème siècle*, 2 vols. (Lille: Atelier National Reproduction des Thèses, 1985), 2: 213–17 for a detailed comparison of the texts of Dictys and Dares and the *Roman de Troie*.

48. Louis Faivre D'Arcier, *Histoire et géographie d'un mythe: La circulation des manuscrits du De excidio Troiae de Darès le Phrygien (VIIIe–XVe siècles)* (Paris: École des Chartres,2006); Curtius, *European Literature and the Latin Middle Ages*, 174–75.

49. C. David Benson, *The History of Troy in Middle English Literature* (Woodbridge: Boydell & Brewer, 1980), 4.

50. On Guido's career as a poet at the court of Frederick II and after, see Vincent Moleta, "Guido delle Colonne's 'Amor, che lungiamenta m'hai menato': A Source for the Opening Metaphor," *Italica* 54 (1977): 468–84, esp. 478–79. Some scholars have asserted that there were two Guido delle Colonnes, one who was a court poet in the first half of the thirteenth century and another who was a judge and author of the *Historia destructionis Troiae*. Gianfranco Contini, *Poeti del Duecento*, 2 vols. (Milan: Riccardi, 1960), 1: 46, 95–96, cited in Moleta, "Guido delle Colonne's 'Amor, che lungiamente'," n. 51.

51. Guido delle Colonne (Guido de Columnis), *Historia destructionis Troiae*, ed. Nathaniel Edward Griffin (Cambridge, Mass.: Medieval Academy, 1936), Prologue, 4, Epilogue, 276. Hereafter, *HDT.*

52. Benson, *The History of Troy in Middle English Literature*, 35. Sylvia Federico has linked the popularity of the tale of the Trojan War in late fourteenth- and early fifteenth-century England to the monarchy's desire for a connection to the Trojan past, and a way to use that connection to project an imperial agenda. See Sylvia Federico, *New Troy: Fantasies of Empire in the Late Middle Ages* (Minneapolis: University of Minnesota Press, 2003).

53. Joly, *Benoît de Sainte-Maure et le Roman de Troie*, 1: 857–65; Young, *Troy and Her Legend*, 63.

54. "Premierement l'ont desarmé / E de vin blanc set feiz lavé / En cheres especes boilli. / Anceis qu'il fust enseveli, / L'ont mout bien aromatizié, / E le ventre del cors sachié. / Ostee en ont bien la coraille, / Feie e poumon e l'autre entraille. / Le cors dedenz ont embasmé, / Sin i mistrent a grant plenté, / E si refirent il dehors," *Roman de Troie*, ll. 16507–16517, 3: 89.

55. Katharine Park, *Secrets of Women: Gender, Generation and the Origins of Human Dissection* (New York: Zone, 2007), 16, 127.

56. Truitt, "The Virtues of Balm," 722–23.

57. Curtius, *European Literature and the Latin Middle Ages*, 174–75.

58. "Prout in duobus libris eorum inscriptum quasi una uocis consonantia inuentum est in Athenis," *HDT*, 4. Benson, *The History of Troy in Middle English Literature*, 5.

59. "Verum quia corpus Hectoris, cadauer effectum, sicut est fragitilitatis humane, diu non poterat supra terram sine corrupcione seruari, in multorum consilio magistrorum rex Priamus subtiliter perquisuit si corpus ipsum absque sepulture clausura posset in aspectu hominum semper esse sic quod absque alicuius horribilitatis odore corpus mortuum ficticie quasi uiuum uideretur," *HDT*, 177.

60. "Magistros eosdem ualde artificiose discretos," *HDT*, 177.

61. "Corpus uero ipsius Hectoris in mirabilis magisterii eorum artificio statuerunt in medio, ipsius solii subnixa firmitate, sedere, sic artificiose locatum ut quasi uiuum se in sua regeret sessione, propriis indutum uestibus preter pedum extrema. Apposuerunt enim in eius uertice, quodam artificioso foramine constituto, quoddam uas, plenum puro et precioso balsamo, quibusdam aliis mixturis rerum uirtutem conseruacionis habencium intermixtis. Cuius balsami et rerum liquor primo deriuabatur ad frontis ambitum per partes intrinsecas, deinde ad oculos et nares, necnon rector decursu descendendo per easdem partes intrinsecas perueniebat ad genas, per quas gingiuas et dentes conseruabat ipsius, sic quod tota eius facies cum suorum multitudine capillorum in sua conseruacione uigebat. Deinde liquor ipse per guttur eius et ipsius gule catenas descendendo eius deriuabatur ad pectus et per ossa brachiorum intrinseca perueniebat ad manus et usque ad digitorum extrema. Sic et liquor ipse descendens per utrunque latus, copiose diffusus, latera ipsa sic conseruabat in statu ut quasi uiui latera uiderentur. Qui continuis instillacionibus ad continencias pectoris emanabat et per eas perueniebat ad crura, a quibus continuo cursu perueniebat ad pedes. In cuius pedibus erat quoddam aliud uas balsamo puro plenum. Et

sic per has apposiciones cadauer Hectoris quasi corpus viui ficticie presentabat, in multa durabilitatis custodia conseruatum," *HDT*, 177–78.

62. Hugo Buchthal, *Historia troiana: Studies in the History of Mediaeval Secular Illustration* (Leiden: Brill, 1971), 29. The vessel of balm pouring over Hector's head also recalls sanctified healing oils. See Alice-Mary Talbot, "Pilgrimage to Healing Shrines: The Evidence of Miracle Accounts," *Dumbarton Oaks Papers* 56 (2002): 153–73.

63. See Jacques de Vitry on the smell of the decaying body of Pope Innocent III, n. 43.

64. See Paravincini-Bagliani, *The Pope's Body*, 179–80, 207–8.

65. Aristotle, *De meteorologica*, 3.1–3.3.379a. In Latin, see Pieter L. Schoonheim, *Aristotle's Meteorology in the Arabico-Latin Tradition: A Critical Edition of the Texts, with Introduction and Indices* (Leiden: Brill, 2000), 142; in English, see H. D. P. Lee, ed., *The Complete Works of Aristotle*, Loeb Classical Library (Cambridge, Mass.: Harvard University Press, 1952), 295–97. On *De meteorologica* in medieval Europe, see Joëlle Ducos, *La météorologie en français au Moyen Age (XIIIe et XIVe siècles)* (Paris: Champion, 1998); Lorenzo Minio-Paluello, "Henri Aristippe, Guillaume de Moerbeke et les traductions latines médiévales des météorologiques et du De Generatione d'Aristote," *Revue Philosophique de Louvain* 45 (1947): 206–35.

66. This is the notion of *humidum radicale*, mentioned above.

67. Aristotle, *Meteorologica*, 3.1, 295.

68. Aristotle, *Meteorologica*, 3.3.379a, 297.

69. *Le Roman d'Alexandre*, ll. 7176–7182, 700.

70. The text survives in at least 136 manuscripts. *HDT*, ed. Griffin, xi; *HDT*, trans. Meek, xiv.

71. "Nonnulli enim iam eius ystorie poetice alludendo ueritatem ipsius in figurata commenta quibusdam fictionibus transsumpserunt, vt non uera que scripserunt uiderentur audientibus perscripsisse sed pocius fabulosa," *HDT*, 3–4.

72. John Lydgate, *Troy Book*, ed. Henry Bergen, 3 vols., EETS (Millwood, N.J.: Kraus, 1975), Prologue, ll. 113–115.

73. On the English tradition of using poetry to convey history, see Benson, *The History of Troy in Middle English Literature*, 37–38.

74. *Troy Book*, 3, ll. 5601–5603, 2: 556.

75. *Troy Book*, 3, ll. 5592–5598, 2: 556.

76 *Troy Book*, 3, ll. 5676–5680, 2: 558.

77. *Troy Book*, 3, l. 5664, 2: 558; ll. 5682–5684, 2: 559.

78. In Middle English "licour" was a term closely related to "baume." The general definition carried a figurative meaning of any natural liquid vital to sustaining life, such as sap or blood. Like balm, it could also mean a therapeutic or revitalizing liquid, prepared in accordance with natural knowledge (including magic), and could be used to mean an unguent used to anoint a corpse. *Middle English Dictionary*, s.v. "licour."

79. Paravincini-Bagliani, *The Pope's Body*, xiv. For Bacon's writing on alchemy and rejuvenation, see William Newman, "An Overview of Roger Bacon's Alchemy," in *Roger*

Bacon and the Sciences, ed. Hackett 317–36; Newman, "The Philosophers' Egg: Theory and Practice in the Alchemy of Roger Bacon," *Micrologus* 3 (1995): 75–101.

80. William Newman, *Promethean Ambitions: Alchemy and the Quest to Perfect Nature* (Chicago: University of Chicago Press, 2004), 63–75; Jonathan Hughes, *The Rise of Alchemy in Fourteenth-Century England: Plantagenet Kings and the Search for the Philosopher's Stone* (London: Continuum, 2012), 41–54, 165–202.

81. *Troy Book*, 3, ll. 5696–5700, 2: 559.

82. *Middle English Dictionary*, s.v. "proces."

83. Paravincini-Bagliani, *The Pope's Body*, 207.

84. *Middle English Dictionary*, s.v. "craft."

85. *Troy Book*, 3, l. 5664, 2: 558; *Middle English Dictionary*, s.v. "avise," "aviseness."

86. *Middle English Dictionary*, s.v. "maisteres" See *Troy Book*, 3, ll. 5655–5657, 2: 558; ll. 5663–5673, 2: 558.

CHAPTER 5. FROM TEXTS TO TECHNOLOGY: MECHANICAL
MARVELS IN COURTLY AND PUBLIC PAGEANTRY

1. On Villard and his milieu, see Roland Bechmann, *Villard de Honnecourt: La pensée technique au XIIIème siècle et sa communication* (Paris: Picard, 1991).

2. Bechmann gives a more nuanced view of the anachronistic term "architect," especially as applied to Villard. See Bechmann, *Villard de Honnecourt*, 24.

3. Alain Erlande-Brandenburg, "Villard de Honnecourt, l'architecture et la sculpture," in *Le carnet de Villard de Honnecourt*, ed. Alain Erlande-Brandenburg, Regine Pernoud, Jean Gimpel, and Roland Bechmann (Paris: Stock, 1986), 17–25, 17.

4. The availability and extent of Latin translations of the *Pneumatica* remains under debate, although scholars do agree that at least part of this work was available, in Latin (though not French), from the twelfth century. See Grant, "Henricus Aristippus, William of Moerbeke, and Two Alleged Mediaeval Translations of Hero's *Pneumatica*"; Boas, "Hero's *Pneumatica*."

5. "Vesci une cantepleure c'on puet fair en i henap et tel maniere q'ens enmi le henap dont avoir une torete et ens en miliu de le tourete doit avoir i behor qui tiegne ens el fons del henap mais que li behos soit ausi lons com li henap et parfons et ens en le torete doit avoir iii travecons par sontre le fons del henap si que li vins del henap puist aler al behot, et par de seur le torete doit avoir i oziel qui doit tenir son biec si bas, que qant le hanap iert plains quil boive. A dont sen corra li vins parmi le behor et parmi le piet de henap qui est dobles; et sentendes bien que li doit estre crues," Villard de Honnecourt, *Carnet*, Paris, BnF, MS Fr. 19093, fol. 9r. See Bechmann, *Villard de Honnecourt*, 297–300.

6. Villard's drawing is misleading, for in order for the design to work, the bird's beak needs to reach below the rim of the basin. A cup of similar design, from the fifteenth century, is held at Corpus Christi College, Cambridge. See Sherwood, "Magic and Mechanics," 586.

7. The crossbow and the hydraulic saw are not immediately central to a discussion of medieval automata, although the latter does further underscore the innovations made in water power in the thirteenth century, and the former enriches the discussion below on the use of the crank in medieval machinery. There has been some interest in the technological aspects of Villard's drawings. See Jean-Pierre Adam and Pierre Varene, "La scie hydraulique de Villard de Honnecourt et sa place dans l'histoire des techniques," *Bulletin Monumental* 143 (1985): 317–22; Bechmann, *Villard de Honnecourt*, 278–86; Carlo Maccagni, "Il disegno di macchine come fonte per la storia delle tecnica del Rinascimento," *Quaderni Storici* 70 (1989): 13–24.

8. "Par chu fait on un ange tenir son doit ades vers le solel," Villard, *Carnet*, fol. 22v.

9. "Par chu fait om dorner la teste de lagile vers la diachene kant list la Vangile," Villard, *Carnet*, fol. 22v. The full design for the lectern is on fol. 7r. See Bechmann, *Villard de Honnecourt*, 300.

10. On the development and proliferation of mill technology, including gear wheels and cams, see George Brooks, "The 'Vitruvian Mill' in Roman and Medieval Europe," in *Wind and Water in the Middle Ages*, ed. Steven A. Walton, MRTS (Tempe, Ariz.: ACMRS, 2006), 1–39; Long, *Technology and Society in the Medieval Centuries*, 45–48.

11. Frances Gies and Joseph Gies, *Cathedral, Forge, and Water-Wheel: Technology and Invention in the Middle Ages* (New York: HarperCollins, 1994), 114–18.

12. The Arabic title is *Kitab al-Jami' bayn al'ilm wa-'l-'amal al-nafi' fi sinat'at al-hiyal*. Translated into English the title is *Book of the Knowledge of Ingenious Geometrical Contrivances*, also called *Work That Combines Theory and Practice and Is Profitable to the Craft of Ingenious Contrivances*. See Ananda K. Coomaraswamy, *The Treatise of Al-Jazari on Automata* (Boston: Museum of Fine Arts, 1924), 5. See also Al-Jazari, *The Book of Ingenious Mechanical Devices*, trans. Donald R. Hill (Dordecht: Reidel, 1974); Kurt Weitzmann, "The Greek Sources of Islamic Scientific Illustrations," in *Archaeologica Orientalia in memoriam Ernst Herzfeld*, ed. George Carpenter Miles (Locust Valley, N.Y.: Augustin, 1952), 244–66, 245–50.

13. Further bolstering his claim to authority, al-Jazari stated that he invented the reversible cup and many other devices. See Coomaraswamy, *The Treatise of Al-Jazari*, 5–6.

14. Wetzel Collection, Fogg Art Museum, 1919.138, Harvard University. See Eric Schroeder, *Persian Miniatures in the Fogg Museum of Art* (Cambridge, Mass.: Harvard University Press, 1942), 21–28; Coomaraswamy, *The Treatise of Al-Jazari*, 18–19; Rudolph Riefstahl, "The Date and Provenance of the Automata Miniatures," *Art Bulletin* 11 (1929): 206–15.

15. Donald Hill, "From Philo to al-Jazari," in *Learning, Language, and Invention: Essays Presented to Francis Maddison*, ed. W. D. Hackmann and A. J. Turner (Aldershot: Variorum, 1994), 188–206; Hill, "Medieval Arabic Mechanical Technology," 222–37.

16. See Banu Musa, *The Book of Ingenious Devices*, trans. Donald Hill (Dordrecht: Kluwer, 1978), 22. Pamela O. Long mentions that the fifteenth-century inventor and physician Giovanni Fontana drew inspiration from the writings of the Alexandrian school and Arabic treatises, but is not more specific. Long, *Openness, Secrecy, Authorship: Technical Arts and the Culture of Knowledge from Antiquity to the Renaissance* (Baltimore: Johns

Hopkins University Press, 2001), 110. For the impact of manuscript drawings in Alexandrian and Arabic technological texts on Europeans, see Jane Andrews Aiken, "Truth in Images: From the technical drawings of Ibn Al-Razzaz Al-Jazari, Campanus of Novara, and Giovanni de'Dondi to the perspective projection of Leon Battista Alberti," *Viator* 25 (1994): 325–59.

17. Villard, *Carnet*, fol. 2r. A drawing of a traveler with the caption underneath: "Villard de Honnecourt, celui ki est alle en Hongrie" ["Villard of Honnecourt, who went to Hungary"].

18. Banu Musa, *The Book of Ingenious Devices*, trans. Donald Hill, 23.

19. *The Journey of William of Rubruck to the Eastern Parts of the World, 1253–55*, 176–78, 208–12.

20. *Inventaire-Sommaire des Archives Départmentales Antérieures à 1790, Pas-des-Calais, Archives Civiles, Series A*, ed. Jules-Marie Richard, 2 vols. (Arras, 1878), A 2 (1298), 1: 4; A 161 (1308), 1: 178–79 (henceforth cited as Richard, Arras); AN, Montheil MS KK 393, fol. 13r; *Le compte general du receveur d'Artois pour 1303–1304*, ed. Bernard Delmaire (Brussels: Palais des Académies, 1977), xlvii, lx–lxii; Jean Dunbabin, *The French in the Kingdom of Sicily 1266–1305* (Cambridge: Cambridge University Press, 2011), 115, 212, 232. See also Marguerite Chargeat, "Le parc d'Hesdin, création monumental du XIIIème siècle," *Bulletin de la Société de l'Histoire de l'Art Français* (1950): 94–104; Anne Hagopian van Buren, "Reality and Literary Romance in the Park of Hesdin," in *Medieval Gardens*, ed. Elisabeth Blair MacDougall (Washington, D.C.: Dumbarton Oaks, 1986), 115–34, 125–27. Coignet disappears from the Artois archives in 1299; four years later Mahaut sent a letter to the king of Naples explaining that Coignet had been accused of embezzling funds and had fled. He appears in Lucera, in the kingdom of Naples, as a tax collector and royal administrator at the end of 1300. See van Buren, "Reality and Literary Romance," 126; *Codice Diplomatico dei Saraceni di Lucera*, ed. Pietro Egidi (Naples: L. Pierro et Figlio, 1917), docs. 320, 328, 330–31, 334, et passim.

21. Sharon Farmer, "Aristocratic Power and the 'Natural' Landscape: The Garden Park at Hesdin, ca. 1291–1302," *Speculum* 88 (2013): 644–80, 645. This article contains the most comprehensive description of the chateau and the estate under Robert's rule.

22. The deer, rabbits, and carp were not native to northern France, but had been introduced from southern regions in the late twelfth and early thirteenth centuries. The heron species was native, but needed significant oversight in order to be kept on the estate year-round. See Farmer, "Aristocratic Power," 648.

23. The "pavillon du Marès" was later called the "pavillion des fontaines." See Anne-Élisabeth Cléty, "Les machines extraordinaires d'Hesdin aux XIVème et XVème siècles," *Sucellus* 44 (1997): 1–59, 14; Richard, Arras, A 237 (1308), 1: 229–30.

24. *Archives Départmentales du Pas-de-Calais*, A 147 (1299), ed. in Chrétien C. A. Dehaisnes, *Documents et extraits divers concernant l'histoire de l'art dans la Flandre, l'Artois, le Hainaut avant le XVème siècle*, 2 vols. (Lille: Daniel, 1886), 1:107–9; Richard, Arras, A 237 (1308), 1: 229–30. See also Farmer, "Aristocratic Power," 645; Chargeat, "Le parc d'Hesdin," 94–104.

25. Richard, Arras, A 155 (1300), 1: 171.

26. Richard, Arras, A 147 (1296–1299), 1: 165; A 163 (1301), 1: 179; AN, Montheil KK 393, fol. 21 (1304). On the *gloriette* and its inspiration, see Sharon Farmer, "La Zisa/Gloriette: Cultural Interaction and the Architecture of Repose in Medieval Sicily, France and Britain," *Journal of the British Archaeological Association* 166 (2013): 99–123, 114.

27. Cléty, "Les machines extraordinaires d'Hesdin," 22.

28. "Engiens d'esbattement."

29. The county of Burgundy should not be confused with the duchy of Burgundy; the county of Burgundy corresponds to Franche-Comté.

30. A bill from 1304 indicates that over 300 nails were needed to repair the monkeys. AN, Montheil MS KK 393, fol. 32v. See also Richard, Arras, A 168 (1301), 1: 182; Farmer, "Aristocratic Power," 679–81; Cléty, "Les machines extraordinaires d'Hesdin," 22. One can only imagine what the tanner thought about this. Perhaps he set aside badger furs for this commission.

31. Richard, Arras, A 237 (1308), 1: 230; Cléty, "Les machines extraordinaires d'Hesdin," 22–23.

32. "Pour ouvrer à sauder as engiens du pavillon, pour ouvrer à revestir les singes du pavillon et mettre unes cornes," Richard, Arras, A 290 (1312), 1: 265.

33. Richard, Arras, A 315 (1314), 1: 278–79. See also Jules-Marie Richard, *Une petite-nièce de Saint Louis: Mahaut, comtesse d'Artois et de Bourgogne (1302–1329)* (Paris: Champion, 1887), 337.

34. "Pour fair .i. siege a mettre sus le roy de le gloriete," Richard, Arras, A 333 (1315), 1: 290–91; Dehaisnes, *Documents et extraits divers*, 1: 216. See also Cléty, "Les machines extraordinaires d'Hesdin," 33–34.

35. AN Montheil, KK 393, fol. 98; Richard, *Une petite-nièce*, 342; Cléty, "Les machines extraordinaires d'Hesdin," 23.

36. See Chapter 3, n. 19.

37. As Sharon Farmer has observed, the interesting difference between Hesdin and *La Zisa* is that although the landscape of Hesdin was artificially constructed and maintained, the overall aesthetic was naturalistic. Farmer, "Aristocratic Power," 646.

38. Farmer, "La Zisa/Gloriette," 114; Cléty, "Les machines extraordinaires d'Hesdin," 20; David Abulafia, *Frederick II: A Medieval Emperor* (London: Penguin, 1988), 267; Houben, *Roger II of Sicily*, 104; Eva Baer, *Ayyubid Metalwork with Christian Images*, Studies in Islamic Art and Architecture 4 (Leiden: Brill, 1989), 45; Chargeat, "Le parc d'Hesdin," 94–104. See also the *Oxford Companion to Gardens*, ed. Patrick Goode and Michael Lancaster (Oxford: Oxford University Press, 1986), s.v. "pleasance."

39. Farmer, "La Zisa/Gloriette," 102; Cléty, "Les machines extraordinaires d'Hesdin," 21; Ruggles, *Islamic Gardens and Landscapes*, 82; Chargeat, "Le parc d'Hesdin," 100, n 2.

40. Van Buren, "Reality and Literary Romance," 131–33. However, van Buren then goes on to state that the devices at Hesdin could have been built using Villard's designs, which is unlikely, as they were not extensive enough.

41. *Aymeri de Narbonne*, ll. 3504–3523, 2: 148–49. The "pleasance" or pleasure-garden (*locus amoenus*), was, by the late twelfth century an ekphrastic trope that poets were expected to master. See Curtius, *European Literature and the Latin Middle Ages*, 195–97.

42. "Quant li oisel ont grignor vent, / adont cantent plus doucement, / et el vergier, au tans seri, / des oisiaus i a si douç cri, / et tant de faus et tant de vrais, / merles et calendres et gais/ et estorniaus et rosignos, / et pinçonés et esprinos/ et autres oisiaus qui i sont/ qui par le vergier joie font, / qui les sons ot et l'estormie/ molt est dolans s'il n'a s'amie," *Le Conte de Floire et Blancheflor*, ll. 1963–1986, 100. Leclanche notes that the text may be corrupted, given the shift from "bird" to "birds." *Le Conte de Floire et Blancheflor*, 101, n1.

43. ".xm. oisiaus a en la trelle / grans et petis a grant mervelle / d fin or . . . ," *Éneas*, 2: 390, interpolation of mss. G, F, and D, no line numbers.

44. *Éneas*, 2: 389–90.

45. For the date of the composition of *Walewein*, which is difficult to assess with any certainty, see *Dutch Romances: Roman van Walewein*, ed. David F. Johnson and Geert H. M. Classens, 3 vols. (Woodbridge: Brewer, 2000), 1: 4–7. See also W. P. Ker, "The Roman van Walewein (Gawain)," *Folk-Lore* 5 (1894): 121–27.

46. *Dutch Romances: Roman van Walewein*, ll. 3534–3548, 1: 175.

47. See Chapter 1, n. 46; Farmer, "Aristocratic Power," 646; Farmer, "*La Zisa/Gloriette*," 100–102; Delumeau, *Une histoire du paradis*, 1:167–68.

48. Farmer, "Aristocratic Power," 648.

49. There were culinary techniques for removing the skin and feathers of a bird and then reattaching them to the cooked fowl for presentation. It is possible that these techniques could have been modified for decorating avian automata. Richard, Arras, A 168 (1301), 1: 182.

50. Richard, *Une petite-nièce*, 7.

51. See van Buren, "Reality and Literary Romance," 123; Derek Pearsall and Elizabeth Salter, *Landscapes and Seasons of the Medieval World* (Toronto: University of Toronto Press, 1973), 173; Bruno Danvin, *Vicissitudes, heur et malheur du Vieil-Hesdin* (St.-Pol: Bécart-Renard, 1866), 89.

52. *Oeuvres de Guillaume de Machaut*, ed. Ernest Hoepffner, SATF, 3 vols. (Paris: Firmin-Didot, 1908–21), 1: lxiv–lxv; 2: i–iii. See also Guillaume de Machaut, *Le Jugement du roy de Behaigne and Remede de Fortune*, ed. and trans. James Wimsatt and William Kibler (Athens: University of Georgia Press, 1988), 33.

53. "Tristes, pensis, et souspirans," l. 773, 211; "Tant que vi .i. trop bel jardin/ Qu'on claimme le Park de Hedin," ll. 785–786, 211–13, Machaut, *Remede de Fortune*, ed. and trans. Wimsatt and Kibler. I have used my own translation of this text here and following.

54. "Et les merveilles, les deduis, / Les arts, les engins, les conduis, / Les esbas, les estranges choses/ qui estoient dedens encloses, / Ne saroie jamais descrire," Machaut, *Remede de Fortune*, ed. and trans. Wimsatt and Kibler, ll. 813–817, 213.

55. For example, the mechanical monkeys were supposed to appear, at least at first glance, to be live monkeys. See Farmer, "Aristocratic Power," 679–80.

56. François Avril, *Manuscript Painting at the Court of France: The Fourteenth Century*, trans. Ursule Molinaro and Bruce Benderson (New York: Braziller, 1978); Avril, "Les manuscrits enluminés de Guillaume de Machaut," in *Guillaume de Machaut*, Colloque-Table Ronde Organisé par l'Université de Rheims, Actes et Colloques 23 (Paris: Klincksieck, 1982), 117–33. This manuscript, BnF, MS. Fr. 1586, is the C manuscript of the poem, and forms the basis for Wimsatt and Kibler's edition.

57. Dora Panofsky, "The Textual Basis of the Utrecht Psalter Illustrations," *Art Bulletin* 25 (1943): 50–58; White, *Medieval Technology*, 110.

58. Donald Hill, "Arabic Fine Technology and Its Influence on European Mechanical Engineering," in *The Arab Influence in Medieval Europe*, ed. Dionisius A. Agius and Richard Hitchcock (Reading: Ithaca, 1994), 25–43, 29.

59. Richard Vaughan, *Philip the Good: The Apogee of Burgundy*, 2nd ed. (Woodbridge: Boydell, 2002), 136–37.

60. "Ouvrages ou chastel de Hesdin. A Colard le Voleur, valet de chambre et paintre de Monseigneur le duc, la somme de mil livres du pris de XL groz, monnoie de Flandres, la livre, laquelle mondit seigneur a ordonné luy estre bailliée et délivrée comptant, pour, par son commandement et ordonnance et par marchié à luy fait en tâche, avoir faiz et fait faire, de painterie et aultrement, en son chastel de Hesdin, les ouvraiges et devises cy après déclairés. C'est assavoir d'avoir paint la galerie dudit chastel pareillement et de la devise qu'elle estoit paravant, bien richement et des plus fines estoffes de paintrerie que fait (faire) a peu. Item avoir fait et renouvelé les ystoires et paintures de trois personnages qui vuident eaue et moullent les gens quant l'en vault; et à l'entrée d'icelle galerie a ung engine pour moullier les dames en marchant par dessus et ung mirouer où l'on voit plusieurs abuz; et avec ce fait à l'entrée d'icelle galerie ung engine, lequel au toucher aux boucles ledit angien doit venir frapper au visaige de ceulx qui sont dessoubz et broulliez tous noirs ou blans; et aussi une fontaine en icelle galerie, la où il courra eaue quant l'en vouldra et yra tousjours dont elle vient. Item à l'issue d'icelle galerie a ung aultre engine que tous ceulx qui passent parmi seront feruz et batus de bonnes boulées sur leurs testes et espaules. Item en la sale devant l'ermite qui fait plouvoir tout par tout comme l'eaue qui vient du ciel, et aussi tonner et neger, et aussi esclitrer comme se on le voit ou ciel. Item ou plus prez de ladicte sale a ung hermite de bois pour parler aux gens qui vendront en icelle sale. Item avoir fait faire pavement pour pave icelle sale semblable comme devant estoit la moitié ou environ, et là a une place que quant les gens vont par dessus pour eulx garantir de la pluie, ilz chéent du hault en bas en ung sac là ou ilz sont tous emplumez et très bien brouilliez. A fair lesquelz ouvraiges mondit seigneur luy a fait livrer bois, charpenterie et maçonnerie pour faire les edifices proices à faire les choses dessus dictes. Item lui a convenu mettre jus et sus, oultre la devise avant dicte, la plus grant partie du ciellement d'icelle sale et lamb-rouciet là où doit plouvoir, pur ce que trop estoit faible et meschans pour faire les engiens ad ce appartenans. Item a fait, d'abondance, que en icelle galerie a ung pont que, quant l'en vault, l'en fait cheoir en l'eaue ceulx qui vont par dessuz. Item sont en plusieurs lieux engiens que, quant l'en vault touchier à aucunes touches y estans, on fait cheoir grande habondance d'eaue sur les gens. Item sont en la galerie six personnages, plus que paravant

il n'y avoit, qui moillent les gens et par plusieurs manières. Ita à l'entrée d'icelle vii conduiz pour moullier les dames par dessoubz, et trois contuiz que, quant les gens arrestent
par devant, ilz sont tous blanchiz et broullez de farine. Item une fenestre que, quant les
gens la veulent ouvrir, il y a ung personage par devant qui moulle les gens et reclot la fenestre a parelle. Item y a ung estaplel ouquel a ung livre de balades que, quant l'en y vault
lire, les gens se treuvent tous broulliez de moir et tantost qu'ilz regardent dedans aussi
sont ilz moulliez d'eaue quant on vault; et se y a ung aultre mirouer là où l'on envoie les
gens pour eulx voir quant ilz sont tous broulliez, et quant ilz regardent dessus ilz sont de
rechief tous embouserez de farine et tous blancs. Item y a ung personage de bos qui vient
par dessus ung bang ou milieu de la galerie et doit tromper, et faire un cry de par Monseigneur que tout home s'en voit hors la galerie, et ceulx qui iront a ce cry seront batus de
grans personages en manière de sots et sottes, lesquelz tendront les boulées dessus dictes
où il faudra qu'ilz chéent en l'eaue à l'entrée du pont, et ceulx qui ne se vouldront partir
seront telement moulliezqu'ilz ne saront où aler pour eschever l'eaue. Item y a une fenestre en laquele est une boiste pendue en l'air, et sus icelle boiste a ung buet, lequel fait plusieurs contenances en regardant les gens et fait bailler response de tout ce que on lui vault
demander et en peut l'en oir la voix en icelle boiste ou en voirre . . . et que depuis les devises dessus dictes mondi seigneur luy ordonna faire, tout du long la galerie dessus dicte
au dessoubz du mur d'un pré par embas, conduis et aultres engiens qui jetteront eaue par
tant de lieux qu'il n'est personne en la galerie qu'il sache luy sauver qu'il ne soit moullié,
et par tout dessoubz le pavement aultres conduiz et engiens pour moullier les dames par
dessoubz." *Inventaires-Sommaires des archives départmentales antérieures à 1790, Nord: Archives civiles, Série B*, ed. Chrétien Dehaisnes, vol. 4 (Lille, 1881) (henceforth Dehaisnes,
Lille), B. 1948 (1433), 123–24; also quoted in Comte de Laborde, *Les ducs de Bourgogne*, 3
vols. (Paris: Plon, 1849), 2, pt. 1: 268–71.

   61. Dehaisnes, Lille, B. 1948 (1433), 124.

   62. For example, the movement of Philip's court in 1435 from Dijon to Arras took a
month, and required seventy-two carts and over four hundred horses. Seven carts were
needed to transport the duke's and duchess's jewels. Vaughan, *Philip the Good*, 142. For
an inventory of Philip's treasure at the start of his reign, in 1420, see Vaughan, *Philip the
Good*, 151–52.

   63. Daston and Park, *Wonders*, 103. The authors also make the point that the emphasis on artifice and the exotic at the court of Burgundy "reflected the duchy's liminal and
'unnatural' position between the Empire and France."

   64. On the splendor and pageantry of Philip's court, see Vaughan, *Philip the Good*,
esp. 136–63; Richard McLanathan, *The Pageant of Medieval Art and Life* (Philadelphia: Westminster Press, 1966), 95–98. By claiming Jason of Troy as patron of the Order of the Golden
Fleece, Philip claimed descent from the Trojans just as the Anglo-Norman and French
rulers had done centuries earlier, thereby placing Burgundy (and himself) on a par with
England and, especially, France. On the foundation of the Order and the political uses of
Troy in identity politics, see Yvon Lacaze, "Le rôle des traditions dans la genèse d'un sentiment national au XVème siècle: La Bourgogne de Philippe le Bon," *Bibliothèque de l'École*

des Chartres 129 (1971): 303–85, esp. 303–5. The foundation of the Order and the importance of splendor in Burgundian courtly culture are also discussed in Daston and Park, *Wonders*, 100–108. On the importance of chivalric culture and the chivalric ideal in fifteenth-century Burgundy, see Johan Huizinga, *The Autumn of the Middle Ages*, trans. Rodney J. Payton and Ulrich Mammitzsch (Chicago: University of Chicago Press, 1996), chaps. 4–6.

65. Klaus Oschema, "Liquid Splendor—Table-Fountains and Wine-Fountains at the Burgundian Courts," in *Staging the Court of Burgundy: Proceedings of the Conference "The Splendor of Burgundy"*, ed. Wim Blockmans, Till-Holger Borchert, Nele Gabriëls, Johan Oosterman, and Anne van Oosterwijk (Turnhout: Brepols, 2013), 133–42, 137.

66. Oschema, "Liquid Splendor," 139.

67. Vaughan, *Philip the Good*, 160.

68. "Wetting ladies from below" is mentioned several times in the account, strongly suggesting that there may have been an aspect of sexual titillation involved in these devices. Philip had a reputation for being quite courteous to women; he also had over a dozen mistresses. Vaughan, *Philip the Good*, 130–34.

69. Jesús-Francesc Massip Bonet, "The Cloud: A Medieval Aerial Device, Its Origins, and Its Use in Spain Today," *Early Drama, Art, and Music Review* 16 (1994): 65–77.

70. Poor Borra. *Crónica de Juan II*, Garcia de Santamaría, fol. 204, cited and translated in *The Staging of Religious Drama in Europe in the Later Middle Ages*, ed. Peter Meredith and John E. Taliby (Kalamazoo, Mich.: Medieval Institute Publications, 1983), 94–95. Scott Lightsey examines this incident at length in *Manmade Marvels*, 2–12.

71. Lightsey, *Manmade Marvels*, 3.

72. Susan Crane, *The Performance of Self: Ritual, Clothing, and Identity During the Hundred Years War* (Philadelphia: University of Pennsylvania Press, 2002); Patricia Eberle, "The Politics of Courtly Style at the Court of Richard II," in *The Spirit of the Court*, ed. Glyn S. Burgess and Robert A. Taylor (Cambridge: Brewer, 1985); Louis Green, "Galvano Fiamma, Azzone Visconti, and the Revival of the Classical Theory of Magnificence," *Journal of the Warburg and Courtauld Institutes* 53 (1990): 98–113.

73. From Juvenal des Ursins, quoted in Paul Lacroix [P. L. Jacob], *Moeurs, usages et costumes au moyen âge et à l'époque de la renaissance* (Paris: Firmin Didot, 1871), 253.

74. Mathieu d'Escouchy, *Chronique de Mathieu d'Escouchy*, 2 vols. (Paris: Renouard, 1863–64), 1: 113–237, 119, 137–38, et passim; Olivier de la Marche, *Memoire: Maître d'hôtel et capitaine des gardes de Charles le Temeraire*, 4 vols. (Paris: Renouard, 1884), 1: 340–80, 342, 346, 352–53.

75. "Maistre des engiens du chastel et des peintres," Richard, Arras, A 237 (1308), 1: 229–30.

76. Richard, *Une petite-nièce*, 326–27. Costs are not attributed to particular objects or engines, but instead to a collective group (e.g., "the monkeys on the bridge"). For a breakdown of the relative costs, see Cléty, "Les machines extraordinaires d'Hesdin," 27–29.

77. For example, records from 1308 mention vermilion, ochre, azure, and gold leaf in the decorations in the *gloriette*; see n. 75. See also Long, *Openness, Secrecy, Authorship*, 210–43.

78. AN, Montheil MS KK 393, fols. 27, 31; Richard, Arras, A 147 (1296–99), A 166 (1301), 1: 165, 1: 181; Cléty, "Les machines extraordinaires d'Hesdin," 30–32.

79. Richard, Arras, A 147 (1299), 1: 165; AN, Montheil MS KK 393, fol. 1r.

80. Richard, Arras, A 147 (1296–99), 1: 165, A 166 (1301), 1: 181. *Ymage* or *ymagete* could refer to a moving or nonmoving statue.

81. AN Montheil, KK 393, fol. 27 (1306–7) mentions fine metalworkers; fol. 31 (1307–8) discusses replumbing the pipes for the *engiens* and work in the *gloriette*.

82. AN, Montheil MS KK 393, fol. 32v; Richard, Arras, A 290 (1312), 1: 264.

83. Richard, Arras, A 315 (1314), 1: 278; Richard, *Une petite-nièce*, 337.

84. This was due in part to Arabic notions of craft, which contrasted with the Aristotelian notion of craft knowledge and manual labor as servile. Arabic classifications of the sciences and the role of craft knowledge became more widely known in the thirteenth century. See Whitney, *Paradise Restored*, 134–37.

85. See Lightsey, *Manmade Marvels*, 54–81, for a detailed analysis of this pageant and the goldsmiths' role.

86. Clifford Davidson, *Technology, Guilds, and Early English Drama* (Kalamazoo, Mich.: Medieval Institute Publications, 1997), 57–100; Carol Symes, *A Common Stage: Theater and Public Life in Medieval Arras* (Ithaca, N.Y.: Cornell University Press, 2007), especially chaps. 2 and 3.

87. Davidson, *Technology, Guilds, and Early English Drama*, 2–8, 13.

88. Cf. *OED*, s.v. "mystery."

89. For example, the twelfth-century work on the mechanical arts, *De diversis artibus*, by Theophilus, a Benedictine monk. See Theophilus, *On Diverse Arts*, ed. and trans. C. R. Dodwell (Oxford: Clarendon, 1986). See also Long, *Openness, Secrecy, Authorship*, 85–88.

90. Long, *Openness, Secrecy, Authorship*, 89–96.

CHAPTER 6. THE CLOCKWORK UNIVERSE: KEEPING SACRED
AND SECULAR TIME

1. McCluskey, *Astronomies and Cultures*, 51–96.

2. Psalm 119: 61, 164. Benedict of Nursia, *Regula Sancti Benedicti*, ch. 16. In English: http://www.ccel.org/ccel/benedict/rule2/files (accessed 20 June 2013).

3. Benedict of Nursia, *Regula Sancti Benedicti*, chs. 9–10. In English: http://www.ccel.org/ccel/benedict/rule2/files (accessed 20 June 20 2013).

4. Gregory of Tours, *De cursu stellarum, MGH SS rer. Ger.*, ed. Bruno Krusch, vol. 1, pt. 2 (Hanover: Hahn, 1885), 854–72; Park, "Observation in the Margins, 500–1500," 15–44, esp. 21–22; Stephen C. McCluskey, "Gregory of Tours, Monastic Timekeeping, and Early Christian Attitudes to Astronomy," *Isis* 81 (1990): 8–22; McCluskey, *Astronomies and Cultures*, 101–10.

5. Bede, *The Reckoning of Time*, ed. and trans. Faith Wallis (Liverpool: Liverpool University Press, 1999). See Chapters 2 and 3 for a discussion of computus and *cumpas*.

6. Hourglasses, also called sandglasses, are not attested to until the fourteenth century. See Dorhn-van Rossum, *History of the Hour*, 117.

7. See Chapter 3 n. 18.

8. Donald Hill, "Islamic Fine Technology and its Influence on the Development of European Horology," *Al-Abhath* 35 (Beirut: American University of Beirut, 1987), reprinted in Donald Hill, *Studies in Medieval Islamic Technology: From Philo to al-Jazari—from Alexandria to Diyar Bakr*, ed. David A. King (Aldershot: Ashgate, 1998), 9–28, 20; F. Maddison, B. Scott, and A. Kent, "An Early Medieval Water-Clock," *Antiquarian Horology* 3 (1962): 348–53; C. B. Drover, "A Medieval Monastic Water-Clock," *Antiquarian Horology* 1 (1954): 54–58.

9. See Chapter 1.

10. "Eadem enim hora cecidit horologium ante horas matutinas," *The Chronicle of Jocelin of Brakelond*, ed. and trans. H. E. Butler (London: Thomas Nelson, 1949), 107.

11. Drover, "A Medieval Monastic Water-Clock," 54–63.

12. Earlier generations of scholars posited that the mechanism to turn the angel was an early form of mechanical escapement, and thus vital to the development of mechanical clockwork in Europe. However, more recent scholars have effectively demonstrated that this is not a mechanical escapement at all, but something much simpler. See Maurice Daumas, "Le faux échappement de Villard de Honnecourt," *Revue d'Histoire des Sciences* 35 (1982): 43–52; Derek J. de Solla Price, "On the Origin of Clockwork, Perpetual Motion Devices, and the Compass," *United States National Museum Bulletin 218: Contributions from the Museum of History and Technology* (Washington, D.C.: Smithsonian Institution, 1959), 82–112, 85. For a comprehensive outline of the scholarship on the mechanical angel and the escapement debate, see Dohrn-van Rossum, *The History of the Hour*, 105–6.

13. Jean Gimpel, "Villard de Honnecourt, Architecte-ingenieur," in *Le carnet de Villard de Honnecourt*, ed. Erlande-Brandenburg, 27–38, 30–31.

14. Hill, "Islamic Fine Technology," 16; Bechmann, *Villard de Honnecourt*, 248–50. However, other scholars assert that the clock was based on a design of Hero of Byzantium. See Dohrn-van Rossum, *History of the Hour*, 81–82; Drover, "A Medieval Monastic Water-Clock," 56. On the notional nature of Villard's and Alfonso's mercury motion wheels, see Dohrn-van Rossum, , 83; Silvio A. Bedini, ""The Compartmented Cylindrical Clepsydra," *Technology and Culture* 3 (1963): 114–41.

15. II Kings, 20.11; Isaiah 38.3.

16. Scholars disagree over the exact design of this clock, and how often the main wheel rotated. Drover, "A Medieval Monastic Water-Clock"; Dohrn-van Rossum, *History of the Hour*, 70–71; J. D. North, "Monasticism and the First Mechanical Clocks," in *The Study of Time II*, ed. J. T. Fraser and N. Lawrence (Berlin: Springer-Verlag, 1975), 381–98, esp. 382–83.

17. On the *Bible moralisée* manuscript and this particular miniature and links to the French royal court see Alexandre de Laborde, *La Bible moralisée*, 5 vols. (Paris: Société Française de Reproductions Manuscrits à Peintures, 1911–27), 1: 183; 5: 181.

18. Flood, *The Great Mosque of Damascus*, 130.

19. Ibid., 114–15.

20. Ibid., 115.

21. Benjamin of Tudela, *The Itinerary of Benjamin of Tudela*, cited in Flood, *The Great Mosque of Damascus*, 132.

22. Flood, *The Great Mosque of Damascus*, 135.

23. "In eodem eiusdem numeri equitibus, qui per duodecim fenestras completis horis exiebant, et inpulsu egressionis suae totidem fenestras, quae prius erant apertae claudebant," *Annales Regni Francorum*, annum 807, 123. See Chapter 1.

24. MFA 14.533. A water clock. Coomaraswamy, *The Treatise of Al-Jazari*, 10–12; Donald R. Hill, "Mechanical Engineering in the Medieval Near East," *Scientific American*, May 1991, 64–69.

25. Flood, *The Great Mosque of Damascus*, 129.

26. Dunstable Priory (1283), Exeter Cathedral (1284), St. Paul's (1286), and Merton College (1288?) in C. F. C. Beeson, *English Church Clocks, 1250–1850: History and Classification* (London: Antiquarian Horological Society, 1971). See also Julian M. Luxford, *The Art and Architecture of English Benedictine Monasteries, 1300–1540* (Woodbridge: Boydell, 2005), 209–11.

27. North, "Monasticism and the First Mechanical Clocks," 384–86; Borlik, " 'More than Art,' 129–44, esp. 136.

28. Dohrn-van Rossum, *History of the Hour*, 103–5.

29. David Glasgow, *Watch and Clock-Making* (London: Cassell, 1885), 124–26; Carlo Cipolla, *Clocks and Culture, 1300–1700* (New York: Norton, 1967, repr. 2003), 31.

30. "The First Mechanical Clocks," in *The Encyclopedia of Time*, ed. Samuel Macey (New York: Garland, 1994), 127–32; F. C. Haber, "The Cathedral Clock and the Cosmological Clock Metaphor," *The Study of Time II: Proceedings of the Second Conference of the International Society for the Study of Time, Lake Yamanaka, Japan*, ed. J. T. Fraser and Nathaniel Lawrence (Berlin: Springer Verlag, 1975), 399–416, 401.

31. Jean Froissart, *L'Horloge amoureuse*, in *Oeuvres de Jean Froissart*, ed. Auguste Scheler, 3 vols. (Brussels: Devaux, 1870), 1: 53–86. See also Julie Singer, "L'horlogerie et la mécanique de l'allégorie chez Jean Froissart," *Médiévales* 49 (2005): 155–72; Sherwood, "Magic and Mechanics in Medieval Fiction," 583–84.

32. The word *jacquemart* appears to have been derived from the French "Jacquème" and "marteau" meaning "a man with a hammer." This was shortened to "jacquemart" and translated into English as "clock-jack." See Silvio A. Bedini, "The Role of Automata in the History of Technology," *Technology and Culture* 5 (1964): 24–42, n 15.

33. Bedini, "The Role of Automata in the History of Technology," 29–31.

34. The phrase "monumental astronomical clock" is from Maurice Klaus, *Die deutsche Räderuhr: Zur Kunst und Technik des mechanischen Zeitmessers in deutschen Sprachraum*, 2 vols. (Munich: Beck, 1976), 1: 38.

35. I have not seen the Sacrists' Rolls, and instead have relied on the excerpts printed in *Archaeological Journal* 12 (1855): 175–77; and North, "Monasticism and the First Mechanical Clocks," 386.

36. *Chronica sive historia de rebus Glastoniensibus*, ed. Thomas Hearne (Oxford, 1726), cited in R. P. Howgrave-Graham, "Some Clocks and Jacks, with Notes on the History of

Horology," *Archaeologia: Or, Miscellaneous Tracts Relating to Antiquity* 77 (1928): 257–312, 288.

37. Beeson, *English Church Clocks*, 18.

38. Nicole Oresme, *Le livre du ciel et du monde*, II, 2, ed. Albert D. Menut and Alexander J. Denomy (Madison: University of Wisconsin Press, 1968), 282 (regularity), 288 (motion). See also Arno Borst, *The Ordering of Time*, trans. Andrew Winnard (Chicago: University of Chicago Press, 1993), 97.

39. Haber, "The Cathedral Clock and the Cosmological Clock Metaphor," 400.

40. J. D. North, *God's Clockmaker: Richard of Wallingford and the Invention of Time* (London: Hambledon, 2005), 179, Plate 33; Dohrn-van Rossum, *History of the Hour*, 50–52.

41. North, *God's Clockmaker*, 202–18.

42. Richard of Wallingford, *Richard of Wallingford: An Edition of His Writings with Introductions, English Translation, and Commentary*, ed. and trans. J. D. North, 3 vols. (Oxford: Clarendon, 1976), 3: 344. The Albion is conceptually similar to the Antikythera Mechanism.

43. Alfred Ungerer, *Les horloges astronomiques et monumentales les plus remarquables de l'antiquité jusqu'à nos jours* (Strasbourg, 1931), 172–73. There are many other examples of monumental astronomical clocks with automata. See, in addition to Beeson and Ungerer, Dohrn-van Rossum, *History of the Hour*, 108–13; Alan H. Lloyd, *Some Outstanding Clocks over Seven Hundred Years, 1250–1950* (London: Leonard Hill, 1958).

44. Matthew 26: 34–75; Mark 13: 32; 13: 35–36; 14: 30–72; Luke 22: 34–61; John 13: 38–18: 27.

45. Théodore Ungerer and l'Abbé André Glory, "L'astrologue au cadran solaire de la cathédrale de Strasbourg (1493)," *Archives Alsaciens d'Histoire de l'Art* 12 (1933): 73–108; Joseph Walter, "Le mystère 'Stella' de trois mages joué à la cathédrale de Strasbourg au XIIème siècle," in *Archives Alsaciens d'Histoire de l'Art* 8 (1929): 39–50.

46. Dasypodius, *Heron mechanicus: Seu de Mechanicis Ejusdem Horologii Astronomici* (Strasbourg, 1580), fol. Hii, "Siuidem ante 200 annos hic ipse gallus gallinaceus affabrefactus fuit: et ueteri horlogio impositus, atque eo tempore quo Passionem Christi in Ecclesia christiana solitum fuerat commemorare: hic suo cantu abnegationis Petri, homines commonefecit," trans. Bernard Aratowsky, introduction and commentary Günther Oestmann (Augsburg: Dr. Erwin Rauner Verlag, 2008), 153.

47. Théodore Ungerer, "Les Habrecht: Une dynastie d'horlogers strasbourgeois au XVIe et au XVIIe siècle," *Archives Alsaciennes d'Historie de l'Art* 4 (1925): 95–146; Ungerer, *Les horloges astronomiques et monumentales*, 172–73.

48. Dasypodius, *Heron mechanicus*, fol. Gii, "Pelicanum uer hunc adhibuimus, ut esset loco Atlantis: et ut aeternitatis referret symbolum, aut etia[m] redemptoris nostri ac Saluatoris." Trans. Aratowsky, 137. The pelican tears the flesh from its breast to feed its young; this was seen as a symbol of Jesus' sacrifice to save humankind.

49. Haber, "The Clock as Intellectual Artifact," in *The Clockwork Universe: German Clocks and Automata, 1550–1650*, ed. Klaus Maurice and Otto Mayr (Washington, D.C.: Smithsonian Institution, 1980), 9–18.

50. Dasypodius, *Heron mechanicus*, fol. Gii, "Singula enim et omnia ita a nobis ordinate et disposita sunt: ut certam, et notatu dignam significationem. Et uel ex sacris paginis, uel ex poetarum fabulis, uel historiarum et annalium." Trans. Aratowsky (2008), 137.

51. Ibid., fol. Hv, "tamen necessum nobis uidebatur esse: haec oblectamenti, et admirationis gratia addere: non tamen absq[ue] singulari quadam significatione." Trans. Aratowsky (2008), 151.

52. Ibid., fol. Fiv, "Et in eo [horologium] aeternitatem, seculum, periodos planetarum, Solis, et Lune annuas, et menstruas conuersiones, septimanarum, dierum, horarum, partium horariarum, ac minitorum distinctiones: hec inquam omnia, conspicienda exhibemus: adiecimus etiam ornatus, et splendoris, atque admioationis gratia, uaria machinamenta, pneumatica, sphaeropoetica, automatopoetica, ex historiis, atque poetarum fabullis, sacris, et prophanis scriptis quoque, omnia: in quibus temporis aliqua est aut esse potest descriptio." Trans. Aronowsky (2008), 129.

53. Ibid., fol. A, "Cum atrium et disciplinarum, maxima sit uarietas: non tantum earum quae animo res certunt: set et illarum quae moliuntur et faciunt aliquid: inter eas, quarum opus est in agendo atque faciendo: non postremum locum tenet mechanica. Quam qui apprime olim tenebant: in philosophi rerum naturas, uires, et effectus, perscrutantur contemplando: ita mechanici opera manuum et industria, atque ingenio et arte ea efficient: quae uel ad uitam sunt necessaria: uel ad delectationem faciunt: uel usui quotidiano accomodantur." Trans. Aratowsky, 37.

54. René Descartes, *Principles of Philosophy*, Part 4, §188. Trans. Valentine Rodger Miller and Reese P. Miller (Dordrecht: Reidel, 1983), 275–76; Thomas Hobbes, *Leviathan*, intro. and ed. Noel Malcolm, 3 vols. (Oxford: Clarendon, 2012), 2: 16; Robert Boyle, *The Usefullnesse of Natural Philosophie*, part 1 (1663), *Works* 3: 248; *Selected Philosophical Papers of Robert Boyle*, ed. M. A. Stewart (Indianapolis: Hackett, 1991), xv–xvi. Steven Shapin draws attention to the use of clock metaphors, because the clock more than any other mechanical device "appealed to early modern natural philosophers." Shapin, *The Scientific Revolution*, discussion on 32–37, quote on 32. Descartes's and Boyle's versions of mechanical philosophy are central to Shapin's narrative in chap. 4, "What Was Known?" 47–57.

BIBLIOGRAPHY

UNPUBLISHED PRIMARY SOURCES

Abrégé des histoires divines. MS. 751. New York, Pierpont Morgan Library.

Alexandre de Paris. *Roman d'Alexandre.* MS. Bodley 264. Oxford, Oxford University Library.

———. *Roman d'Alexandre.* MS. Fr. 791. Paris, BnF.

Al-Jazari. *The Book of Ingenious Mechanical Devices.* Wetzel Collection, Fogg Art Museum, 1919.138. Cambridge, Mass., Harvard University.

———. *Book of Ingenious Mechanical Devices.* MFA 4.533. Boston, Museum of Fine Arts.

Benoît de Sainte-Maure. *Roman de Troie.* MS. Fr. 60. Paris, BnF.

———. *Roman de Troie.* MS. Fr. 17. Venice, Biblioteca Marciana.

Bible. MS. M. 638. New York, Pierpont Morgan Library.

Bible moralisée. MS. Bodley 270b. Oxford, Oxford University Library.

Corsini, Matteo. *Rosaio della vita.* MS. Ricc. 656. Florence, Biblioteca Riccardiana.

———. *Rosaio della Vita.* MS. Ricc. 1159. Florence, Biblioteca Riccardiana.

———. *Rosaio della Vita.* MS. Ricc. 1735. Florence, Biblioteca Riccardiana.

———. *Rosaio della Vita.* MS. Ricc. 1736. Florence, Biblioteca Riccardiana.

Curtius, Quintus. *Historia Alexandri magni.* MS. Fr. 711. Paris, BnF.

———. *Historia Alexandri magni.* MS. 20311. Paris, BnF.

Grande chroniques de France. MS. Fr. 2610. Paris, BnF.

Guido delle Colonne. *Historia destructionis troiae.* MS. Cod. Bodmer 78. Cologny, Fondation Martin Bodmer.

Guillaume de Lorris and Jean de Meun. *Roman de la Rose.* MS. 416. New Haven, Conn., Yale University Library.

Guillaume de Machaut. *Remede de Fortune.* MS. Fr. 1586. Paris, BnF.

Histoire ancienne jusqu'à César. MS. Fr. 301. Paris, BnF.

Histoire du saint graal. MS. Fr. 113. Paris, BnF.

Horoscope. MS. Royal App. 85. London, BL.

Household accounts for Hesdin. Montheil Collection. MS KK 393. Paris, AN.

James le Palmer. *Omne Bonum.* MS. Royal E VI. London, BL.

Johannes de Colomna. *Mare historiarum.* MS. Lat. 4915. Paris, BnF.

Lancelot do lac. MS. Fr. 112. Paris, BnF.

Lancelot do lac. MS. Fr. 118. Paris, BnF.

Polo, Marco. *Livres du grant caam*. MS. Bodley 264. Oxford, Oxford University Library.

Polonus, Martinus. *Chronicon pontificum et imperatorum*. Cod. Pal. Germ. 137. Heidelberg, Universitätsbibliothek Heidelberg.

S. Gregorii moralia in Iob. MS. Lat. 83. Manchester, John Rylands Library, University of Manchester.

Villard de Honnecourt. *Carnet*. MS. Fr. 19093. Paris, BnF.

William of Conches. *De philosophia mundi*. LJS 384. Philadelphia, University of Pennsylvania.

PUBLISHED PRIMARY SOURCES

Adhémar of Chabannes. *Historiarum*. In *Adémar de Chabannes: Chronique*, ed. Jules Chavanon. Paris: Picard, 1897.

———. *Historiarum libre tres*. In *PL*, 141.

Alan of Lille. *Anticlaudianus*. In *The Anglo-Latin Satirical Poets and Epigrammatists of the Twelfth Century*, ed. Thomas Wright. RS 59. Weisbaden: Kraus, 1964.

Alexandre de Paris. *Le Roman d'Alexandre*. Paris: Livre de Poche, 1994.

Al-Jazari. *The Book of Knowledge of Ingenious Mechanical Devices*. Trans. Donald R. Hill. Dordrecht: Reidel, 1974.

Anglo-Saxon Chronicle. Ed. and trans. M. J. Swanton. New York: Routledge, 1998.

Annales regni Francorum. In *Annales regni Francorum inde a. 741 usque ad 829, qui dicuntur Annales Laurissenses maiores et Einhardi, MGH, SS. rer. Ger*, ed. F. Kurze and G. H. Pertz. Hanover: Hahn, 1895.

Aquinas, Thomas. *Summa contra Gentiles*. Leonine edition. Rome: Marietti, 1961.

Aristotle. *De spiritu*. In *The Works of Aristotle*, trans. J. F. Dobson, ed. W. D. Ross. Oxford: Clarendon, 1931.

———. *Metaphysica*. In *Metaphysical Lib. I–XIV: Recensio et translatio Guillelmi de Moerbeka*, ed. Gudrun Vuillemin-Diem. Leiden: Brill, 1939.

———. *The Complete Works of Aristotle*. Ed. H. D. P. Lee. Loeb Classical Library. Cambridge, Mass.: Harvard University Press, 1952.

———. *The Complete Works of Aristotle: The Revised Oxford Translation*. Trans. Jonathan Barnes. 2 vols. Princeton, N.J.: Princeton University Press, 1984.

———. *Aristotle's Meteorology in the Arabico-Latin Tradition: A Critical Edition of the Texts, With Introduction and Indices*. Ed. Pieter L. Schoonheim. Leiden: Brill, 2000.

Arnold of Lübeck. *Chronica Slavorum*. In *MGH, SS. rer. Ger.*, ed. Lappenberg. Hanover: Hahn, 1868.

Augustine. *The City of God Against the Pagans*. Trans. David S. Wiesen. 7 vols. Loeb Classical Library. Cambridge, Mass.: Harvard University Press, 1918.

———. *De doctrina christiana*. Ed. and trans. R. P. H. Green. Oxford: Clarendon, 1995.

Aymeri de Narbonne, chanson de geste. Ed. Louis Demaison. 2 vols. SATF. Paris: Firmin Didot, 1887.

Aymeri of Narbonne: A French Epic Romance. Trans. Michael A. H. Newth. New York: Italica Press, 2005.

Banu Musa. *The Book of Ingenious Devices (Kitab al-Hiyal)*. Trans. Donald R. Hill. Dordrecht: Kluwer, 1978.

Bede. *The Reckoning of Time*. Ed. and trans. Faith Wallis. Liverpool: Liverpool University Press, 1999.

Beno. *Benonis aliorumque cardinalium schismaticorum contra Gregorium VII et Urbanum II*. In *MGH, SS. Ldl. Scripta contra Gregorium VII et Urbanum II*, ed. K. Francke. Hanover: Hahn, 1892.

Bernard of Chartres. *The Glossae super Platonem of Bernard of Chartres*. Ed. Paul Dutton. Toronto: PIMS, 1991.

Bernard Silvestris. *Cosmographia*. Trans. Winthrop Wetherbee. New York: Columbia University Press, 1973.

Boyle, Robert. *Selected Philosophical Papers of Robert Boyle*. Ed. M. A. Stewart. Indianapolis: Hackett, 1991.

———. *The Usefullnesse of Natural Philosophie*. London, 1663.

Chalcidius. *Timaeus: A Calcidio translatus commentarioque instructus*. Ed. J. H. Waszink. In *Plato Latinus: Corpus Platonicum Medii Aevii*, ed. Raymond Kiblansky. Vol. 4. London: Warburg, 1962.

La Chanson de Roland. Ed. Luis Cortés. Paris: Nizet, 1994.

Chaucer, Geoffrey. "The Squire's Tale." In *The Riverside Chaucer*, 3rd ed., ed. Larry Benson. Boston: Houghton Mifflin, 1987.

Chronica sive historia de rebus Glastoniensibus. Ed. Thomas Hearne. Oxford, 1726.

Chronicon Novaliciense. In *MGH, SS. rer. Ger.*, ed. G. H. Pertz. Hanover: Hahn, 1846.

Codice Diplomatico dei Saraceni di Lucera. Ed. Pietro Egidi. Naples: L. Pierro et Figlio, 1917.

Le compte general du receveur d'Artois pour 1303–1304. Ed. Bernard Delmaire. Brussels: Palais des Académies, 1977.

Constantine VII Porphyrogennetos. *The Book of Ceremonies*. Trans. Anne Moffat and Maxeme Tall. 2 vols. Canberra: Australian Association for Byzantine Studies, 2012.

Le Conte de Floire et Blancheflor. Ed. Jean-Luc Leclanche. Paris: Champion, 1980.

Corsini, Matteo. *Rosaio della Vita*. Ed. Filippo Luigi Polidori. Florence: Societá Poligrafica Italiana, 1845.

Dares Phrygius. *De excidio troiae historia*. Ed. F. Meister. Leipzig: Teubner, 1873.

Dasypodius, Conrad. *Heron mechanicus: Seu de Mechanicis Ejusdem Horologii astronomici*. Strasbourg, 1580. Trans. Bernard Aratowsky, with an introduction and commentary by Günther Oestmann. Augsburg: Dr. Erwin Rauner Verlag, 2008.

Descartes, René. *Principles of Philosophy*. Trans. Valentine Rodger Miller and Reese P. Miller. Dordrecht: Riedel, 1983.

Dictys Cretensis. *Ephemeris belli troiani*. Ed. F. Meister. Leipzig: Teubner, 1872.

Die nordische Version der Tristan Sage. Ed. and trans. Eugen Kölbing. Hildesheim: Georg Olms, 1978.

Dutch Romances: Roman van Walewein. Ed. Johnson, David F. and Geert H. M. Classens. 3 vols. Woodbridge: Brewer, 2000.

Einhard. *Annales.* In *Annales regni Francorum inde a. 741 usque ad 829, qui dicuntur Annales Laurissenses maiores et Einhardi, MGH, SS. rer. Ger.*, ed. F. Kurze and G. H. Pertz. Hanover: Hahn, 1895.

Éneas. Ed. J.-J. Salverda de Grave. 2 vols. Geneva: Slatkine, 1975 [1891].

Epistola Alexandri Macedonis ad Aristotelem magistrum suum de itinere suo et de situ Indiae. Ed. and trans. Lloyd L. Gunderson. Meisenheim am Glan: Verlag, 1980.

Epistola Alexandri Macedonis ad Aristotelem magistrum suum de itinere suo et de situ Indiae. Ed. W. Walther Boer. Beitrage zur Klassichen Philologie. Meisenheim am Glan: Verlag, 1980.

Fredegarius. *Chronicari quae dicuntur Fredegarii Scholastici continuationes.* In *Fredegarii et aliorum chronica vitae sanctorum.* 2 vols. In *MGH, SS. rer. Mer.*, ed. Bruno Krusch. Hanover: Hahn, 1888.

Froissart, Jean. *L'Horloge amoureuse.* In *Oeuvres de Jean Froissart*, 1: 53–86, ed. Auguste Scheler. 3 vols. Brussels: Devaux, 1870.

Gerald of Wales. *History and Topography of Ireland.* Trans. John J. O'Meara. Harmondsworth: Penguin, 1982.

———. *Topographia Hiberniae.* In *Geraldi Cambrensis Opera*, ed. James Dimock. 8 vols. RS 21. Weisbaden: Kraus, 1964.

Gerbert of Aurillac. *De rationale et ratione uti. PL* 139. Paris, 1844–64.

———. *Lettres de Gerbert.* Ed. Julien Havet. Librairie des Archives Nationales et de la Société de l'École des Chartres. Paris: Picard, 1889.

———. *Gerbert d'Aurillac: Correspondance.* Ed. Pierre Riché and J. P. Callu. 2 vols. Paris: Belles Lettres, 1993.

Gervase of Tilbury. *Otia imperialia: Recreation for an Emperor.* Ed. and trans. S. E. Banks and J. W. Binns. Oxford: Clarendon, 2002.

Gottfried von Strassburg. *Gottfried von Strassburg: Tristan, with the Surviving Fragments of the Tristran of Thomas.* Ed. and trans. A. T. Hatto. New York: Penguin, 1960.

Gower, John. *Confessio Amantis.* Ed. G. C. Macaulay. EETS. 2 vols. London: Oxford University Press, 1969.

Greene, Robert. *Friar Bacon and Friar Bungay.* Ed. Daniel Seltzer. Lincoln: University of Nebraska Press, 1963.

Gregory of Tours. *De cursu stellarum.* In *MGH, SS. rer. Ger.*, ed. Bruno Krusch. Hanover: Hahn, 1885.

Grosseteste, Robert. *De artibus liberalibus.* In *Die philosophischen Werke des Robert Grosseteste, Bischofs von Lincoln*, ed. Ludwig Baur. BGPM. Munster: Aschendorff, 1912.

———. *De cometis.* In *Die philosophischen Werke des Robert Grosseteste, Bischofs von Lincoln*, ed. Ludwig Baur. BGPM. Munster: Aschendorff, 1912.

———. *De impressionibus aeris seu de prognosticatione.* In *Die philosophischen Werke des Robert Grosseteste, Bischofs von Lincoln*, ed. Ludwig Baur. BGPM. Munster: Aschendorff, 1912.

Guido delle Colonna. *Historia Destructionis Troiae*. Ed. Nathaniel Edward Griffin. Cambridge, Mass.: Medieval Academy, 1936.

———. *Historia Destructionis Troiae*. Ed. and trans. Mary Elizabeth Meek. Bloomington: Indiana University Press, 1974.

Guillaume de Lorris and Jean de Meun. *Roman de la Rose*. Ed. Ernest Langlois. 5 vols. SATF. Paris: Firmin Didot, 1914.

Guillaume de Machaut. *Oeuvres de Guillaume de Machaut*. Ed. Ernest Hoepffner. 3 vols. SATF. Paris: Firmin Didot, 1908–21.

———. *Le Jugement du roy du Behaigne and Remede de Fortune*. Ed. and trans. James Wimsatt and William Kibler. Athens: University of Georgia Press, 1988.

Helgaud of Fleury. *Vie de Robert le Pieux*. Ed. Robert-Henri Bautier. Paris: CNRS, 1965.

Higden, Ranulf. *Polychronicon*. In *Polychronicon Ranulphi Higden monachi cestrensis, Together with the English Translation of John Trevisa and an Unknown Writer of the Fifteenth Century*, ed. Churchill Babington. 9 vols. RS 41. London, 1865–86.

Hobbes, Thomas. *Leviathan*. Ed. Noel Malcolm. 3 vols. Oxford: Clarendon, 2012.

Homer. *The Iliad*. Trans. Michael Reck. New York: HarperCollins, 1994.

Hugh of Flavigny. *Chronicon. PL* 154. Paris, 1844–64.

Hugh of St. Victor. *Didascalicon*. Ed. Charles Henry Buttimer. Washington, D.C.: Catholic University of America Press, 1939.

———. *Didascalicon: A Medieval Guide to the Arts*. Trans. and intro. Jerome Taylor. New York: Columbia University Press, 1961.

Inventaire-Sommaire des Archives Départmentales Antérieures à 1790. Pas-des-Calais, Archives Civiles, Series A. Ed. Jules-Marie Richard. 2 vols. Arras, 1878.

Inventaires-Sommaires des Archives départmentales antérieures à 1790. Nord, Archives civiles, Série B. Ed. Chrétien C. A. Dehaisnes. 4 vols. Lille, 1881.

Isidore of Seville. *Etymologiarum sive originum libri XX*. Ed. W. M. Lindsay. 2 vols. Oxford: Clarendon, 1911.

Jacques de Vitry. *Lettres de Jacques de Vitry*, ed. R. B. C. Huygens. 2 vols. Leiden: Brill, 1960.

Jocelin of Brakelond. *The Chronicle of Jocelin of Brakelond*. Ed. and trans. H. E. Butler. London: Thomas Nelson, 1949.

John of Salisbury. *Letters. PL*, 199. Paris, 1844–64.

———. *Policraticus, sive nugis curialium et vestigiis philosophorum, libri VIII*. Ed. Charles Webb. 2 vols. Oxford: Clarendon, 1909.

———. *The Letters of John of Salisbury*. Ed. W. J. Millor and C. N. L. Brooke, trans. C. N. L. Brooke. Oxford: Clarendon, 1979.

Knighton, Henry. *Chronicon Henrici Knighton*. Ed. J. R. Lumby. 2 vols. RS 92. London, 1895.

Lancelot do Lac: The Non-Cyclic Old French Prose Romance. Ed. Elspeth Kennedy. 2 vols. Oxford: Clarendon, 1980.

Liudprand of Cremona. *Antapodosis*. In *Opera Omnia. MGH. SS. rer. Ger.*, ed. J. Becker. Hanover: Hahn, 1915.

————. *The Embassy to Constantinople and Other Writings*. Ed. John Julius Norwich, trans. F. A. Wright. London: J. M. Dent, 1993.

Lydgate, John. *Troy Book*. Ed. Henry Bergen. 3 vols. EETS 1906–35. Millwood, N.J.: Kraus, 1975.

Macrobius. *Commentarius in Somnium Scipionis*. Ed. Franz Eyssenhardt. Leipzig: Teubner, 1868.

————. *Macrobius' Commentary*. Trans. William Harris Stahl. New York: Columbia University Press, 1952.

Mandeville, John. *Mandeville's Travels*. Ed. M. C. Seymour. Oxford: Clarendon, 1967.

————. *The Book of John Mandeville with Related Texts*. Ed. and trans. Iain MacLeod Higgins. Indianapolis: Hackett, 2011.

Martin of Laon. *Scholica graecarum glossarum*. *Bulletin of the John Rylands Library* 7 (1922–23): 421–56.

Mathieu d'Escouchy. *Chronique de Mathieu d'Escouchy*. 2 vols. Paris: Renouard, 1863–64.

Neckam, Alexander. *De naturis rerum*. Ed. Thomas Wright. RS 34. London, 1863.

Odoric of Pordenone. *Relatio*. In *Sinica franciscana*, vol. 1, *Itinera et relationes fratrum Minorum saeculi XIII et XIV*. Florence: Quaracchi, 1929.

Olivier de la Marche. *Mémoires d'Olivier de la Marche: Maître d'hôtel et capitaine des gardes de Charles le Téméraire*. 4 vols. Paris: Renouard, 1884.

Oresme, Nicole. *Le livre du ciel et du monde*. Ed. Albert D. Menut and Alexander J. Denomy. Madison: University of Wisconsin Press, 1968.

Paris, Matthew. *Chronica Majora*. Ed. Henry Richard Luard. 7 vols. London: Longman, 1877.

Le Pèlerinage de Charlemagne. Ed. and trans. Glyn S. Burgess, intro. Anne Elizabeth Cobby. New York: Garland, 1988.

Perceval le Gallois, ou le conte du Graal. Ed. Charles Potvin. 6 vols in 3. 1866–71. Geneva: Slatkine, 1977.

Polo, Marco. *The Book of Ser Marco Polo the Venetian, Concerning the Kingdoms and Marvels of the East*. Ed. and trans. Henry Yule. 2 vols. London: Murray, 1875.

————. *The Travels of Marco Polo the Venetian*. Intro. John Masefield. New York: Dutton, 1908.

Richard of Bardney. *Vita Roberti Grosthead Episcopi Lincolniensis*. In *Anglia Sacra*, ed. Henry Wharton. London, 1691.

Richard of Wallingford. *Richard of Wallingford: An Edition of His Writings with Introductions, English Translation, and Commentary*. Ed. and trans. J. D. North. 3 vols. Oxford: Clarendon, 1976.

Richer of Rheims. *Historiarum Libri Quatuor*. In *MGH, SS. rer. Ger.*, ed. George Waitz. Hanover: Hahn, 1877.

Robert of Clari. *La conquête de Constantinople*. Ed. Philippe Lauer. Paris: Champion, 1924.

Le Roman de Thèbes. Ed. Léopold Constans. 2 vols. SATF. Paris: Firmin Didot, 1890.

Le Roman de Thèbes. Ed. Guy Reynaud de Lage. 2 vols. Paris: Champion, 1966, 1968.

The Saga of Tristram and Ísönd. Ed. and trans. Paul Schach. Lincoln: University of Nebraska Press, 1973.

Sainte-Maure, Benoît de. *Le Roman de Troie*. Ed. Léopold Constans. 6 vols. SATF. Paris: Firmin Didot, 1904–12.

Sigebert of Gembloux. *Chronologium*. In *PL* 160. Paris, 1844–64.

Srngaramanjarikatha. Ed. and trans. K. M. Munshi. Bombay: Bharatiya Vidya Bhavan, 1959.

Statius, P. Papinius. *Thebaid*. Ed. and trans. D. R. Shackleton Bailey. Loeb Classical Library. Cambridge, Mass.: Harvard University Press, 2003.

Theophilus. *De diversis artibus*. Ed. and trans. C. R. Dodwell. Oxford: Clarendon, 1986.

Thietmar of Merseburg. *Thietmari Merseburgensis Episcopi Chronicon*. In *MGH, SS. rer. Ger.*, ed. F. Kurze. Hanover: Hahn, 1889.

———. *Ottonian Germany: The Chronicon of Thietmar of Merseburg*. Trans. David A. Warner. Manchester: Manchester University Press, 2001.

Thomas of Britain. *Le Roman de Tristran par Thomas, poème du XIIème siècle*. Ed. Joseph Bédier. 2 vols. SATF. Paris: Firmin Didot, 1902–5.

———. *The Romance of Tristram and Ysolt by Thomas of Britain, translated from the Old French and the Old Norse*. Trans. Roger Loomis. New York: Columbia University Press, 1931.

———. *Tristran*. Ed. and trans. Stewart Gregory. New York: Garland, 1991.

Vitruvius. *De architectura libri decem*. Ed. Curt Fensterbusch. Darmstadt: Wissenschaftliche Buchegesellschaft, 1976.

Le Voyage de Charlemagne à Jérusalem et à Constantinople. Ed. Paul Aebischer. Geneva: Droz, 1965.

Wharton, Henry. *Anglia Sacra*. London, 1691.

Wilkins, D. *Concilia Magnae Britanniae et Hiberniae*. 2 vols. London, 1737.

William of Auvergne. *De universo*. In *Opera Omnia*, ed. Peter Aubouin. 2 vols. Paris: Aureliae, 1674.

William of Malmesbury. *Gesta regum anglorum*. Ed. Bishop William Stubbs. 2 vols. 1887–89. Wiesbaden: Kraus, 1964.

———. *De gestis regum Anglorum libri quinque*. Ed. and trans. R. A. B. Mynors, Rodney M. Thomson, and Michael Winterbottom. 2 vols. Oxford: Clarendon, 1998.

———. *Gesta pontificum anglorum*. Ed. and trans. Rodney M. Thomson and Michael Winterbottom. 2 vols. Oxford: Clarendon, 2007.

William of Rubruck. *The Journey of William of Rubruck to the Eastern Parts of the World, 1253–55*. Ed. and trans. William Woodville Rockhill. London: Hakluyt Society, 1900.

Yasastilakacampu. Ed. P. Sivadatta and Kasinath Pandurang Parab. Bombay: Tukaram Javaji, 1901.

SECONDARY SOURCES

Abulafia, David. *Frederick II: A Medieval Emperor*. London: Penguin, 1988.

Adam, Jean-Pierre and Pierre Varene. "La scie hydraulique de Villard de Honnecourt et sa place dans l'histoire des techniques." *Bulletin Monumental* 143 (1985): 317–22.

Aiken, Jane Andrews. "Truth in Images: From the technical drawings of Ibn Al-Razzaz Al-Jazari, Campanus of Novara, and Giovanni de'Dondi to the Perspective Projection of Leon Battista Alberti." *Viator* 25 (1994): 325–59.

Akbari, Suzanne Conklin. *Idols in the East: European Representations of Islam and the Orient, 1100–1450.* Ithaca, N.Y.: Cornell University Press, 2009.

Albert, Jean-Pierre. *Odeurs de sainteté: La mythologie chrétienne des aromates.* Paris: École des Hautes Études en Sciences Sociales, 1990.

Ali, Daud. "Gardens in Early Indian Court Life." *Studies in History* 19 (2003): 221–52.

Alidori, Laura. "Il Plut. 20.56 della Laurenziana. Appunti sull'iconografia dei manoscritti della *Genealogia* di Petrus Pictaviensis." *Rivista di Storia della Miniatura* 6–7 (2001–2002): 157–70.

Althoff, Gerd. *Otto III.* Trans. Phyllis G. Jestice. University Park: Pennsylvania State University Press, 2003.

Alverny, Marie-Thérèse. *La transmission des textes philosophiques et scientifiques au moyen âge.* Aldershot: Variorum, 1994.

Alverny, Marie-Thérèse and Franchise Hudry. "Al-Kindi, *De Radiis.*" *Archives d'Histoire Doctrinale et Littéraire du Moyen Âge* 61 (1974): 139–259.

Amartin-Serin, Annie. *La Création défiée: L'homme fabriqué dans la littérature.* Paris: Presses Universitaires de France, 1996.

Anderson, Benjamin. "Public Clocks in Late Antique and Early Medieval Constantinople." *Jahrbuch der Österreichischen Byzantinistik* 64 (2014): 24–32.

Andrea, Alfred J. "Essay on Primary Sources." In *The Fourth Crusade: The Conquest of Constantinople,* ed. Donald E. Queller and Thomas F. Madden, 299–313. Philadelphia: University of Pennsylvania Press, 1993.

Aubé, Pierre. *Roger II de Sicile.* Paris: Payot et Rivages, 2001.

Avril, François. *Manuscript Painting at the Court of France: The Fourteenth Century.* Trans. Ursule Moliano with the assistance of Bruce Benderson. New York: Braziller, 1978.

———. "Les manuscrits enluminés de Guillaume de Machaut." In *Guillaume de Machaut: Colloque-table ronde,* organisé par l'Université de Rheims. Actes et Colloques 23. Paris: Klincksieck, 1982.

Baer, Eva. *Ayyubid Metalwork with Christian Images.* Studies in Islamic Art and Architecture 4. Leiden: Brill, 1989.

Bardill, Jonathan. "Monuments and decoration of the Hippodrome." In *Hippodrome/Atmeydanı: A Stage for Istanbul's History,* ed. Brigitte Pitarakis, 149–84. Istanbul: Pera Müzesi, 2010.

Barron, Roger. *Science et sagesse chez Hugues de Saint-Victor.* Paris: Lethielleux, 1957.

Barton, Tamsyn. *Ancient Astrology.* London: Routledge, 1994.

Baswell, Christopher. *Virgil in Medieval England: Figuring the Aeneid from the Twelfth Century to Chaucer.* Cambridge: Cambridge University Press, 1995.

Battles, Dominique. "Trojan Elements in the Old French *Roman de Thèbes.*" *Neophilologus* 85 (2001): 163–76.

Baum, Paul Franklin. "The Young Man Betrothed to a Statue." *PMLA* 34 (1919): 523–79.

Beaune, Colette. "L'utilisation politique du mythe des origines troyennes en France à la fin du moyen âge." In *Lectures médiévales de Virgile: Actes du colloque organisé par l'École française de Rome (Rome, 25–28 octobre, 1982)*, 331–55. Rome: École Française de Rome, 1985.

Bechmann, Roland. *Villard de Honnecourt: La pensée technique au XIIIème siècle et sa communication*. Paris: Picard, 1991.

Bedini, Silvio A. "The Compartmented Cylindrical Clepsydra." *Technology and Culture* 3 (1963): 114–41.

———. "The Role of Automata in the History of Technology." *Technology and Culture* 5 (1964): 24–42.

———. "Sylvester II, Pope." In *Dictionary of the Middle Ages*, ed. Joseph Strayer. 12 vols. New York: Scribner, 1982–89.

Beer, Rudolf. "Die Handschriften des Klosters Santa Maria de Ripoll." *Sitzungsberichte der Akademie der Wissenschaften, Philosophisch-historische Klasse* 155 (1908), Abhandlung III.

Beeson, C. F. C. *English Church Clocks, 1250–1850: History and Classification*. London: Antiquarian Horological Society, 1971.

Benson, C. David. *The History of Troy in Middle English Literature*. Woodbridge: Boydell, 1980.

Bernheimer, Richard. *Wild Men in the Middle Ages: A Study in Art, Sentiment, and Demonology*. New York: Octagon, 1970.

Berryman, Sylvia. "Ancient Automata and Mechanical Explanation." *Phronesis* 48 (2003): 344–69.

———. "The Imitation of Life in Ancient Greek Philosophy." In *Genesis Redux: Essays in the History of Philosophy and Artificial Life*, ed. Jessica Riskin, 35–45. Chicago: University of Chicago Press, 2007.

Beumann, Jutta. *Sigebert von Gembloux und der Traktat de investitura episcoporum*. Sigmaringen: Jan Thorbecke, 1976.

Bezzola, Reto. *Les origines de la formation de la littérature courtoise en Occident*. 3 vols. Paris: Champion, 1944–63.

Blacker, Jean. *The Faces of Time: Portrayal of the Past in Old French and Latin Historical Narrative of the Anglo-Norman Regnum*. Austin: University of Texas Press, 1994.

Blumenfeld-Kosinski, Renate. "Old French Narrative Genres: Towards a Definition of the *roman antique*." *Romance Philology* 34 (1980–81): 143–59.

———. *Reading Myth: Classical Mythology and Its Interpretations in Medieval French Literature*. Palo Alto, Calif.: Stanford University Press, 1997.

Boas, Marie. "Hero's *Pneumatica*: A Study of Its Transmission and Influence." *Isis* 40 (1949): 38–48.

Bolens, Guillemette. "La momification dans la littérature médiévale: L'embaument d'Hector chez Benoît de Sainte-Maure, Guido delle Colonne, et John Lydgate." *Micrologus* 13 (2005): 213–31.

Bond, John David. "Richard Wallingford." *Isis* 12 (1922): 459–65.

Borlik, Todd Andrew. "'More Than Art': Clockwork Automata, the Extemporizing Actor, and the Brazen Head in *Friar Bacon and Friar Bungay*." In *The Automaton in English Renaissance Literature*, ed. Wendy Hyman, 129–44. Surrey: Ashgate, 2011.

Borst, Arno. *The Ordering of Time: From the Ancient Computus to the Modern Computer*. Trans. Andrew Winnard. Chicago: University of Chicago Press, 1993.

Boudet, Jean-Patrice. *Entre science et nigromance: Astrologie, divination et magie dans l'Occident médiéval (XIIe–XVe siècle)*. Paris: Publications de la Sorbonne, 2006.

Brett, Gerard. "The Automata in the Byzantine 'Throne of Solomon'." *Speculum* 29 (1954): 477–88.

Brians, Paul. "Paul Aebischer and the 'Gab d'Olivier.'" *Romance Notes* 15 (1973–74): 164–71.

Brooks, George. "The 'Vitruvian Mill' in Roman and Medieval Europe." In *Wind and Water in the Middle Ages*, ed. Steven A. Walton, 1–39. MRTS. Tempe, Ariz: ACMRS, 2006.

Brown, Peter. *The Cult of the Saints: Its Rise and Function in Latin Christianity*. Chicago: University of Chicago Press, 1981.

Bruce, Douglas. "Human Automata in Classical Tradition and Medieval Romance." *Modern Philology* 10 (1913): 511–26.

Brumbaugh, R. S. *Ancient Greek Gadgets and Machines*. New York: Cromwell, 1966.

Bruyne, Edgar de. *Études d'esthétique médiévale*. 3 vols. Bruges: De Tempel, 1946.

Buchthal, Hugo. *Historia troiana: Studies in the History of Mediaeval Secular Illustration*. Leiden: Brill, 1971.

Buettner, Brigitte. "Profane Illuminations, Secular Illusions: Manuscripts in Late Medieval Courtly Society." *Art Bulletin* 74 (1992): 75–90.

Burnett, Charles. *Adelard of Bath: An English Scientist and Arabist of the Early Twelfth Century*. London: Warburg, 1987.

———. *The Introduction of Arabic Learning into England*. London: British Library, 1997.

———. "King Ptolemy and Alchandreus the Philosopher: The Earliest Texts on the Astrolabe and Arabic Astrology at Fleury, Micy and Chartres." *Annals of Science* 55 (1998): 329–68.

———. *Magic and Divination in the Middle Ages: Texts and Techniques in the Islamic and Christian Worlds*. Aldershot: Variorum, 1996.

———. "Mathematics and Astronomy in Hereford and Its Region in the Twelfth Century." In *Hereford: Medieval Art, Architecture, and Archaeology*, ed. David Whitehead. British Archaeological Association Conference Transactions. Leeds: Maney, 1995.

———. "The Works of Petrus Alfonsi." *Medium Aevum* 66 (1997): 42–79.

Burnett, Charles and Danielle Jacquart, eds. *Constantine the African and the 'Ali ibn al-'Abbas al-Magusi: The "Pantegni" and Related Works*. Studies in Ancient Medicine 10. Leiden: Brill, 1994.

Butler, E. M. *The Myth of the Magus*. Cambridge: Cambridge University Press, 1948.

Bynum, Caroline Walker. "Wonder." *AHR* 102 (1997): 1–26.

Cadden, Joan. "Charles V, Nicole Oresme, and Christine de Pizan: Unities and Uses of Knowledge in Fourteenth-Century France." In *Texts and Contexts in Ancient and*

Medieval Science: Studies on the Occasion of John E. Murdoch's Seventieth Birthday, ed. Edith Sylla and Michael McVaugh, 208–44. Leiden: Brill, 1997.

———. *Meanings of Sex Difference in the Middle Ages*. Cambridge: Cambridge University Press, 1993.

Cameron, Averil. "The Construction of Court Ritual: The Byzantine *Book of Ceremonies*." In *Rituals of Royalty: Power and Ceremonial in Traditional Societies*, ed. David Cannadine and Simon Price, 106–36. Cambridge: Cambridge University Press, 1987.

Camille, Michael. *The Gothic Idol: Ideology and Image Making in Medieval Art*. Cambridge: Cambridge University Press, 1989.

Campbell, Mary Baine. *The Witness and the Other World: Exotic European Travel Writing, 400–1600*. Ithaca, N.Y.: Cornell University Press, 1988.

———. *Wonder and Science: Imagining Worlds in Early Modern Europe*. Ithaca, N.Y.: Cornell University Press, 1999.

Carey, Hilary M. *Courting Disaster: Astrology at the English Court and University in the Later Middle Ages*. London: Macmillan, 1992.

Carruthers, Mary. *The Book of Memory: A Study of Memory in Medieval Culture*. 2nd ed. Cambridge: Cambridge University Press, 2008.

Cary, George. *The Medieval Alexander*. Cambridge: Cambridge University Press, 1956.

Chandès, Gérard, ed. *Le merveilleux et la magie dans la littérature*. Amsterdam: Rodopi, 1992.

Chapuis, Alfred. *Les automates dans les oeuvres de l'imagination*. Neuchatel: Griffon, 1947.

Chapuis, Alfred and Edmond Droz. *Les automates, figures artificielles d'hommes et d'animaux*. Neuchatel: Griffon, 1949.

Chapuis, Alfred and Edouard Gelis. *Le monde des automates*. Paris: Griffon, 1928.

Chargeat, Marguerite. "Le parc d'Hesdin, création monumental du XIIIe siècle." *Bulletin de la Société de l'Histoire de l'Art Français* (1950): 94–104.

Chazan, Mireille. *L'empire et l'histoire universelle de Sigebert de Gembloux à Jean de Saint-Victor*. Paris: Champion, 1999.

Chenu, Marie-Dominique. *Nature, Man, and Society in the Twelfth Century*. Trans. Jerome Taylor and Lester K. Little. Chicago: University of Chicago Press, 1968.

Cipolla, Carlo. *Clocks and Culture, 1300–1700*. New York: Collins, 1978.

Clagget, Marshall. *The Science of Mechanics in the Middle Ages*. Madison: University of Wisconsin Press, 1961.

Clark, Frederic N. "Authenticity, Antiquity, and Authority: Dares Phrygius in Early Modern Europe." *Journal of the History of Ideas* 72 (2011): 183–207.

Clark, Stuart. *Thinking with Demons*. Oxford: Oxford University Press, 1997.

Cléty, Anne-Elisabeth. "Les machines extraordinaires d'Hesdin aux XIVème et XVème siècles." *Sucellus* 44 (1997): 1–59.

Cochrane, Louise. *Adelard of Bath: The First English Scientist*. London: British Museum, 1994.

Cohen, H. Floris. *How Modern Science Came into the World: Four Civilizations, One 17th-Century Breakthrough*. Amsterdam: Amsterdam University Press, 2011.

Cohen, John. *Human Robots in Myth and Science*. London: Allen and Unwin, 1966.

Collins, D. J. "Albertus, 'Magnus' or Magus? Magic, Natural Philosophy, and Religious Reform in the Late Middle Ages." *Renaissance Quarterly* 63 (2010): 1–44.

Colvile, K. N. "The Tale of Troy." *Greece & Rome* 10 (1940): 1–11.

Comparetti, Domenico. *Vergil in the Middle Ages*. Trans. E. F. M. Benecke, intro. Jan M. Ziolkowski. Princeton, N.J.: Princeton University Press, 1997.

Contini, Gianfranco. *Poeti del Duecento*. 2 vols. Milan: Riccardi, 1960.

Contreni, John J. *The Cathedral School of Laon, 850–930: Its Manuscripts and Masters*. Munich: Arbeo-Gesellschaft, 1978.

Coomaraswamy, Ananda K. *The Treatise of Al-Jazari on Automata*. Boston: Museum of Fine Arts, 1924.

Cooper, Helen. "Magic That Does Not Work." *Medievalia et Humanistica* 7 (1976): 131–46.

Copenhaver, Brian. "Hermes Trismegistus, Proclus, and the Question of Philosophy of Magic in the Renaissance." In *Hermeticism and the Renaissance: Intellectual History and the Occult in Early Modern Europe*, ed. Ingrid Merkel and Allan Debus. Washington, D.C.: Folger Books, 1998.

———. "Natural Magic, Hermetism, and Occultism in Early Modern Science." In *Reappraisals of the Scientific Revolution*, ed. David C. Lindberg and Robert S. Westman, 261–301. Cambridge: Cambridge University Press, 1990.

———. "Scholastic Philosophy and Renaissance Magic in the *De vita* of Marsilio Ficino." *Renaissance Quarterly* 37 (1984): 523–54.

Crane, Susan. *The Performance of Self: Ritual, Clothing, and Identity During the Hundred Years War*. Philadelphia: University of Pennsylvania Press, 2002.

Cubitt, Catherine. "Folklore and Historiography: Oral Stories and the Writing of Anglo-Saxon History." In *Narrative and History in the Early Medieval West*, ed. Elizabeth M. Tyler and Ross Balzaretti, 189–223. Turnhout: Brepols, 2006.

Curtius, Ernst Robert. *European Literature and the Latin Middle Ages*. Trans. Willard R. Trask. Bollingen Series 36. Princeton, N.J.: Princeton University Press, 1953.

Dalby, Andrew. *Dangerous Tastes: The Story of Spices*. London: British Museum, 2000.

Dalché, Patrick Gautier. "Le 'Tuyau' de Gerbert, ou la légende savante de l'astronome: origines, thèmes, échos contemporains (avec un appendice critique)." *Micrologus* 21 (2013): 243–76.

Daniel, Norman. *Heroes and Saracens: An Interpretation of the Chansons de Geste*. Edinburgh: Edinburgh University Press, 1984.

Danvin, Bruno. *Vicissitudes, heur et malheur du Vieil-Hesdin*. St.-Pol: Bécart-Renard, 1866.

D'Arcier, Louis Faivre. *Histoire et géographie d'un mythe: la circulation des manuscrits du De excidio Troiae de Darès le Phrygien (VIIIe–XVe siècles)*. Paris: École des Chartres, 2006.

Darlington, Oscar. "Gerbert, the Teacher." *AHR* 52 (1947): 456–76.

Daston, Lorraine and Katharine Park. *Wonders and the Order of Nature*. New York: Zone, 1998.

Daumas, Maurice. "Le faux échappement de Villard de Honnecourt." *Revue d'Histoire des Sciences* 35 (1982): 43–52.

Davidson, Clifford. "Heaven's Fragrance." In *The Iconography of Heaven*, ed. Clifford Davidson, 110–27. Kalamazoo, Mich: Medieval Institute Publications, 1994.

———. *Technology, Guilds, and Early English Drama*. Early Art, Drama, and Music Monograph Series 23. Kalamazoo, Mich: Medieval Institute Publications, 1997.

Dear, Peter. *Revolutionizing the Sciences: European Knowledge and Its Ambitions, 1500–1700*. 2nd ed. Princeton, N.J.: Princeton University Press, 2009.

Dehaisnes, Chrétien C. A. *Documents et extraits divers concernant l'histoire de l'art dans la Flandre, l'Artois, le Hainaut avant le XVème siècle*. 2 vols. Lille: Daniel, 1886.

Delumeau, Jean. *Un histoire du Paradis*. 2 vols. Paris: Fayard, 1992.

Deluz, Christian. *Le Livre de Jehan de Mandeville: Une "géographie" au XIVe siècle*. Louvain-la-Neuve: Institut d'Études Médiévales de l'Université Catholique de Louvain, 1988.

Dickson, Arthur. *Valentine and Orson: A Study in Late Medieval Romance*. New York: Columbia University Press, 1929.

Dictionary of Old French. Ed. A. Hindley, Frederick William Langley, and B. J. Levy. Cambridge: Cambridge University Press, 2000.

Dictionnaire de l'ancienne langue française et tous ses dialects du IXe au XVe siècle. Ed. Frédéric Godefroy. 8 vols. Geneva: Slatkine, 1982.

Dictionnaire étymologique de la langue française. Ed. Gilles Ménage. 2 vols. Geneva: Slatkine, 1973.

Dictionnaire historique de la langue française. Ed. Alain Rye. 2 vols. Paris: Robert, 1992.

Dohrn-van Rossum, Gerhard. *The History of the Hour: Clocks and Modern Temporal Orders*. Trans. Thomas Dunlap. Chicago: University of Chicago Press, 1996.

Döllinger, Johann Joseph. *Die Pabst-fabeln des Mittelalters*. Munich: Cotta, 1863.

Drachmann, A. G. *Ktesibios, Philon, and Heron, a study in ancient pneumatics*. Copenhagen: Munksgaard, 1948.

———. *The Mechanical Technology of Greek and Roman Antiquity*. Copenhagen: Munksgaard, 1963.

Drover, C. B. "A Medieval Monastic Water-Clock." *Antiquarian Horology* 1 (1954): 54–63.

Duc de la Salle de Rochemaure. *Gerbert. Silvestre II. Le savant, le "faiseur de rois," le pontife*. Paris: Émile-Paul Frères, 1914.

Ducos, Joëlle. *La météorologie en français au Moyen Age (XIIIe et XIVe siècles)*. Paris: Champion, 1998.

Dunbabin, Jean. *The French in the Kingdom of Sicily 1266–1305*. Cambridge: Cambridge University Press, 2011.

Dykmans, Marc. *Le cérémonial papal de la fin du Moyen Age à la Renaissance*. 4 vols. Brussels: Institut Historique Belge de Rome, 1977–85.

Eamon, William. *Science and the Secrets of Nature: Books of Secrets in Medieval and Early Modern Culture*. Princeton, N.J.: Princeton University Press, 1994.

———. "Technology as Magic in the Late Middle Ages and the Renaissance." *Janus* 70 (1983): 171–212.

Eastwood, Bruce. "The Astronomies of Pliny, Martianus Capella, and Isidore of Seville in the Carolingian World." In *Science in Western and Eastern Civilization in Carolingian Times*, ed. P. L. Butzer and D. Lohrmann, 161–80. Basel: Verlag AG, 1993.

———. "Astronomy in Christian Latin Europe, c. 500–c. 1150." *Journal for the History of Astronomy* 28 (1997): 235–58.

Eberle, Patricia. "The Politics of Courtly Style at the Court of Richard II." In *The Spirit of the Court*, ed. Glyn S. Burgess and Robert A. Taylor. Cambridge: Brewer, 1985.

Economou, George. *The Goddess Natura in Medieval Literature*. Cambridge, Mass.: Harvard University Press, 1972.

Edson, Evelyn. "The Medieval World View: Contemplating the Mappamundi." *History Compass* 8/6 (2010): 503–17.

Eley, Penny. "Author and Audience in the *Roman de Troie*." In *Courtly Literature: Culture and Context; Selected papers from the 5th Triennial Congress of the International Courtly Literature Society, Dalfsen, The Netherlands, 9–16 August, 1986*, ed. Keith Busby and Erik Kooper, 179–90. Amsterdam: Benjamins, 1990.

———. "Translation and Adaption in the *Roman de Troie*." In *The Spirit of the Court. Selected Proceedings of the Fourth Congress of the International Courtly Literature Society (Toronto, 1983)*, ed. Glyn S. Burgess and Robert A. Taylor, 350–59. Woodbridge: Brewer, 1985.

The Encyclopedia of Time. Ed. Samuel Macey. New York: Garland, 1994.

Erlande-Brandenburg, Alain. "Villard de Honnecourt, l'architecture et la sculpture." In *Le carnet de Villard de Honnecourt*. Ed. Alain Erlande-Brandenburg, Regine Pernoud, Jean Gimpel, and Roland Bechmann, 17–25. Paris: Stock, 1986.

Faral, Edmond. *Les arts poétiques du XIIème et du XIIIème siècle: Recherches et documents sur la technique littéraire du moyen âge*. Paris: Champion, 1924.

———. "Le merveilleux et ses sources dans les descriptions des romans français du XIIème siècle." In *Recherches sur les sources latines des contes et romans courtois du Moyen Âge*. Paris: Champion, 1913.

Farmer, D. H. "William of Malmesbury's Life and Works." *Journal of Ecclesiastical History* 13 (1962): 39–54.

Farmer, Sharon. "Aristocratic Power and the 'Natural' Landscape: The Garden Park at Hesdin, ca. 1291–1302." *Speculum* 88 (2013): 644–80.

———. "*La Zisa/Gloriette*: Cultural Interaction and the Architecture of Repose in Medieval Sicily, France and Britain." *Journal of the British Archaeological Association* 166 (2013): 99–123.

Federico, Sylvia. *New Troy: Fantasies of Empire in the Late Middle Ages*. Minneapolis: University of Minnesota Press, 2003.

Feldhaus, Franz Maria. *Die Technik der Antike und des Mittlealters*. Potsdam: Akademische verlagsgesellschaft Athenaion, 1931.

Finucane, Ronald. *Miracles and Pilgrims: Popular Beliefs in Medieval England.* Totowa, N.J.: Rowman and Littlefield, 1977.

Fisher, John. *John Gower: Moral Philosopher and Friend of Chaucer.* New York: New York University Press, 1964.

Fleischman, Suzanne. "On the Representation of History and Fiction in the Middle Ages." *History and Theory* 22 (1983): 278–310.

Flint, Valerie. *The Rise of Magic in Early Medieval Europe.* Princeton, N.J.: Princeton University Press, 1991.

Flood, Finbarr Barry. *The Great Mosque of Damascus: Studies on the Making of an Umayyad Visual Culture.* Leiden: Brill, 2001.

Flusche, Anna Marie. *The Life and Legend of Gerbert d'Aurillac: The Organ-Builder Who Became Pope Sylvester II.* Lampeter, Wales: Edwin Mellen, 2005.

Fox, George G. *The Medieval Sciences in the Works of John Gower.* Princeton, N.J.: Princeton University Press, 1931.

Franke, Birgit. "Gesellshaftsspiele mit Automaten: 'Merveilles' in Hesdin." *Marburger Jahrbuch für Kunstwissenschaft* 24 (1997): 135–58.

Freeman, Michelle. *The Poetics of translatio studii and conjointure: Chrétien de Troyes' Cligès.* Lexington, Ky.: French Forum, 1979.

———. "Problems in Romance Composition: Ovid, Chrétien de Troyes, and the *Romance of the Rose.*" *Romance Philology* 30 (1976): 158–68.

Freeth, Tony, Alexander Jones, John M. Steele, and Yanis Bitsakis. "Calendars with Olympiad Display and Eclipse Prediction on the Antikythera Mechanism," *Nature* 454 (31 July 2008): 614–17.

French, Roger. "Foretelling the Future: Arabic Astrology and English Medicine in the Late Twelfth Century." *Isis* 87 (1996): 453–80.

Frenzel, Elisabeth. *Stoffe de Weltliteratur: Ein Lexikon dichtungsgeschichtlicher längshnitte.* 4th ed. Stuttgart: Kröner, 1976.

Freud, Sigmund. "The Uncanny." In *The Uncanny*, trans. David McLintock, 121–98. New York: Penguin, 2003.

Friedman, John Block. *The Monstrous Races in Medieval Art and Thought.* 2nd ed. Syracuse, N.Y.: Syracuse University Press, 2000.

Gabriele, Matthew. "Otto III, Charlemagne, and Pentecost A.D. 1000: A Reconsideration Using Diplomatic Evidence." In *The Year 1000: Religious and Social Response to the Turning of the First Millennium*, ed. Michael Frassetto, 111–32. New York: Palgrave, 2003.

Galison, Peter. *Image and Logic: A Material Culture of Microphysics.* Chicago: University of Chicago Press, 1997.

Geary, Patrick. *Furta Sacra.* Princeton, N.J.: Princeton University Press, 1978.

Gies, Frances and Joseph Gies. *Cathedral, Forge, and Water-Wheel: Technology and Invention in the Middle Ages.* New York: HarperCollins, 1994.

Gimpel, Jean. "Villard de Honnecourt, Architechte-ingenieur." In *Le carnet de Villard de Honnecourt*, ed. Alain Erlande-Brandenburg, Regine Pernoud, Jean Gimpel, and Roland Bechmann. Paris: Stock, 1986.

Glasgow, David. *Watch and Clock-Making*. London: Cassell, 1885.

Glossarum mediae et infimae latinitatis. Ed. Charles DuCange. 10 vols. Paris: Librairie des Sciences et des Arts, 1937–38.

Goode, Patrick and Michael Lancaster, eds. *The Oxford Companion to Gardens*. Oxford: Oxford University Press, 1986.

Gordon, R. L. "The Real and the Imaginary: Production and Religion in the Graeco-Roman World," *Art History* 2 (1979): 5–34.

Görich, Knut. "Otto III öffnet das Karlsgrab in Aachen." In *Herrschaftsrepräsentation im ottonischen Sachsen*, ed. Gerd Althoff and Ernst Schubert, 381–430. Sigmaringen: Thorbecke, 1998.

Gosman, Martin. "La propagande politique dans *Le Voyage de Charlemagne à Jérusalem et à Constantinople*." *Zeitschrift für romanische Philologie* 102 (1986): 53–66.

Gransden, Antonia. *Historical Writing in England c. 550 to c. 1307*. Ithaca, N.Y.: Cornell University Press, 1974.

Grant, Edward. "Henricus Aristippus, William of Moerbeke and Two Alleged Mediaeval Translations of Hero's *Pneumatica*." *Speculum* 46 (1971): 656–69.

Green, Louis. "Galvano Fiamma, Azzone Visconti, and the Revival of the Classical Theory of Magnificence." *Journal of the Warburg and Courtauld Institutes* 53 (1990): 98–113.

Green, R. H. "Alan of Lille's *De planctu naturae*." *Speculum* 31 (1956): 649–74.

Grigsby, John L. "A Note on the Genre of the *Voyage de Charlemagne*." In *Essays in Early French Literature Presented to Barbara M. Craig*, ed. Norris J. Lacy and Jerry C. Nash, 1–8. New York: French Literature Publications, 1982.

Groom, Nigel. *Frankincense and Myrrh: A Study of the Arabian Incense Trade*. London: Longman, 1981.

Gros i Pujol, Miquel dels Sants. "La vila de Vic i el monestir de Ripoll en els anys 967–970." In *Actes del Congrés international Gerbert d'Orlhac i el seu temps: Catalunya i Europa a la fi del 1r milleni. Vic-Ripoll, 10–13 de novembre de 1999*, 747–61. Vic: Eumo, 1999.

Gross, Kenneth. *The Dream of the Moving Statue*. Ithaca, N.Y.: Cornell University Press, 1992.

Gutas, Dimitri. *Greek Thought, Arabic Culture: The Graeco-Arabic Translation Movement in Baghdad and Early 'Abbasid Society (2nd–4th/8th–10th Centuries)*. Abingdon: Routledge, 1998.

Guyotjeannin, Olivier and Emmanuel Poulle. *Autour de Gerbert d'Aurillac, le Pape de l'an mil*. Paris: Champion, 1996.

Haber, F. C. "The Cathedral Clock and the Cosmological Clock Metaphor." In *The Study of Time II: Proceedings of the Second Conference of the International Society for the Study of Time, Lake Yamanaka, Japan*, ed. J. T. Fraser and Nathaniel Lawrence, 339–416. Berlin: Springer-Verlag, 1975.

———. "The Clock as Intellectual Artifact." In *The Clockwork Universe: German Clocks and Automata, 1550–1650*, ed. Klaus Maurice and Otto Mayr, 9–18. Washington, D.C.: Smithsonian Institution, 1980.

Hackett, Jeremiah. "Roger Bacon on Astronomy-Astrology: The Sources of the *Scientia experimentalis.*" In *Roger Bacon and the Sciences*, ed. Jeremiah Hackett, 175–99. Leiden: Brill, 1997.

Hanning, Robert. *The Vision of History in Early Britain: From Gildas to Geoffrey of Monmouth.* New York: Columbia University Press, 1966.

Haskins, Charles Homer. "The Reception of Arabic Science in England." *English Historical Review* 30 (1915): 56–69.

———. *The Renaissance of the Twelfth Century.* Cambridge, Mass.: Harvard University Press, 1927.

———. *Studies in the History of Medieval Science.* Cambridge, Mass.: Harvard University Press, 1924.

Haynes, D. E. L. "Philo of Byzantium and the Colossus of Rhodes." *Journal of Hellenic Studies* 77 (1957): 311–12.

Head, Thomas. *Hagiography and the Cult of Saints: The Diocese of Orléans, 800–1200.* Cambridge: Cambridge University Press, 1990.

Healy, Patrick. *The Chronicle of Hugh of Flavigny: Reform and the Investiture Contest in the Late Eleventh Century.* Aldershot: Ashgate, 2006.

Henkin, Leo. "The Carbuncle in the Adder's Head." *Modern Language Notes* 58 (1943): 34–39.

Henry, John. "Occult Qualities and the Experimental Philosophy." *History of Science* 24 (1986): 335–81.

Higgins, Iain Macleod. *Writing East: The "Travels" of Sir John Mandeville.* Philadelphia: University of Pennsylvania Press, 1997.

Higley, Sarah Lynn. "The Legend of the Learned Man's Android." In *Retelling Tales: Essays in Honor of Russell Peck*, ed. Thomas Hahn and Alan Lupack, 127–60. Rochester, N.Y.: Brewer, 1997.

Hill, Donald. "Arabic Fine Technology and Its Influence on European Mechanical Engineering." In *The Arab Influence in Medieval Europe*, ed. Dionisius A. Aigus and Richard Hitchcock, 25–43. Reading: Ithaca Press, 1994.

———. "From Philo to al-Jazari." In *Learning, Language, and Invention: Essays Presented to Francis Maddison*, ed. W. D. Hackmann and A. J. Turner, 188–206. Aldershot: Variorum, 1994.

———. "Islamic Fine Technology and Its Influence on the Development of European Horology." *Al-Abhath* 35. Beirut: American University of Beirut, 1987. Rep. in Donald Hill, *Studies in Medieval Islamic Technology: From Philo to al-Jazari—from Alexandria to Diyar Bakr*, ed. David A. King, 9–28. Aldershot: Ashgate, 1998.

———. "Mechanical Engineering in the Medieval Near East." *Scientific American* (May 1991): 64–69.

———. "Medieval Arabic Mechanical Technology." In *Proceedings of the First International Symposium for the History of Arabic Science, Aleppo, April 5–12, 1976.* Aleppo: Institute for the History of Arabic Science, 1979. Rep. in Donald Hill, *Studies in Medieval Islamic Technology: From Philo to al-Jazari—from Alexandria to Diyar Bakr*, ed. David A. King, 222–37. Aldershot: Ashgate, 1998.

Horden, Peregrine and Emilie Savage Smith, eds. *The Year 1000: Medical Practice at the End of the First Millennium*. Social History of Medicine 13, 2. Oxford: Oxford University Press, 2000.

Houben, Hubert. *Roger II: A Ruler Between East and West*. Trans. Graham A. Loud and Diane Milburn. Cambridge: Cambridge University Press, 2002.

Howgrave-Graham, R. P. "Some Clocks and Jacks, with Notes on the History of Horology." *Archaeologia: Or, Miscellaneous Tracts Relating to Antiquity* 77 (1928): 257–312.

Hughes, Jonathan. *The Rise of Alchemy in Fourteenth-Century England: Plantagenet Kings and the Search for the Philosopher's Stone*. London: Continuum, 2012.

Huizinga, Johan. *The Autumn of the Middle Ages*. Trans. Rodney J. Payton and Ulrich Mammitzsch. Chicago: University of Chicago Press, 1996.

Hutchinson, Keith. "What Happened to Occult Qualities in the Scientific Revolution?" *Isis* 73 (1982): 233–53.

Hyman, Wendy, ed. *The Automaton in English Renaissance Literature*. Surrey: Ashgate, 2011.

Ingham, Patricia. "Little Nothings: The Squire's Tale and the Ambition of Gadgets." *SAC* 31 (2009): 53–80.

Jaeger, C. Stephen. *The Envy of Angels: Cathedral Schools and Social Ideas in Medieval Europe, 950–1200*. Philadelphia: University of Pennsylvania Press, 2000.

Jenkins, A. D. Fraser. "Cosimo de'Medici's Patronage of Architecture and the Theory of Magnificence." *Journal of the Warburg and Courtauld Institutes* 33 (1970): 162–70.

Joly, Aristide. *Benoît de Sainte-Maure et le Roman de Troie ou les Métamorphoses d'Homère et l'épopée gréco-latine au Moyen-Age*. 2 vols. Paris: F. Vieweg, 1870–71.

Jones, George. *The Ethos of the Song of Roland*. Baltimore: Johns Hopkins University Press, 1963.

Jones, Timothy and David Sprunger, eds. *Marvels, Monsters, and Miracles: Studies in the Medieval and Early Modern Imagination*. Kalamazoo, Mich.: Medieval Institute Publications, 2002.

Jones, W. R. "The Political Uses of Sorcery in Medieval Europe." *Historian* 34 (1972): 670–87.

Juste, David. *Les alchandreana primitifs: Études sur les plus anciens traits astrologiques latins d'origine arabe, Xe siècle*. Leiden: Brill, 2007.

Kaczynski, Berenice M. "Some St. Gall Glosses on Greek Philanthropic Nomenclature." *Speculum* 58 (1983): 1008–17.

Kang, Minsoo. *Sublime Dreams of Living Machines: The Automaton in the European Imagination*. Cambridge, Mass.: Harvard University Press, 2011.

Karnes, Michelle. "Wonder, Marvels, and Metaphor in *The Squire's Tale*." *English Literary History* 82 (2015), forthcoming.

Kelly, Douglas. *The Art of Medieval French Romance*. Madison: University of Wisconsin Press, 1992.

———. *The Conspiracy of Allusion: Description, Rewriting, and Authorship from Macrobius to Medieval Romance*. Leiden: Brill, 1999.

Ker, W. P. "The Roman van Walewein (Gawain)." *Folk-Lore* 5 (1894): 121–27.

Kieckhefer, Richard. *Forbidden Rites: A Necromancer's Manual of the Fifteenth Century*. University Park: Pennsylvania State University Press, 1997.

———. *Magic in the Middle Ages*. Cambridge: Cambridge University Press, 1989.

———. "The Specific Rationality of Medieval Magic," *AHR* 99 (1994): 813–36.

Kinoshita, Sharon. *Medieval Boundaries: Rethinking Difference in Old French Literature*. Philadelphia: University of Pennsylvania Press, 2006.

Klaus, Maurice. *Die deutsche Räderuhr: Zur Kunst und Technik des mechanischen Zeitmessers im deutschen Sprachraum*. 2 vols. Munich: Beck, 1976.

Knight, Alan. *Aspects of Genre in Late Medieval French Drama*. Manchester: Manchester University Press, 1983.

Koopmans, Rachel. *Wonderful to Relate: Miracle Stories and Miracle Collections in High Medieval England*. Philadelphia: University of Pennsylvania Press, 2011.

Labbé, Alain. *L'Architecture des palais et des jardins dans les chansons de geste: Essai sur le thème du roi en majesté*. Paris: Champion-Slatkine, 1987.

Laborde, Comte Alexandre de. *La Bible moralisée*. 5 vols. Paris: Societé Française de Reproductions Manuscrits à Peintures, 1911–27.

———. *Les ducs de Bourgogne*. 3 vols. Paris: Plon, 1849.

Lacaze, Yvon. "Le rôle des traditions dans la genèse d'un sentiment national au XVème siècle: La Bourgogne de Philippe le Bon." *Bibliothèque de l'École des Chartres* 129 (1971): 303–85.

Lacroix, Paul [P. L. Jacob]. *Moeurs, usages, et costumes au moyen âge et à l'époque de la renaissance*. Paris: Firmin Didot, 1871.

Ladner, G. B. *Ad Imaginem Dei: The Image of Man in Medieval Art*. Latrobe, Pa.: Archabbey Press, 1965.

LaGrandeur, Kevin. *Androids and Intelligent Networks in Early Modern Literature and Culture: Artificial Slaves*. New York: Routledge, 2013.

———. "The Talking Brass Head as a Symbol of Dangerous Knowledge in *Friar Bacon* and *Alphonsus, King of Aragon*." *English Studies* 5 (1999): 408–22.

Langer, R. E. "Alexandria: Shrine of Mathematics." *American Mathematical Monthly* 48 (1941): 109–25.

Lavezzo, Kathy. *Angels on the Edge of the World: Geography, Literature, and English Community, 1000–1534*. Ithaca, N.Y.: Cornell University Press, 2006.

Le Goff, Jacques. *Time, Work, and Culture in the Middle Ages*. Trans. Arthur Goldhammer. Chicago: University of Chicago Press, 1980.

Legros, Huguette. "Connaissance, réception, et perceptions des automates orientaux au XIIe siècle." In *Le merveilleux et la magie dans la littérature*, ed. Gérard Chandès, 103–36. Amsterdam: Rodopi, 1992.

Levy, M. L. "As Myn Auctor Seyth." *Medium Aevum* 12 (1943): 25–39.

Lewis, C. S. *The Discarded Image: An Introduction to Medieval and Renaissance Literature*. Cambridge: Cambridge University Press, 1964.

Leyser, Karl. "*Theophanu divina gratia imperatrix augusta*: Western and Eastern Emperorship in the Later Tenth Century." In *The Empress Theophano: Byzantium and the West at the Turn of the First Millennium*, ed. Adelbert Davis, 1–27. Cambridge: Cambridge University Press, 1995.

Lightsey, Scott. "Chaucer's Secular Marvels and the Medieval Economy of Wonder." *SAC* 23 (2001): 289–316.

———. *Manmade Marvels in Medieval Culture and Literature*. New York: Palgrave Macmillan, 2007.

Lindberg, David C., ed. *Science in the Middle Ages*. Chicago: University of Chicago Press, 1980.

———. "The Transmission of Greek and Arabic Learning to the West." In *Science in the Middle Ages*, ed. David C. Lindberg. Chicago: University of Chicago Press, 1980.

Lindgren, Uta. *Gerbert von Aurillac und das Quadrivium: Untersuchungen zur Bildung im Zeitalter der Ottonen*. Sudhoffs Archiv 18. Weisbaden: Steiner, 1976.

Lloyd, Alan H. *Some Outstanding Clocks over Seven Hundred Years, 1250–1950*. London: Leonard Hill, 1958.

Long, Pamela O. *Openness, Secrecy, and Authorship: Technical Arts and the Culture of Knowledge from Antiquity to the Renaissance*. Baltimore: Johns Hopkins University Press, 2001.

———. *Technology and Society in the Medieval Centuries: Byzantium, Islam, and the West, 500–1300*. Washington, D.C.: Society for the History of Technology and American Historical Association, 2003.

Luxford, Julian M. *The Art and Architecture of English Benedictine Monasteries, 1300–1540*. Woodbridge: Boydell, 2005.

Maccagni, Carlo. "Il disegno di macchine come fonte per la storia delle tecnica del Rinascimento." *Quaderni Storici* 70 (1989): 13–24.

Maddison, F., B. Scott, and A. Kent. "An Early Medieval Water-Clock." *Antiquarian Horology* 3 (1962): 348–53.

Magnier, Thierry, ed. *Une renaissance: L'art entre Flandre et Champagne de 1150–1250*. Paris: Réunion des Musées Nationaux, 2013.

Marenbon, John. *Early Medieval Philosophy*. London: Routledge, 1983.

———. "Twelfth-Century Platonism: Old Paths and New Directions." In *Aristotelian Logic, Platonism, and the Context of Early Medieval Philosophy in the West*, 1–21. Aldershot: Ashgate, 2000.

Marigny, François Augier de. *Histoire des Arabes sous le gouvernement de califes*. 4 vols. Paris: La Veuve Estienne et fils, 1750.

Massip Bonet, Jesús-Francesc. "The Cloud: A Medieval Aerial Device, Its Origins, and Its Use in Spain Today." *Early Drama, Art, and Music Review* 16 (1994): 65–77.

Maurice, Klaus and Otto Mayr, eds. *The Clockwork Universe: German Clocks and Automata, 1550–1650*. Washington, D.C.: Smithsonian Institution, 1980.

McCaffery, Ellen. *Astrology: Its History and Influence in the Western World*. New York: Scribner's, 1942.

McCluskey, Stephen C. *Astronomies and Cultures in Early Medieval Europe*. Cambridge: Cambridge University Press, 1997.

———. "Gregory of Tours, Monastic Timekeeping, and Early Christian Attitudes to Astronomy." *Isis* 81 (1990): 8–22.

McEvoy, James. *Robert Grosseteste*. Oxford: Oxford University Press, 2000.

McKeon, Richard. "Poetry and Philosophy in the Twelfth Century: The Renaissance of Rhetoric." *Modern Philology* 43 (1945–46): 217–34.

McLanathan, Richard. *The Pageant of Medieval Art and Life*. Philadelphia: Westminster Press, 1966.

McVaugh, Michael. "The 'Humidum Radicale' in Thirteenth-Century Medicine." *Traditio* 30 (1974): 259–83.

Meier, Christel. *Gemma Spiritalis*. Munich: Fink, 1977.

Méjean, Suzanne. "A propos de l'arbre aux oiseaux dans *Yvain*." *Romania* 91 (1970): 392–99.

Melberg, Arne. *Theories of Mimesis*. Cambridge: Cambridge University Press, 1995.

Mercier, Raymond. "Astronomical Tables in the Twelfth Century." In *Adelard of Bath: An English Scientist and Arabist of the Early Twelfth Century*, ed. Charles Burnett, 87–118. London: Warburg, 1987.

———. "Studies in the Medieval Conception of Precession." In *Studies on the Transmission of Medieval Mathematical Astronomy*, ed. Raymond Mercier, 197–220. Aldershot: Ashgate, 2004.

Meredith, Peter and John E. Taliby, eds. *The Staging of Religious Drama in Europe in the Later Middle Ages*. Early Drama, Art, and Music Monograph Series 4. Kalamazoo, Mich.: Medieval Institute Publications, 1983.

Merkel, Ingrid and Allan Debus, eds. *Hermeticism and the Renaissance: Intellectual History and the Occult in Early Modern Europe*. Washington, D.C.: Folger Shakespeare Library, 1988.

Middle English Dictionary. Ed. Hans Kurath, Sherman Kuhn, et al. 23 vols. Ann Arbor: University of Michigan Press, 1959–2001.

Minio-Paluello, Lorenzo. "Henri Aristippe, Guillaume de Moerbeke et les traductions latines médiévales des Météorologiques et du De Generation d'Aristote." *Revue Philosophique de Louvain* 45 (1947): 206–35.

Modersohn, Mechtild. *Natura als Göttin im Mittelalter: Ikonographische Studien zur Darstellung der personifzierten Natur*. Berlin: Akademie Verlag, 1997.

Moleta, Vincent. "Guido delle Colonne's 'Amor, che lungiamenta m'hai menato': A Source for the Opening Metaphor." *Italica* 54, 4 (1977): 468–84.

Murphy, Susan. "Heron of Alexandria's *On Automaton-Making*." *History of Technology* 17 (1995): 1–45.

Nelson, Victoria. *The Secret Life of Puppets*. Cambridge, Mass.: Harvard University Press, 2001.

Newman, William R. "An Overview of Roger Bacon's Alchemy." In *Roger Bacon and the Sciences*, ed. Jeremiah Hackett, 317–36. Leiden: Brill, 1997.

———. "The Philosophers' Egg: Theory and Practice in the Alchemy of Roger Bacon." *Micrologus* 3 (1995): 75–101.

———. *Promethean Ambitions: Alchemy and the Quest to Perfect Nature.* Chicago: University of Chicago Press, 2004.

Niebyl, Peter H. "Old Age, Fever, and the Lamp Metaphor." *Journal of the History of Medicine and the Allied Sciences* 26 (1971): 351–68.

Noble, David. *The Religion of Technology.* New York: Knopf, 1997.

North, J. D. *God's Clockmaker: Richard of Wallingford and the Invention of Time.* London: Hambledon, 2005.

———. "Medieval Concepts of Celestial Influence: A Survey." In *Astrology, Science, and Society: Historical Essays*, ed. Patrick Curry, 5–18. Woodbridge: Boydell, 1987.

———. "Monasticism and the First Mechanical Clocks." In *The Study of Time II: Proceedings of the Second Conference of the International Society for the Study of Time, Lake Yamanaka, Japan*, ed. J. T. Fraser and Nathaniel Lawrence, 381–98. Berlin: Springer-Verlag, 1975.

Norwich, John Julius. *Byzantium: The Decline and Fall.* 1995. Reprint London: Folio Society, 2003.

———. *The Kingdom in the Sun, 1130–1194.* London: Longman, 1970.

Novum glossarium mediae Latinitatis, 350–1250, ed. Franz Blatt et al. Copenhagen: Munksgaard, 1957–69.

Oldoni, Massimo. "'A fantasia dicitur fantasma.' Gerberto e la sua storia, II, Fine." *Studi Medievali* 23 (1983): 167–245.

———. "Gerberto e la sua storia, I." *Studi Medievali* 18 (1977): 629–704.

Olsan, Lea. "The Inscription of Charms in Anglo-Saxon Manuscripts." *Oral Tradition* 14 (1999): 401–19.

———. "Latin Charms of Medieval England: Verbal Healing in a Christian Oral Tradition." *Oral Tradition* 7 (1992): 116–42.

Oostrom, Fritz van. *Maerlants Wereld.* Amsterdam: Prometheus, 1996.

Oschema, Klaus. "Liquid Splendor: Table-Fountains and Wine-Fountains at the Burgundian Courts." In *Staging the Court of Burgundy: Proceedings of the Conference "The Splendor of Burgundy,"* ed. Wim Blockmans, Till-Holger Borchert, Nele Gabriëls, Johan Oosterman, and Anne van Oosterwijk, 133–42. Turnhout: Brepols, 2013.

Otter, Monika. *Inventiones: Fiction and Referentiality in Twelfth-Century English Historical Writing.* Chapel Hill: University of North Carolina Press, 1996.

Ovitt, George, Jr. *The Restoration of Perfection.* New Brunswick, N.J.: Rutgers University Press, 1987.

Page, Sophie. *Astrology in Medieval Manuscripts.* London: British Library, 2002.

———. *Magic in Medieval Manuscripts.* Toronto: University of Toronto Press, 2004.

Panafieu, Christine Woesler de. "Automata—A Masculine Utopia." In *Nineteen Eighty-Four: Science Between Utopia and Dystopia*, ed. Everett Mendelsohn and Helga Nowotny. Dordrecht: Reidel, 1984.

Panofsky, Dora. "The Textual Basis of the Utrecht Psalter Illustrations." *Art Bulletin* 25 (1943): 50–58.

Panofsky, Erwin. *Renaissance and Re-Nascences in Western Art*. New York: Harper and Row, 1960.

Paravincini-Bagliani, Agostino. "La légende médiévale d'Albert le Grand (1270–1435): Prèmieres recherches." *Micrologus* 21 (2013): 295–368.

———. *The Pope's Body*. Trans. David S. Peterson. Chicago: University of Chicago Press, 2000.

Parent, Joseph-Marie. *La doctrine de la création dans l'École de Chartres*. Paris: J. Vrin, 1938.

Paris, Gaston. "*La chanson du pèlerinage du Charlemagne.*" *Romania* 9 (1880): 1–50.

Park, Katharine. "The Meaning of Natural Diversity: Marco Polo on the 'Division' of the World." In *Texts and Contexts in Medieval Science: Studies on the Occasion of John E. Murdoch's Seventieth Birthday*, ed. Edith Sylla and Michael McVaugh. Leiden: Brill, 1997.

———. "Observation in the Margins." In *Histories of Scientific Observation*, ed. Lorraine Daston and Elizabeth Lunbeck, 15–44. Chicago: University of Chicago Press, 2011.

———. *Secrets of Women: Gender, Generation, and the Origins of Human Dissection*. New York: Zone, 2007.

Partner, Nancy F. *Serious Entertainments: The Writing of History in Twelfth-Century England*. Chicago: University of Chicago Press, 1977.

Patterson, Lee. *Negotiating the Past: The Historical Understanding of Medieval Literature*. Madison: University of Wisconsin Press, 1987.

Pearsall, Derek and Elizabeth Salter. *Landscapes and Seasons of the Medieval World*. Toronto: University of Toronto Press, 1973.

Pedersen, Olaf. "Astronomy." In *Science in the Middle Ages*, ed. David C. Lindberg, 303–37. Chicago: University of Chicago Press, 1978.

Peek, Wendy Chapman. "King by Day, Queen by Night: The Virgin Camille in the *Roman d'Éneas*." In *Menacing Virgins: Representing Virginity in the Middle Ages and the Renaissance*, ed. Kathleen Coyne Kelly and Marina Leslie, 71–82. London: Associated University Presses, 1999.

Peron, Gianfelice. "Meraviglioso e versimile nel romanzo francese medievale: Da Benoît de Sainte-Maure e Jean Renart." In *Il meraviglioso e il versimile tra antichità e medioevo*, ed. Diego Lanza and Oddone Longo. Florence: L.S. Olschki, 1989.

Peters, Edward. *The Magician, the Witch, and the Law*. Philadelphia: University of Pennsylvania Press, 1978.

Petit, Aimé. *L'anachronisme dans les romans antiques du XIIème siècle: Le Roman de Thèbes, le Roman d'Éneas, le Roman de Troie, et le Roman d'Alexandre*. Paris: Champion, 2002.

———. *Naissances du roman: Les techniques littéraires dans les romans antiques du XIIème siècle*. 2 vols. Lille: Atelier National Reproduction des Thèses, 1985.

Phillips, Jonathan. *The Fourth Crusade and the Sack of Constantinople*. New York: Viking, 2004.

Picavet, François. *Gerbert: Un pape philosophe, d'après la legende*. Paris: E. Leroux, 1897.

Pingree, David. "Astrology." In *Religion, Learning, and Science in the 'Abbasid Period*, ed. M. J. L. Young, J. D. Latham, and R. B. Serjeant, 290–300. Cambridge: Cambridge University Press, 1990.

Pleij, Hermann. *Dreaming of Cockaigne: Medieval Fantasies of the Perfect Life*. Trans. Diane Webb. New York: Columbia University Press, 2001.

Poirion, Daniel. "Eddypus et l'énigme du roman médiéval." In *L'enfant du Moyen Age*, 285–98. Senefiance 9. Aix-en-Provence, 1980.

———. "De *l'Eneide* à *l'Éneas*: Mythologie et moralisation." *CCM* 19 (1976): 213–29.

Polak, Lucie. "Charlemagne and the Marvels of Constantinople." In *The Medieval Alexander Legend and Romance Epic: Essays in Honour of David J. A. Ross*, ed. Peter Noble, Lucie Polak, and Claire Isoz, 159–71. London: Kraus, 1982.

Poulle, Emmanuel. "L'Astronomie de Gerbert." In *Gerberto: Scienza, storia, e mito: Atti del Gerberti Symposium, Bobbio 25–27 Iuglio 1983. Archivium Bobiense II* , ed. M. Tosi, 597–617. Piacenza: Archivi Storici Bobiense, 1985,

———. "Le Traité de l'astrolabe d'Adélard de Bath." In *Adelard of Bath: An English Scientist and Arabist of the Early Twelfth Century*, ed. Charles Burnett, 119–32. London: Warburg, 1987.

Price, Derek J. de Solla. "Automata and the Origins of Mechanism and Mechanistic Philosophy." *Technology and Culture* 5 (1964): 9–23.

———. "Clockwork before the Clock and Timekeepers Before Timekeeping." In *The Study of Time II: Proceedings of the Second Conference of the International Society for the Study of Time, Lake Yamanaka—Japan*, ed. Julius T. Fraser and Nathaniel Lawrence, 367–80. Berlin: Springer-Verlag, 1975.

———. "Gears from the Greeks. The Antikythera Mechanism: A Calendar Computer from ca. 80 B.C." *TAPS* 64 (1974): 1–70.

———. "On the Origin of Clockwork, Perpetual Motion Devices, and the Compass." *U.S. National Museum Bulletin 218: Contributions from the Museum of History and Technology* (1959): 82–112.

———. *Science Since Babylon*. New Haven, Conn.: Yale University Press, 1975.

V. Raghavan. "Somadeva and King Bhoja." *Journal of the University of Gauhati* 3 (1952): 35–38.

Ramey, Lynn Tarte. *Christian, Saracen, and Genre in Medieval French Literature*. New York: Routledge, 2001.

Richard, Jules-Marie. *Une petite-nièce de Saint Louis: Mahaut, comtesse d'Artois et de Bourgogne (1302–1329)*. Paris: Champion, 1887.

Riché, Pierre."Fulbert de Chartres et son école." In *Le temps de Fulbert. Actes de l'Université d'été du 8 au 10 juillet, 1996*, 27–32. Chartres: Société Archéologique d'Eure-et-Loir, 1996.

———. *Gerbert d'Aurillac: Le pape de l'an mil*. Paris: Fayard, 1987.

Riefstahl, Rudolph. "The Date and Provenance of the Automata Miniatures." *Art Bulletin* 11 (1929): 206–15.

Riskin, Jessica. "Le canard, l'homme, et le robot." *Le Recherche* 350 (2002): 36–40.

———. "The Defecating Duck, Or, The Ambiguous Origins of Artificial Life." *Critical Inquiry* 29 (2003): 599–633.

Riskin, Jessica, ed. *Genesis Redux: Essays in the History of Philosophy and Artificial Life.* Chicago: University of Chicago Press, 2007.

Robinson, I. S. *Authority and Resistance in the Investiture Contest: The Polemical Literature of the Late Eleventh Century.* New York: Holmes and Meier, 1978.

Rollo, David. *Glamorous Sorcery: Magic and Literacy in the High Middle Ages.* Minneapolis: University of Minnesota Press, 2000.

———. *Historical Fabrication, Ethnic Fable, and French Romance in Twelfth-Century England.* Lexington, Ky.: French Forum, 1998.

Romm, James. *The Edges of the Earth in Ancient Thought.* Princeton, N.J.: Princeton University Press, 1992.

Ruggles, D. Fairchild. *Islamic Gardens and Landscapes.* Philadelphia: University of Pennsylvania Press, 2008.

Salmon, Georges. *Introduction topographique à l'histoire de Bagdad d'Abou Bakr Ahmad ibn Thabit al-Kathib al-Bagdadi.* Paris: Bouillon, 1904.

Sandler, Lucy Freeman. *Omne Bonum: A Fourteenth-Century Encyclopedia of Universal Knowledge.* London: Harvey Miller, 1996.

Scafi, Allesandro. *Mapping Paradise: A History of Heaven on Earth.* Chicago: University of Chicago Press, 2006.

Schlauch, Margaret. "The Palace of Hugon de Constantinople." *Speculum* 7 (1932): 500–514.

Schroeder, Eric. *Persian Miniatures in the Fogg Museum of Art.* Cambridge, Mass.: Harvard University Press, 1942.

Schulthess, Daniel. "Zur Infinitisierung der Automaten: Descartes und Leibniz." In *Androïden: zur Poetologie der Automaten,* ed. Jürgen Söring, 85–98. Frankfurt: P. Lang, 1997.

Sénac, Philippe. "Note sur les relations diplomatiques entre les comtes de Barcelone et le califat de Cordoue au Xe siècle." In *Histoire et archéologie des terres catalanes au Moyen Âge,* ed. Philippe Sénac, 87–101. Centre de Recherche sur les Problèmes de la Frontière. Perpignan: Presses Unitaires de Perpignan, 1995.

Sezgin, Ursula. "Pharaonische Wunderwerke bei Ibn Wasif as-Sabi' und al-Mas'udi. Einige Remeniszenzen an Ägyptens vergagene Grösse und an Meisterwerke der Alexandrinischen Gelehrten in arabischen Texten des 10. Jahrhunderts n. Chr. Teil I-V." Published in five parts in *Zeitschrift für Geschichte der Arabisch-Islamischen Wissenschaften* I, 9 (1994): 229–91; II, 11 (1997): 189–250; III, 14 (2001): 217–56; IV, 15 (2002/03): 281–312; V, 16 (2004/05): 149–209.

Shapin, Steven. *The Scientific Revolution.* Chicago: University of Chicago Press, 1996.

Sherwood, Merriam. "Magic and Mechanics in Medieval Fiction." *Studies in Philology* 44 (1947): 567–92.

Sicard, Patrice. *Hugues de Saint-Victor et son école: Introduction, choix de texte, traduction et commentaires.* Turnhout: Brepols, 1991.

Singer, Julie. "L'horlogerie et la mécanique de l'allégorie chez Jean Froissart." *Médiévales* 49 (2005): 155–72.

Siraisi, Nancy G. *Medieval and Early Renaissance Medicine*. Chicago: University of Chicago Press, 1990.

Söhring, Otto. "Werke bildener Kunst in altfranzösischen Epen." *Romanische Forshungen* 12 (1900): 491–640.

Söring, Jürgen, ed. *Androïden: zur Poetologie der Automaten*. Frankfurt: P. Lang, 1997.

Southern, R. W. *The Making of the Middle Ages*. New Haven, Conn.: Yale University Press, 1953.

———. *Medieval Humanism and Other Studies*. Oxford: Blackwell, 1970.

———. *Robert Grosseteste: The Growth of an English Mind in Medieval Europe*. Oxford: Clarendon, 1986.

———. *Scholastic Humanism and the Unification of Europe*. Vol. 1, *Foundations*. Oxford: Blackwell, 1995.

———. *Western Views of Islam in the Middle Ages*. Cambridge, Mass.: Harvard University Press, 1962.

Spargo, John Webster. *Vergil the Necromancer*. Cambridge, Mass.: Harvard University Press, 1934.

Standage, Tom. *The Turk: The True Story of the Chess-Playing Machine That Fooled the World*. London: Penguin, 2002.

Stock, Brian. "Science, Technology, and Economic Progress in the Early Middle Ages." In *Science in the Middle Ages*, ed. David C. Lindberg. Chicago: University of Chicago Press, 1980.

Sturlese, Lois. "Saints et magiciens: Albert le Grand en face d'Hermès Trismégeste." *Archives de Philosophie* 43 (1980): 615–41.

Stürner, Wolfgang. *Friedrich II*. 2 vols. Darmstadt: Wissenschaftliche Buchgesellschaft, 1992–2000.

Sullivan [Eley], Penny. "Medieval Automata: The 'Chambre des Beautés' in Benoît de Sainte-Maure's *Roman de Troie*," *Romance Studies* 6 (1985): 1–20.

Symes, Carol. *A Common Stage: Theater and Public Life in Medieval Arras*. Ithaca, N.Y.: Cornell University Press, 2007.

Talbot, Alice-Mary. "Pilgrimage to Healing Shrines: The Evidence of Miracle Accounts." *Dumbarton Oaks Papers* 56 (2002): 153–73.

Tatarkiewicz, Wladyslaw. *History of Aesthetics*. 3 vols. The Hague: Mouton, 1970.

Taylor, Jerome. *The Origin and Early Life of Hugh of St. Victor: An Evaluation of the Tradition*. South Bend, Ind.: Medieval Institute, University of Notre Dame, 1957.

Thomson, Rodney M. *William of Malmesbury*. Woodbridge: Boydell, 2003.

Thorndike, Lynn. *The History of Magic and Experimental Science*. 8 vols. New York: Columbia University Press, 1923–58.

———. *The Place of Magic in the Intellectual History of Europe*. New York: Columbia University Press, 1905.

Thurlow, A. G. G. "The Bells of Norwich Cathedral." *Norfolk Archaeology* 29 (1946): 89–90.

Trannoy, Patricia. "De la technique à la magie: Enjeux des automates dans *Le voyage de Charlemagne à Jérusalem et à Constantinople*." In *Le merveilleux et la magie dans la littérature*, ed. Gérard Chandès, 227–52. Amsterdam: Rodopi, 1992.

Trilling, James. "Daedalus and the Nightingale: Art and Technology in the Myth of the Byzantine Court." In *Byzantine Court Culture from 829–1204*, ed. Henry Maguire, 217–30. Washington, D.C.: Dumbarton Oaks, 1997.

Truitt, E. R. "Celestial Divination and Arabic Science in Twelfth-Century England: The History of Gerbert of Aurillac's Talking Head." *Journal of the History of Ideas* 73 (2012): 201–22.

———. "Fictions of Life and Death: Tomb Automata in Medieval Romance." *postmedieval* 1 (2010): 194–98.

———. "'Trei poëte, sages dotors, qui mout sorent di nigromance': Knowledge and Automata in Twelfth-Century French Literature." *Configurations* 12 (2004): 167–93.

———. "The Virtues of Balm in the Late Medieval Period." *Early Science and Medicine* 14 (2009): 711–36.

Tybjerg, Karin. "Wonder-Making and Philosophical Wonder in Hero of Alexandria." *Studies in History and Philosophy of Science* 34 (2003): 443–66.

Ungerer, Alfred. *Les horloges astronomiques et monumentales les plus remarquables de l'antiquité jusqu'à nos jours*. Strasbourg: author, 1931.

Ungerer, Théodore. "Les Habrecht: Une dynastie d'horlogers strasbourgeois au XVIe et au XVIIe siècle." *Archives Alsaciennes d'Historie de l'Art* 4 (1925): 95–146.

Ungerer, Théodore and l'Abbé André Glory. "L'astrologue au cadran solaire de la cathédrale de Strasbourg (1493)." *Archives Alsaciens d'Histoire de l'Art* 12 (1933): 73–108.

Van Buren, Anne Hagopian. "Reality and Literary Romance in the Park of Hesdin." In *Medieval Gardens*, ed. Elisabeth Blair MacDougall, 115–34. Washington, D.C.: Dumbarton Oaks, 1986.

Vance, Eugene. "Semiotics and Power: Relics, Icons, and the *Voyage de Charlemagne à Jérusalem et à Constantinople*." *Romance Review* 79 (1988): 164–83. Rep. in *The New Medievalism*, ed. Marina S. Brownlee. Baltimore: Johns Hopkins University Press, 1991.

Vanden Berghe, Marc. "Technique et utopie au siècle des lumières: Les androïdes Jaquet-Droz dans l'Encyclopédie d'Yverdon." In *Androïden: zur Poetologie der Automaten*, ed. Jürgen Söring, 99–131. Frankfurt: P. Lang, 1997.

Vaughan, Richard. *Philip the Good: The Apogee of Burgundy*. 2nd ed. Woodbridge: Boydell, 2002.

Voskuhl, Adelheid. *Androids in the Enlightenment: Mechanics, Artisans, and Cultures of the Self*. Chicago: University of Chicago Press, 2013.

Wagner, Robert-Leon. *"Sorcier" et "Magicien": Contribution à l'histoire du vocabulaires de la magie*. Paris: Droz, 1939.

Walter, Joseph. "Le mystère 'Stella' de trois mages joué à la cathédrale de Strasbourg au XIIIème siècle." *Archives Alsaciens d'Histoire de l'Art* 8 (1929): 39–50.

Warner, David A. *Ottonian Germany: The Chronicon of Thietmar of Merseburg*. Manchester: Manchester University Press, 2001.

Waswo, Richard. "Our Ancestors, the Trojans: Inventing Cultural Identity in the Middle Ages." *Exemplaria* 7 (1995): 269–90.

Weill-Parot, Nicolas. *Les "images astronomiques" au moyen âge et à la renaissance*. Paris: Champion, 2002.

Weisheipl, James. "The Nature, Scope, and Classification of the Sciences." In *Science in the Middle Ages*, ed. David C. Lindberg, 461–82. Chicago: University of Chicago Press, 1980.

Weitzmann, Kurt. "The Greek Sources of Islamic Scientific Illustrations." In *Archaeologica orientalia in memoriam Ernst Herzfeld*, ed. George Carpenter Miles, 244–66. Locust Valley, N.Y.: J.J. Augustin, 1952.

Wetherbee, Winthrop. "The Function of Poetry." *Traditio* 25 (1969): 85–125.

White, Lynn, Jr. *Medieval Technology and Social Change*. Oxford: Oxford University Press, 1962.

Whitney, Elspeth. *Paradise Restored: The Mechanical Arts from Antiquity Through the Thirteenth Century. TAPS* 80 (1990): 1–169.

Williams, Peter. *The Organ in Western Culture, 750–1250*. Cambridge: Cambridge University Press, 1993.

Wood, Gaby. *Edison's Eve: A Magical History of the Quest for Mechanical Life*. New York: Knopf, 2002.

Wright, Michael T. "Epicyclic Gearing and the Antikythera Mechanism, part 1." *Antiquarian Horology* 27 (2003): 270–79.

———. "Epicyclic Gearing and the Antikythera Mechanism, part 2." *Antiquarian Horology* 29 (2005): 54–60.

Yeager, Robert F. *John Gower's Poetic: The Search for a New Arion*. Rochester, N.Y.: Brewer, 1990.

Young, Arthur M. *Troy and Her Legend*. Pittsburgh: University of Pittsburgh Press, 1948.

Yule, Henry, ed. *Cathay and the Way Thither: Being a Collection of Medieval Notices of China*. 4 vols. New Delhi: Munishram Manoharlal Publishers, 1916.

Zambelli, Paola. "Scholastic and Humanist Views of Hermeticism and Witchcraft." In *Hermeticism and the Renaissance: Intellectual History and the Occult in Early Modern Europe*, ed. Ingrid Merkel and Allen G. Debus, 125–35. Washington, D.C.: Folger Shakespeare Library, 1988.

———. *The Speculum Astronomiae and Its Enigma: Astrology, Theology, and Science in Albertus Magnus and His Contemporaries*. Dordrecht: Kluwer, 1992.

Zink, Michel. *Medieval French Literature: An Introduction*. Trans. Jeff Rider. Binghamton, N.Y.: MRTS, 1995.

Ziolkowski, Jan M. *Alan of Lille's Grammar of Sex: The Meaning of Grammar to a Twelfth-Century Intellectual*. Cambridge, Mass.: Medieval Academy, 1985.

Ziolkowski, Jan M. and Michael C. J. Putnam, eds. *The Virgilian Tradition*. New Haven, Conn.: Yale University Press, 2008.

Ziolkowski, Theodore. *Varieties of Literary Thematics*. Princeton, N.J.: Princeton University Press, 1983.

Zuccato, Marco. "Gerbert of Aurillac and a Tenth-Century Jewish Channel for the Transmission of Arabic Science to the West." *Speculum* 80 (2005): 742–63.

ACKNOWLEDGMENTS

Writing this book has taken me in directions I never expected and to places I never imagined. Many people and institutions provided support, stimulating environments, and exquisite generosity along the way. Above all, I thank Katharine Park for her sustained commitment to my development as a scholar and a human being. I am also grateful to Jan Ziolkowski for guiding me through the landscape of medieval literature with comity and humor, and Joan Cadden for patiently introducing me to the rigors of natural philosophy. Allan Brandt, Kate Cooper, Conrad Leyser, Henrietta Leyser, Charis Thompson, and Nicholas Watson also gave me the benefit of their time, goodwill, and knowledge.

The financial support I received to research and write this book was instrumental to its completion. The Embassy of France in the United States, the Lurcy Foundation, The Folger Library, and Harvard University provided funding during the early stages of my research. More recently, the Mellon Foundation, the Humanities Forum at the University of Pennsylvania, and Bryn Mawr College, especially the Provost's Office and the Center for International Studies, provided grants for travel and research. A Scholar's Award from the National Science Foundation made it possible for me to spend a year reconceiving this project, and a Dibner Fellowship from The Huntington Library allowed me to do the final research and revisions.

Every medievalist depends on curators, librarians, and archivists. I would have been adrift without the expertise and goodwill of the special collection librarians at the Kislak Center at the University of Pennsylvania, the Pierpont Morgan Library, the John Rylands University Library at the University of Manchester, the Bodleian Library at the University of Oxford, the Biblioteca Riccardiana, The Huntington Library, and the Bibliothèque nationale de France; the reference librarians at Villa I Tatti, The Getty Research Institute, The Warburg Institute, and Harvard University; and the archivists at the Archives nationales de France, especially Ghislain Brunel. Ingrid Sonvilla welcomed me to Schloss Hellbrunn and Thomas Schneider showed me the automata there at close range. Eric Pumroy, at Bryn Mawr College, supported my research with library acquisitions. Jerry Singerman, Ruth Mazo Karras, and the anonymous readers of the Press of the University of Pennsylvania provided sage editorial advice; Cali Buckley sourced some of the images and secured permissions for all of them; Alison Anderson, Hannah Blake, Caroline Hayes and Caroline Winschel shepherded the book through the stages of its development with élan.

When I first began this project Minsoo Kang, Scott Lightsey, Scott Maisano, Alexander Marr, and Adelheid Voskuhl encouraged me to think about automata in broader contexts and multiple disciplines. The participants in seminars and colloquia at Harvard University, The Folger Library, Princeton University, Indiana University–Bloomington, the University of Pennsylvania, The Johns Hopkins University, Cornell University, and Rutgers University offered interventions at different stages, as did Charles Burnett and his colleagues and students at the Warburg Institute in London and Gerhard Wolff and his colleagues at the Kunsthistorisches-Institut in Florence. Benjamin Anderson, Sharon Farmer, Justine Firnhaber-Baker, Finbarr Barry Flood, Shirin Fozi, Eva Helfenstein, James Palmer, Peter Stallybrass, and Ittai Weinryb made bibliographic recommendations that enriched my research; Daud Ali, Patricia Ingham, and Michelle Karnes graciously shared their unpublished work with me; Babak Ashrafi, Kathleen Biddick, Susan Brandt, Jeremy Greene, Joel Klein, Nichole Miller, Shannon Miller, Lawrence Principe, Jessica Rosenberg, Jonathan Seitz, Lauren Shohet, Gabrielle Spiegel, Walter Stephens, Eric Song, and Laura Weigert read parts of this book in draft and asked all the right questions. Ari Ariel, Kim Cassidy, David Cast, Catherine Conybeare, Ignacio Gallup-Diaz, Bridget Gurtler, Homay King, Dale Kinney, Anita Kurimay, Steven Levine, Peter Magee, Kalala Ngalamulume, Lisa Saltzman, Bethany Schneider, Elliott Shore, Rosi Song, Jamie Taylor, Kate Thomas, Dan Torday, Sharon Ullman, and Alicia Walker, my colleagues—past and present—at Bryn Mawr College, offered fellowship, insightful comments on my work, and some excellent meals. Alexander Harper made a serendipitous discovery and shared it with me. My students in my seminar on ancient and medieval automata taught me how to think about this topic in exciting new ways.

Warmest thanks to Karley Ausiello, David Berz, Sherry Berz, Alex Boxer, Matt Brackett, Alexis Alcantara Brock, Chris Brock, Stephen Cave, Jordan Crane, Rebecca Hall Crane, Nicholas de Fleury, Ethan Gilsdorf, Elizabeth Goldberg, Jesse Goldberg, Leah Gotcsik, Jay Hannon, Jon Karpinos, Jenni McKee, Rosamond Purcell, Stephen Truitt, John Vine, Kirsten Westlake, and

Stian Westlake for their unfeigned interest in medieval robots; to Pamela Daniels for her insights about creativity; and to Darin Hayton, Timothy McCall, and Katherine Rowe for showing me the way out of a dead end. Carl Pearson and Dave Unger made the dizzyingly complex perfectly intelligible. Kerry Ahearn read and commented on an entire draft of this book; his dry marginal glosses brought some much-needed levity to the revision process. Conversations with Jennifer Borland, Andrew Cole, Rob Dorit, Clare Gillis, Julie Livingston, James McHugh, Mara Mills, Alex Medico More, Christopher Phillips, Alisha Rankin, Bill Rankin, Sophie Roux, Matthew Stanley, John Tresch, Matthew Underwood, Marco Viniegra, Jeffrey Webb, Alex Wellerstein, and Nasser Zakariya galvanized my ideas, changed my mind, and made me laugh. Deborah Levine got me out of a jam more than once. Ellen Bales, Sean Cairncross, Beth Ann Corr, Steve Fischer, Ross Flournoy, Joshua Frost, Liz Greene, Christina Greer, Jake Kantrowitz, Sarah Kantrowitz, Josh Kletzkin, Lynn Kletzkin, Morris Kletzkin, John Kuczwara, Jennifer Paull, Marsha Pinson, Max Pinson, Rachel Pinson, Lillian Potter, Tarun Ramadorai, Samuel Roberts, Suzanne Schneider, Mathew Schwartz, Emily Skor, Coach Staples, Kellie Staples, Paul Sutherland, Dominic Tierney, Chris Timmerman, Adam Vine, David Vine, and Emily Yacus provided moral support that I could not have done without.

My mother, Joan Greenbaum, first noticed and then fostered my early obsessions with science fiction and *medievalia*; she created the conditions of possibility for this book. My incredible siblings—Kendall Truitt Barrett, Matthew Bretz, Sarah Bretz, Shawn Greenbaum, Randall Lavelle, Anne O'Rell Owen, Lindsey Truitt, Paul Truitt, Rebecca Truitt, and Sally Truitt—and their families are some of the neatest people I know, and the most encouraging. And the best for last: I want to thank Tick Ahearn, for everything.